# THE BUSH ADMINISTRATION (1989-1993) AND THE DEVELOPMENT OF A EUROPEAN SECURITY IDENTITY

# The Bush Administration (1989-1993) and the Development of a European Security Identity

SOPHIE VANHOONACKER
*European Institute of Public Administration,*
*Maastricht, The Netherlands*

LONDON AND NEW YORK

First published 2001 by Ashgate Publishing

Reissued 2018 by Routledge
2 Park Square, Milton Park, Abingdon, Oxon OX14 4RN
711 Third Avenue, New York, NY 10017, USA

*Routledge is an imprint of the Taylor & Francis Group, an informa business*

Copyright © Sophie Vanhoonacker 2001

All rights reserved. No part of this book may be reprinted or reproduced or utilised in any form or by any electronic, mechanical, or other means, now known or hereafter invented, including photocopying and recording, or in any information storage or retrieval system, without permission in writing from the publishers.

Notice:
Product or corporate names may be trademarks or registered trademarks, and are used only for identification and explanation without intent to infringe.

Publisher's Note
The publisher has gone to great lengths to ensure the quality of this reprint but points out that some imperfections in the original copies may be apparent.

Disclaimer
The publisher has made every effort to trace copyright holders and welcomes correspondence from those they have been unable to contact.

A Library of Congress record exists under LC control number: 2001087937

ISBN 13: 978-1-138-71266-9 (hbk)
ISBN 13: 978-1-138-71265-2 (pbk)
ISBN 13: 978-1-315-19932-0 (ebk)

# Table of Contents

| | |
|---|---:|
| *Preface* | *ix* |
| *Acknowledgements* | *xi* |
| *Abbreviations* | *xiii* |

**1 Transatlantic Relations in the Post-Cold War Period:**
**New Challenges Ahead** ............................................................... 1
    **Setting the Scene** ...................................................................... 2
        Trade: Globalisation versus Regionalisation .......................... 4
        The End of the Cold War ......................................................... 6
        The Bush Administration ......................................................... 7
    **The Research Question** ............................................................ 12
        What is the Future for the US in Europe? ............................. 12
        The Conceptual Lenses ............................................................ 15
        Sources .......................................................................................... 17
        Structure ....................................................................................... 18

**2 Realism and the End of the Cold War** ....................................... 27
    **The Realist Tradition** ............................................................... 29
    **The International System After Berlin** ................................. 31
        The "US in Decline" Debate .................................................... 32
        Change and the International System ..................................... 34
    **Maintaining the Pax Americana: Primacy Matters** ............ 37
    **Filling the Lippmann Gap** ..................................................... 41
    **Primacy or Selective Engagement?** ...................................... 45
    **Selecting the Cases** .................................................................. 46

**3 The US and the Development of a European Security**
**Identity: A Historic Perspective** ................................................. 57
    **Introduction** .............................................................................. 57
    The European Defence Community (EDC):

|   |   |   |
|---|---|---|
| | **Setting the Tone** | 59 |
| | Background | 59 |
| | Lessons and Consequences of a Failure | 61 |
| | **The Fouchet Proposals** | 64 |
| | Strains in the Alliance | 64 |
| | President de Gaulle's Dream of a United Europe | 66 |
| | – Political Union and the European Communities | 67 |
| | – The British Connection | 67 |
| | – Political Union Versus NATO | 68 |
| | – France Turns to Germany | 70 |
| | An Alternative Approach: Kennedy's Grand Design | 70 |
| | Two Competing Designs | 73 |
| | **European Political Cooperation (EPC)** | 75 |
| | Origins of the EPC | 75 |
| | The EPC and European Security | 80 |
| | The US Reaction to the EPC: Nixon and the "*Year of Europe*" | 82 |
| | The US and the EPC Beyond 1973 | 85 |
| | **Conclusion** | 86 |
| 4 | **American Reactions to Common Foreign and Security Policy (CFSP)** | 95 |
| | **The Intergovernmental Conference on Political Union** | 96 |
| | The Franco-German Linchpin | 97 |
| | From EPC to a Common Foreign and Security Policy | 99 |
| | A Europeanist or Atlanticist Approach? | 101 |
| | Why a Temple Proved Stronger than a Tree | 103 |
| | CFSP as Defined in Maastricht: A First Evaluation | 104 |
| | **The Bush Administration and Its Response to CFSP** | 105 |
| | A New Europe, A New Atlanticism | 105 |
| | The Transatlantic Declaration | 108 |
| | Washington and German Reunification | 110 |
| | NATO and CFSP: Rivals or Partners? | 116 |
| | France: *l'enfant terrible* | 120 |
| | External Events Influencing the European and Transatlantic Security Debate: The Case of the Gulf Conflict | 123 |

|   |   |
|---|---|
| Implementing Rome and Maastricht | 127 |
| **Conclusion** | **130** |
| **5 Transatlantic Relations and the Yugoslav Crisis** | **147** |
| **Introduction** | **147** |
| **Yugoslavia: An Accident of History?** | **149** |
| The Two Yugoslavias | 149 |
| **The EC and the Yugoslav Crisis** | **152** |
| EC-Yugoslav Relations Prior to the Crisis | 154 |
| The Crisis Breaks Out | 155 |
| The Military Option | 157 |
| Germany Breaks Ranks | 159 |
| Explaining Germany's *Alleingang* | 163 |
| When the UN Comes In | 164 |
| Lessons for the European Community | 167 |
| **The US and the Yugoslav Crisis** | **169** |
| The Cold War Period | 170 |
| Keeping Hands Off | 173 |
| Supporting the European Community | 175 |
| The Recognition Question | 177 |
| The War Spreads to Bosnia and Herzegovina | 180 |
| Strengthening Humanitarian Relief Efforts | 181 |
| Evaluating the Role of the Bush Administration | 184 |
| **Yugoslavia and the Transatlantic Relationship** | **186** |
| **6 Conclusions** | **205** |
| **Maintaining NATO as the Prime European Security Organisation** | **207** |
| **Washington and CFSP: Mixed Feelings** | **211** |
| **Yugoslavia: The First Test for Europe's Emerging Security Architecture** | **214** |
| **US Policy Towards Western Europe in the Post-Cold War Period** | **219** |
| **Evaluating the Results** | **224** |
| **Is Realism Still Relevant?** | **226** |
| **Beyond the Bush Administration** | **229** |

| | |
|---|---:|
| **Bibliography** | 233 |
| **Official Documents and Reports** | 233 |
| **Speeches** | 239 |
| **Interviews** | 240 |
| – Case One – American Reactions to CFSP | 240 |
| – Case Two – The Bush Administration and Yugoslavia | 240 |
| **Articles and Books** | 241 |
| **Index** | 263 |

# Preface

Since the establishment of NATO, which led to the inextricable link between US and European security, the development of an independent European security identity has been a very sensitive issue in transatlantic relations. President de Gaulle's proposals for Political Union in the 1960s and the establishment of European Political Cooperation from the 1970s onwards were always viewed with suspicion on the other side of the Atlantic. Washington seldom refrained from countering these European initiatives with new transatlantic partnership proposals.

With the end of the cold war, the Member States of the European Community saw a chance to give new impetus to their attempts at foreign policy cooperation and, in the framework of the 1991 Intergovernmental Conference on Political Union, they agreed to develop a Common Foreign and Security Policy (CFSP). Despite the radically changed international environment the Bush administration (January 1989 – January 1993) adopted the same ambivalent attitude as its predecessors. While it argued, on the one hand, that the time had come for the Europeans to take a larger share of the transatlantic security burden, it was on the other hand extremely wary of the Europeans going their own way. For Washington the essential forum for addressing European security affairs was to remain NATO.

The four years of the Bush administration were too short to digest and handle all the consequences of the end of the cold war for transatlantic security. Nevertheless, some first important steps were made, heading in a direction which would be developed further and to some extent adjusted by the Clinton administration. By the mid-1990s the shape that CFSP was taking had already become much clearer and it was obvious that for the time being it was not a serious alternative to NATO.

Notwithstanding the many hurdles CFSP has faced and despite the continuing central role of NATO, the attempts to develop the EU into a mature foreign policy and security player on the international scene are still ongoing. Parallel to the negotiations of the Nice Treaty, the Fifteen are discussing the development of a European Security and Defence Policy (ESDP). The relationship between and cooperation of ESDP and NATO remain central themes of discussion for the EU and the US. By putting the debate on the development of a European security identity in a historic perspective and by analysing the reactions of America's first post-cold war administration to CFSP, this study aims at contributing to a better understanding of US security policy towards Europe and at providing a context to the current transatlantic security debate.

Maastricht, October 2000

# Acknowledgements

The idea for this research first originated at one of the annual seminars on "EC Institutions and Decision-making and Transatlantic Relations" organised by the European Institute of Public Administration (EIPA), Maastricht, and the Brookings Institution, Washington D.C. The first of these seminars was organised in 1987 in Maastricht for high-level officials from various US Departments who wished to learn more about European integration and the main issues on the transatlantic agenda.

These seminars, which are still taking place, give a good picture of the "mood" in US-European relations. While, in the beginning, the debates were very much dominated by the 1992 internal market programme and American fears of a "fortress Europe", the late 1980s and the early 1990s again brought the issue of security high on the agenda. There were many uncertainties on both sides of the Atlantic and, after more than 40 years of a high degree of continuity, relations seemed to have come to a crossroads. In Europe fears arose that, following the collapse of communism, neo-isolationist forces would again emerge, leading to a withdrawal of US troops from the European continent. Washington, on the other hand, was worried that the Europeans would grasp the chance provided by the fall of the Berlin Wall to further develop their own security identity, undermining the central US position on the European security scene.

This research looks at how the end of the cold war has affected the transatlantic security relationship and, more particularly, studies the reaction of the Bush administration towards attempts by the EC Member States to develop an independent European security pillar.

Since this study deals with the US-European relationship, research was required on both sides of the Atlantic. Although most of my work was done at EIPA, the research topic also required regular stays in the United States. In this respect I would like to give special thanks to Desmond Dinan, Associate Professor at the Institute of Public Policy, George Mason University, who was one of the first to invite me to Washington D.C. and who gave me the opportunity to spend some time at his University. Throughout my work he was of great support. I also enjoyed the hospitality of the Brookings Institution where Larry Korb, the then Director at its Center for Public Policy Education and Barbara Littell, a Senior Staff Member, gave me the opportunity to work in a stimulating environment. They were also very helpful in arranging interviews with high-level US officials. Chris and Susan Buchanan were incredible hosts, allowing me to use their guest house and giving me the opportunity to become acquainted with American daily life. Towards the end of my research I had the chance to spend seven months at the Institute on Western Europe at Columbia University in New York. I am very grateful to Glenda Rosenthal, the Director of the Institute, whose encouragement in the final stages of my work I particularly appreciated.

This research would not have been possible without the support of my colleagues at EIPA. First of all, I would like to express my gratitude to my former colleagues Panos Tsakaloyannis and Finn Laursen who stimulated my interest in international relations and, through their comments, helped me in defining and elaborating the research topic. I am also indebted to my EIPA colleagues Les Metcalfe, Edward Best, Adriaan Schout, Simon Duke, Rita Beuter and Veerle Deckmyn all of whom supported me and encouraged me to pursue my work until its completion. I would also like to express my appreciation to Jacqueline Walkden and Suzanne Habraken from EIPA's linguistic services and to Denise Grew for the type-setting and lay-out of the book.

Last but not least, I should mention my husband Bernard who, as an "outsider", was always a good discussion partner and challenged my ideas on the European security architecture.

This study is dedicated to my parents who created a stimulating environment at home and encouraged me to look beyond the Flemish-Belgian horizon.

Maastricht, October 2000

# Abbreviations

| | |
|---|---|
| APEC | Asian Pacific Economic Cooperation |
| ARRC | Allied Rapid Reaction Force |
| CFSP | Common Foreign and Security Policy |
| CJTF | Combined Joint Task Forces |
| CSCE | Conference on Security and Cooperation in Europe |
| EC | European Community |
| ECSC | European Coal and Steel Community |
| EDC | European Defense Community |
| EFTA | European Free Trade Association |
| EMU | Economic and Monetary Union |
| EPC | European Political Cooperation |
| EU | European Union |
| FAWEU | Forces Answerable to the WEU |
| FDI | Foreign Direct Investment |
| IGC | Intergovernmental Conference |
| JNA | Yugoslav National Army |
| NACC | North Atlantic Cooperation Council |
| NAFTA | North Atlantic Free Trade Agreement |
| NATO | North Atlantic Treaty Organisation |
| NSC | National Security Council |
| SDI | Strategic Defense Initiative |
| SNF | Short Range Nuclear Forces |
| SRNMs | Short Range Nuclear Missiles |
| UN | United Nations |
| UNPROFOR | United Nations Protection Force |
| WEU | Western European Union |

# 1 Transatlantic Relations in the Post-Cold War Period: New Challenges Ahead

In 1992, the United States celebrated the 500th anniversary of the Christopher Columbus' discovery of the New World, an event that also marked the beginning of a long and colourful relationship between both sides of the Atlantic. Be it through cultural bonds, intense trade links, or the participation in the same alliance, relations between the US and Europe have always been close and have never been characterised by indifference. On the contrary, generations of Europeans have been fascinated by the unlimited opportunities offered by this huge country and Americans continue to be intrigued by what for many of them is the continent of their ancestors.

This study is about the transatlantic security relationship during the period January 1989 to January 1993. These years, which correspond with those of the one-term Presidency of the Bush administration, were an extremely interesting, but also very challenging, time for US-European relations as they coincided with the end of the cold war, which was undeniably one of the major events in twentieth-century international relations.[1]

In 1989, after more than 40 years of superpower rivalry, the structures that had been underpinning the international system collapsed and the principles that had been guiding the foreign policy of its major players had to be rethought in a fundamental way. For the United States, its policy of containment had become obsolete and being the only superpower left, it had to reconsider its role in the world and to formulate a new grand strategy determining how to define and defend its vital interests. For Europe, the impact of the collapse of communism can also hardly be overstated. The crumbling of the Berlin Wall implied that Europe was no longer confined to Western Europe and that it was no longer immune from the economic and security problems facing its eastern neighbours. Although Central Europe was not a concrete issue on the agenda of the European Community's Intergovernmental Conference on Political Union which took place in 1991, it was certainly on the minds of EC policy makers when they considered the next steps on the road towards closer European integration.

While both the European Community (EC)[2] and the US were struggling to cope with the new international environment, transatlantic relations were also facing important challenges. Bereft of its common enemy, the Alliance was coming to a crossroads. Having achieved its ultimate purpose of defeating communism, the North Atlantic Treaty Organisation (NATO) had the choice of going in two entirely opposite directions: either it could disintegrate, or it could adjust to the changed circumstances, redefining its mission and strategy. One of the central questions pending was to what extent the United States would be ready to stay in Europe following the collapse of communism. Would Washington, as some predicted, return to a policy of isolationism, requiring the Europeans to take care of their own security, or would it be willing to take the lead in transforming the Alliance into a body able to deal with the security challenges of the new Europe?

On the European side, it was unclear whether the Member States of the European Community, which represented a consequential economic power, would grasp the end of the cold war as a chance to try to stand on their own feet in the security area or whether they would prefer to continue to embed their security in an Atlantic structure.

It is precisely the evolving US-European security relationship in the immediate aftermath of the 1989 events which will be the central focus of this study. What were the new underlying principles of US policy towards the reunified Europe and more particularly how did the United States respond to initiatives of the European Community to develop a European security and defence identity?

Before further elaborating on the research question and the theoretical framework used, the first part of this introduction will outline the general climate in US-European relations in the late 1980s and early 1990s and will give a brief introduction to the Bush administration and its main actors.

## Setting the Scene

When President Bush came to power in January 1989, relations between Western Europe and the United States were going through a difficult period and both economic and security relations, the twin pillars of the transatlantic relationship, were under strain.

In the trade area, it was a period characterised both by further globalisation as well as by the formation of regional trading blocks. Growing interdependence between their economies incited the two partners to look for ways to realise further liberalisation and Washington and Brussels were the main catalysts behind the Uruguay Round of GATT: an ambitious new round of multilateral negotiations. Simultaneously, however, there was also a trend towards regionalisation – in the EC through the 1992 internal market programme and in the US through the further enlargement of the North American Free Trade Association (NAFTA) – and there were concerns that this might lead each side to become inward-looking and protectionist.

The term that best describes the transatlantic relationship in the field of security in the second half of the 1980s is "ambiguous". Washington, while pleading for the Europeans to take a greater share of the burden, was showing little willingness to allow the Europeans to match their increased responsibilities with an increase in their weight in the Alliance's decision making. The Europeans were shocked to learn that President Reagan, during his meeting with President Gorbachev in Reykjavik, in October 1986, had agreed to major reductions in strategic forces without consulting his European allies. This, together with Reagan's Strategic Defence Initiative (SDI), raised fears in Europe that the US was gradually abandoning the strategy of nuclear deterrence, raising the spectre of a denuclearised Europe.[3]

The Europeans on their side, while complaining about the inequality of the partnership, were doing little to show that they were able to assume larger responsibilities and proved incapable of speaking with one voice. An example in point was the disagreement with regard to the modernisation and the possible reduction of short-range nuclear forces (SNF). While in Germany, *glasnost* and *perestroika* led to raised expectations, France and the United Kingdom took a much more cautious approach towards the changes in the East and fundamentally disagreed with the German desire to start negotiations on the reduction of SNFs in the near future, pointing to the need to first address the problem of the Warsaw Pact's vast superiority in conventional weapons.

The end of the cold war presented the Alliance with even more daunting challenges which caused a questioning of the viability of the Alliance itself and required a fundamental rethink of the transatlantic security relationship. Would the end of the cold war provide the catalyst for a radical and long-overdue transformation of the Alliance or would it gradually disintegrate now that the original purpose of its creation had disappeared?

## Trade: Globalisation versus Regionalisation

Taking into account the importance of transatlantic trade, it is not surprising that during the Bush administration trade questions continued to draw the full attention of both European and US policy-makers. On average, exports to the US during the period 1989-92 represented 17.7% of the European Community's (EC) total exports,[4] while 23.9% of US exports went to the EC.[5] In addition, both regions were also each other's most important foreign direct investment (FDI) partners. Although transatlantic trade was relatively balanced, certainly compared to that with Japan,[6] there were nevertheless serious concerns as to how trade would further evolve.

The Europeans were worried that initiatives for regional trade liberalisation like NAFTA[7] and the launching of a forum for Asian Pacific Economic Cooperation (APEC)[8] might be to the detriment of transatlantic trade relations and they were also afraid that the Americans would increasingly resort to the creation of regional trade blocks as an instrument to open third country markets. Following the 1989 events, it was widely believed that economic rather than military power had become the major yardstick of international influence, and it was feared that the US would adopt a more aggressive approach when pursuing the implementation of its economic policy objectives. At the confirmation hearing before the Senate Finance Committee, US Trade Representative Carla Hill announced that foreign markets would be opened "with a crowbar or a handshake"[9] and, now that the cold war had ended, some analysts did not hesitate to define the pursuit of economic interests as the most important objective of US foreign policy.[10]

In the United States, on the other hand, a real phobia had developed around the European Community's so-called 1992 project, which proposed to remove all internal barriers to trade and to create a single European market characterised by the free movement of goods, services, capital and persons by the end of 1992.[11] American firms not only feared that an increasingly competitive Europe might constitute a serious threat for the US in global markets, they also believed that the internal liberalisation process would be compensated by the creation of new barriers to third countries. They expected the single market to result in the establishment of a fortress Europe, into which it would be hard for American products to gain access.[12]

From 1987 onward, the US Government and more particularly US Secretary of Commerce Robert Moschbacher engaged in intense talks with the EC and its Member States, trying to obtain guarantees that the EC-wide norms being set would not be to the detriment of US goods. While some authors emphasised the long-term benefits of the internal market for American manufacturers, especially for those who had subsidiaries in Europe,[13] others, like Lester Thurow, anticipated a much more gloomy scenario, going as far as predicting that the earlier military contest between the US and the Soviet Union would be replaced by a contest for economic primacy between the US, Europe and Japan.[14] If by the early 1990s the commotion around the internal market project had considerably calmed down, it had nevertheless one important lasting effect in that the United States, who before had primarily relied on bilateral relations with the individual EC Member States, also discovered the EC institutions and more particularly the European Commission as an important negotiating partner. In May 1989, President George Bush made an appeal to develop closer consultative links between the US and the European Community[15] and, in November 1990, both partners adopted the "Declaration on EC-US Relations", establishing for the first time formal institutional links between the EC and the US.[16] A further signal reflecting a recognition of the increased role of the EC institutions was the acceptance by the US in July 1989 that the European Commission would become the central coordinator for Western aid to the countries of Central Europe.[17]

In hindsight the concerns around "Europe 1992" seem to have been wildly exaggerated and totally out of proportion. This partly had to do with misunderstandings and a bad communication policy on behalf of the EC, but the strong American reactions were also a reflection of a much broader concern in the US about its declining international economic position. From the 1970s onwards, the message had gradually come home that the US was no longer the unchallenged economic superpower it had been in the immediate post-war period and many American observers were extremely pessimistic about the US' capacity to maintain its predominant position on the international scene.[18]

Besides the discussions around 1992, a second issue of intense debate among the US and the European Community at the time was the deliberations on trade liberalisation taking place in the framework of the Uruguay Round of GATT, which had been dragging on since 1986. This was one of the most ambitious rounds of talks in the history of trade liberalisation because it aimed to produce an agreement for the first time on the liberalisation of trade in services. It also aimed to include the liberalisation of heavily protected sectors until then exempted from GATT rules, such as agriculture and textiles and to provide for the stronger protection of intellectual property rights.[19] After talks had broken down in December 1990 because of a deadlock between the US and the EC over the issue of agricultural subsidies,[20] a final agreement was only reached under the Clinton administration in December 1993.

## The Bush Administration (1989-1993)

Throughout the Bush administration, the difficulties surrounding the Uruguay Round negotiations caste a shadow over transatlantic relations, seemingly confirming the projection of certain analysts that now that the Soviet threat had disappeared the Atlantic partners would no longer suppress economic conflicts for political and military reasons and would adopt a less flexible attitude in trade matters.

### The End of the Cold War

If today we can say that the above-mentioned difficulties in the trade area have been less dramatic than they at first seemed, the challenges facing the security relationship have been much more fundamental in nature. The momentous events of 1989 in Central Europe and the waning of the Soviet threat were so shocking that they had the potential to radically overturn more than 40 years of transatlantic relations, raising a whole range of questions, including that of the continuing viability of the Alliance itself.[21]

Several analysts argued that following the collapse of the Soviet Empire, NATO had become an anachronism and many believed that it would not survive the defeat of its former enemy. They expected that the United States, coping with a huge budget deficit, would no longer be willing to defy George Washington's advice to stay out of entangled alliances and would withdraw its troops from Europe. Fearing that isolationist forces would again prevail, there were voices in Europe saying that it had better start to take care of its own security, rather than to place its fate in the hands of an outside power. They argued that as a civilian power, the European Community was much better placed to cope with the challenges of the post-cold war period than any other player.

The foregoing reflections illustrate that it was far from clear in which direction the organisation of European security would develop further. Besides the highly unattractive direction of the re-nationalisation of European security and defence policies, two major options were open: either the United States would remain actively involved and European security would continue to be organised on an Atlantic basis, possibly with a more important European contribution, or, alternatively, the Europeans would start to take care of their own security. In which case they would have to develop proper defence capacities in a purely European framework in which the United States would therefore not participate. The most probable fora for doing this were the European Community and the Western European Union (WEU). Although the main emphasis of the EC had always been on economic integration, the

Member States from 1970 onwards had cooperated in the foreign-policy area. Following the EC's increasing importance on the international trade scene, discussions had started to translate this economic weight into political responsibility and to move towards the development of a European foreign and security policy. A possible partner in realising "the Twelve's" ambitions was the Western European Union (WEU), the only purely Western European security organisation. It was, however, clear that the WEU still had a long way to go before it could fulfil such aspirations. Following the creation of the North Atlantic Treaty Organisation, the WEU's tasks in defending Europe had been transferred to this body[22] and the WEU had for most of the time led a dormant existence.

Since the great uncertainties surrounding the events of 1989 required a prompt reaction, not leaving much time for long and philosophical debates, and since there were divergent opinions as to how to best react to the challenges posed by the new developments, both those favouring an "Atlanticist" and those proposing a purely European answer to the new political realities started to work on their preferred solution. While the United States took the lead in the reorganisation of the Atlantic Alliance, the Member States of the European Community, primarily at the instigation of France and Germany and in the framework of an Intergovernmental Conference (IGC), discussed how European Political Cooperation (EPC) could be developed into a fully-fledged European foreign and security policy.

Although both processes took place simultaneously and had the same objective of addressing the new European security challenges there was barely any coordination between them. On the contrary, competition existed between the two projects and there was a tendency to see progress in one framework as reducing the chances of success in the other.

This study examines the independent European initiatives which were launched to deal with the new European security environment and focuses more particularly on how the United States – as an outside, but nevertheless very much concerned actor – reacted to them. Before further elaborating the research question, a brief introduction is first given on the Bush administration and its principal players.

*The Bush Administration*

When recalling the Bush administration, some of the major events that immediately come to mind are not so much the achievements at the domestic level, but the end of the superpower conflict and the Gulf crisis, which are both related to the realm of the external relations of the United States. Although foreign policy had hardly been an issue in the 1988 presidential elections, it very much dominated the US agenda in the period 1989 to January 1993.[23] As the only superpower left, the United States bore a major responsibility in guaranteeing a peaceful transition towards the so-called "post-cold world" and it was therefore undoubtedly an advantage that when succeeding Ronald Reagan in January 1989, George Bush (b. 1924) had not only a long experience in government but had also had an impressive career in foreign policy.[24]

Under the Nixon and Ford administrations, Bush had successively served as Ambassador to the United Nations (March 1971-January 1973), Chairman of the Republican National Committee (RNC)(1973-1974), Head of the American liaison office in Beijing (1974-December 1975)[25] and as Director of the Central Intelligence Agency (CIA)(January 1976-January 1977).[26] The various high-level posts the future President occupied in the 1970s were of major importance in shaping his views and allowed him to build up considerable experience as well as a broad network of contacts both in the US and abroad. The eight years during which he served as President Ronald Reagan's Vice-President (January 1981-January 1989) allowed him to further develop this expertise.[27]

Despite Bush's clear preference for foreign policy over domestic politics, it is nevertheless difficult to distil from his speeches the core of his views in this area. As in the domestic field, Bush favoured the adoption of a pragmatic approach and dreaded what he used to call the "vision thing".[28] In his inaugural address, he only referred to the vague goal of making "gentler the face of the world", expressing his strong belief that the United States, as a great nation was to play a leading role in international affairs.[29] At that moment he was not aware yet of the historic changes over which he would be presiding, and which would require a substantial rethinking of US foreign policy.

Even though certain actions under his Presidency such as a confidential visit of Henry Kissinger to Moscow to discuss a potential deal on the management of the changes in Eastern Europe[30] and the secret China mission by National Security Adviser Brent Scowcroft and Deputy-Secretary of State Lawrence Eagleburger after the massacre on the Tiananmen Square bring to mind the Nixon-Kissinger approach to international relations, the Bush administration missed the clearly articulated foreign-policy objectives of the former administration. Bush did not believe in grand designs and he refused to perceive leadership as "high drama and the sounds of trumpets calling". For him, history was "a book with many pages, and each day we fill a page with acts of hopefulness and meaning".[31] Continuity was to be one of the central guiding principles of US foreign-policy. It is therefore highly ironic that it was during the Bush Presidency that the 40 year-old cold war structures collapsed and that the world saw the most dramatic changes in international relations since the Second World War.

When it comes to portraying the foreign-policy style of George Bush, the characteristic that immediately comes to mind is the importance he placed on the development of personal contacts with his foreign colleagues. Throughout his four years in office, Bush undertook numerous trips all over the world,[32] and he used to personally call political leaders to discuss important foreign-policy issues. This working method, which is commonly referred to as "Rolodex diplomacy", is not without risks. His almost blind faith in President Mikhail Gorbachev and his neglect to develop relations with other upcoming leaders in the Soviet Union such as Boris Yeltsin illustrates this case in point.

In contrast to Ronald Reagan, who was notorious for his total lack of interest in details, George Bush was very much a hands-on President, who liked to be in charge.[33] In that sense he much more corresponds to Isaiah Berlin's category of the fox rather than that of the hedgehog.[34] He knew his dossiers well and was very much involved in the decision-making process.[35] But unlike Carter, he succeeded in not falling in the trap of micromanagement. When important decisions were to be taken, he was able to take them and act upon them. This is well illustrated by his handling of the Gulf conflict, the first major post-cold-war crisis. Relying on his huge network of contacts, he succeeded in forging a world-wide alliance against Iraq and was actively involved in handling the crisis.

However, Bush was not able to exploit the unprecedented levels of popularity reached during the Gulf war to tackle a number of difficult questions at the domestic level.[36] In the second half of 1990, an economic crisis broke out, which lasted for all of 1991 and most of 1992, but Bush was very slow to come up with an economic plan. His neglect of domestic problems in favour of US foreign policy finally resulted in the US electorate refusing to nominate him for a second term.[37]

As concerns his foreign-policy team, Bush was surrounded by people who, like himself, were very much in favour of a pragmatic approach to foreign policy. Loyalty was a very important quality and several of the top-level members of the foreign-policy team were his personal friends. Besides the President, the two most important players in the foreign-policy area were Secretary of State James Baker and Secretary of Defence Richard Cheney.

The advisory body of the National Security Council (NSC), on the other hand, was not to play an important role during the Bush administration. The

President estimated that the US "didn't need two secretaries of State and two secretaries of Defence" and that the NSC was to stick to its original goals which were to see "that the views of all Council members were accurately and objectively reported to the President".[38]

Through his choice of Brent Scowcroft as National Security Adviser, Bush appointed somebody whom he expected would respect his narrow definition of the job.[39] Knowing his work from when Scowcroft had been Deputy National Security Adviser in the Nixon administration and then National Security Adviser (November 1975-January 1977) under the Ford administration,[40] Bush very much appreciated his low-key, behind-the-scenes operating style.

The President's main foreign-policy adviser was Secretary of State James A. Baker. The latter's nomination to this important post did not come as a surprise. Baker, originally from Texas, had been a close friend to George Bush for more than 20 years and had been the chairman of Bush's presidential campaign both in 1980 and 1988. Baker had very little foreign-policy experience, but this was at least partly offset by the fact that he had had a long experience in government. He had served as Under-Secretary of Commerce in the Ford administration and in 1976 had been his presidential campaign manager. He had also served as White House Chief of Staff during Ronald Reagan's first term and as Secretary of the Treasury in his second term.[41] James Baker was known as a pragmatist, "more inclined toward negotiation than confrontation in dealing with Congress and foreign governments".[42]

To the discontent of the State Department's staff and US career diplomats,[43] James Baker relied very much on a small team around him, excluding the bureaucracy from the most important decisions. The main players of the team of top officials around Baker were Deputy-Secretary of State Lawrence Eagleburger,[44] Under-Secretary of State and White House Deputy Chief of Staff Robert Zoellick[45] and the Under-Secretary for foreign-policy affairs, Robert Kimmitt.[46] As concerned the Middle East and Soviet Union, a major role was played by Dennis Ross, Director of the State Department's policy planning staff. It is interesting to note that the only career diplomat in the team was Lawrence Eagleburger.

As Secretary of Defence, the President appointed Richard ("Dick") Cheney.[47] Cheney also had a long experience in Washington, first as White House Chief of Staff in the Ford administration and from 1978 as member of the House representing Wyoming. He had served on the House Intelligence Committee from 1985.[48] Richard Cheney had never served in the military but had dealt with defence and intelligence issues in the course of his career. The

Senate unanimously confirmed his nomination.

Bush had the habit of maintaining direct contacts with his cabinet secretaries, and more particularly with the Secretary of State. He often used the telephone, directly calling upon people he wanted to speak to or whose opinion he wanted to hear.[49] The fact that there was clarity about the respective roles of his personal staff on the one hand and his cabinet secretaries on the other meant that their mutual relations were rather smooth.

Relations with Congress, where the Democrats had the majority in both the House and the Senate,[50] were, in contrast, rather difficult.[51] Although in his inaugural address Bush had referred to "the new breeze" blowing between Congress and the executive,[52] once he was in the Oval Office, he manifested himself as a jealous guardian of his presidential prerogatives and he proved anxious to assert his executive authority.[53]

Bush was particularly eager to assert his power in the field of foreign policy.[54] In his Princeton address on the separation of powers in May 1991, he stated that "It is the President who is responsible for guiding and directing the nation's foreign policy ...Our founders noted the necessity of performing this duty with 'secrecy and dispatch', when necessary".[55] Although there were cases of successful cooperation between Congress and the President in the foreign-policy area such as the bipartisan agreement on Contra aid to Nicaragua and the adoption of sanctions against South Africa, on other issues such as the policy towards China after Tiananmen Square, or the course to be followed with regard to Iraq (prior to August 1990), the two branches often defended diverging positions. Congress was also very critical with regard to the administration's very cautious approach to the events in the Soviet Union and Eastern Europe.

The executive-congressional competition culminated in the course of the Gulf crisis when Bush argued that UN Security Council Resolution 678 made Congress' authorisation to go to war with Iraq superfluous. Although he never explicitly recognised the need for such approval, he ultimately addressed a letter to Congress asking for legislative authorisation.[56]

Despite the good intentions at the beginning of the Presidency, relations between the legislative and executive branch continued to be confrontational. Rather than directly appealing to Congress and trying to convince its members of his point of view, Bush, through the instrument of the presidential veto,[57] or by relying on the use of internal and therefore unaccountable channels to realise his objectives, tried to overcome the limits the Framers of the Constitution had imposed upon presidential power.

## The Research Question

*What is the Future for the US in Europe?*

The years immediately following the end of the cold war have been crucial for transatlantic relations and for the future position of the US in Europe. It was a period of transition where the European order established after the end of the Second World War and based on a divided Europe and Germany was moving into a new still-to-be-established arrangement. As in 1815, 1918 or 1945, it was the beginning of an era where new players would probably start to take the lead and where different rules would be applied.

What the future American position in Europe would be, was rather uncertain and it was doubtful whether it could maintain the same dominant position as before. The post-war order had been established at a time when a victorious US was at the height of its power and when the Western European countries were exhausted from the war and entirely dependent on the US both for economic assistance and military support. In contrast, in 1989, the circumstances were quite different. The Member States of the European Community were in good economic shape and had become an important competitor of the US in the global market. Following the collapse of the Soviet Empire, the relative dependence of Western Europe, i.e. the extent to which it needed the US to guarantee its security, had considerably declined and what Snyder has called "the risks of abandonment" of the Alliance had increased.[58] As a matter of fact, many students of international relations predicted that with the decline of the Soviet threat the Alliance would break up or at least considerably weaken.[59]

Even very early on in the debate, the United States made it clear that it would not simply accept such a doom-laden scenario and Washington was quick to stipulate its own preferred design for the new European security architecture. Barely one month after the Wall fell, Secretary of State James Baker, in a speech in Berlin, declared that the United States remained fully committed to European security and he pleaded for an adapted Alliance to continue to be the linchpin of transatlantic relations.[60] Although Baker's address also referred to the increasingly important roles of the EC, he made it very clear that the function of political-military arm of European security should continue to be attributed to NATO and that a further development of the EC's political functions should be developed in parallel with closer transatlantic links.

Having these rather outspoken views about the design of the new

European security architecture, the Bush administration did its utmost to try to realise its preferred option and followed a double strategy of providing leadership in adapting the existing structure of NATO, while at the same time trying to influence the shape of the independent European initiatives as much as possible.

Although it had always pleaded for increased burden-sharing and for a long time had paid lip service to the idea of the Europeans taking more responsibility in the security area, the United States was traditionally wary of Europe following its own course in the foreign-policy and security area. Even so, the Americans had not forgotten that twice in the twentieth century they had been drawn into a European war and the idea that the Europeans would once again be left on their own for their security was not very reassuring.

Secondly, Washington also realised that over the past 40 years it had occupied an extremely powerful position on the European continent and that, if it wanted to maintain some of the related advantages, the preservation of the Alliance, even in a extensively revised form, was an important asset. Since it was unclear to what extent the development of a European security identity would be compatible with the continuing existence of NATO, they looked upon such a development with suspicion.

Thirdly, the Bush administration considered it important to be able to count on its European allies when dealing with what it considered to be one of the principal challenges of the immediate post-cold war period, namely to "manage the international effects" of the decline of the Soviet Union "productively and peacefully".[61] After the collapse of the Wall, there were no guarantees that the process towards democracy in Central and Eastern Europe would continue to be peaceful and a successful transition towards market economies was uncertain. The US fully realised that it could never address the multiple challenges on its own and considered it of prime importance to be able to count on the support of its European allies. Maintenance of Western unity was considered to be one of the principal assets for dealing with the emerging New World.

From the beginning, the attitude of the United States towards the aspirations of some European countries to establish an independent European security identity was therefore rather ambiguous. Although the perspective of a more responsible European partner on the international scene was attractive, certainly from a financial point of view, its compatibility with the continuance of a central position for the North Atlantic Alliance was much more doubtful and this was a cause of major concern in Washington.

The central focus of this study is how the United States reacted to the independent European initiatives in the security area during the period of the Bush administration. The question is of interest because it gives an indication of the possible new direction of US foreign policy in the post-cold war period and more particularly of the future role of the United States in Europe. It is both a test of the willingness of the United States to remain further committed to European security as well as of its readiness to accept a more balanced relationship between Western Europe and the United States in the security area. Although the four years of the Bush administration did not provide sufficient time to entirely assimilate the changes provoked by the 1989 events, the steps being made had potentially very important implications for the future of transatlantic relations and set a certain trend.

For the empirical part of this study two case studies have been selected which teach us more about how the US has reacted to attempts by the European Community to develop an independent European security identity. The first looks at the American response to the endeavours of the EC in the framework of the 1991 Intergovernmental Conference (IGC) to upgrade its foreign-policy cooperation to include all aspects of security, including defence.[62] The second focuses on how the Bush administration reacted to European efforts to play a leading role in addressing the Yugoslav crisis.[63]

The choice of these two case studies is motivated by several factors.[64] The attempts of the 1991 IGC to move beyond economic integration to closer cooperation and even integration in the security and defence area has been the most ambitious attempt of the immediate post-1989 period to develop an independent European security identity. Since it was an initiative taking place outside the frame of the Alliance, it had the potential to be a real challenge to NATO. It attracted considerable attention from the United States, and is therefore an interesting test of American willingness to accept an increased European role in security issues.

The second case study focuses on the Yugoslav crisis. Its interest not only lies in the fact that it constitutes the first major post-cold war crisis in Europe, but also in that the European Community, very soon after its outbreak in June 1991, presented itself as the main mediator in the conflict. The crisis not only illustrated the extent to which the Twelve's rhetoric about a European security identity was matched by reality, but it was also a test for Washington's continued commitment to European security. In contrast to the first case study, which concerns a project that initially only existed on paper in the form of a series of Treaty articles, the second pertains to a tangible challenge to security.

On the basis of the facts collected from the two case studies, an attempt will be made to draw some conclusions on US policy towards Europe in the immediate post-war period. What were its main underlying principles? Was there a new division of tasks among the US and its European allies? Were Europe's new security challenges addressed in a primarily Atlantic or a purely European framework? To which extent was there a break from the past?

## *The Conceptual Lenses*[65]

The US response to the development of a European security identity can be studied from two entirely different angles. Either one can focus primarily on the impact of domestic politics and look at the US strategy from within; alternatively one can examine the process from without and focus on the external forces that have had an impact on US policy.

This study opts for the second approach and is primarily interested in examining the impact of structural factors on the national strategy of the United States.[66] It aims to test the explanation offered by structural realism, a systemic theory of international relations.

The end of the cold war provides an excellent opportunity to test the pertinence of systemic theories since the collapse of bipolarity has initiated a period of transformation of the international system. The changes affecting the international system have to do with two parallel developments: the demise of the Soviet Union, one of the two principal actors of the post-war period, on the one hand, and the declining position of the United States, on the other.

This study is interested in the behaviour of the United States, the only remaining superpower after the end of the cold war. It more particularly focuses on how the newly emerging international system has affected US policy towards Western Europe. The analysis will be limited to US' role in transatlantic security, an area in which the US had indisputably been the dominant partner since the end of the Second World War and where the 1989 events had the most dramatic impact.

Structural realism is based on the premise that states are the principal actors in an anarchic international environment and considers that their overriding goal is to safeguard their security. Their prime concern is how their capabilities relate to the other states in the system since it is the distribution of power, which determines whether or not they will be able to survive in an anarchical world.

Realist scholars are generally rather pessimistic about international relations in the post-cold-war world. Having identified bipolarity as one of the principal reasons for the "Long Peace"[67] after the Second World War,[68] they are not enthusiastic about a newly emerging multipolar system,[69] which they expect to succeed the US hegemony of the "unipolar moment".[70] They argue that multipolarity is much more subject to attempts to maintain the balance in power and is therefore inherently more unstable and unpredictable than a world where there are only two main rivals.[71]

Realists also have rather low expectations about the possibilities for a successful security cooperation in Europe fearing a return, rather than the end, of history. In an article with the revealing title *"Back to the Future"*, John Mearsheimer argues that the new Europe will be much more prone to conflicts and major crises than the post-1945 period.[72] He expects that the end of the superpower domination of Europe will result in the European nations once again fearing each other and returning to attempts to redress the balance of power. Realists therefore generally argue that Washington can still play an important role in helping to protect the European states, this time not against the Soviet Union but against themselves. Although they do not agree about the likelihood of a continued US involvement in European security, they acknowledge its desirability.[73]

One of the countries which would be most affected by the transition towards multipolarity is the United States. In the period following the end of the Second World War, the US' position was extremely powerful. In a world with multiple players, in contrast, there are competing forces of other states striving for influence. It is therefore not surprising that several scholars, when warning the US of the rise of other emerging powers, have recommended the US at least try to maintain the *status quo ante*. Charles Krauthammer for example does not hesitate to advocate a perpetuation of the unipolar moment as long as possible and to do the utmost to preserve the primacy of the United States, arguing that American leadership is the best guarantee for continuing order and stability.[74]

Also Robert Gilpin, who in his study *"War and Change in World Politics"* primarily focuses on the question of hegemonic decline, expects a power which is being challenged by other rising powers to resort either to a policy of primacy or to try to restore the disturbed equilibrium in the system by balancing its commitments and resources.[75] Translated to the transatlantic relationship, this means that the US, in order to maintain the advantages associated with its earlier position of privilege as much as possible, is expected to defend its dominant position on the European security scene. Since increased European security cooperation, certainly if it took place outside the framework of the Atlantic Alliance, would constitute a threat to the US position, it can be expected that the American reactions to such initiatives would be negative.

*Sources*

In conducting this research, we were fully aware that the period being studied is extremely recent and that due to a lack of sufficient hindsight, its results can only be preliminary and will have to be tested against later studies. Furthermore, the shocks caused by the 1989 events have been so colossal that the process of adaptation to the new realities it shaped has continued on well beyond the Bush administration and the responses developed during that period can therefore not be considered final. In that respect, it is indeed significant to see that so far this new period in international relations has not even received a name of its own. As the parameters that will determine the main characteristics of the new era are not fully clear yet we continue to speak about the post-cold war period, maintaining the nomenclature of the previous era.

The recent character of the period being studied has influenced the research method in an important way. It will still take several decades before the archives of the Bush administration[76] and the different European governments are available and therefore the number of in-depth studies on the period in question is still limited. There were, however, a wide range of other sources, both written and oral on which we were able to rely for our information. Furthermore, this study does not have the ambition to give a complete overview of transatlantic relations during the Bush years. The events and more particularly the changes in the international system in that period were in the first place used as an opportunity to test some of the central premises of realism.

As concerns the written material, use was made of a large variety of sources, including official documents of the US and the European governments and international institutions, articles in the international press,[77] memoirs by some of the major actors,[78] as well as articles and monographs by academics. George Bush himself has not written his memoirs, but in a joint publication with his National Security Adviser, Brent Scowcroft, he has given what he calls a "personal account" of some of the major foreign-policy events of his administration limiting himself to the period 1989 to 1991.[79] Both Bush and Scowcroft present their views on important international events and the text is interspersed with excerpts of Bush's diary.

The fact that this study was conducted in the immediate aftermath of the end of the cold war had the advantage that direct contact with some of the players involved could be arranged relatively easily. For each of the two case studies, interviews with officials on both sides of the Atlantic were conducted. Since this research primarily focuses on the US response to the development of a European security identity, interviews with American officials were slightly more numerous. Those questioned include representatives of different US departments such as the National Security Council, the State Department, and the Pentagon. The openness of the US governmental system permitted contacts at very high levels, allowing interviews with some of the major actors involved including Deputy-Secretary of State Lawrence Eagleburger and Under-Secretary of State and White House Deputy-Chief of Staff, Robert B. Zoellick. On the European side, meetings were arranged both with representatives of national administrations as well as with officials of the EC institutions.

In order to allow open and frank interviews, it was agreed with those being questioned that they would not be directly quoted. In the bibliographical part, there is a full list of those interviewed, including a reference to the position they occupied at the time of the Bush administration. Transcripts of the interviews have been typed out and are available from the author.

The focus of the current study is quite narrow and well specified. While several authors have addressed the broader question of the future of the transatlantic relationship in the post-cold-war world,[80] so far little research has been done on the more specific question of the US response to the development of a European security identity. William C. Cromwell, in his study *"The United States and the European Pillar"*, places the debate of the development of a European security identity in a broader historic perspective, but only devotes one chapter to the events of the post-1989 period.[81]

So far, one of the most in-depth studies on US policy towards Europe during the period 1989 to 1993 is that by Robert L. Hutchings, who during the Bush administration served as director for European Affairs with the National Security Council. In his study, *"American Diplomacy and the End of the Cold War"*, he looks into the conduct of American foreign policy with respect to the revolutions in Central and Eastern Europe and attempts to give a first evaluation of the American strategy during the immediate post-war period.[82] Contrary to this research which concentrates on US policy towards Western Europe, Hutchings however primarily focuses on Central and Eastern Europe.

*Structure*

Following this introduction sketching the general background of transatlantic relations during the Bush administration and outlining the research question, the next chapter presents the theoretical framework that will serve as a background to the empirical research. Following a presentation of the principals of realism, this chapter studies the main characteristics of the international system following the fall of the Berlin Wall. It looks at the implications of unipolarity for the position and role of the US in the international system and presents realist scholars' views as to how the US can best deal with the opportunities and constraints resulting from the systemic changes that have occurred in the late 1980s.

The third chapter will place transatlantic relations in a historic perspective and will examine how the United States has traditionally responded to European attempts to play an increased role in the security area. Once the Western European countries had recovered from the war losses and started to become economic competitors of the United States in the 1960s, the question arose as to what extent both partners could also come to a more balanced relationship in the security area. Both Kennedy's Grand Design (1962) and Kissinger's Year of Europe (1973) were attempts to realise such an alliance among equals but they were unsuccessful. It may be interesting to see to what extent factors explaining this failure have continued to play a role in the period following the events of 1989 and to what degree the situation created by the end of the cold war opened the possibility for a more balanced relationship. However revolutionary the collapse of the Berlin Wall may have been, it did not constitute a total break with the arrangements developed during the cold war period and it remains therefore important to examine how far the patterns that have characterised the past, are of relevance in explaining the European and American policies of 1989 and its immediate aftermath.

Chapter four and five present the results of the empirical research. The first case study looks at how the United States has responded to the initiatives of the European Community in the framework of the 1991 Intergovernmental Conference to upgrade European Political Cooperation to a fully-fledged foreign and security policy. The second case study investigates American policy towards the conflict in Yugoslavia and focuses more particularly on Washington's response toward the EC's ambitions to handle the crisis independently.

The concluding chapter examines what the two empirical case studies teach us about US security policy towards Western Europe in the post-1989 period and explores to what extent realism is helpful in addressing this question. Why did the end of the cold war not lead to a return of isolationist forces and a withdrawal of US troops from Europe as some predicted? To what extent was there continuity with the past? What were the main motives and guiding principles behind the US policy and to what extent the realist assumptions are helpful in understanding the policy of the Bush administration towards the newly unified Europe?

## Notes

1. Robert O. Keohane and Joseph S. Nye define the "end of the cold war" in terms of two dimensions: firstly, the withdrawal of Soviet military power from Central Europe; secondly, the reunification of Germany. See Robert O. Keohane and Joseph S. Nye, "Introduction: The End of the Cold War in Europe", in Robert O. Keohane, Joseph S. Nye, Stanley Hoffmann (eds.), *After the Cold War. International Institutions and State Strategies in Europe, 1989-1991* (Cambridge, Massachusetts: Harvard University Press, 1993), 1-19, 1-2.
2. We use the term European Community since the denomination "European Union" has only been formally introduced after the entering into force of the Treaty on European Union in November 1993.
3. William C. Cromwell, *The United States and the European Pillar: The Strained Alliance* (London: Macmillan, 1992), 159 and 174-175.
4. These figures exclude the intra-European trade. *External Trade. Statistical Yearbook. Recapitulation 1958-1993* (Luxembourg: Statistical Office of the EC, 1994).
5. *US-EC Facts and Figures* (Brussels: US Mission to the EC, March 1993).
6. In the first two years of the Bush administration, the deficit with Japan accounted for almost half of the US total trade deficit and in the last two years it accounted for even more than 50%. See *Statistical Abstract of the United States 1991* (Washington D.C.: US Department of Commerce, 1991), No.1387 and *Statistical Abstract of the United States 1993* (Washington D.C.: US Department of Commerce, 1993), No.1330. In the period 1989-92, the US had a slight trade surplus with the EC. See "External Trade and Balance of Payments. Monthly Statistics", *Eurostat* (Luxembourg: Statistical Office of the European Communities, 1992-93), Nos 1-12.
7. M. Delal Baer, "North American Free Trade", *Foreign Affairs*, vol.70, No.4, 1991, 132-149; Peter Morici, "Free Trade with Mexico", *Foreign Policy*, vol.87, 1992, 88-104.
8. Stephen W. Bosworth, "The United States and Asia", *Foreign Affairs*, vol.71, No.1, 1992, 113-129, 122.
9. *President Bush. The Challenge Ahead* (Washington D.C.: Congressional Quarterly, 1989), 102.
10. FC. Fred Bergsten, "The Primacy of Economics", *Foreign Policy*, vol.87, summer 1992, 3-24.
11. Paolo Cecchini, *The European Challenge 1992: The Benefits of a Single Market* (Aldershot: Gower, 1988); Jacques Pelkmans and L. Alan Winters, *Europe's Domestic Market* (London: Royal Institute for International Affairs, 1988).
12. James A. Baker III (with Thomas A. Defrank), *The Politics of Diplomacy. Revolution, War and Peace 1989-1992* (New York: G.P. Putnam's Sons, 1995), 44.
13. See, for example, Michael Calingaert, *The 1992 Challenge From Europe: Development of the European Community's Internal Market* (Washington D.C.: National Planning Association, 1988); Gary Clyde Hufbauer (ed.), *Europe 1992. An American Perspective* (Washington D.C.: The Brookings Institution, 1990).
14. Thurow was extremely negative about the impact of further European integration on the US: "Realistically, outsiders have to face the fact that European integration will hurt them. It wouldn't work if it didn't". See Lester Thurow, *Head to Head. The Coming Economic Battle Among Japan, Europe and America* (New York: William Morrow and Company, 1992), 69.

15 "Remarks at the Boston University Commencement Ceremony in Massachusetts", 21 May 1989, in *Public Papers of the Presidents of the United States. George Bush. 1989* (Washington D.C.: US Government Printing Office, 1990), vol. 1, 582-585, 583.
16 "Declaration on EC-US Relations", *Europe Documents*, No.1662, 23 November 1990. *Cf. infra*, Chapter 4.
17 Initially only Poland and Hungary were given assistance. Later aid was extended to other countries of Central and Eastern Europe. See Simon Nuttall, "The Commission: The Struggle for Legitimacy", in Christopher Hill (ed.), *The Actors in Europe's Foreign Policy* (London: Routledge, 1996), 130-147, 142.
18 The question of the declining position of the US will be discussed in more detail in Chapter 2.
19 On the Uruguay Round negotiations, see Hugo Paemen and Alexandra Bensch, *Du Gatt à l'OMC: la Communauté européenne dans l'Uruguay Round* (Leuven: Leuven University Press, 1995); Terence P. Stewart, *The Gatt Uruguay Round: A Negotiating History (1986-1992)*(Deventer: Kluwer, 1993).
20 Washington had counted on considerable EC concessions with regard to the liberalisation of agricultural trade, hoping to win the support of developing countries for new rules on trade in services and stricter intellectual property rights. See Jagdish Bhagwati, "Jumpstarting GATT", *Foreign Policy*, vol.83, summer 1991, 105-118, 105.
21 For an account on the end of the cold war, see, for example, Michael R. Beschloss and Strobe Talbott, *At the Highest Levels. The Inside Story of the End of the Cold War* (Boston: Little, Brown and Company, 1993); Henry Kissinger, *Diplomacy* (New York: Touchstone, 1994), 702-803.
22 Article IV of the "Protocol amending and modifying the Brussels Treaty" stated that "the Council and its Agency will rely upon the appropriate military authorities of NATO for information and advice on military matters".
23 In that respect, it is interesting to note that in the account he gave on his Presidency, together with his National Security Adviser Brent Scowcroft, Bush limits himself to the events in the area of foreign policy. See George Bush and Brent Scowcroft, *A World Transformed* (New York: Alfred A. Knopf, 1998).
24 For the most elaborate biography on George Bush, see Herbert S. Parmet, *George Bush: The Life of A Lone Star Yankee* (New York: Scribner, 1997). See also Fitzhugh Green, *George Bush. An Intimate Portrait* (New York: Hippocrene Books, 1989); Nicholas King, *George Bush. A Biography* (New York: Dodd, Mead and Company, 1980). For an autobiography of George Bush prior to his years as President, see George Bush (with Victor Gold), *Looking Forward* (New York: Doubleday, 1987).
25 He preferred the post of head of the US liaison office to China to the posts of Ambassador to France or Great Britain. George Bush, *Looking Forward*, 128. His nomination in Beijing was intended to support the newly established relationship between the US and China, which had resulted from the Nixon-Kissinger diplomacy.
26 *President Bush. The Challenge Ahead*, 92-95.
27 When George Bush failed to win the 1980 Republican presidential nomination, he was invited by his earlier competitor Ronald Reagan to become his vice-presidential running mate on the Republican national ticket.
28 Bert A. Rockman, "The Leadership Style of George Bush", in Colin Campbell and Bert A. Rockman (eds.), *The Bush Presidency. First Appraisals* (Chatham, New Jersey: Chatham Publishers, 1991), 1-35, 24-26.

29 "Inaugural Address", January, 20, 1989, in *Public Papers of the Presidents of the United States. George Bush. 1989* (Washington D.C.: US Government Printing Office, 1990), vol.1, 1-4, 2.
30 The visit took place briefly before the inauguration of George Bush. See Michael R. Beschloss and Strobe Talbott, *op. cit.*, 13-17.
31 "Inaugural Address", January, 20, 1989, 3-4.
32 By the end of 1990, Bush had visited 29 countries, almost as many as Reagan after 8 years in office. See Larry Berman and Bruce W. Jentleson, "Bush and the Post-Cold War World: New Challenges for American Leadership", in Colin Campbell and Bert A. Rockman (eds.), *op. cit.*, 93-128, 99.
33 See President Bush himself: "I intended to be a 'hands-on' president. I wanted the key foreign policy players to know that I was going to involve myself in many of the details of defense, international trade, and foreign affairs policies, yet I would not try to master all the details and complexities of policy matters. I planned to learn enough so I could make informed decisions without micromanaging. I would rely heavily on department experts and, in the final analysis, on my cabinet secretaries and the national security advisor for more studied advice. A president must surround himself with strong people and then not be afraid to delegate." See George Bush and Brent Scowcroft, *op. cit.*, 17-18.
34 See Isaiah Berlin, "The Hedgehog and the Fox. An Essay on Tolstoy's View of History", in Henry Hardy and Roger Hauscher (eds.), *The Proper Study of Mankind. An Anthology of Essays* (New York: Farrar, Straus and Giroux, 1998), 436-498.
35 Colin Campbell, "The White House and Presidency Under the 'Let's Deal' President", in Colin Campbell and Bert A. Rockman (eds.), *op. cit.*, 185-222, 189-194.
36 Public approval ratings raised to 89% in early March 1991, the highest presidential approving rating ever reached in a Gallup poll. See George C. Edwards, "George Bush and the Public Presidency", in Colin Campbell and Bert A. Rockman (eds.), *op. cit.*, 129-154, 131-138.
37 Pippa Noris, "The 1992 Presidential Election: Voting Behaviour and Legitimacy", in Gillian Peele, Christopher J.Bailey et al. (eds.), *Developments in American Politics* (London: Macmillan, 1994)(second edition), 279-280.
38 George Bush, *Looking Forward*, 172.
39 Early in his career, Brent Scowcroft (b. 1925, Utah) who had graduated from the US Military Academy in 1947, held several operational, administrative and teaching positions in the US military. He entered the White House in February 1972 as military assistant to President Nixon. Following his positions in the Nixon and Ford administrations, he chaired the President's Commission on Strategic Forces (1983), was a member of the President's Blue Ribbon Commission on Defense Management. In the period 1986-87, he was a member of the Tower commission investigating the Iran-contra affair. Prior to joining the Bush administration, he was vice chairman of the consulting firm Kissinger Associates Inc. Taken from: *President Bush. The Challenge Ahead*, 103-104.
40 This was the time that Bush was director of the CIA.
41 *President Bush. The Challenge Ahead*, 70-71.
42 *Ibid.*, 70.
43 Kegley and Wittkopf quote a senior diplomat complaining that Baker was "running a mini-NSC, not State". Charles W. Kegley and Eugene R. Wittkopf, *American Foreign Policy. Pattern and Process* (New York: St Martin's Press, 1991), 370.
44 Lawrence Eagleburger was a career diplomat who retired from the US foreign service in

1984. He was a close friend of Brent Scowcroft with whom he had worked at the US Embassy in Belgrade. In the 1970s, he worked under Kissinger, first as member of the National Security staff and later at the State Department. Before joining the Bush administration, he was President of Kissinger Associates. See Michael R. Beschloss and Strobe Talbott, *op. cit.*, 26-27.
45 Robert Zoellick had also worked under Baker at the Department of the Treasury. *Ibid.*, 26.
46 Robert Kimmitt had served on the Carter and Reagan National Security Council staffs. Later in the Bush administration, he was succeeded by Arney Canter.
47 The Senate refused to confirm John Tower, Bush's initial nominee for Secretary of Defence.
48 *President Bush. The Challenge Ahead*, 75-76; and Bob Woodward, *The Commanders* (New York: Simon and Schuster, 1991), 60-67.
49 At the first meeting of the cabinet, before the inauguration, Bush has been quoted as saying: "This is going to be an open Presidency. I want you all to feel free to call me at any time; I'm going to call you." Taken from Fitzhugh Green, *op. cit.*, 254.
50 When Bush came to power, the Democrats had a majority of 260 to 175 in the House and 55 to 45 in the Senate. In the period 1991-92, the Democrats increased their number of seats in the House to 268 versus 166 held by the Republicans; in the Senate, the proportion was 57:43 respectively. See Roger H. Davidson and Walter J. Oleszek, *Congress and Its Members* (Washington D.C.: Congressional Quarterly Press, 1994)(fourth edition), 457.
51 On the respective role of the Presidency and Congress in the area of foreign policy, see Cecil C. Crabb and Pat M. Holt, *Invitation to Struggle. Congress, the President, and Foreign Policy* (Washington D.C.: Congressional Quarterly Press, 1992) (fourth edition); Thomas E. Mann, "Making Foreign Policy: President and Congress", in *Id., A Question of Balance. The President, the Congress, and Foreign Policy* (Washington D.C.: The Brookings Institution, 1990), 1-34; John G. Tower, "Congress Versus the President: The Formulation and Implementation of American Foreign Policy", *Foreign Affairs*, vol.60, No.2, 1981-82, 229-246.
52 "A new breeze is blowing – and the old bipartisanship must be made new again. To my friends – and yes, I do mean friends – in the loyal opposition – and yes, I mean loyal: I put out my hand. ... For this is the thing: This is the age of the offered hand." "Inaugural Address, January, 20, 1989", 3.
53 For a critical overview of Bush's relations with Congress, see Charles Tiefer, *The Semi-Sovereign Presidency. The Bush Administration's Strategy for Governing Without Congress* (Oxford: Boulder, 1994).
54 Larry Berman and Bruce W. Jentleson, *op. cit.*, 99.
55 "Remarks at Dedication Ceremony of the Social Sciences Complex at Princeton University in Princeton, New Jersey, May 10, 1991", in *Public Papers of the Presidents of the United States. George Bush. 1991* (Washington D.C.: US Government Printing Office, 1992), vol.1, 496-499.
56 Michael J. Glennon, "The Gulf War and the Constitution", *Foreign Policy*, vol.70, No.2, 1991, 84-101.
57 Examples of foreign policy bills vetoed by Bush are: a congressional resolution restricting the FS-X deal with Japan; the 1989 foreign appropriations bill; the 1991 intelligence authorization bill; a chemical weapons sanctions bill (1990). Taken from Larry Berman and Bruce W. Jentleson, *op. cit.*, 105-106.
58 See Glenn Snyder, "The Security Dilemma in Alliance Politics", *World Politics*, vol.36,

No.4, July 1984, 461-495, 471-472.
59  See, for example, Hugh de Santis, "The Graying of NATO", *Washington Quarterly*, vol.14, No.4, autumn 1991, 51-65; John J. Mearsheimer, "Back to the Future. Instability in Europe After the Cold War", *International Security*, vol. 15, No. 1, summer 1990, 5-56.
60  "A New Europe, A New Atlanticism, Architecture for a New Era", *US Policy Information and Texts*, No. 175, 12 December 1989.
61  James Baker, *op. cit.*, 41.
62  See Chapter 4.
63  See Chapter 5.
64  Robert K. Yin, *Case Study Research. Design and Methods* (Newbury Park, London: Sage Publications, 1989).
65  The term comes from Graham Allison, *Essence and Decision. Explaining the Cuban Missile Crisis* (Boston: Little Brown, 1971), 2 and 245.
66  The theoretical framework that will be used in this study will be further elaborated in Chapter 2.
67  The term "Long Peace" has first been used by John Lewis Gaddis, "The Long Peace: Elements of Stability in the Post-war International System", *International Security*, vol. 10, No. 4, spring 1986, 5-58.
68  Kenneth N. Waltz, "The Stability of A Bipolar World", *Daedalus*, vol. 93, No. 3, summer 1964, 881-909.
69  An exception is Henry Kissinger. He praises the multipolar international system established at the Congress of Vienna (1815) and based on a balance of power among the big players as extremely stable and he recommends a similar set-up for the post-1989 world. See Henry Kissinger, *Diplomacy* (New York: Touchstone, 1994), 811-812.
70  The unipolar moment refers to the post-1989 period where the US is the only superpower left. See Charles Krauthammer, "The Unipolar Moment", *Foreign Affairs*, vol. 70, No. 1, 1990-91, 23-33; Christopher Layne, "The Unipolar Illusion: Why New Great Powers Will Arise", *International Security*, vol. 17, No. 4, spring 1993, 5-51.
71  Kenneth N. Waltz, "The Emerging Structure of International Politics", *International Security*, vol.18, No.2, fall 1993, 44-79, 454-52.
72  John J. Mearsheimer, "Back to the Future. Instability in Europe After the Cold War", *International Security*, vol.15, No.1, summer 1990, 5-56.
73  Mearsheimer, for example, expected that NATO might perhaps continue to exist on paper but would cease to exist as an alliance. See John J. Mearsheimer, *op. cit.*, 188. Others like Charles L. Glaser are however more optimistic. See Charles L. Glaser, "Realists as Optimists. Cooperation as Self-Help", *International Security*, vol.19, No.3, winter 1994-95, 50-90.
74  Charles Krauthammer, *op. cit.*, 23-33.
75  Robert Gilpin, *War and Change in World Politics* (Cambridge: Cambridge University Press, 1981), 187-188.
76  All Bush presidential records are at the George Bush Presidential Library which is located on the campus of the Texas A & M University in College Station, Texas.
77  Use has been made of the daily press review edited by the General Secretariat of the Western European Union. This review includes articles of the *Corriere della Sera*, *Daily Telegraph*, *Die Welt*, *El Pais*, the *Financial Times*, the *Frankfurter Allgemeine*, the *International Herald Tribune*, *La Repubblica*, *La Stampa*, *Le Figaro*, *Neue Zürcher Zeitung*, *Le Monde*, *Le Soir*, *Libération*, *The Christian Science Monitor*, *The Economist*,

*The Guardian, The Independent, The Times, The Wall Street Journal Europe.*
78  See for example: James A. Baker III (with Thomas A. Defrank), *The Politics of Diplomacy. Revolution, War and Peace 1989-1992* (New York: Putnam's Sons, 1995); Helmut Kohl, *Ich Wollte Deutschlands Einheit.* Dargestellt von Kai Diekmann und Ralf Georg Reuth (Berlin: Ullstein Buchverlage, 1996); Margaret Thatcher, *The Downing Street Years* (London: Harper Collins, 1993).
79  George Bush and Brent Scowcroft, *A World Transformed* (New York: Alfred A. Knopf, 1998). The book discusses the following issues: the end of the cold war; the turmoil in China; Operation Desert Storm; the collapse of the Soviet Union; the emergence of the US as the pre-eminent power.
80  Kevin Featherstone and Roy H. Ginsberg, *The United States and the European Community in the 1990s. Partners in Transition* (London: St. Martin's Press, 1993); Nanette Gantz and John Roper (eds.), *Towards A New Partnership. US-European Relations in the Post-Cold War Era* (Paris: The Institute for Security Studies, WEU, 1993); David Gompert and F. Stephen Larrabee, *America and Europe: A Partnership for A New Era* (Cambridge and Santa Monica: Cambridge University Press and Rand, 1997); Peter Ludlow, *Europe and North America in the 1990s* (Brussels: Centre for European Policy Studies, 1992); John Peterson, *Europe and America. The Prospects for Partnership* (London and New York: Routledge, 1996)(first edition in 1993); Michael Smith and Stephen Woolcock, *The United States and the European Community in a Transformed World* (London: The Royal Institute of International Affairs, 1993).
81  William C. Cromwell, *The United States and the European Pillar. The Strained Alliance* (London: Macmillan, 1992).
82  Robert L. Hutchings, *American Diplomacy and the End of the Cold War: An Insider's Account of US Policy in Europe, 1989-1992* (Washington D.C.: The Woodrow Wilson Center Press and John Hopkins University Press, 1997).

# 2 Realism and the End of the Cold War

The end of the cold war has not only led to a fierce debate on the possible future course of international relations, it also provoked a heated discussion on the role and relevance of international relations theory.[1] The fact that most scholars were taken entirely by surprise by the revolutionary developments of 1989 has raised serious questions about the role and validity of theory when studying and trying to understand international relations and has led some to reject the theory tool all together.

Undeniably, the sudden and unexpected termination of the superpower conflict has given researchers a lesson in modesty. It has been a reminder of the complexity of reality, where many variables are involved and where human beings are "conscious entities capable of reacting to, and often modifying, the variables and conditions they encounter".[2] However, it would be an overreaction, and perhaps too facile a solution, to simply drop theory as an instrument. Even if theory manifestly has its limits, it can help us in the formulation of our research question and in the selection of the research data. Furthermore, it reminds us that we are studying a problem through particular lenses and that our views will inevitably always overlook certain aspects of an incredibly complex reality. Rather than throwing the baby out with the bath water, the collapse of the bipolar system should be grasped as an opportunity to put some of the central premises of different theoretical approaches to the test and see what their relevance is to understanding international developments following the end of the cold war.[3]

For a theory like realism, which emphasises the impact of system-level forces on international relations, the post-1989 period, in particular, constitutes an extremely interesting testing ground. Contrary to earlier changes which had taken place within the configuration of power as it developed in the post-war period and merely presented modifications in the interactions among the actors of the system, the momentous events of 1989 constituted a veritable systemic change, i.e. a change in the governance of the international system, "entailing changes in the international distribution of power, the hierarchy of prestige, and the rules and rights embodied in the system."[4]

The period of the Bush administration was one in which the position of the two major players who had been dominating international relations since the end of the Second World War was subject to change. The Soviet Empire fell apart and the United States, even though it was the only superpower left, was increasingly being challenged by other emerging economic powers. The cold war order collapsed but no new order had yet replaced it. The key question being addressed in this study is how the changes in the international system have affected US international conduct, and more particularly how they have influenced American security policy towards its cold war allies in Europe.

Besides its attention to systemic explanations, there are also a couple of other factors which make the use of realism as the principal conceptual framework for this study particularly attractive. For realists, the overriding goal of a state is to guarantee its security and all other requirements are subordinate to this central preoccupation. The fact that this research primarily looks at the transatlantic relationship from the security point of view, further motivated the choice.

A third factor influencing our decision is the prime attention realist theory gives the role of great powers in the international system. Realism reminds us that the rules in international relations best reflect the interests of the big players. Since we are interested in the conduct of the only remaining superpower after the end of the cold war, realism, perhaps more than other approaches, has the potential to provide us with useful keys to understand US behaviour.

Finally, realism also has the advantage that it is a parsimonious theory. It looks at states as a single rational actor, making it possible to account for US behaviour in general terms.[5] While this will allow us to reduce the number of variables and facilitate the organisation of our research, we have nevertheless to remain conscious of the fact that it is rare that a phenomenon can be explained by one single cause or explanation. Generally there are several causal variables, often situated at different levels of analysis and it can therefore not to be excluded that at a later stage the black box will have to be opened and realism will have to be complemented by other approaches, like those emphasising explanations situated at the domestic level.[6] As a first step, this study will however limit itself to the examination of the systemic forces that have moulded US behaviour.

## The Realist Tradition

Realism has been the dominant analytical model in international relations since the end of the Second World War.[7] It originated as a reaction against the utopian and prescriptive character of the idealist school and has the ambition of studying and explaining the world and the behaviour of states as they are, rather than as they should be. Its earliest interpreters, Edward Hallett Carr and Hans Morgenthau, radically rejected the idealists' optimism and their belief that once universal moral principles were rationally defined, a world order based on international law would automatically be established and conflicts would simply become impossible.[8]

In the United States, it was especially the work of Hans Morgenthau, a German national who had emigrated shortly before the outbreak of the Second World War, which was influential. His first major publication *Politics Among Nations* (1947) coincided with a period in which the US was starting to assume an international role and was widely read by the US foreign-policy establishment.[9]

There are many variants of realist thought and different scholars tend to emphasise different aspects of the theory. Generally a distinction is made between classical realism as developed by Hans Morgenthau, and structural realism, a later variant designed in the 1970s by Kenneth Waltz and aimed at addressing some of the deficiencies of his predecessor.[10]

Despite differences, it is nevertheless possible to identify a series of basic assumptions subscribed by most authors of the school in question. One of the central premises of realism is that the principal units in the international system are states.[11] These states are defined as unitary and rational actors, who before taking a decision rationally examine the different alternatives and select the option that best fulfils their national security interests.[12]

Relying on the legacy of authors such as Thucydides, Machiavelli and Hobbes, realists are generally pessimistic about human nature and international relations. In an anarchical world where there is no world government setting the rules, states primarily pursue their own sovereign interests and struggle for security and power. International politics tend toward the model of a zero-sum game and the possibilities for cooperation are rather bleak. States are in the first place concerned about their position *vis-à-vis* others, i.e. about relative rather than absolute gains. Cooperation is not attractive because it always involves the risk that some states may gain more than others, or that one of the partners will defect.[13] It will therefore only occur to the extent that it helps states to realise some of their own purposes.[14]

One of the key assumptions driving the work of neorealists is the view that international relations are in the first place shaped by the structure of the international system. It is considered to be the primary task of the study of international relations to disclose the constraints and opportunities created by that structure.[15] In his classic study *Theory of International Politics* (1979), Kenneth N. Waltz defines the structure of the international system as being determined by two factors: by the "arrangement" of the parts that compose it and by the "principle" by which the system is ordered.[16] Depending on the distribution of capabilities, units occupy a particular place in the system. In contrast to domestic politics, the ordering principle of international politics is not a hierarchy but anarchy. Anarchy is a permanent characteristic of the system, while the arrangement of the parts can change.

It follows from the above definition that the structure of the international system, also referred to as its systemic forces, influences the behaviour of states in a two-fold manner. Firstly, states, depending on their place in the system, behave differently.[17] The determining impact of the distribution of capabilities among the states on the structure means that the latter is primarily moulded by the dominant states of the system and that the structure best reflects the interests of these most powerful units.[18] As a result, great powers will always adopt a behaviour favouring the preservation of the system.

A second factor which determines the behaviour of states is the anarchical character of international politics. Since there is no supranational authority capable of imposing its rules or of controlling the behaviour of states, the international system can best be characterised as a self-help system.[19] Feeling very insecure, states consider it as their primary task to fight for their survival and subordinate other goals to this objective. Consequently, international relations become a continuous struggle for life where moral considerations play a negligible role[20] and where possibilities for cooperation are scarce.[21] The structure further encourages the struggle for preservation by rewarding those states trying to maintain or to improve their place in the system and penalising those who do not.[22]

Even though Waltz places major emphasis on the system-level, the unit-level is not considered to be unimportant as both levels are considered to mutually influence one another.[23] The structure itself finds its origin in the interaction between the units[24] and when there is a change in the distribution of capabilities among the units, this change at the unit-level will affect the structure of the international system and both unit-level and system-level causes will interact.[25]

Waltz insists that he has developed a theory of international relations and that it is his objective to explain international outcomes rather than the foreign-policy behaviour of specific states.[26] At the same time, however, he accepts that the place of the units in the system has an impact on their behaviour and recognises that "units differently juxtaposed and combined behave differently and in interacting produce different outcomes".[27] Also in a more recent article, he admits that the place of states in the international system accounts for a good deal for their behaviour.[28] Together with authors such as Michael Mastanduno and Colin Elman, we therefore defend the view that neorealism is more than a tool to explain international outcomes, but is also relevant when trying to understand national foreign policies, especially those of the major states in the system.[29]

This study examines to what extent the change in the international structure following the end of the cold war has had an impact and accounts for new developments in US foreign-policy behaviour at the time of the Bush administration. A first question which therefore has to be addressed is what were the main characteristics of the international system during that period. Given that anarchy is a permanent feature, the issues to be investigated are the number of great powers dominating the international system as well as the question of the distribution of capabilities among the different units of the system.

## The International System After Berlin

One of the factors which makes the study of the years 1989 to 1993 particularly interesting is that it is a period coinciding with a change in the number of big players[30] and in the governance and the rules of the system.[31] When in January 1989 President George Bush came to power, the international system was dominated respectively by the United States and the Soviet Union and it was still characterised as bipolar.[32] By the time that he passed the helm to his successor William J. Clinton, in January 1993, the United States was the sole remaining superpower and the system had become unipolar.[33]

The historic events of 1989 confronted Washington, as one of the big players in international relations, with important new challenges. On the one hand, the collapse of the Soviet Union brought the long-awaited victory over communism and seemed to suggest that as the only remaining superpower the US was at the height of its influence. On the other hand, the reduced importance of military capabilities as yardstick of power and the rise of economic competitors like Japan and the European Community brought new and, according to some, even more serious challenges to the position of the US.[34] In other words, the end of the cold war presented the United States with the paradoxical situation of having eliminated its arch rival while at the same time and perhaps more than before, having to worry about its position in the international system.

Secondly, the fall of the Berlin Wall deprived the US of the grand strategy that had been guiding its foreign policy for the last 40 years.[35] Its post-war policy of containment had become obsolete and the question of defining US security interests and how they could best be safeguarded was again open for discussion and led to heated debates. Should the US continue to adopt an activist foreign policy or did the collapse of communism allow for a considerable reduction of its involvement abroad? Was it now permitted and advisable for the sole superpower to act alone or was it better to try to operate in a multilateral framework?

The above-mentioned issues of the changing US position in the international system and the need to develop a new grand strategy are closely linked. Depending on whether scholars were taking a more positive or negative view on the American position, they came to different conclusions with regard to the strategy that should best be followed by Washington in the post-1989 period. The next section briefly sketches the debate on the changing place of the US in the international system and then elaborates the strategy recommended by realist scholars to address the situation.

*The "US in Decline" Debate*

Even though the end of the cold war certainly added a new dimension to the discussion, it has to be noted that the debate on the changing place of the United States in the international system was not new but had already started to take shape from the 1970s onwards.[36] By that time it had become increasingly clear that the American position could no longer be compared to that of the immediate post-war era when it accounted for more than one third of world GDP, half of the global production of manufactured goods, and had the monopoly on the atomic bomb.[37] Although the US undoubtedly continued to be one of the major players in international relations, the rise of other powers like Japan and the European Community implied, that at least relatively, its power had declined.[38]

While most scholars did not deny that the United States' position had changed, there was no agreement on what this implied for its influence nor was there a consensus on what should best be done to address, or to stop, this downward trend. Authors like Paul Kennedy[39] and David Calleo[40] belong to those who believed that the relative power of the US would probably continue to decrease and rather than trying to win a lost battle, they recommended that American policy makers try to manage the redistribution of power as well as possible by reducing the nation's commitments and by opting for burden-sharing with other rising powers.

Other scholars, however, challenged their pessimistic view that it was very likely that the US would ultimately share the fate of previous great powers and stressed America's continuing overwhelming absolute power, referring to the country's enormous natural resources, its huge military capacity, its vast economy and its well-trained population.[41] In his study *Bound to Lead*, Joseph S. Nye introduced the notion of "soft power", referring to the huge attraction and influence of American culture and ideology, and to its leading role in international institutions. Nye defends the view that due to greater interdependence and the increasing importance of transnational non-governmental actors, traditional sources of power such as military force have become more costly and difficult to use, whereas soft power is becoming increasingly important in leading other nations to develop preferences or define their interests in ways consistent with those of the US.[42] A similar reasoning is followed by Henry R. Nau who argues that America needs less power today than in the post-1945 period as its democratic and free market model is admired and followed around the world. The *pax Americana* has been replaced by a western era in which increasingly more countries share American values.[43]

While the debate between the "declinists" and "revivalists" was still going on and – as the success of Paul Kennedy's *Rise and Fall* illustrates – the sudden end of the cold war added a new dimension to the discussion on decline and further intensified the debate. For optimists like Francis Fukuyama, the collapse of communism confirmed the triumph of the West and the universal victory of liberal ideology.[44] All twentieth century alternatives to liberalism, from Marxism to fascism had proven not to be viable and as a result, we had reached "the end of history". Or in Fukuyama's words, we had come to "the end point of mankind's ideological evolution and the universalisation of Western liberal democracy as the final form of human government".[45]

Fukuyama's triumphalism was most fiercely attacked by the realist school of thought. Far from reducing the chances of global conflict, the end of the cold war was considered to be the harbinger of a much more insecure rather than a safer world. Sooner or later US primacy would be challenged by other rising powers who would try to redress the balance in relation to the predominant American position, and an unstable multipolar world with many powers competing for influence would arise.[46] Because of the increasing importance of economics rather than military capacities in the post-1989 world, it was thought that it had become easier than before for new powers to emerge.

The main reason why realists generally consider a multipolar world to be less stable lies in the way states balance in such a system.[47] In bipolarity the main players primarily balance through internal means, i.e. by relying on their own capabilities rather than on those of their allies. This considerably reduces the risk of miscalculation and the associated uncertainty. In contrast, in a multipolar world the great powers depend on the conclusion of alliances with other states to right imbalances in the system. Not only is it easy to misjudge the capacities of a possible ally, there is always the danger that a partner might defect. In a multipolar world, realignment by one of the partners with the other side might prove dramatic: in a world of only two, changes in the alliances will hardly be noticed.[48]

Some realists, however, take a different view. Henry Kissinger, for example, argues that under certain conditions multipolar systems can provide stability. He quotes the example of the international system established at the Congress of Vienna (1815), which was based on a balance among the big powers and provided peace for a long time.[49]

At the time of the Bush administration, however, the multipolar world was not in place yet. The United States was the sole remaining superpower, but it was expected that sooner or later other emerging powers would challenge that position. In order to better grasp this process of transition, we will first give an overview of what realism says about the conditions under which change in the international system takes place and how it expects the challenged power to react.

*Change and the International System*

Despite the fact that change is one of the few certainties in history, the subject of change in the international system has generally received little attention from students of international relations. A literature survey by Ned Lebow and Thomas Risse-Kappen of a number of international-relations reviews for the period 1970 to 1990 resulted in the identification of only half a dozen articles on systemic change.[50] Also Waltz himself, although recognising that the bipolar system was unlikely to last as long as its predecessor, pays relatively little attention to the question in his study *Theory of International Politics* (1979).[51] As anarchy is a permanent characteristic of the structure, he attributes a change of the system to modifications in the distribution of capabilities across units, ultimately leading to a variation in the number of principal parties constituting the system.[52] In other words, a system is transformed when the number of great powers changes.[53] Waltz, however, does not elaborate on the conditions under which change takes place, nor on its possible effects. He seems to be much more intrigued by the endurance of the bipolar system and an important part of his research focuses on the question of why it proved so remarkably stable.[54]

One of the few exceptions with regard to the study of change in the international system and its impact on great powers is Robert Gilpin. In his study *War and Change in World Politics* (1981), he formulated a number of assumptions both on the conditions under which ascending powers try to change the system as well as on how the challenged nation will react.[55] He situates the principal cause for a change in the international system in a growing disequilibrium between the system and the distribution of capabilities among its units. Such disequilibrium or "disjuncture between the basic components of the existing international system and the capacity of the dominant state to maintain the system"[56] finds its origin in the differential growth in power among the different units.[57] States whose capacities have grown more rapidly than that of the dominant power will at a given moment, which is indeed completely subjective, consider it profitable to try to change the system so that it better reflects their own interests and will engage in balancing behaviour.[58]

Of central interest to our research is how the leading country will react to the assault on its position. As Gilpin starts from the realist premise that the international system is primarily determined by its dominant powers and consequently very much conducive to their interests, he expects that they will defend the system and try to preserve the *status quo* as much as possible. Gilpin identifies two major possible strategies for a state when trying to halt its declining position in the international system. The first and preferred approach[59] consists of attempting to increase the resources necessary to sustain its preeminence, and primarily embodies measures such as increased taxes, inflationary policies, recourse to increased spending or a more efficient use of the available resources.[60]

The second possible strategy for a great power to try to reverse or at least halt the decline is "to reduce its existing commitments (and associated costs) in a way that does not ultimately jeopardise its international position".[61] Gilpin defines three alternative ways of realising this objective as being: the launching of a preventive war against the oncoming power(s), a further expansion through the conquest of less costly territories, and the reduction of foreign-policy commitments. When choosing the option of reducing its foreign-policy commitments, a state has multiple ways to do so. The most radical and certainly also the most risky way for a state to retrench is to unilaterally renounce some of its foreign-policy commitments. A more prudent approach consists in the conclusion of alliances with other friendly powers who are invited to carry part of the burden in exchange for receiving a share of the benefits of maintaining the *status quo*. A third way to retrench is the recourse to a policy of "appeasement", i.e. to try to accommodate the rising power(s) by making certain concessions with regard to their demands.

There is no guarantee that the challenged power, applying these methods, will be successful. Much will depend on how the other states of the system react to its policy, whether allies accept the concept of burden-sharing and whether the rival powers consider that the concessions made to their demands are satisfactory. It remains that a state always resorts to a policy of retrenchment from a position of weakness and that it is therefore tempting for other players in the system to exploit the situation by trying to obstruct its attempts to reduce its commitments. Consequently, neither the second strategy of reducing commitments and costs will provide the state whose supremacy is challenged with miraculous solutions.

Gilpin's study is extremely interesting for this research as it presents us with a key to the two principal strategies recommended to the United States by realist scholars for the post-1989 period: a strategy of primacy on the one hand, and that of selective engagement on the other hand. Both approaches share the objective of formulating recommendations as to how US interests and security can best be defended, but they differ as to how this goal can be realised. While the strategy of primacy pleads for a policy whereby the US tries to perpetuate its global pre-eminence, the strategy of selective engagement considers that further decline can best be stopped by balancing resources and commitments. The advocates of a primacy policy want the US to remain a hegemonic nation, while for those supporting selective engagement it suffices that the US continues to be a leading nation, possibly together with others.

The following pages will describe the main premises of the two strategies and will present in more detail the views of some of its main interpreters. In the concluding chapter, we will consider what the dominant strategy of the Bush administration was and to what extent the realist premises are helpful in explaining its policy.

## Maintaining the Pax Americana: Primacy Matters

As one of its key players, the United States has played a central role in the shaping of the post-1945 international system and has ensured that it was propitious to its cherished values of free trade and democracy and that it was highly conducive to its interests. Hence it is not surprising that when in 1989 the system was challenged, US policy-makers came to its defence and looked at possible ways of preserving it. They found a very willing ear with realists pleading for a US policy of primacy.[62]

For these scholars the end of the cold war was not a cause for lengthy celebrations or complacency. On the contrary, even though the collapse of the Soviet Union had elevated the United States to the status of being the number one in the international system, it was very uncertain how long it could maintain such a position. Balance of power theory teaches us that unipolar systems are generally short lived and predicts that other powers will rise up and try to balance the hegemon's power so that sooner or later a new international system, either bipolar or multipolar will arise.[63] Although it is commonly accepted that the unipolar moment will not continue forever, there is no agreement as to how long this "geopolitical interlude"[64] can last and several realist scholars have been arguing that by following a policy of preponderance or primacy, it is possible, if not to perpetuate, to at least prolong unipolarity.[65] The main concern of the advocates of a primacy policy is therefore that strategies allowing the American dominant position to be safeguarded as long as possible should be devised which prevent other emerging states from challenging it.

States present both competitive as well as cooperative motives when trying to justify a strategy of preponderance.[66] They may argue that they want to prevent other powers from ascending because they want to avoid the outbreak of a war or because they see other countries as a challenge to their economic well-being. Others justify their policy primarily by cooperative reasons, maintaining that they provide the international system with certain collective goods such as security or an open economic system, which other players are not able to deliver. In Duncan Snidal's words, the central premise of these advocates of a hegemonic stability theory is that "the presence of a single, strongly dominant actor in international politics leads to collectively desirable outcomes for all states in the international system."[67] The hegemon is seen as the best safeguard against disorder and instability.[68]

A typical example of an author advocating a policy of primacy for competitive reasons is Huntington in his early works.[69] In an article published in *International Security* in 1993, he defends the view that now that the cold war is over, it is no longer military but economic primacy that matters and he anticipates that the main conflicts of the future will be of economic nature.[70] Pointing to Japan as the principal challenge to US primacy he recommends Washington to take bold measures to counter Tokyo's policy of "economic warfare". Arguing that no other country can substitute for the US as the main guarantor of order and stability, it is not only in the interest of the US, but also in that of the world that America is not replaced by Japan as the prime nation of the world.

A similar position is taken by Edward N. Luttwak. He introduces the concept of "geo-economics", defending the view that the ancient struggle for territory has been replaced by a rivalry in the economic area, resulting in a declining importance of military power. Trade quarrels will not be fought with weapons but with the instruments of commerce such as import restrictions, subsidies, or competitive structures. Also Luttwak defines Japan as America's fiercest competitor and as a country having a high propensity to act geo-economically. His recommendations to counter the Japanese challenge are primarily situated at the domestic level. He pleads for improved education, more emphasis on investment and a sound industrial policy.[71]

Other scholars have been emphasising non-competitive or cooperative reasons for seeking dominance. They present America as the benign hegemon, the personification of universal values such as democracy and free trade, and as the only power able to maintain world order in an anarchical environment. Krauthammer, for example, sees a continued active US involvement on the international scene as the only way to guarantee a continuing open world economy. The proliferation of weapons of mass destruction have replaced the communist threat as the principle challenge to stability and the United States is the only power which has the capacity and the resources to fight it.[72] He states that "if America wants stability, it will have to create it",[73] "unashamedly laying down the rules of world order and being prepared to enforce them".[74] It is typical of America's missionary ambitions and moralistic approach to foreign policy that Krauthammer not only considers such an approach to be necessary, he also describes it as being "noble".[75]

Another plea for a continued American world leadership based on cooperative arguments can be found in the work of Joshua Muravcik.[76] In his book *The Imperative of American Leadership*, he argues that as the most prosperous and powerful nation, the United States is the only country that can prevent the world from sliding into chaos and instability. Japan, China, the European Union nor the United Nations can provide credible alternatives to

American leadership. Muravcik uses the Yugoslav crisis to prove his case. The decision to let the Europeans and later the United Nations take the lead, had catastrophic consequences and is illustrative for the type of Hobbesian world order that might arise should the US abdicate. The imbalance of power resulting from the unipolar moment is not negative but is one of the best guarantees for continuing peace. Muravcik refutes any fears of the abuse of US power by arguing that the *pax Americana*, unlike the *pax Romana* or *Britannica* "consists only of influence, not of empire"[77] and that America has shown "a vision of the global well-being that others have not".[78]

Whether they underpin it with competitive or cooperative arguments, scholars pleading for the maintenance of primacy all consider that the best way to safeguard US security is by opting for a policy of foreign entanglement. Despite the end of the cold war, US vital interests cannot be reduced to the holding off of a physical attack on its territory. As a trading nation with investments all over the world, its well-being depends on a stable world stage and Washington should be willing to invest in fostering such an environment. As the EC is a major trading partner, it is considered important to closely follow the process of European integration and if possible try to influence it so that it does not develop in a direction which is detrimental to US interests. From a security point of view, Europe, more than other parts of the world, is seen as a partner which can be helpful in realising US objectives abroad and which can provide the necessary military bases for certain military interventions. Proponents of a policy of primacy reject the argument that American involvement abroad is too costly and a factor leading to further decline. On the contrary, the advantages are considered to largely outweigh the costs.

A policy of entanglement is also seen as an important instrument in accommodating emerging powers and in such a way as to prolong the unipolar moment. It provides rising states with security, aiming to discourage them from increasing their own military capacities. In other words it is a way of convincing other states to bandwagon with the Unites States, rather than provide a counter balance against it.[79]

With regard to Europe, the advocates of a policy of predominance advocate a continuing deployment of US troops. In his article *Back to the Future*, John Mearsheimer is extremely pessimistic about the prospects for stability and peace in a Europe no longer dominated by the two superpowers.[80] Uncertainty about the future behaviour of a united Germany, increased risk of the proliferation of nuclear weapons and re-emerging nationalism make him fear the worst for the "old continent". Unable to overcome "cold war thinking", he not only defends a continuing overseas presence of US troops, but he also argues in favour of maintaining a divided European continent, including East-West confrontation.[81]

To what extent US policy-makers during the Bush administration have ultimately decided to follow the primacy option will be discussed in the concluding chapter of this study, following the presentation of the case study material. For the moment we will limit ourselves to formulating some initial critical thoughts with regard to this approach.

The policy of primacy is very much a policy of the *status quo*. Even though only a minority agrees with Mearsheimer's recommendation that it would have been desirable to prolong the cold war conflict, most of the "primacy scholars" support his view that the end of the superpower confrontation created more problems than it resolved. They are so obsessed with the "long peace" of the post-war period that they have difficulties thinking in different terms and overlook the fact that past solutions might not necessarily be suitable for the new international situation.

Furthermore, it may not be as simple to perpetuate the unipolar moment as the primacy advocates suggest. If one takes the view of Waltz and Gilpin that structural constraints are determining factors in the behaviour of states, it might be extremely difficult to prevent growing powers from emerging when the structure of the international system impels them to do so.[82] By not abiding by the rules of the game (i.e. the structure), a state is putting its security in jeopardy and it is indeed very doubtful that it would be ready to take such risk.

A further difficulty with the recommendation that the unipolar moment should be sustained as long as possible is that it stems from a consideration of international relations very much from the point of view of the dominant power in the system. The argument that perpetuating unipolarity is also beneficial for the other players raises certain question marks. Robert Keohane for example seriously questions whether a continued US leadership is needed to maintain international cooperation.[83] Although he recognises that the leadership of a dominant nation makes cooperation easier, he argues that once international regimes have been established they will in most cases continue to exist, even when the hegemon's power has eroded.[84]

What will happen in a situation whereby the interests of the sole superpower do not coincide with those of the others? States are no saints. However "benign" the US may be, it would be against the premises of realism to put the interests of others before its own. It is therefore to be expected that in a situation where there were conflicting views, Washington will always think of itself first. This brings us to the question of how power is checked in a unipolar system. The temptation to abuse the situation or blackmail the other players might become too great to resist.[85] It would not be the first time that the US has used its predominance in the security area as a leverage in trade negotiations for example.

Last but not least, the policy of primacy is a very arrogant policy. It presumes that America knows what is best for the world and can impose its "insights" upon others. Even though the majority of countries in the international community may share the American goals of democracy and free trade, they may disagree with the way the US tries to implement these objectives. A hegemonic system provides few incentives for the pre-eminent player to consult others about their views and preferences. So, even if a policy of primacy is very attractive from the US point of view, it is extremely doubtful whether the other emerging states in the system will accept a vulnerable position.

## Filling the Lippmann Gap

A second group of scholars, even though they also start from realist premises and share the pessimistic views about the emerging multipolar system, are quite critical with regard to the major assumptions of the primacy strategy.

They do not believe that the unipolar moment can be perpetuated for long[86] and argue that since the emergence of great powers is a structurally driven phenomenon, it is an illusion and a waste of resources to try to prevent the rise of the multipolar system. Differential growth rates will very soon push rising states to balance the dominant power and this is an inevitable process which cannot be stopped by a hegemon, however benign his intentions may be. By opposing the transition towards multipolarity, the hegemon will not only antagonise its competitors, it will also further hasten the process of its own decline.

Therefore, rather than striving to sustain the unipolar moment as long as possible, it is recommended that the US try to manage the process of change as well as possible. This can best be done by following Walter Lippmann's well-known recommendation of bringing "the nation's commitments and the nation's power" into balance.[87] America's global ambitions mean that the country lives above its means, which has led to a situation of imperial overstretch. If it is difficult in the short-term to change the relative position of the US *vis-à-vis* other powers, it might at least be possible to prevent a further decline by correcting the imbalance between its capacities and its foreign-policy commitments.

The best way to realise this objective is to become more selective with regard to foreign entanglements and to concentrate on regions where instability and war can constitute a real threat for American security. Most authors agree that the players that really matter for the US are the great powers of Eurasia: the European Union, Russia, China and Japan, as well as the Middle East.[88] They follow the geopolitical logic of George Kennan who argued that it should be one of the prime goals of US foreign policy to see that no single power dominates Eurasia.[89] The father of containment policy opposed America's global ambitions, defending the view that besides the US, there were only four more regions that really mattered and that they were where Washington had to focus its attention. If the US could guarantee the political independence of these players in question (the Soviet Union, the Rhine valley, the United Kingdom, and Japan), its security was safeguarded.

Henry Kissinger expects the emerging post-cold war world to contain at least six major powers, those being the US, Europe, China, Japan, Russia, and probably also India.[90] Although it will still be powerful, the United States will be "a nation with peers, the *primus inter pares* but nonetheless a nation like others".[91] Arguing that international relations will resemble the European state system of the eighteenth and the nineteenth century, he recommends the US base the rising new order "on some concept of equilibrium".[92] Inspired by the international system following the Congress of Vienna, Kissinger advocates a policy based on a combination of balance of power and shared values. In other words, the traditional American idealistic approach towards international relations should be complemented by a policy based on the defence of US national interests. Contrary to nineteenth-century British diplomacy which only intervened when the equilibrium was under threat, Kissinger favours a balance of power model along Bismarckian lines, which aims at restraining power in advance and tries to develop alliances with many parties, not just the weakest one in the system.[93] However, the relationship with Western Europe and more particularly the Atlantic Alliance continues to occupy a special place since both partners share common values and can assist each other in realising common goals. Those pleading for a policy of selective engagement generally support a continued presence of US troops in Europe. Although they do not expect it to be very likely, both Robert J. Art and Stephen Van Evera consider that the possibility of an outbreak of war in Europe or Asia cannot be excluded. Such a war always has the potential of ultimately dragging in the United States and seriously affecting American commercial interests. The objective of a continued US presence in the region is however primarily preventative: by maintaining a limited number of troops, the US signals that it still remains committed to the stability of the region and it preserves an important instrument to influence developments. Also the risk of further nuclear proliferation is an important reason for remaining engaged in Eurasia. Even if the US might not always be able to prevent it, it might at least try to help directing and managing the process.

In contrast to Eurasia, most third world regions are not strategically important to the US as they will never have the potential to tip the balance of power. Arguments that these regions matter because they provide raw materials[94] or military bases are refuted as is the point that the US should be concerned with promoting human rights and democracy in these countries.[95] Even if a democratic third world which respects human rights is preferable, the US lacks both the means and the political support to pursue an activist policy in that part of the world. Only in exceptional cases and fulfilling strict conditions such as a high probability of success and a low number of casualties, may intervention in a third world country be considered.[96]

While all above-mentioned authors strongly recommend the US remain present in Europe and Asia in order to reach its foreign-policy objectives and plead for a policy of balancing from within, Christopher Layne, also driven by the concern that the US adjust its commitments in accordance with its decreasing resources, advocates a strategy of balancing from without. For Layne, the goal of safeguarding stability in Eurasia can best be preserved without a direct American presence. He pleads for a policy of "strategic independence" whereby the United States assumes the role of an offshore balancer, which only comes in when the other states of the region in question prove incapable of regaining their balance against a rising state.[97]

The role Layne is recommending for the US is similar to that assumed by the United Kingdom in the nineteenth century and which Josef Joffe has succinctly coined as a strategy of "anti-hegemonism without entanglement".[98] Rather than committing itself to a permanent alliance, London only interfered when the balance of power on the European continent was disturbed, joining with the weaker states. Equally, Layne recommends the US "rely on global and regional power balances" to prevent one single power from dominating the European continent.[99] Washington should "stay outside the central balance until the moment when its intervention can be decisive".[100]

Although he does not elaborate on the question, Layne's approach seems to suggest the end of, or at least a US withdrawal from, NATO.[101] He does not appear to be concerned about the associated loss of American influence in Europe, nor about the possible destabilising effects of such an act. Attractive from the economic point of view, the strategy of the offshore balancer requires the appropriate diplomatic skills. If the balancer comes in too late, it can prove extremely difficult to redress the balance and, even though it may appear initially to be cheaper, the experience of the Second World War shows that when balancing is done too late or is not successful, it may in the end prove extremely expensive.

An author who is perhaps less concerned about the decreasing US resources, but for his own reasons also recommends a policy of selective engagement, is Samuel Huntington. In his book *The Clash of Civilisations* (1996),[102] he abandons his earlier support for a strategy of primacy and argues that a competition between civilisations is replacing the ideological struggle of the cold war.[103] By trying to impose its own Western values on the rest of the world as the strategy of primacy suggests, the United States risks provoking an inter-civilisational clash.[104] He therefore recommends that the US confine itself to the West.[105] By further strengthening and rejuvenating American-European relations, the US can halt Western decline and assure a continuing central place on the world scene. The revived transatlantic community which he is projecting is however not one of equal partners, but one where the US as "the most powerful Western country" is taking the lead.[106]

If the policy of selective engagement may present a less optimistic picture of the US than the strategy of primacy, the fact that it responds to budgetary constraints and pressures to concentrate more on domestic problems, makes it particularly appealing. It seems to strike the right balance between maintaining a sufficient American involvement abroad while guarding it from becoming the world's policeman. At the same time however, we cannot escape the impression that the recommended policy is somewhat misleading. Considering that it recommends a continuing engagement on the Eurasian continent and the Middle East as well as in the Gulf, the question arises of how selective the strategy really is and to what extent it really differs from the policy of primacy.

Furthermore, the implementation of the policy presents certain difficulties. US foreign policy does not operate in a vacuum. The fact that Washington decides not to intervene in a particular conflict or problem can never go unnoticed and may backfire or weaken its position on other occasions when it considers it has interests at stake. Furthermore, the distinction between regions that matter and those that do not is not always as clear-cut as one might hope. Small conflicts often have the potential to escalate and ultimately involve the greater powers of the region. Intervention at an earlier stage by a big and influential power such as the United States may sometimes prevent such escalation and is in most cases also much less expensive than coming in later.

## Primacy or Selective Engagement?

The end of the cold war has presented US foreign-policy-makers with challenges of an amplitude comparable to that of the immediate post-war period. The collapse of communism and the changing US position in the international system implied that questions of how to define US vital interests had to be looked at from a new angle and novel policies taking into account the changed situation had to be formulated.

Realist scholars have actively contributed to this debate. Starting from assumptions such as the continuing centrality of states as the main players in the international system and the priority of relative over absolute gains in international relations, they have formulated recommendations as to the strategies to be adopted by future American administrations. Two main schools of thought can be distinguished: one which considers that the US, currently at the height of its power, can best guarantee its security by following a policy of primacy or preponderance of power; and another one which emphasises the declining American position in the international system and recommends the US concentrate on regions which really matter, i.e. states which can affect its well-being.

The advocates of a primacy strategy consider that maintaining the imbalance inherent to the unipolar moment is the best guarantee for a continued peace and stability. Emerging powers should be watched carefully and be convinced of the benefit of bandwagoning with the US, rather than challenging it. As the world's most powerful nation and a country which embodies universal values, the United States should assume its responsibilities and become the leader of the emerging international order. It should therefore adopt an activist and engaged foreign policy. The question of resources and finances are not considered to be a problem.

For the second group, the United States, despite its size and resources has become a country as others and should therefore respect what Lippmann has called "the self-evident common principle of all genuine foreign policy", namely "to maintain its purposes within its means".[107] The US should not strive to stay a hegemonic power, but try to manage the transition to a multipolar world as far as possible and accept being simply a great power. America's declining position forces it to make certain choices in its foreign-policy commitments and to limit its engagements to regions that really matter, i.e. Eurasia.

As to their recommendations with regard to Europe, both schools broadly share the same views. They consider it in the absolute interest of the US to stay actively engaged on the European continent. The need to counterbalance Russia and Germany, to fight re-emerging nationalism, and to prevent the risk of a re-nationalisation of defence policies means that a continuing deployment of American troops remains fully justified. The possibility of a war on the old continent, even though it has been considerably reduced, can never be entirely excluded. The lessons from American intervention, learnt at high costs during two world wars, have still not been forgotten. NATO is seen as the most suitable instrument for realising American objectives in Europe and should also be enlarged to the countries of Central Europe. The presence of American troops, even in considerably reduced numbers, is the best proof that Europe continues to matter and it is also a very effective way to guarantee a lasting influence on the developments in that part of the world.

While the supporters of selective engagement press for increased burden-sharing in the Alliance, the advocates of a primacy policy are in the first place concerned about maintaining America's central position and the related advantages and influence. They prove not very receptive to any arguments about equal partnership. Germany is identified as one of the emerging powers which could possibly challenge the United States' preponderance in Europe. By paying special attention to its interests, Germany should be convinced of bandwagoning with the US rather than trying to balance it. It is not excluded that in the long term this may imply the need to provide Germany with nuclear weapons.

Both the "primacy" and the "selective engagement" schools formulate a series of interesting, though to some extent differing assumptions as to what they expect to be the behaviour of the United States in Europe following its changing position in the international system. The best way to test the validity of these assumptions is to confront them with reality and see, through a series of case studies, to what extent they are helpful in understanding the policy of the Bush administration towards Europe.

## Selecting the Cases[108]

The central focus of this research is on the attempts of the Western European countries to foster their own security identity in the post-1989 period and on the question of how the United States has reacted to these initiatives and what has been its underlying strategy. Were the European initiatives indeed welcomed by the US as a pretext to gradually disengage from the old continent, or were they, on the contrary, seen as a threat to the Atlantic-based model for European security which had so far been prevalent. The question is of interest because it gives us a first indication of Washington's future intentions in Europe. While an encouraging or indifferent attitude might point to a willingness of the United States to start handing over European security responsibilities to the Europeans themselves, expressions of reluctance or even obstruction may indicate an American preference for a continuing Atlantic organisation of European security.

Realism, looking at the impact of structural factors on a state's behaviour, expects that a power whose position is being challenged will defend its place and the associated advantages. In order to see whether and how Washington has concretely done so, we have selected two case studies which have had the potential of challenging Washington's central place on the European security scene. Both concern initiatives by the European Community, which had developed into an important player on the international economic scene, and which was the only body that could realistically have ambitions to replace NATO.

The first case study looks at the reaction of the Bush administration towards the EC's ambitions to develop a common European foreign and security policy. In June 1990, the Heads of State and Government of the Twelve decided that besides an Intergovernmental Conference (IGC) on Economic and Monetary Union (EMU), they would also convene one on Political Union and discuss amongst a series of other issues on the agenda, ways of developing European Political Cooperation (EPC), the existing form of loose foreign-policy cooperation among the Member States, into a more fully-grown foreign policy which would also include security and possibly defence aspects. The events in Central Europe and the prospect of a reunified Germany confronted the Western European countries with a wide range of challenges both from the economic, political and security point of view. If the EC was to be successful in addressing them, it was necessary that it first put its own house in order, further strengthening its political capacities.

For the United States, the IGC and more particularly the debates on a European foreign and security policy could have far-reaching effects. If successful, a fully-fledged Common Foreign and Security Policy (CFSP) could develop into a viable alternative to NATO, ultimately making a continuing US presence in Europe superfluous or certainly drastically reducing the American influence in Europe.

The first case study looks at how the United States has responded to this potential challenge to its predominant position in Europe. What does it teach us about US views with regard to the new European security architecture and about its own role in it? Did the Bush administration opt for a radical break with the past or was it, despite the changed circumstances, still very much guided by the principles of the post-1945 period? Was the CFSP welcomed as a sign that the Europeans were finally developing the capabilities to take care of their own security, or was it seen as a rival, undermining the powerful position of the United States?

The second case study, the results of which will be presented in chapter 5, looks at the Yugoslav crisis, the first major conflict in the post-cold war Europe. Following the frustrations about its limited role in the Gulf crisis, the EC saw the conflict in Yugoslavia as presenting a chance to prove that it was developing into a mature foreign-policy actor and eagerly took the lead in trying to address it. If successful, it could be important in supporting those who argue that now that the cold war is over, the European Community is well-placed to take care of its own security, no longer requiring the presence of the United States. The chapter explores how the Bush administration has responded to Europe's ambitions in Yugoslavia and how the crisis has had an impact on the emerging European security architecture. In contrast to the first case study where the examined proposals to a large extent only existed on paper, this concerns a concrete foreign-policy crisis, in which both sides' rhetoric can be tested with regard to their role and relevance for the future of European security.

Although it concerns recent events, a considerable number of articles and books have been written, both on the IGC debate on CFSP as well as on the Yugoslav crisis. In addition, the two developments have been covered widely by official documents and the press both on the EC and the US side. The written information has been complemented by a series of interviews with officials directly involved on both sides of the Atlantic. The list of those that have been interviewed is reproduced in the bibliography.[109] In order to allow for open discussions, an agreement was made with the interviewees that they would not be quoted directly. The full text of the interviews is available from the author.

## Notes

1    See for example: John Lewis Gaddis, "International Relations Theory and the End of the Cold War", *International Security*, vol.17, No.3, winter 1992-93, 5-58; Charles W. Kegley, "The Neoidealist Moment in International Studies? Realist Myths and the New International Realities", *International Studies Quarterly*, vol.37, No.2, June 1993, 131-146; Richard Ned Lebow and Thomas Risse-Kappen, "Introduction: International Relations Theory and the End of the Cold War", in *Id.* (eds.), *International Relations Theory and the*

*End of the Cold War* (New York: Columbia University Press, 1995), 1-21.
2. John Lewis Gaddis (1992-93), *op.cit.*, 55.
3. See for example: Robert O. Keohane, "Institutional Theory and the Realist Challenge after the Cold War", in David A. Baldwin (ed.), *Neorealism and Neoliberalism. The Contemporary Debate* (New York: Columbia University Press, 1993), 269-300.
4. Robert Gilpin distinguishes three broad types of change characteristic of international systems: the system change which constitutes "a change in the nature of the actors or diverse entities that compose an international system" (see for example the rise and decline of the Greek city-state); systemic change, which entails "changes in the international distribution of power, the hierarchy of prestige, and the rules and rights embodied in the system"; interaction change, which refers to modifications in the political, economic, and other interactions or processes among the actors in an international system. See Robert Gilpin, *War and Change in World Politics* (Cambridge: Cambridge University Press, 1981), 39-44.
5. Lynn Eden, "The End of US Cold War History?", *International Security*, vol.18, No.1, summer 1993, 174-207, 179-182.
6. Rather than being an alternative to one another, both the "international level of analysis" approach and the domestic model illuminate and explain different sides and aspects of the same coin. Some authors like Robert Keohane argue that the international level of analysis is a precondition for an analysis at the domestic level. He maintains that "Without a conception of the common external problems, pressures and challenges... we lack an analytic basis for identifying the role played by domestic interests and powers." It is "a question of stages, rather than either-or-choices". See Robert O. Keohane, "Theory of World Politics", in Robert O. Keohane, *Neorealism and Its Critics* (New York: Columbia University Press, 1986), 187-188.
7. For an introduction to realism, see Benjamin Frankel (ed.), "Roots of Realism", *Security Studies*, vol.5, No.2, winter 1995 (special issue); Michael Joseph Smith, *Realist Thought from Weber to Kissinger* (Baton Rouge: Louisiana State University Press, 1986); A. van Staden, "De heerschappij van staten: het perspectief van het realisme", in R.B. Soetendorp, K. Koch, A. van Staden (eds.) *Internationale Betrekkingen: Theorieën en Benaderingen* (Utrecht: Het Spectrum, 1994)(2nd revised edition), 11-39.
8. Edward Hallett Carr, *The Twenty Years' Crisis 1919-1939. An Introduction to the Studies of International Relations* (London: Macmillan, 1940)(second print); Hans J. Morgenthau, *Politics Among Nations: The Struggle for Power and Peace* (New York: Knopf, 1978)(5th revised edition).
9. Ashley J. Tellis, "Reconstructing Political Realism. The Long March to Scientific Theory", *Security Studies*, vol.5, No.2, winter 1995, 2-94, 52.
10. Kenneth N. Waltz, *Theory of International Politics* (Reading, Massachusetts: Addison-Wesley Publishing Company, 1979).
11. Most realists, when trying to define the concept of the state, describe as its principle role the protection of the welfare of its citizens, which, within its territory, legitimises the use of force. See for example the definition of the state by Max Weber, in Michael Joseph Smith, *op.cit.*, 24: "a state is a human territory which successfully claims the monopoly of the legitimate use of physical force within a given territory ... The state is considered the sole source of the 'right' use of force."
For a similar definition, see also: Kenneth N. Waltz (1979), *op.cit.*, 104: "An effective government, ..., has a monopoly on the legitimate use of force, and legitimate here means

that public agents are organised to prevent and to counter the private use of force." See also Robert Gilpin, *op.cit.*, 15: The state is an "organisation that provides protection and [welfare]...in return for revenue". Gilpin himself follows the definition of North and Thomas (in: Douglas C. North and Robert Paul Thomas, *The Rise of the Western World – A New Economic History* (Cambridge: Cambridge University Press, 1973).

12  See, for example, Hans Morgenthau, *op.cit.*, 4-5.

13  Joseph M. Grieco, *Cooperation Among Nations: Europe, America and Non-Tariff Barriers to Trade* (Ithaca: Cornell University Press, 1990); Jan Q.Th. Rood, *Hegemonie, Machtsspreiding en Internationaal-Economische Orde Sinds 1945* (Den Haag: Nederlands Instituut voor Internationale Betrekkingen, 1996), 25-38.

14  This scepticism towards the chances of cooperation has been strongly criticised by so-called liberal institutionalists like Robert O. Keohane. See Robert O. Keohane, *After Hegemony. Cooperation and Discord in the World Political Economy* (Princeton: Princeton University Press, 1984).

15  Realism considers it incorrect to reduce the system in which the states are operating to the sum of its interacting units, but considers that there is an additional element to it, made up by the structure. It is the structure which makes it possible to think of the system as a whole. See Kenneth N. Waltz (1979), *op.cit.*, 79. See also: Robert Jervis, "Systems Theories and Diplomatic History" in Paul Gordon Lauren (ed.), *Diplomacy: New Approaches in History, Theory, and Policy* (New York: Free Press, 1979), 212; Robert Gilpin, *op.cit.*, IX.

16  Kenneth N. Waltz (1979), *op.cit.*, 80.

17  *Ibid.*, 81.

18  Robert Gilpin, *op.cit.*, 29. See also Raymond Aron, *Paix et guerre entre les nations* (Paris: Calmann-Levy, 1984), III: "certaines unités, par leurs dimensions, par leur puissance, exercent un pouvoir de fait sur l'ensemble du système."

19  Kenneth N. Waltz (1979), *op.cit.*, 111. See also Joseph M. Grieco, "Anarchy and the Limits of Cooperation: A Realist Critique of the Newest Liberal Institutionalism", *International Organization*, vol.42, No.3, summer 1988, 485-507, 497: "international anarchy means the absence of a common inter-state government". Realists believe that in anarchy "there is no overarching authority to prevent others from using violence, or the threat of violence, to destroy or enslave them".

20  Hans Morgenthau, *op.cit.*, 10-11.

21  Joseph M. Grieco (1988), *op.cit.*

22  One of the chief instruments for a state to maximise its interests is to engage in balancing behaviour. Waltz defines two possible ways to do so, either through the use of internal means such as for example an increase of military or economic capabilities or by external ways, such as the conclusion of alliances. See Kenneth N. Waltz (1979), *op.cit.*, 118.

23  *Ibid.*, 40.

24  *Ibid.*, 91: Structures emerge from the co-existence of states. No state intends to participate in the formation of a structure by which it and others will be constrained. International political systems ... are individualist in origin, spontaneously generated, and unintended.

25  Kenneth N. Waltz, "The Emerging Structure of International Politics", *International Security*, vol.18, No.2, autumn 1993, 44-79, 49.

26  Kenneth N. Waltz (1979), *op.cit.*, 60-78.

27  *Ibid.*, 81.

28  Kenneth N. Waltz (1993), *op.cit.*

29  See Colin Elman, "Why Not Neorealist Theories of Foreign Policy?", Security Studies,

vol.6, No.1, autumn 1996, 7-53; Michael Mastanduno, "Preserving the Unipolar Moment. Realist Theories and US Grand Strategy After the Cold War", *International Security*, vol.21, No.4, 1997, 49-88.
30  Kenneth N. Waltz speaks of a "consequential variation". Consequential variations in number are changes of number that lead to different expectations about the effect of structure on units. See Kenneth N. Waltz (1979), *op.cit.*, 162.
31  *Cf. supra*, footnote 4.
32  Kenneth N. Waltz defines bipolarity as a situation where "there is a great gap between the power of the two leading countries and the power of the next most considerable states". See Kenneth N. Waltz, "The Stability of a Bipolar World", *Daedalus*, vol.93, No.3, 1964, 881-909, 892.
33  Christopher Layne gives the following definition of unipolarity: it is a system in which "a single power is geopolitically preponderant because its capabilities are formidable enough to preclude the formation of an overwhelming coalition against it". See Christopher Layne, "The Unipolar Illusion. Why New Great Powers Will Rise", *International Security*, vol.17, No.4, spring 1993, 5-51. For scholarly attempts to get a grip on the succession of great powers having dominated the international system since the Treaty of Westphalia (1648), see, for example, Joshua S. Goldstein, *Long Cycles. Prosperity and War in the Modern Age* (New Haven and London: Yale University Press, 1988); Richard N. Rosecrance, *Action and Reaction in World Politics. International Systems in Perspective* (Boston-Toronto: Little, Brown and Co., 1963), 232-237; Kenneth N. Waltz (1979), *op.cit.*, 162.
34  See, for example, Samuel P. Huntington, "Why International Primacy Matters", *International Security*, vol.17, No.4, spring 1993, 68-118.
35  Stephen Walt gives the following definition for the term "grand strategy": "grand strategy identifies the objectives that must be achieved to produce security, and describes the political and military actions that are believed to lead to this goal." See Stephen N. Walt, "The Case for Finite Containment. Analyzing US Grand Strategy", *International Security*, vol.14, No.1, summer 1989, 5-49, 6.
36  See, for example, Richard N. Rosecrance (ed.), *America as an Ordinary Country. US Foreign Policy and the Future* (Ithaca and London: Cornell University Press, 1976). Rosecrance argues that the *pax Americana* is over and that the US has become an ordinary country in international relations, no longer able to pursue its role as maintainer of the international system.
37  Joseph Nye, "American Strategy After Bipolarity", *International Affairs*, vol.66, No.3, July 1990, 513-521.
38  By 1960, the American share of world GDP had dropped to 25.9%. It went further down to 23% in 1970 to reach the level of 21.5% in 1980. From 1980 onwards, it stayed more or less stable. See Paul Kennedy, *The Rise and the Fall of the Great Powers. Economic Change and Military Conflict from 1500 to 2000* (London: Fontana Press, 1989) (first print in 1988), 558 and 563. Other figures illustrating the changing position of the US were its reduced share of world exports (from 17% in 1950 to 10% in 1988), the slowing down in the growth of its productivity rate (from 2.7% in the period 1947-68 to 1.4 % in the 1980s) and the fall in its share of aggregate production for all OECD countries (from 58% in 1953 to 38% in 1975). Joseph S. Nye, *Bound to Lead. The Changing Nature of American Power* (New York: Basic Books, 1990), 210 and Stephen Krasner, "Declining American Leadership in the World Economy", *The International Spectator*, vol. 26, No.3, July-September 1991, 49-74, 53 (note 13).

39  Paul Kennedy, *The Rise and Fall of the Great Powers. Economic Change and Military Conflict from 1500 to 2000* (London: Fontana Press, 1989)(first print in 1988).
40  David Calleo, *Beyond American Hegemony: The Future of the Western Alliance* (New York: Basic Books, 1987).
41  See, for example, John Chancellor, *Peril and Promise. A Commentary on America* (New York: Harper and Row Publishers, 1990); Joseph S. Nye (1990), *op. cit.*
42  Nye refers to this power as "cooptive behavioural power", i.e. power which occurs when one country gets other countries to want what it wants. Joseph S. Nye (1990), *op.cit.*, 173-201.
43  Henry R. Nau, *The Myth of America's Decline. Leading the World Economy into the 1990s* (New York-Oxford: Oxford University Press, 1990), 10.
44  Francis Fukuyama, "The End of History?", *The National Interest*, vol.16, summer 1989, 3-18.
45  *Ibid.*, 4.
46  Christopher Layne (1993), *op.cit.*, 7: "unipolar systems contain the seeds of their own demise because the hegemon's unbalanced power creates an environment conducive to the emergence of new great powers; and the entry of new great powers into the international system erodes the hegemon's relative power, and ultimately, its pre-eminence."
47  Kenneth N. Waltz (1979), *op.cit.*, 163-170.
48  Waltz gives the example of China in the post-war world. The break between Russia and China hardly affected the balance between the United States and the Soviet Union. See Kenneth N. Waltz (1979), *op.cit.*, 169.
49  Henry Kissinger, *Diplomacy* (New York: Touchstone, 1994), 811-812.
50  The reviews that were being checked were *International Organisation*, *World Politics*, *International Studies Quarterly*. See Ned Lebow and Thomas Risse-Kappen, *op.cit.*, 19 (footnote 14).
51  Kenneth N. Waltz (1979), *op.cit.*, 162.
52  *Ibid.*, 100-101.
53  Waltz recognises that the link between change in the number of principal members and change in the system is not absolute in the sense that some powers might gain the great power status at the expense of others while the number of principal players remains the same. See Kenneth N. Waltz (1979), *op.cit.*, 162.
54  Kenneth N. Waltz (1979), *op.cit.*, 161-183. He had earlier elaborated the theme in: "The Stability of A Bipolar World", *Daedalus*, vol.93, No.3, 1964, 881-909.
55  Robert Gilpin, *War and Change in World Politics* (Cambridge: Cambridge University Press, 1981).
56  *Ibid.*, 156.
57  *Ibid.*, 13.
58  *Ibid.*, 50-55.
59  *Ibid.*, 186-190.
60  The Chinese Empire and the Venetian city-state are cited as two examples of dominant powers which were extremely successful in innovating the resources over which they disposed.
61  *Ibid.*, 188-192.
62  Samuel Huntington defines international primacy as follows: "international primacy means that a government is able to exercise more influence on the behaviour of more actors with respect to more issues than any other government can." In Samuel Huntington (1993),

op.cit., 68. Those who are critical of this approach use the term "imperialism". See, for example, Michael Parenti, *Against Empire* (San Francisco: City Light Books, 1995); Stephen Rosskamm Shalom, *Imperial Alibis. Rationalizing US Intervention After the Cold War* (Boston: South End Press, 1993).
63 Christopher Layne (1993), op.cit., 7.
64 Ibid.
65 Charles Krauthammer, for example, referring to the need for a great power to be strong in all categories of power, expects unipolarity to last for several decades. See Charles Krauthammer, "The Unipolar Moment", *Foreign Affairs*, vol.70, No.1, 1990-91, 23-33, 23-24.
66 This distinction has been borrowed from Robert Jervis, "International Primacy. Is the Game Worth the Candle?", *International Security*, vol.17, No.4, spring 1993, 52-67. Jervis himself does not approve of a policy of primacy.
67 Duncan Snidal, "The Limits of Hegemonic Stability Theory", *International Organization*, vol.39, No.4, autumn 1985, 579-614, 579.
68 The concept of the "benign hegemon" was first presented by Charles Kindleberger, *The World in Depression, 1929-1939* (Berkeley: University of California Press, 1973).
69 Later on Huntington changed his views. *Cf. infra*, 47.
70 Samuel Huntington (1993), 71-72.
71 Edward N. Luttwak, "From Geopolitics to Geo-Economics", *The National Interest*, vol.20, summer 1990, 17-23. He further elaborated these ideas in a book entitled: *The Endangered American Dream. How to Stop the United States from Becoming a Third-World Country and How to Win the Geo-Economic Struggle for Industrial Supremacy* (New York: Simon and Schuster, 1993).
72 Charles Krauthammer, op.cit., 27.
73 Ibid., 29.
74 Ibid., 33.
75 Ibid.
76 Joshua Muravcik, *The Imperative of American Leadership. A Challenge to Neo-Isolationism* (Washington D.C.: American Enterprise Institute, 1996).
77 Ibid., 207.
78 Ibid., 70.
79 An interesting but somehow peculiar variation to this strategy is suggested by Josef Joffe. Rather than proposing that the US balances the emerging powers, he suggests that Washington bandwagon with them. See Josef Joffe, "'Bismarck' or 'Britain'. Toward an American Grand Strategy after Bipolarity", *International Security*, vol.19, No.4, spring 1995, 94-117. For a critical analysis of the strategy recommended by Joffe, see Alfred van Staden, "A Return of the Classical Balance of Power", *Studia Diplomatica*, vol.49, No.6, 1996, 77-92, 91-92.
80 John Mearsheimer, "Back to the Future. Instability in Europe After the Cold War", *International Security*, vol.15, No.1, summer 1990, 5-56.
81 If the US nevertheless decides to leave Europe and NATO disintegrates, Mearsheimer proposes the alternative of a well-managed nuclear proliferation limited to Germany and the US balancing against emerging aggressors. Ibid., 52.
82 Kenneth N. Waltz (1979), op.cit., 91-92; Robert Gilpin, op.cit., 85-86.
83 Robert Keohane, *After Hegemony. Cooperation and Discord in the World Political Economy* (Princeton: Princeton University Press, 1984).

84  For a similar view, see Duncan Snidal, *op.cit.*, 579-614.
85  See also Kenneth N. Waltz: "I believe that America is better than most nations, I fear that it is not as much better as many Americans believe. In international politics, unbalanced power constitutes a danger even when it is American power that is out of balance." In "America as a Model for the World? A Foreign Policy Perspective", *Political Science and Politics*, vol.24, No.4, 1991, 667-670, 670.
86  Layne for example expects that the unipolar moment will give way to multipolarity between 2000 and 2010. See Christopher Layne (1993), *op.cit.*, 7.
87  Walter Lippmann, *US Foreign Policy: Shield of the Republic* (Boston: Little, Brown, 1943), 9.
88  See, for example, Robert J. Art, "A Defensible Defense. America's Grand Strategy After the Cold War", *International Security*, vol.15, No.4, spring 1991, 5-53; Stephen Van Evera, "Why Europe Matters, Why the Third World Doesn't: American Grand Strategy After the Cold War", *Journal of Strategic Studies*, vol.13, No.2, June 1990, 1-51.
89  See George Kennan, *American Diplomacy, 1900-1950* (Chicago: University of Chicago Press, 1951).
90  Henry Kissinger, *op. cit.*, 22.
91  *Ibid.*, 809-810.
92  *Ibid.*, 19.
93  *Ibid.*, 835.
94  The only exception is oil. This is also the reason why proponents of a selective engagement policy still recommend an American presence in the Middle East and the Gulf.
95  Stephen Van Evera, *op.cit.*, 15-31.
96  Art defines four conditions which are to be present before an American intervention can be justified: the nation that is invaded should be small and weak; the intervention should be welcomed by the majority of the population; the number of American casualties should be low; and the probability of success should be high. See Robert J. Art, *op.cit.*, 43.
97  Christopher Layne (1993), *op.cit.*, 46-50.
98  Josef Joffe, *op.cit.*, 102-105.
99  Christopher Layne (1993), *op.cit.*, 47.
100  *Ibid.*, 48.
101  Also before the end of the cold war Layne had already pleaded for a US disengagement from Europe. See Christopher Layne, "Atlanticism without NATO", *Foreign Policy*, vol. 67, summer 1987, 22-45; *Id.*, "Continental Divide: Time to Disengage in Europe", *The National Interest*, vol.13, autumn 1988, 13-27.
102  Samuel P. Huntington, *The Clash of Civilizations and the Remaking of World Order* (New York: Simon and Schuster, 1996).
103  According to Huntington, there are seven or eight major civilisations (depending on whether one recognises a distinct African civilisation). They are the Sinic, Japanese, Hindu, Islamic, Orthodox, Western, and Latin American civilisations. See Samuel P. Huntington (1996), *op.cit.*, 40-48.
104  Huntington does not hesitate to define Western intervention in other civilisations as "the single most dangerous source of instability and potential global conflict in a multicivilisational world". *Ibid.*, 312.
105  He defines the Western civilisation as including Europe, North America, Australia and New Zealand. See Samuel P. Huntington (1996), *op.cit.*, 46.
106  *Ibid.*, 311.

107 Walter Lippmann, *op.cit.*, 6-7.
108 On the selection and use of case studies, see Robert K. Yin, *Case Study Research. Design and Methods* (Newbury Park-London: Sage Publications, 1989).
109 See 237-238.

# 3 The US and the Development of a European Security Identity: A Historic Perspective

**Introduction**

The fall of the Berlin Wall and the end of the cold war will undoubtedly be defined by future historians as events which played a significant part in determining twentieth century history. The collapse of communism and German reunification caused shock waves throughout international relations and it was clear that their effects would reach far beyond 1989. These events seriously challenged the rules of the international system which had been developed following the end of the Second World War.

Whatever the magnitude of the above-mentioned changes and their consequences, one should keep in mind that there are rarely complete breaks in history[1] and that despite the momentous events, there are very important elements of continuity between the pre- and the post-1989 period. If it is manifest that the fall of communism in Central and Eastern Europe has had radical implications for European security, it is important to remember that the debate on its reorganisation did not take place in a vacuum, nor did it start from scratch. On the contrary, important use was made of the existing structures and bodies, as attempts were made to adapt them to the challenges posed by the new international environment.

As this study is interested in the attitude of the United States towards attempts to develop an independent European security identity in the immediate post-1989 period, it cannot confine itself to an examination of the period 1989 to 1993, but also needs to try to get a better understanding of the American role in European security during the cold war period and examine how the United

States traditionally reacted to European attempts to play an increased role in the security and defence area.

The great interest with which the US has followed the security debate in Europe, and has tried to influence the outcome of the 1991 Intergovernmental Conference, cannot be understood without placing the transatlantic relationship, as it has taken shape since the end of the Second World War, in a historic perspective. Throughout the cold war era, the United States occupied a central place in European security. After having been involved in the fighting of two European wars in a time span of less than 25 years, the US abandoned its traditional policy of non-involvement in Europe's political and military affairs and gradually started to assume a key role in guaranteeing the security of the "old world".

Besides the experience of the Second World War, rivalry with the Soviet Union was also a major catalyst. From 1947 onwards, the containment of the Soviet threat became the prime objective of US policy in Europe, the continent where the expansion of communism appeared most imminent.

The Truman doctrine (1947)[2] and the Marshall Plan (1948 to 1951)[3] were the first concrete expressions of containment policy and of the United States' determination to become actively involved in European affairs. Through the Truman doctrine, Washington assisted Greece and Turkey in combating communism, while the Marshall Plan contributed significantly to the economic recovery of Western Europe, including the western part of Germany. Due to its size and geographical position, the latter was seen as a major asset for the recovery and security of Western Europe and the policy of discriminating against this former enemy was totally reversed.

The most decisive step in the gradual process of US entanglement in European affairs was made with the signature of the North Atlantic Treaty on 4 April 1949, committing the signatories to mutual assistance in case of an attack.[4] In the 1950s, the North Atlantic Treaty Organisation (NATO), which was initially a loose body, developed an integrated military command and provided the framework to embed a rearmed Germany firmly in the West. To compensate for the overwhelming conventional superiority of the Soviet Union, NATO chose to heavily rely on nuclear weapons.

Throughout the cold war period, NATO remained Western Europe's principal security organisation. As a nuclear power with a huge military capacity, the United States *de facto* dominated the Alliance. By considerably reducing the possibility of a Soviet attack on Western Europe, NATO directly served US security interests, and in addition it provided Washington with an extremely powerful instrument with which to exert influence on Europe.

Although there were occasional tensions with the European partners due to diverging interests and to the hegemonic character of the Alliance, the centrality of NATO in European security was never questioned. All Western European countries, including France, were all too conscious of the fact that the credibility of their defence was contingent upon the guarantee of American nuclear capability and the presence of US troops on European soil. The Alliance supplied them with a relatively cheap security guarantee against the Soviet Union, whose position they could not possibly balance on their own.

Taking into account the United States' entanglement in European security affairs, it is understandable that any efforts made by the Europeans to assume an increased role in political, security and defence matters has always been regarded with a certain suspicion in Washington, especially when such cooperation was intended to take place outside the traditional NATO framework.

Throughout the cold war period, there have been three major attempts by the Western European countries to establish closer cooperation in the foreign-policy and security area. The first two endeavours to establish a European Defence Community (1950 to 1954) and a European Political Union (1960 to 1962) failed. Only the third and least ambitious bid, establishing European Political Cooperation (EPC) in 1970, was successful.

In an effort to better understand the US response to the European efforts to develop its own security identity in the post-1989 period, the following chapter will place the debate on the development of a European foreign and security policy in a historic perspective and will examine how the United States has reacted to the three above-mentioned European initiatives. This should permit us to get a clearer picture of the US' views with regard to the role of the Europeans in the security and defence of their continent and should provide us with an insight into the elements of continuity and change in US policy towards Europe in the post-1989 era.

## The European Defence Community (EDC): Setting the Tone

*Background*

The first serious proposal to develop a European security and defence identity goes back to the early 1950s when the French Prime Minister, René Pleven, inspired by Jean Monnet, proposed the creation of a European Defence Community (24 October 1950). The launching of this very ambitious initiative – proposing a common defence policy, a European minister of defence in charge of implementing the guidelines of the Council of Ministers,[5] and the creation of a European army, responsible before a European assembly – has to be seen against the background of the increasing East-West tensions at the time.[6]

The first Soviet test of the atomic bomb in July 1949 and the outbreak of the Korean war (25 June 1950) considerably increased the feeling of insecurity in the West and put the question of German rearmament and the restoration of its sovereignty firmly on the transatlantic agenda.[7] The US considered the inclusion of German troops to be a crucial element in the defence of Western Europe and decided to exploit the tense international situation in order to address this controversial and sensitive issue.

Conscious of how very dependent the Europeans were, the Truman administration was able to negotiate from a position of strength. At a meeting of the NATO Council in September 1950, Secretary of State Dean Acheson launched a "one package proposal"[8] according to which the sending of extra American troops and the appointment of an American Supreme Commander in Europe was made conditional upon the re-establishment of Germany's armed forces.[9]

For most European countries and particularly for France, the reconstitution of a *Wehrmacht* was an extremely delicate issue so shortly after the end of the Second World War and Paris made it clear that it would refuse to accept German rearmament if it was to form a national military force. As an alternative solution the French Prime, Minister Pleven, proposed the creation of a European army in which German troops would be progressively integrated. The troops provided by the participating countries were to be included "on the level of the smallest possible unit".[10]

The initial response of the Truman administration to the so-called Pleven proposal was rather reticent.[11] The EDC was rightly interpreted as a French manoeuvre to delay an effective contribution to the common European defence and the creation of a European army was considered to be impractical.

Parallel to the EDC negotiations, which were taking place in Paris, there were negotiations on an Atlantic solution to the German problem in Petersberg near Bonn. There, the occupying powers France, the UK and the US negotiated with the government of the Federal Republic on how German troops could be integrated into the NATO framework.[12] When, due to French intransigence, the Petersberg negotiations failed and it became increasingly clear that a European army constituted the only possible way for France to accept German rearmament, President Truman agreed to give the Pleven proposal a chance.

In July 1951, following lobbying by Jean Monnet, General Dwight D.

Eisenhower, the Supreme Allied Commander in Europe, also became supportive of the proposal, and Washington even started to actively promote the EDC project.[13] When in 1953 Eisenhower succeeded Truman as President of the United States, his Secretary of State John Foster Dulles, also a personal friend of Monnet, made the EDC project an end in itself and went as far as staking his personal reputation on it. When it became more and more doubtful whether there would be sufficient support in the French national assembly to ratify the treaty, he did not hesitate to exert strong pressure on the European allies and even threatened "an agonising reappraisal" of American policy, including the withdrawal of the US troops from the European continent.[14]

US coercion remained however without effect. By 1954, following the end of the Korean war and the death of Stalin (March 1953), tensions in East-West relations had calmed down as had the pressure to deal with Europe's security challenges. With a large number of soldiers in Indochina, France's major preoccupation was that the European army would be dominated by Germany. The prospect that Paris would give up full sovereignty in the defence field, while London would remain completely in charge of its security policy, was a further reason why France found it increasingly difficult to accept the EDC as a viable option.

Ultimately, the EDC project would die in the country where it had originated. On 30 August 1954, the EDC proposal was on the agenda of the French National Assembly, but its opponents introduced a so-called "*motion préalable*" allowing for an issue to be conclusively rejected without prior consideration and discussion. The motion was adopted by 319 against 264 votes.[15] The EDC had received a fatal blow without even having received the chance of being seriously debated between the different political groups.

*Lessons and Consequences of a Failure*

The European Defence Community and the European army were never established, and so far no European project in the security area has equalled the EDC in its ambitions. Despite its failure, the EDC project, which presented the European allies with crucial questions concerning the organisation of their security, constitutes an important episode in the history of Western European security.

The difficulties around the negotiations and the ratification of the treaty illustrate very well the high degree of sensitivity surrounding the question of European defence integration. The fact that the EDC negotiations were much more problematic than those of the European Coal and Steel Community

(ECSC) demonstrates that the giving up of sovereignty in the security area is more complex than the transfer of competencies in the economic field. Defence of the home territory is one of the core responsibilities of a nation state and by transferring this task to the European level, the EDC touched an extremely sensitive chord.

A study of the EDC is also instructive as to the different perspectives of the Western countries on European security and defence cooperation. At the basis of the EDC initiative was Franco-German determination to overcome former rivalry and to cooperate in a joint European structure. For France, the EDC primarily provided a way to firmly embed Germany into a European framework. For Germany on the other hand, it permitted participation on an equal basis with the other five states and provided them with the status of being one of the founding members of this organisation.

The countries participating in the French adventure were the same as those who had signed the Treaty of Paris, establishing the European Coal and Steel Community. Although all European NATO members were invited to participate in the EDC, only Italy and the Benelux countries associated themselves with this process.[16] The United Kingdom made it immediately clear that it would not participate in a proposal where key powers would be transferred to a supranational authority.[17]

The absence of the British proved to be a determining factor in the ultimate failure of the EDC. Without the presence of the UK, France did not feel sufficiently confident to face Germany on its own. Furthermore, Paris felt reluctant to give up its sovereignty in the security area while the UK remained fully independent.

The United States was not a direct participant in the EDC, but nevertheless played an extremely important role in the treaty negotiations as an observer.[18] Considering that German rearmament was indispensable for the credibility of Europe's defence and looking forward to an active European participation in the defence of the continent, the Truman and later the Eisenhower administration followed the course of the EDC negotiations very closely. Furthermore, the Eisenhower administration, as mentioned above, did not hesitate to exert strong pressure on the ratification of the EDC treaty.

Since the European army was to be an integral part of NATO and to operate under an American Supreme Allied Commander (SACEUR), the creation of the EDC was not seen as a threat but as a support for the Alliance. As was stated by Secretary of State Dean Acheson, the EDC was a form of "European cooperation within and in support of NATO". The European army would strengthen Atlantic defence and therefore directly serve US security interests. If ratified, the EDC treaty would positively contribute to the realisation of some of the United States' prime objectives in Europe: Franco-German rapprochement, the cementing of Germany into the West, the strengthening of the common Atlantic defence and closer association between Europe and the Atlantic community.[19]

In the end it was not in the United States but in the country that originally launched the proposal, France, that the EDC treaty ultimately failed to pass the test. However, the response to the central and extremely sensitive question of German rearmament was ultimately given by the UK. In September 1954, the British Foreign Secretary Anthony Eden proposed enlarging the Brussels Treaty Organization by the inclusion of Germany and Italy and making Germany a full member of NATO.[20] Allied troops would remain in Germany and the latter would have to agree not to produce atomic, biological and chemical weapons. To win support for its proposal, the UK agreed to maintain four divisions on the continent.[21]

Eden's solution, leading to the signature of the Paris Agreements on 23 October 1954, was in two respects a victory for London.[22] Firstly, it implied that the intergovernmental approach would prevail over the supranational solution of the EDC. Secondly, it constituted a purely Atlantic response to the central question of German rearmament.

By accepting the British solution, France who had rejected the establishment of a European army because it did not provide sufficient guarantees against a resurgent Germany, now accepted German rearmament on a national basis. Paris appeared to be more comfortable facing a rearmed Germany in the framework of the Alliance, where it would be on the same side as the US and the UK, rather than in the framework of the EDC, where it would be facing Germany on its own.

The controversy around the EDC dominated the European security debate for more than four years. Although the European army was not established, it cannot be denied that the period 1950 to 1954 was an important time in that it laid the foundations that would be underpinning European security for the next 40 years and even beyond.

It was in the early 1950s that NATO was turned into an effective military organisation with an integrated military command and that Germany was incorporated into Western defence. By opting for an Atlantic rather than a European solution, the Western European countries lost an important opportunity to become more active players on the European security scene and their choice further strengthened the already dominant position of the United States in Europe.

Interestingly enough, this situation was not so much the result of US pressure, but of the deliberate choice of the Western European countries themselves, not least of France. Dependent on the US nuclear umbrella and dwarfed by the US' overwhelming power both in economic and military terms, the European countries, after four years of squabbling, ultimately decided to put all their eggs in the NATO basket, promoting this organisation as the central Western security organisation.

## The Fouchet Proposals

*Strains in the Alliance*

A second critical episode for any scholar interested in the debate on the development of a European security identity and its bearings on transatlantic relations is the period following the coming to power of President Charles de Gaulle in France (June 1958). The French President was the first to seriously challenge Washington's dominant position in the Alliance and to try to counterbalance US preponderance by strengthening the position of the European partners through the creation of a European Political Union.

The French initiative has to be situated against the background of the changed European and international environment of the time. By the late 1950s, the Western European economies had recovered from their war losses and the six Member States of the European Economic Community (EEC), who had engaged in a process of intense trade liberalisation, were no longer dependent on American aid. On the contrary, they were on their way to becoming important competitors of the United States, which in 1958 was confronted with its first balance of payments deficit.[23]

In contrast, in the political-military arena Western Europe very much continued to be Washington's junior partner. Having given priority to their economic recovery, the Western European countries remained entirely dependent on NATO for their security, the organisation in which Washington was the predominant player. A series of events and developments on the international scene in the mid- and late 1950s confronted the Europeans with the drawbacks of a policy which entailed absolute dependence on an outside and much more powerful partner.

In 1956, the outbreak of the Suez crisis illustrated for the first time in a dramatic way that the US and Western Europe did not necessarily always see things in the same way and the incapacity of France and the United Kingdom to act on their own was blatantly clear.[24] Through the events in Suez, both European countries learned the hard way that when Washington did not share their views, they were inevitably condemned to be the losers.

A further reason for concern in transatlantic relations was the Soviet launching of Sputnik in October 1957, indicating that it would not take long before American cities would become vulnerable to a Soviet attack.[25] This raised doubts about the credibility of the American nuclear guarantee and about NATO's strategy of massive retaliation. As an alternative, US Secretary of Defence Robert McNamara, in the early 1960s, proposed the strategy of flexible response according to which the US would have a range of conventional and nuclear options to be able to respond to an eventual Soviet attack.

This provoked fears in Europe that the US would no longer come to its nuclear defence in all cases and raised the spectre of a limited European war. As a result, the US monopoly over the decision to use nuclear weapons was increasingly being questioned and there was a mounting desire on the European side to acquire some control over the use of nuclear force.[26]

A final factor which caused strains in the Alliance was the tense situation in Berlin.[27] When in late 1958, the Soviet leader, Khrushchev, questioned the rights and the presence of the Western powers in West-Berlin, the allies disagreed over whether or not to open negotiations with the Soviet Union over this issue. The conciliatory stance of the United States was strongly opposed by France and the Federal Republic of Germany. It led to concerns that the American interest in Europe was diminishing and that international relations would increasingly be based on a situation of superpower bilateralism. Washington's acquiescence in the building of the Berlin Wall (August 1961) further strengthened this uneasiness.

The above-mentioned developments led both sides of the Atlantic to consider possible ways of adjusting their relationship to the altered situation and the new challenges. Two major, and to some extent competitive, proposals were being launched. In Europe, there was the proposal by President de Gaulle to develop a European Political Union among the Member States of the European Community. While in the United States, the Kennedy administration launched its project for a Grand Design or a new Atlantic association between Europe and the United States.

The following pages will examine the two undertakings in more detail and study their impact on the transatlantic relationship.

## President de Gaulle's Dream of a United Europe

The European leader who was undoubtedly most preoccupied with Europe's and especially France's dependent position in the political-military field was the French President de Gaulle.

Very soon after he came to power in June 1958, de Gaulle addressed a memorandum to President Eisenhower and to the British Prime Minister, Harold Macmillan, in which he proposed a "*directoire*" among the US, the UK and France, which would give Paris not only a say in the determination of global strategy, but which would also attribute it with a finger on the nuclear trigger.[28] It is interesting to note that Germany was not included in the French proposal.

Not surprisingly such a proposal for a triumvirate leadership by a non-nuclear power was not received with much enthusiasm in Washington. In his reply, President Eisenhower uttered that it would be inappropriate to give the other European allies "the impression that basic decisions affecting their own vital interests are being made without their participation" and he expressed his objections against a special status for any NATO country.[29]

Being rebuffed in his attempt to become one of the three major Western powers on equal footing with the United States and the United Kingdom, de Gaulle turned to Europe to realise his global power ambitions. If France itself no longer had the necessary resources to claim the status of a great power, it could perhaps do so if it was able to speak on behalf of Europe.

At a press conference on 5 September 1960, during which he attacked both the European Communities and NATO, de Gaulle made an appeal to the Member States of the EEC to start regular consultations with the objective of trying to harmonise their actions in the political, economic, cultural, and defence area.[30] The main forum for such cooperation was to be regular meetings of the heads of state and government or the responsible ministers.

In line with his view that states are the only realities in politics, de Gaulle's proposals did not include the establishment of a supranational body such as the High Authority of the European Coal and Steel Community or the European Commission. Specialised committees, supported by a permanent secretariat in Paris, were to do the preparatory work. A European assembly composed of delegations of the national parliaments would have the power to make recommendations. A referendum would give the cooperation the indispensable support of the European people.

Even though they were critical about certain aspects of the proposal, the EC Member States agreed that some form of closer political cooperation among the European countries was desirable and they agreed to start discussions.[31] At a first meeting of the Heads of State and Government on 10 to 11 February 1961 in Paris, a committee composed of representatives of the six governments and chaired by the French Ambassador to Denmark, Christian Fouchet, was asked to elaborate concrete proposals.

The meetings of the so-called Fouchet committee and the negotiations in general were soon dominated by three major questions: the relationship of the emerging Political Union with the European Communities, the participation of the United Kingdom in the Political Union and the Union's links with the Atlantic Alliance.

*Political Union and the European Communities* A first controversial question in the discussions among the Six was how the future Political Union would relate to the European Communities. President de Gaulle's suggestion of integrating the EC into the overarching structure of the intergovernmental Political Union was seen as a threat to the position of the European Commission.

Especially the smaller Member States like Belgium and the Netherlands for whom the supranational institutions constituted a guarantee against domination by the bigger Member States were wary of such development. They therefore demanded that the competencies of the Political Union and the European Communities were kept separate and that the Political Union would not deal with economic matters.

As a result of their demands, in which they were also supported by Germany and Italy, the declarations adopted at the Paris (10 to 11 February 1961) and Bonn (18 July 1961) summits explicitly refer to the EC Treaties of Paris and Rome. The first draft treaty submitted by the French in early November 1961 and more commonly referred to as Fouchet I, no longer included economic cooperation as one of the core competencies of the Political Union.[32]

Throughout the negotiations suspicions with regard to the French intentions *vis-à-vis* the European Communities persisted. This distrust was not unfounded. When in January 1962, France submitted a second draft treaty, the so-called Fouchet II proposal, economics was once again introduced as one of the fields of action of the Political Union.[33] The prospects for the conclusion of an agreement on Political Union started to look increasingly slim.

*The British Connection* A further issue receiving considerable attention from the Fouchet committee was the question of British participation in the negotiations on Political Union, a position defended with fervour by the

Netherlands.[34] Although London had not yet officially applied for EC membership, The Hague expected them to do so in the near future and considered therefore that their participation in the negotiations was justified. In the early phase of the discussions, the Netherlands and its Minister of Foreign Affairs, Joseph Luns, were not supported in this demand, all the more since London was only asking to be informed about the course of the debate among the Six.

The situation changed in 1961, when the UK applied for EC membership in the August and accession negotiations finally started in the November. The Dutch demand was no longer without any foundation and the Belgian Minister of Foreign Affairs, Paul-Henri Spaak, declared that his country now also supported the so-called *"préalable anglais"*.[35] The Dutch-Belgian position was further strengthened in March 1962, when the British themselves proclaimed that they were interested in participating in the negotiations.

The debate on British participation reached a climax when at a meeting in Paris on 17 April 1962, Spaak and Luns announced that they would refuse to sign a treaty on Political Union as long as the UK was not a member of the EC. The negotiations ran into a complete deadlock and the meeting ended without fixing a date for a new one, without a communiqué and without giving a new mandate to the preparatory committee. The negotiations were not resumed and de Gaulle's dream of a political Europe with France providing the lead was shattered. Once again the position of the UK was an important if not a determining factor in the failure of the negotiations.

The positions of Belgium and the Netherlands have often been criticised for being inconsistent. While criticising the intergovernmental character of the French proposal, they at the same time pleaded for the membership of the United Kingdom, the most fierce opponent of the supranational Community method.

The reasoning behind this apparently contradictory attitude is that if they had had to accept a Political Union along de Gaulle's intergovernmental premises, the Belgian and Dutch governments would have preferred the United Kingdom to have been a member of such a Union.[36] London was not only considered to provide a solid counterweight against the Franco-German axis, its close relationship with the United States would have guaranteed the Political Union's respect for Atlantic interests.

*Political Union Versus NATO* The third question generating heated debate during the Fouchet negotiations was the relationship of the Political Union with the Atlantic Alliance and the United States. Even though most Member States supported the idea of closer political cooperation among the Six, they did not want it to be at the detriment of NATO, the ultimate guarantor of their security.

Not only the smaller Member States but also Germany and Italy questioned de Gaulle's intentions towards the Alliance and it was only after having received assurances that the Union would not interfere with NATO competencies, that Chancellor Adenauer decided to support the French proposal. The Netherlands defended a more radical position, arguing that defence questions were not to be discussed at all outside the NATO framework.[37]

The first Fouchet proposal specifically mentioned that a common defence policy would be adopted in cooperation with other free nations (i.e. the United States), but in Fouchet II (January 1962) any such reference was again dropped. This was unacceptable for the others and in the joint counterproposal which they submitted, they explicitly referred to the Atlantic Alliance.[38]

The debate on the relationship with the Alliance reflects the existence of two different visions of the future of European security among the Six: that of a European versus that of an Atlantic Europe. Even though de Gaulle recognised the continuing importance of NATO in a bipolar world, he considered that its organisation and structures no longer reflected the existing power relations and that its European scope was not adapted to the political and strategic challenges of the time which were of a global nature.[39] The French President argued that Europe should also have the possibility of discussing defence matters outside NATO, in the framework of a European Political Union. By speaking with one voice, Europe could considerably strengthen its position on the international scene and also bring about a more balanced relationship within the Alliance.

In de Gaulle's view it was France which should become Europe's main interlocutor with Washington. Germany was still too much burdened by its past and the other EEC Member States were simply not in a position to compete for such role. By assuming this function, France would be able to accomplish its prime foreign-policy objective of restoring its independence and realising its ambitions of being a great power.

For most EC Member States the French leadership was not as evident as it might have seemed from de Gaulle's point of view. As long as the Soviet threat continued to exist, there was no way that a much weaker France could be a credible substitute for US leadership. In addition, they considered it preferable to be led by a faraway power like the United States than by an immediate neighbour like France.

The reservations towards French leadership are best reflected by the Dutch insistence on Britain's membership of the Political Union. London was considered to serve the double objective of preventing French supremacy and guaranteeing respect for Atlantic interests.

*France Turns to Germany* Following the impasse in the Fouchet negotiations in April 1962, there were several attempts to relaunch the Political Union debate among the Six, but without result.[40] Ultimately de Gaulle turned to Germany to realise his project on a bilateral basis, setting the example for the other European partners and hoping that they would join at a later stage.

On 22 January 1963, de Gaulle and Adenauer signed the Franco-German Treaty on Friendship and Cooperation, providing for political, military, cultural and economic cooperation, the same areas of consultation as in the draft treaty on Political Union.[41] What he had not succeeded to realise with the Six, the French President now attempted to do with Bonn.

Although this was meant to be the symbol of Franco-German reconciliation, the treaty met a lot of resistance. Many in Germany, both in the opposition as well as in Adenauer's CDU, feared that the treaty would give the wrong signal to the United States on whom Germany continued to be fully dependent for its defence. When the German *Bundestag* ultimately ratified the text, it did so only after having added a preamble which referred to close cooperation with the United States, NATO's integrated command, EC membership of the United Kingdom and German unification.[42] All issues over which the Fouchet negotiations had foundered were back again and the text was deprived of substance even before it had entered into force. It would take until the early 1980s before the treaty really took off.[43]

*An Alternative Approach: Kennedy's Grand Design*

In contrast to the negotiations on the European Defence Community where it was a participant all but in name, the United States was not directly involved in the debate on Political Union. Nonetheless, the Kennedy administration very closely followed the developments in Europe and through its embassies and some of its allies was well-informed about the state of the negotiations.

Having learned the lesson during the EDC that getting involved in European affairs could adversely affect its influence on the debate, the US did not try to intervene in the Fouchet negotiations but reacted to the French challenge to US leadership in Europe by launching its own blueprint for a restructured transatlantic relationship.[44]

In a speech on 4 July 1962 in Philadelphia, President John Kennedy launched an appeal for "a concrete Atlantic partnership between the new union now emerging in Europe and the old American Union founded here 175 years ago". With his so-called Grand Design, Kennedy hoped to adapt the transatlantic relationship to the new economic and political realities of the 1960s. He tried to deal with a double concern on the American side: the increasing economic competitiveness of the EEC on the one hand and the fears for nuclear proliferation in Europe following the increased Russian strategic nuclear capabilities on the other hand.[45]

The important tariff reductions in the European Community and the introduction of the Common External Tariff (CET) had led to fears in Washington that transatlantic trade might significantly be reduced, further increasing the already considerable American balance of payments deficit. To remedy the situation President Kennedy proposed a further liberalisation of trade and, in January 1962, he submitted the Trade Expansion Bill to Congress, which would allow the US President to conduct multilateral trade negotiations reducing tariffs by up to 50%.[46] Besides the promotion of US trade interests, a major objective of the initiative was to strengthen transatlantic ties and realise what in the Grand Design would be the economic pillar of the Atlantic partnership.

If in the economic area, the idea of an equal partnership between both sides of the Atlantic was a viable option, in the security field it was much more problematic and fraught with contradictions. The US' greater weight in NATO continued to be overwhelming and it was indeed questionable whether this situation could be overcome in the short term.

The most pressing challenge in transatlantic security relations at the time of the Kennedy administration was not a minor one. It was to restore confidence in the credibility of the American deterrent and to prevent the European countries from developing their own nuclear capacities as a result of Soviet nuclear parity.

In an attempt to maintain effective control over the use of nuclear weapons, while at the same time giving the European allies a sense of nuclear participation, the US launched the idea of a Multilateral Nuclear Force (MLF) in NATO.[47]

The proposal had first been launched in 1960 by the Eisenhower administration and was then renewed by President Kennedy. According to this proposition the decision to launch nuclear weapons would be taken by an intergovernmental council of MLF participants. The United States would however in all cases preserve its veto right and control over the MLF was to be in the hands of the Supreme Allied Commander in Europe, clearly showing the limits of the US' willingness to really share power.[48]

The MLF proposal obtained only a lukewarm reception in Europe. France, who had successfully exploded its first nuclear bomb in February 1960, regarded the plan as a devise to obstruct its own ambitions in the nuclear field.[49] An independent *force de frappe* was one of the central instruments for realising his objective to restore French *grandeur* and privately de Gaulle did not hesitate to refer to the project as a "multilateral farce".[50] The MLF would furthermore undermine France's nuclear monopoly as it would give other continental powers in Western Europe, including Germany, a say in the use of nuclear weapons.[51]

Western Europe's other nuclear power also lacked enthusiasm for the American plans. The United Kingdom considered the proposal as a threat to its privileged relationship with Washington and preferred to discuss nuclear matters on a bilateral basis. If they were to participate, the British wanted to have the possibility of withdrawing their own nuclear weapons from the MLF when supreme national interests were at stake.

It was only in Bonn that the idea of a Multilateral Nuclear Force could count on support. After the German frustration with the US over Berlin, the German government was extremely pleased with the renewed US interest in European affairs. Contrary to the other big countries, Germany was not allowed to develop nuclear weapons and the MLF would therefore improve Bonn's position. As a matter of fact, fears that the Germans might have an appetite for nuclear weapons had been an important consideration in the development of the American plans.

Besides multilateral trade negotiations and the MLF, a third instrument in the strategy to realise the American objective of an Atlantic community was that of British membership of the European Community.[52] Now that the Europeans had embarked upon the plan to start closer political integration, it was considered to be in the interest of the United States that the United Kingdom would also be part of such a Union. London could fulfil the double function of counterbalancing French dominance and defending Atlantic interests.[53] Realising that if it remained aloof of the developments in Europe the US might loose interest in its special relationship with London, the British themselves also started to consider the membership option and in August 1961 Prime Minister Macmillan asked to start accession negotiations.[54]

American hopes of strengthening the Atlantic orientation of the EEC through British membership were however soon shattered when President de Gaulle at a press conference on 14 January 1963 expressed his veto against accession. The Nassau deal between Kennedy and Macmillan in December 1962 according to which the UK was to receive Polaris missiles from the US, had confirmed de Gaulle's worst suspicions about the "Anglo-Saxons" and proved that London was definitely choosing military integration with the US rather than with Europe.[55] Having been frustrated in his attempts to establish a European Europe, de Gaulle did not hesitate to undermine the Atlantic alternative and said *"non"* to the United Kingdom.

Conceiving grand designs on paper is different from making them work in reality. If the idea of an equal partnership was certainly an attractive one, in the security area it did not correspond with the real state of affairs and it was therefore condemned to be artificial and unrealistic. The Americans had to learn the hard way that the appearance of enhanced European participation in security matters was not sufficient for the realisation of a viable restructuring of the Alliance. It was not with a proposal like the MLF, where the Europeans were only given the illusion of being involved in the nuclear decision-making process, that the existing imbalance in NATO could be addressed.

Ultimately, it was only in the economic area that the Grand Design would lead to some concrete results, with the realisation of a new round of multilateral trade negotiations in the framework of the Kennedy Round.

*Two Competing Designs*

The early 1960s brought to the fore two different designs trying to cope with the changes and challenges facing transatlantic relations in that period. Although neither of the projects was ultimately to be realised, they are of interest as they are illustrative for the difficulties involved in transforming the transatlantic relationship into a true partnership and because they give a clear indication of how two of the key actors in the Alliance, the United States and France saw the further development of the organisation of European security.

The Kennedy administration recognising the need to give the Europeans a bigger say in the organisation of their security, proposed to give them this within the existing framework of the Alliance. Kennedy's ideal was that of an Atlantic association between Western Europe and the United States, where both partners would discuss economic and security matters and where they would form a unified Western bloc against the Soviet Union. Closer European integration was possible and even desirable on the condition that it led to the strengthening of Atlantic cooperation.

The French President, de Gaulle, on the other hand, considered that European and American interests were not necessarily always the same and that the Alliance no longer reflected the power relations between both partners and therefore wanted Europe to follow a more independent course in the foreign-policy area. He proposed combining European forces in the framework of a Political Union, which would if necessary be able to defend specific European interests and which would increase Europe's weight on the international scene.

The French President's proposals for Political Union were not to be realised, but this had less to do with US opposition than with the diverging perceptions of the EC Member States on foreign-policy and security cooperation. If most of them were sympathetic to the idea of increasing cooperation in the foreign-policy field, they were all extremely reticent about undertaking any action that might negatively affect NATO, which provided the central underpinning of their security.

Most Western European countries did not share France's eagerness to follow a course which was independent from the US. On the contrary, they were worried about a possible de-coupling of US and European security, and they were certainly not willing to embark upon any adventures which might hasten such a process. The failure of the Fouchet negotiations showed that if de Gaulle wanted them to choose between France and the United States, they definitely preferred to entrust their security to a nuclear superpower rather than to a middle-ranking European country with global ambitions.

Contrary to what de Gaulle might have hoped, increased questions about the reliability of the US nuclear guarantee did not lead to greater European solidarity. On the contrary, it made the Western European countries extremely cautious about not undertaking any action which might further loosen the links with the US.

The Fouchet episode is also instructive as concerns the position of the United States *vis-à-vis* independent European security initiatives. Although there were no threats of "agonising reappraisals" as during the EDC negotiations, there is no doubt that the US was not enthusiast about the French plans, which were undeniably a direct challenge to US leadership in Europe.

The Kennedy administration's proposal for a more balanced relationship between both sides of the Atlantic should in the first place therefore be seen as an attempt to safeguard American interests in Europe. Increased trade across the Atlantic had to offset the effects of the creation of the EEC's common market and the Multilateral Nuclear Force was to guarantee continued American control of the West's nuclear deterrent.

In order to realise its own preferred option, the Kennedy administration did not hesitate to lobby with its closest European allies. Pressure on the UK to apply for EC membership is a case in point. Also Germany was an important pawn on the transatlantic chessboard, especially after the French vetoed

Macmillan in January 1963. In an attempt to counteract the increasingly close cooperation between de Gaulle and Adenauer, the US government did not lose any efforts to court Bonn. The MLF and President Kennedy's visit to Berlin in June 1962 were all part of the same strategy to anchor Germany firmly to the Alliance and to prevent the Franco-German axis from developing at the expense of closer American-German relations.[56]

Neither de Gaulle's Political Union, nor Kennedy's Grand Design would in the end be realised. Each blueprint, representing its own answer for dealing with the challenges facing transatlantic relations, was being discussed in different fora and there was no real exchange of views among the advocates of the different options. As each side rejected the proposals made by the other, transatlantic security relations to a large extent continued to be organised on the same basis as in the early 1950s, with the US unquestionably being the dominant partner. The discrepancy between Western Europe's economic weight and its political and security role continued to grow. As it was highly improbable that the conditions which had created the exceptional situation of the 1950s would return, ever-more serious structural problems were plaguing transatlantic relations.

## European Political Cooperation (EPC)

### Origins of the EPC

Following the two ill-fated attempts of the 1950s and the 1960s, the Six finally started to cooperate in the foreign-policy area from 1970 onwards in the framework of European Political Cooperation (EPC). The ultimate success of this third bid by the Member States to move beyond economic integration can be related both to the rather modest goals of European Political Cooperation as well as to the European and international environment at the time.

After President Charles de Gaulle left the political scene in 1969, there was again a more favourable climate for new European initiatives. Besides reaffirming their commitment to the completion of the internal market process, the Heads of State and Government, meeting in The Hague in December 1969, debated the possibility of starting cooperation in new areas such as foreign-policy and monetary matters and also the question of enlarging the European Community was again placed on the agenda. The triple objective of "completion, strengthening and enlargement" was defined as their main programme of action for the coming years.[57]

It is interesting to note that at The Hague summit, the link between political unification and enlargement made earlier by the Netherlands was accepted without any problems.[58] France, the main instigator behind the meeting and the new efforts for foreign-policy cooperation, was now willing to accept British membership, seeing it as a way to counterbalance an increasingly prosperous and assertive Germany. Simultaneously, Chancellor Brandt was looking for a broader framework to sustain his *Ostpolitik* and was eager to complement his policy towards the East with a more active *Westpolitik*.

If the environment within the EC was rather auspicious for closer political cooperation among the Member States, there were also external factors which pressured the Six to start harmonising their foreign-policy views. The EC's increasing economic weight and its single voice in international economic fora like the GATT contrasted sharply with the total absence of political coordination among the Six, and third countries often had difficulties in coming to grips with this discrepancy between Europe's economic and political capacities.

Especially in the relationship with the United States, this disparity led to a rather uncomfortable situation. While the European Community had become a powerful competitor of the US, it continued to be in a position of total dependence as far as its security was concerned. This placed the EC in a weak negotiating position with its American partner, which was increasingly tempted to link economics and politics and did not hesitate to take advantage of its greater political weight to extract economic concessions from the EC Member States.

The Europeans were, furthermore, increasingly conscious of the fact that American and European foreign-policy objectives were not necessarily always the same. The war which was dragging on in Vietnam was heavily criticised in European capitals and the US policy towards the Soviet Union also led to divergences among the allies. Realising that they would considerably strengthen their position if they started combining their forces in the political area, the EC Member States decided to try once again to overcome the earlier obstacles for closer European political cooperation.

Besides the generally conducive European and international climate, the launching of the EPC was also eased by its modest aspirations. Taking into account the lessons of history, the EC Member States no longer tried to first reach an agreement on detailed treaty provisions outlining their cooperation, nor did they opt for ambitious blueprints like the European Defence Community. They adopted a very pragmatic and flexible approach and decided to develop the EPC in a gradual way, outside the Community framework.[59]

The Luxembourg Report, adopted by the Ministers of Foreign Affairs in

October 1970, and outlining the objectives and instruments of the EPC, did not talk about the development of a European common foreign policy but only refers to modest goals such as the exchange of information, a better mutual understanding of foreign-policy issues, harmonisation of views, coordination of positions, and "where it appears possible and desirable, common actions".[60]

The institutional structure for realising these low-key goals was extremely flimsy. The Ministers of Foreign Affairs of the Six met every six months and a committee of the political directors, the so-called Political Committee was convened at least four times a year to prepare the ministers' meetings.

As the EPC developed step-by-step, new instruments such as working groups, meetings of the Heads of State or Government, a telex network linking the foreign ministries were put into place. The central role of the rotating Presidency in charge of convening and chairing the meetings of the EPC was not conducive to the development of permanent bodies and it was only with the entering into force of the Single European Act (July 1987), that a small secretariat was established.

As closer cooperation gradually came about, the new working habits were laid down in instruments which were successively adopted: the Copenhagen Report (1973), the London Report (1981), the Solemn Declaration on European Union (1983) and the Single European Act (SEA) (July 1987). It is only with the adoption of the SEA that the EPC finally received a basis in a treaty.

It was the result of a deliberate choice that the Luxembourg Report remained vague about the ultimate aim and the final shape of the foreign-policy cooperation among the Member States. The text refers both to the goal of Political Union in Europe as well as to "a Europe composed of states which, while preserving their national characteristics, are united". If this ambiguity prevented a repetition of the Fouchet debates and allowed each Member State to believe that the EPC would ultimately lead to its own preferred version of foreign-policy cooperation, it also created a lack of clarity. The heated debates around the development of CFSP during the 1991 Intergovernmental Conference show that it did not prevent the debate from taking place at a later stage.

Also the question as to whether the EPC was to be organised along supranational or intergovernmental principles was postponed until a later date and the smaller Member States accepted that at least for the time being the intergovernmental approach prevailed. The EPC's main players were the Member States and more particularly their Ministers of Foreign Affairs who decided by consensus.

In the early years in particular, the EC institutions were excluded as much as possible from the EPC decision-making process. EPC decisions were exempted from the jurisdiction by the European Court of Justice, while the European Parliament was in practice excluded from the debate, even though it could in principle try to influence the Ministers of Foreign Affairs through the adoption of resolutions.

At first the Member States were even hesitant about inviting the European Commission to their meetings and in the Luxembourg Report, they only committed themselves to consulting the European Commission if their work affected the activities of the European Communities. It took more than ten years before it was finally stipulated, in the London Report (1981), that the European Commission was "fully associated with political cooperation at all levels".[61] It was only with the entering into force of the Treaty on European Union (November 1993) that the European Commission received the right of initiative in the foreign-policy area.

The very flexible approach towards foreign-policy cooperation had both its advantages and disadvantages and had a determining impact on the EPC's results. Rather than being a framework in which European foreign policy was made, the EPC was primarily a forum for the exchange of information. The most tangible outcome of the discussions among the Member States were declarations. The different historical and geographical backgrounds of the European countries implied that they often perceived international events from a different perspective and since the texts had to be adopted by consensus, their content often lacked stamina.

The two major topics which dominated the debates of European Political Cooperation in the early years were the Middle East and the Conference on Security and Cooperation in Europe (CSCE). The active role of the Six and later the Nine in the launching of the CSCE was helped by the fact that the Western European countries had a common interest in preventing the two superpowers from dominating the CSCE's agenda.[62] The US' initial lack of interest in the process only made it easier for the EC Member States to take a leading role. In addition, the fact that the differentiation of policies was along the lines of that between the EC and EPC was very convenient.

The second topic of close cooperation, that of the Middle East, was more problematic because the Member States had traditionally adopted diverging policies towards the area. As a strategically important region, it was of major concern in the superpower conflict and, as the events following the outbreak of the October 1973 war illustrated, it was not an area where the US was eager to share its sphere of influence with the Europeans.[63]

If in the 1970s the EPC primarily confined itself to the adoption of declarations, from the 1980s onwards, it gradually started to explore new instruments aimed at supporting and strengthening its policy. One of the most visible instruments has been that of sanctions. The negative instrument of sanctions was first imposed against Iran following the hostage crisis in the US embassy in Teheran (April 1980) and also used against the Soviet Union following the imposition of martial law in Poland (February 1982), against Argentina as a result of the Falklands war (April 1982) and against South Africa and its apartheid regime (September 1986).[64] In some cases, the Member States also employed positive incentives to endorse certain policies and in the 1980s for example, they supported the process of closer cooperation among the Central American countries through a series of economic aid measures.

Both sanctions and economic support packages are illustrative of the difficulty of maintaining a strict separation between external economic and political relations. If the political decision to adopt sanctions was taken in the framework of the EPC, it had to be implemented in the framework of the EC's common commercial policy and required an initiative by the European Commission.[65]

While the distinction between the EC and EPC would gradually become vaguer, and Ministers of Foreign Affairs would increasingly be willing to discuss EPC matters in the margin of meetings of the General Affairs Council, it was to take the adoption of the Treaty on European Union before there was a single institutional framework for discussing the Union's external economic and political relations and even then Common Foreign and Security Policy continued to constitute a separate pillar, with the institutions playing a different role from the first EC pillar.[66]

It is beyond the scope of this study to examine in detail the successes and failures of the EPC. Suffice it to say that when interpreting a balance sheet covering more than 20 years of European Political Cooperation it very much depends on whether one evaluates it against the historical context in which it gradually came into being or whether one compares it with the achievements of a national foreign policy.

It is clear that if one does compare it to national foreign-policy achievements, the EPC does not come out very well. Despite its gradual coming to maturity, the EPC continued primarily to be a discussion forum, where its capability to speak with one voice and to act in a unified manner continued to be very limited. Its greatest merit has been that, for the first time in the history of European integration, it allowed Member States to make some timid steps in the foreign-policy area, enabling the different countries to get acquainted with each other's working methods and foreign-policy traditions and gradually creating a habit of consultation and cooperation. As in the 1980s, the EPC further developed and some Member States grew increasingly confident about cooperation, a debate started on the development of a more fully-fledged foreign policy, including the question of whether the Member States should extend their cooperation to the security and even defence area. Since this question is of particular interest to the United States and for transatlantic relations, it will be discussed in more detail.

*The EPC and European Security*

Since the failure of the European Defence Community, the question of cooperation in the security, let alone the defence, area has been a very sensitive issue for the EC Member States and it is no exaggeration to say that in the early years of the EPC it was a taboo issue. Neither in the Luxembourg Report (1970) nor in the Copenhagen Report (1973) was there any reference to cooperation in the security field and it was only with the adoption of the London Report (1981) that the first timid reference to the fact that the EPC discussions could also have a bearing on the political aspects of security appeared.[67]

Although it was the Tindemans Report which first expressed the view that "no foreign policy can disregard threats" and that "security cannot therefore be left outside the scope of European Union",[68] it was only following the launching of a German-Italian proposal, better known as the Genscher-Colombo initiative (1981), that the question of dealing with security matters in the field of the EPC was first seriously debated.[69] Tensions in the transatlantic relationship resulting from different views on the policy towards the Soviet Union, and bickering over the deployment of missiles on European soil, were an important catalyst in this.

The discussion launched by the Foreign Ministers Genscher and Colombo turned out to be very strenuous and, despite more than a decade of European Political Cooperation, time did not seem ripe yet to take any significant decisions on security cooperation. For countries like Greece, Denmark, and Ireland, the proposal clearly proved to be "a bridge too far". The launching of the initiative outside the traditional Franco-German axis was not appreciated by Paris and this further reduced the proposal's chances of success.

The final outcome of the Genscher-Colombo initiative was not a treaty text as Germany and Italy had proposed but a Solemn Declaration on European Union (Stuttgart, 19 June 1983), which confined the scope of the EPC to "the political and economic aspects of security".[70] This restriction was repeated in Title III of the Single European Act.[71]

Following the failure to make any serious progress in the EPC forum, some of the Member States, with France taking the lead, decided to turn to the alternative framework of the Western European Union (WEU) to start discussing security issues. In 1984, after many years of moribund existence, this Western European security organisation was revitalised[72] and in 1987 the WEU adopted a "Platform on European Security Interests", outlining the main principles on which European security was to be based.[73] The WEU had the advantage that countries like Denmark, Greece and Ireland, who fiercely objected the extension of European cooperation to the defence area, were not part of the organisation.[74]

Nevertheless, the reactivation of the WEU did not meet the expectations it had originally raised. As in the EPC, cooperation was organised on a purely intergovernmental basis and therefore entirely dependent on the goodwill of the WEU member countries. A further problem was that the different capitals aspired to realising diverging objectives through the organisation's reactivation. France hoped that increased security cooperation would reduce Western Europe's dependence on the US. The UK on the contrary, saw it primarily as a first step towards a strengthening of the European pillar of NATO.[75]

A further factor seriously weakening the potential of the WEU was its lack of operational capabilities. The organisation's most important achievement in the 1980s was the participation of the naval forces of five WEU member countries in mine-sweeping activities in the Gulf (1987 to 1989).[76] NATO remained the prime forum for any serious discussions and it was clear that as long as the Soviet threat continued to exist, neither the WEU nor EPC could rival it when it came to guaranteeing European security.

The absence of a military component in the EC led François Duchêne to characterise it as a civilian power which emphasises civilian instruments such as trade, aid, and negotiated outcomes in the first place rather than military solutions in order to realise its foreign-policy objectives.[77] For Duchêne, Europe was the first region where "the age-old process of war and indirect violence could be translated into something more in tune with the twentieth-century citizen's notion of civilised politics."

If it was indeed correct that the Member States of the European Community did not have the military means to support their foreign-policy objectives, this was not so much the result of a deliberate policy but of the bare reality that they were far from being in agreement as to how such a policy could possibly be developed. As long as there continued to be a discord between those who wanted an independent European security and defence identity and those who preferred an Atlantic Europe, there was indeed little chance that European countries could move beyond their civilian capacities.

## The US Reaction to the EPC: Nixon and the "Year of Europe"

The question of interest to this study is how the United States has reacted to the EPC and the European attempts to speak with one voice in the political area. Undeniably the EPC's modest approach was less controversial in Washington than the Fouchet plans. Since the Luxembourg Report (1970) did not include any provisions on security and defence cooperation, the EPC was not considered to be an immediate threat to NATO.

Nevertheless, this did not mean that the US did not closely follow the debate on closer political cooperation in Europe. Being freed from the burden of the Vietnam war, the second Nixon administration considered that the time had come to refocus attention on Europe and to address some of the long-standing problems in the transatlantic relationship, both in the economic and political-security area.

The unilateral decision of the first Nixon administration to end the Bretton Woods system and to impose an extra 10% of taxes on all imports into the US had caused serious strains in the US-European relationship. In addition, the heated debates in Congress on the Mansfield amendment to substantially reduce the US presence in Europe had led to fears for a gradual de-coupling of the US from European security and an erosion of US nuclear deterrence.[78]

At the same time there were also concerns in the US that an enlarged and economically powerful Europe would start to pursue its own political interests and increasingly challenge its subordinate role in transatlantic relations. In his memoirs *"Years of Upheaval"*, Henry Kissinger expressed this worry, doubting "that Europe would unite in order to share *our* burdens or that it would be content with a subordinate role once it had the means to implement its own views." He feared that "Europe's main incentive for undertaking a larger cooperative role in the West's affairs would be to fulfil its own distinctive purposes."[79]

It is basically in the light of this mounting concern that one can see the US' decision to declare 1973 as the *"Year of Europe"*. The idea was presented in April 1973, in a speech by US National Security Adviser Henry Kissinger[80] in which he referred to a new era in US-European relations where Europe had become economically unified, America's strategic position *vis-à-vis* the Soviet Union had weakened and where new challenges had arisen.[81] In order to address this new situation, Washington proposed adopting a new Atlantic Charter, dealing both with trade, defence, and East-West relations, as well as with new common problems such as energy and the environment.

To America's embarrassment, none of the three major Western European players reacted positively to the initiative. The United Kingdom had just joined the European Communities and its first priority now was to build up credentials with its European partners. Prime Minister Edward Heath was therefore very cautious and avoided any actions which could provoke the criticism that London was too closely associated with the United States.[82] Germany and Chancellor Brandt were primarily worried about improving relations with their eastern neighbours and considered that a closer Atlantic relationship might negatively affect their efforts for détente.

It was, however, in France that the American proposal received the most lukewarm response, with the French Minister of Foreign Affairs, Michel Jobert, describing the initiative in his memoirs as *"un geste maladroit dans la forme, et qui faisait bon marché à nos intérêts."*[83] In Paris, the initiative was primarily seen as a way to reaffirm the American hegemony over the West. In addition, it was feared that Washington wanted to use the Atlantic Charter to strengthen its position in upcoming talks with Soviet President Brezhnev, permitting President Nixon to present himself as the sole interlocutor of the West.[84]

Besides the different national motives underlying the half-hearted reactions, several European countries were also vexed by Kissinger's relegation of Europe to a purely regional role, while reserving global responsibilities solely as the United States' domain.[85] Although this was undeniably a reality, the explicit allusion to Europe's limited international capacities was resented as a typical expression of US arrogance.[86] Many countries were also puzzled by the US' proposal to associate Japan with the new Atlantic Charter.

In the course of 1973, the debate on the elaboration of a new Atlantic Charter, which had already started under a cloud, encountered a number of additional challenges which further complicated the situation. In June 1973, Presidents Nixon and Brezhnev concluded a "Declaration on the Prevention of Nuclear War", further enhancing the apprehension among the European countries with regard to a possible condominium of the two superpowers.[87]

In October 1973, war broke out in the Middle East. Since the Western European countries were much more dependent on Arab oil than the US, the former adopted a much softer stance towards the Arabs than the US who took sides with Israel.[88] Western solidarity seemed to be non-existent.

A final and perhaps the most important difficulty in reaching an agreement on a new transatlantic charter was the American desire to adopt a comprehensive declaration dealing with both trade, political and security questions. The idea of linking trade and security was for obvious reasons not very popular with the Western European countries. While for security matters, they preferred an agreement in the framework of NATO, for trade issues they favoured a dialogue among equals between the US and the EC. The idea of an Atlantic community where European integration was merely reduced to an instrument to strengthen the West did not appeal to the majority of EC Member States. They also feared that the US would exploit its dominant position in the security area to extract concessions in the economic field.

If the EC Member States recognised their continuing dependence on the US in the security and defence area, they considered it important that in the economic and even in the political field, they had the possibility of speaking on behalf of Europe and its own particular interests. In the "Document on the European Identity", which the Nine adopted in December 1973, the Ministers of Foreign Affairs refer to the close ties with the US, but also assert that these links "do not conflict with the determination of the Nine to establish themselves as a distinct and original entity".[89]

Ultimately, Kissinger's attempt to give new impetus to transatlantic relations resulted in two separate agreements. In the framework of NATO, the allies adopted the Ottawa declaration (19 June 1974) in which for the first time the contributions of the French and British nuclear forces to the overall Alliance deterrent were recognised.[90]

Secondly there was the so-called Gymnich agreement. At an informal meeting of the Ministers of Foreign Affairs at *Schloss* Gymnich near Bonn, the Nine agreed with a German proposal to regularly consult with the US on EPC matters.[91] According to this gentleman's agreement, each Member State could request consultations on EPC questions with the United States and consultations would be conducted by the country holding the Presidency. Changes in government in Paris, London and Bonn had eased the reaching of this agreement.

In practice, the agreement led to regular consultations between representatives of the country holding the Presidency and officials of the State Department. These discussions however never developed into a more structured political dialogue, nor were the meetings extended to the ministerial level.[92]

As with the Kennedy administration, the Nixon one was not able to realise its proposals for an Atlantic community. Ironically, the year of Europe became a year of exceptional animosity in transatlantic relations and it is quite revealing that in his memoirs, Kissinger concludes his chapter on the Year of Europe with a paragraph entitled "The year that never was".[93] The fact that the Nixon administration was increasingly submerged in the Watergate scandal of course did not help bring about an agreement.

## The US and the EPC Beyond 1973

Despite the Gymnich agreement and its possibilities for political consultation between the two allies, the relationship between the US and EPC continued to be rather uncomfortable and Washington remained suspicious of European attempts to speak with one voice.

Two situations in particular repeatedly led to tensions in the transatlantic relationship: one being when the EC Member States tried to adopt an independent position in an area where the US considered it had crucial interests at stake; the other one being when the US urged the reluctant and hesitant EC Member States to act in order to reinforce the American position.

Typical of the first kind of situations were the frictions over policy towards the Middle East and the Soviet Union. Being a key area in the East-West conflict and of strategic importance because of its oil supplies, the Middle East was considered to be a region where the West was to speak with a single voice, i.e. that of the US. The launching of the Euro-Arab dialogue from 1974 onwards and the adoption of the so-called Venice declaration (June 1980)[94] revindicating a special role for Europe in the Middle East and supporting the Palestinian people to fully exercise their right to self-determination were considered to be an intrusion into the American sphere of influence. The pro-Arab stance of the EC Member States heavily disturbed Washington, who did not hesitate to exert pressure to try to prevent the Europeans from launching their own initiatives.[95]

A further important source of tensions was the diverging attitudes towards the Soviet Union and détente.[96] While the European countries were primarily interested in the effects of détente on stability and peace in Europe, the US considered the issue in the light of the global balance of power. Especially during the Reagan era, Western Europe had serious difficulties in accepting the "evil empire" policy of the American President who pressurised them to reduce the increasing trade flows with the countries of Central and Eastern Europe. Considering it important that a policy of dialogue with the Soviet Union was maintained, the EC Member States only reluctantly followed the American example of imposing sanctions against the Soviet Union after the introduction of martial law in Poland in December 1981.[97] They also resisted the US' insistence that they give up on the Western European participation in the construction of a gas pipeline between the Soviet Union and Western Europe.[98] While the Ten considered that the project could have a positive effect on East-West relations, Washington was concerned that new technologies and the availability of hard currency might strengthen the position of the Soviet

Union to the detriment of the West.

Besides the times when Europe was criticised for going its own way, there were also cases where the US blamed the EC Member States for taking a too passive stance. Following the occupation of the US Embassy in Teheran by revolutionary forces in November 1979, the Nine proved extremely reluctant to positively respond to President Carter's call for the imposition of sanctions and it took them several months to come to a decision.[99]

In its attempts to isolate the regime of Colonel Gaddafi and to fight Libyan terrorism, the Europeans also took a more cautious approach than the US wanted. This did however not prevent the US from blunt unilateral action, including an air raid on Tripoli on 14 April 1986, without prior consultation with the European allies.[100] Throughout the more than 20 years of European Political Cooperation, relations between the United States and EPC continued to be a delicate question. While the US wanted European foreign-policy cooperation to reinforce the position of the West in international affairs, the countries participating in the EPC saw it primarily as a forum that could defend specific West-European interests, which did not necessarily always coincide with those of Washington.

The structures for coordination or an exchange of views between the EPC and the United States remained extremely loose and limited. Knowing that their internal unity remained precarious, the Member States participating in the EPC were reluctant to allow a dominant power like the United States to interfere in their discussions. Consultations between the EPC and the US never really took off and remained very much ad hoc. As a result the US continued to rely primarily on bilateral contacts to defend its views and preferred policies in Europe.

## Conclusion

An overview of more than four decades of transatlantic relations brings an entirely different story depending on whether one focuses on economic or security relations between both sides of the Atlantic.

In the economic sphere, American direct intervention in European affairs remained limited to the one-time initiative of the Marshall Plan. When from the 1950s onwards, the European economies were gradually recovering, the transatlantic relationship developed into that of two partners and competitors, soon able to deal with each other on an equal basis.

In the realm of security by way of contrast, the situation was entirely different. Through NATO, which unlike to the Marshall Plan was a permanent structure, the United States became fully engaged in European security. Being established at a time when Europe was still recovering from the damage of the Second World War, Washington was from the beginning the *de facto* dominant partner in the Alliance. This leadership position was not resisted but welcomed and even encouraged by the European countries who appreciated that they could allocate their scarce resources to their economic recovery and who realised that they could not possibly provide a credible defence against the emerging threat of the Soviet Union.[101]

As their economies gradually recovered and they gained increasing weight on the international scene, the Western European countries, with France as its most fierce advocate, also started to have political ambitions and looked for ways to translate their economic weight into political influence. The fate of the European Defence Community and the Fouchet saga illustrate that there was far from a common view as to how to concretely realise these aspirations.

For France and President de Gaulle, there was no doubt that Europe's interests would best be served if it developed its own independent arrangements to translate its views in the political and security area. In this Paris did not want to follow the Monnet method as in the economic area where there was also place for supranational actors like the European Commission, but pleaded for a purely intergovernmental approach according to which the Member States would be the main players.

The majority of EC Member States were not convinced of the desirability to develop foreign-policy and security cooperation outside the NATO framework and there was also heavy criticism, especially on behalf of the small Member States, of the purely intergovernmental approach proposed by de Gaulle.

The United States, who was excluded from the debate among the EC Member States on political identity, and who as a major player in European security had important interests at stake did not hesitate to take advantage of the bickering among the Europeans to try to promote its own favoured option.

Whether through Kennedy's Grand Design or Nixon's Year of Europe, the US left no doubt that its preference was for an Atlantic community in which the US and Europe in a joint forum would discuss economic, political and security issues. This model had the advantage that Washington could remain a direct player in the "game" and was the best guarantee to preserve its interests and central position.

Although both partners were conscious of the need to adjust transatlantic relations to the new political realities, they never succeeded in reaching an agreement on how to realise the required changes. France, who took the lead on the European side, first wanted to assert a more independent role for Europe, which would then allow Europe to negotiate with the US from a position of strength. For Paris, Europe and the US were two independent partners which should closely cooperate but which nevertheless should have the possibility of having their own points of view and if necessary their own policies.

For the US on the contrary, a politically unified Europe had to be fully integrated in the Atlantic community, which should speak with one single voice on behalf of the West. The main problem with this approach was that, with the exception of the economic area, the Western European countries during the cold war period were far from having the capacity to deal with the US as an equal partner. By accepting the proposal of an Atlantic community or association, the European countries realised that they would first and foremost be perpetuating the American hegemony in Atlantic relations.

Neither the French view of an independent European security policy, nor the American proposals for restructuring the Alliance ultimately prevailed. The two blueprints were discussed in parallel, without any real dialogue between them taking place, and with each side being convinced of the superiority of its own solution. Compromises were not possible since each design represented a radically different view of European integration. The French view was that of an autonomous Europe, dealing with the United States on equal footing; the American view was one whereby European integration would always be subordinate and at the service of the Atlantic relationship. When in 1989 the fall of the Berlin Wall marked the end of the division of Europe, the structural problems that had been plaguing the Alliance and transatlantic security relations since the 1960s were still very much the same. Despite the irritations and frustrations on both sides – in Europe, because of its lack of influence, and in the US, because of the disproportionate burden it assumed in guaranteeing European security – all attempts at addressing these problems failed.

In the following chapter, we will see to what extent a major event like the end of the cold war has been a sufficient catalyst to address the problem of the long-awaited structural adaptation of transatlantic relations.

## Notes

1. See Alfred Grosser, *The Western Alliance. European-American Relations Since 1945* (London: Macmillan, 1980), 3-4.
2. On the Truman doctrine, see Richard M. Freeland, *The Truman Doctrine and the Origins of McCartyism. Foreign Policy, Domestic Politics, and Internal Security 1946-1948* (New York and London: New York University Press, 1985), 70-114; Joseph M. Jones, *The Fifteen Weeks (February 21-June 5, 1947)* (New York: The Viking Press, 1955).
3. For an in-depth study on the Marshall Plan, see, Michael Hogan, *The Marshall Plan. America, Britain and the Reconstruction of Western Europe, 1947-1952* (Cambridge: Cambridge University Press, 1987); Alan S. Milward, *The Reconstruction of Western Europe 1945-51* (London: Methuen & Co., 1984).
4. On the origins of NATO, see, Don Cook, *Forging the Alliance. NATO, 1945-1950* (London: Secker and Warburg, 1989); Olav Riste (ed.), *Western Security: The Formative Years. European and Atlantic Defence 1947-1953* (Oslo: Norwegian University Press, 1985); Robert Endicott Osgood, *NATO, the Entangling Alliance* (Chicago: The University of Chicago Press, 1962); Ronald E. Powaski, "The Creation of the North Atlantic Alliance, 1947-1950", in *Id., Toward an Entangling Alliance. American Isolationism, Internationalism, and Europe, 1901-1950* (New York-London: Greenwood Press, 1991), 195-222.
5. Under pressure from the Benelux countries, the idea of a single European defence minister would be dropped and replaced by that of a board.
6. For the most important studies on the EDC, see, Raymond Aron and Daniel Lerner (eds.), *La querelle de la CED* (Paris: Armand Colin, 1956); Armand Clesse, *Le projet de CED du plan Pleven au "crime" du 30 août. Histoire d'un malentendu européen* (Baden-Baden: Nomos Verlag, 1989); Edward Fursdon, *The European Defence Community: A History* (London: Macmillan, 1980).
7. On the US and the question of German rearmament, see Lawrence W. Martin, "The American Decision to Rearm Germany", in Harold Stein, *American Civil-Military Decisions. A Book of Case Studies* (Alabama: University of Alabama Press, 1963), 645-665.
8. Dean Acheson, *Present at the Creation. My Years at the State Department* (London: Hamish Hamilton, 1969), 435-440.
9. The US asked the Europeans to provide 60 divisions, of which ten were to be German. See François Duchêne, *Jean Monnet. The First Statesman of Interdependence* (New York-London: W.W. Norton and Company, 1994), 227.
10. Edward Fursdon, *op.cit.*, 89-90.
11. See the words of Secretary of State Dean Acheson in his memoirs: "We issued phrases of 'welcoming the initiative' and 'sympathetic examination', ... but to me the plan was hopeless, a view confirmed by General Marshall and concurred in by the President ..." In, Dean Acheson, *op.cit.*, 459. See also Pierre Mélandri, "Les Etats-Unis et le plan Pleven", *Relations Internationales*, vol.11, 1977, 201-229.
12. Edward Fursdon, *op.cit.*, 107-108.
13. René Massigli, *Une comédie des erreurs 1943-1956. Souvenirs et réflexions sur une étape de la construction européenne* (Paris: Plon, 1978), 281-282.
14. Dulles pronounced these words at the 12th session of the meeting of the North Atlantic Council in Paris (14-16 December 1953). He added that "It may never again be possible for integration to occur in freedom, although it might be that Western Europe might be

unified, as East Europe has been, in defeat and servitude." Quoted in Ernst H. van der Beugel, *From Marshall Aid to Atlantic Partnership. European Integration as a Concern of American Foreign Policy* (Amsterdam-London-New York: Elsevier, 1966), 292-293.
15  Jacques Fauvet, "Naissance et mort d'un traité", in Raymond Aron and Daniel Lerner (eds.), *op.cit.*, 23-58; Edward Fursdon, *op.cit.*, 296-297.
16  The Netherlands was initially rather reticent to participate in an EDC without the United Kingdom, fearing domination by France and Germany.
17  Anthony Eden, *Full Circle* (London: Casell, 1960), 29-47.
18  *Foreign Relations of the United States (FRUS)*, vol.3, Part I, 1951,760.
19  *Ibid.*, 761.
20  The Brussels Treaty Organization would be renamed Western European Union.
21  Anthony Eden, *op.cit.*, 146-174.
22  For the text of the modified Brussels Treaty and its protocols, see, Arie Bloed and Ramses A. Wessel (eds.), *The Changing Functions of the Western European Union (WEU). Introduction and Basic Documents* (Dordrecht-Boston-London: Martinus Nijhoff Publishers, 1994), 1-38.
23  Over the period 1958-61, the US balance of payments deficit amounted to US $ 3.4 billion. See Pascaline Winand, *Eisenhower, Kennedy, and the United States of Europe* (New York: St.Martin's Press, 1993), 168.
24  See Alfred Grosser, *op.cit.*, 140-147.
25  David N. Schwartz, *NATO's Nuclear Dilemma's* (Washington D.C.: The Brookings Institution, 1983), 61.
26  *Cf. infra*, 69-70.
27  Pierre Gerbet, "In Search of Political Union: The Fouchet Plan Negotiations (1960-62)", in Roy Pryce (ed.), *The Dynamics of European Union* (London: Croom Helm, 1987), 105-129, 105-106.
28  Alfred Grosser, *op.cit.*, 187.
29  For the text of Eisenhower's letter, see Lois Pattison de Ménil, *Who Speaks for Europe? The Vision of Charles de Gaulle* (London: Weidenfeld and Nicholson, 1977), 193-194.
30  For extracts of parts of de Gaulle's speech, see "Le dossier de l'Union politique. Recueil de documents avec préface de M. Emilio Battista" (Luxembourg: Direction générale de la documentation parlementaire et de l'information, January 1964), 5-6.
31  For the most important studies on the Fouchet negotiations, see, Robert Bloes, *Le "plan Fouchet" et le problème de l'Europe politique* (Bruges: College of Europe, 1970); Susanne J. Bodenheimer, *Political Union: A Microcosm of European Politics, 1960-1966* (Leiden: A.W. Sijthoff, 1967); Alessandro Silj, *Europe's Political Puzzle. A Study of the Fouchet Negotiations and the 1963 Veto* (Cambridge, Massachusetts: Center for International Affairs, Harvard University, 1967).
32  For the text of Fouchet I, see Alexander Silj, *op.cit.*, 141-148.
33  For the text of Fouchet II: *Ibid.*, 149-164.
34  On the position of the Netherlands during the Fouchet negotiations, see, Hans Nijenhuis, "De Nederlandse tactiek in de onderhandelingen over een Europese politieke unie (1960-1962): Nee tegen de Gaulle", *Internationale Spectator*, vol.41, No.1, January 1987, 41-49 and Susanne J. Bodenheimer, *op.cit.*, 152-196.
35  On the position of Belgium during the Fouchet negotiations, see, Sophie Vanhoonacker, "La Belgique: responsable ou bouc émissaire de l'échec des négociations Fouchet?", *Res Publica*, vol.31, No.4, 1989, 513-526.

36 The Dutch and Belgian positions are however not completely identical. While the Netherlands had fiercely opposed de Gaulle's plans for a Political Union from the beginning of the negotiations, Belgium's position was more flexible. Sufficient pressure could very probably have convinced the Belgians to drop the *préalable anglais*. This cannot be said of the Netherlands. See Susanne Bodenheimer, *op.cit.*, 77-79.
37 *Ibid.*, 112.
38 For the text of the counterproposal of the Five, see Alexander Silj, *op.cit.*, 149-164.
39 On de Gaulle and the Alliance, see, Stanley Hoffmann, "de Gaulle, Europe, and the Atlantic Alliance", *International Organization*, vol.18, No.1, winter 1964, 1-28.
40 Both the Italian diplomat Attilio Cattani, the successor of Christian Fouchet as chairman of the committee, and the Belgian Minister of Foreign Affairs, Paul-Henri Spaak, undertook such efforts. See Susanne Bodenheimer, *op.cit.*, 64-65 and 68-69.
41 On the Franco-German treaty, see Werner Weidenfeld, "25 Years After 22 January 1963: The Franco-German Friendship Treaty", *Aussenpolitik*, vol.39, No.1, 1988, 3-12.
42 Lois Pattison de Ménil, *op.cit.*, 124.
43 From 1982 onwards, the Ministers of Defence and Foreign Affairs of both countries met twice a year in the framework of the "Franco-German Panel on Defence and Security", a channel through which they tried to coordinate their security policies. In 1988, President Mitterrand and Chancellor Kohl established the "Franco-German Council on Security and Defence", bringing together the Heads of State and Government, the Ministers of Defence and Foreign Affairs, the Chiefs of Staff, as well as the Council's Secretary and Deputy Secretary of both countries.
44 Susanne Bodenheimer, *op.cit.*, 90-91.
45 For a comprehensive study of President Kennedy's Grand Design, see, Pascaline Winand, *Eisenhower, Kennedy, and the United States of Europe* (New York: St.Martin's Press, 1993).
46 For products where the US and the EEC together counted for 80% of world trade, tariffs could even be eliminated. Following an active campaign by the State Department, the bill was adopted by Congress in October 1962. See Simona Toschi, "Washington-London-Paris. An Untenable Triangle", *Journal of European Integration History*, vol.1, No.2, 1995, 81-109, 97-99.
47 On the MLF, see Charles G. Cogan, *Oldest Allies, Guarded Friends. The United States and France Since 1940* (Westport-Connecticut-London: Praeger, 1994), 121-150. See also, David N. Schwartz, *op.cit.*, 82-135.
48 Charles G. Cogan, *op.cit.*, 137-138.
49 The French decision to develop nuclear weapons goes back to the early 1950s and was given absolute priority after General de Gaulle took office.
50 Lois Pattison de Ménil, *op.cit.*, 115.
51 Charles G. Cogan, *op.cit.*, 128.
52 Pascaline Winand, *op.cit.*, 265-284.
53 The same reasoning was also being followed by the Bush administration: "... we wanted Britain's global and Atlantic perspective to influence the outlook of an increasingly cohesive Europe: we needed a more Europeanised Britain because we wanted a more Anglicised Europe." See Robert L. Hutchings, *American Diplomacy and the End of the Cold War. An Insider's Account of US Policy in Europe, 1989-1992* (Washington D.C.: The Woodrow Wilson Center Press and the John Hopkins University Press, 1997), 163.
54 The importance of preserving the special relationship with the US as an important motive

for the British application for EC membership is well explained and argued in: Wolfram Kaiser, "The Bomb and Europe. Britain, France, and the EEC Entry Negotiations 1961-1963", *Journal of European Integration History*, vol.1, No.1, 1995, 65-85, 78-79.
55  On the Nassau agreement, see, Jan Melissen, "Pre-Summit Diplomacy: Britain, the United States and the Nassau Conference", *Diplomacy and Statecraft*, vol.7, No.3, November 1996, 652-687.
56  William C. Cromwell, *The United States and the European Pillar. The Strained Alliance* (London: Macmillan, 1992), 38.
57  "Communiqué of the Conference of the Heads of State and Government of the Member States of the European Community (The Hague, 2 December 1969, excerpts)", in *European Political Cooperation* (Bonn: Press and Information Office, 1988), 22-23.
58  The communiqué adopted in The Hague speaks about "achieving progress in the matter of political unification, within the context of enlargement".
59  For the most important studies on the development of European Political Cooperation, see, Philippe de Schoutheete, *La Coopération Politique Européenne* (Brussels: Labor, 1986)(second edition); Martin Holland (ed.), *The Future of European Political Cooperation. Essays on Theory and Practice* (London: Macmillan, 1991); Panayiotis Ifestos, *European Political Cooperation: Towards A Framework of Supranational Diplomacy?* (Aldershot: Avebury, 1987); Simon J. Nuttall, *European Political Cooperation* (London: Clarendon Press, 1992); Alfred E. Pijpers, Elfriede Regelsberger, Wolfgang Wessels (eds.), *European Political Cooperation in the 1980s: A Common Foreign Policy for Western Europe* (Dordrecht: Martinus Nijhoff, 1988); Alfred E. Pijpers, *Vicissitudes of European Political Cooperation: Towards A Realist Interpretation of the EC's Collective Diplomacy* (Leiden: Rijksuniversiteit Leiden, 1990); Elfriede Regelsberger, Philippe de Schoutheete de Tervarent and Wolfgang Wessels, *Foreign Policy of the European Union: From EPC to CFSP and Beyond* (Boulder, CO: Lynne Rienner Publishers, 1997).
60  "First Report of the Foreign Ministers to the Heads of State and Government of the Member States of the European Community of 27 October 1970 (Luxembourg Report)", in *European Political Cooperation* (Bonn: Press and Information Office, 1988), 24-31.
61  "Report on European Political Cooperation Issued by the Foreign Ministers of the Ten on 13 October 1981 (London Report)", in *European Political Cooperation* (Bonn: Press and Information Office, 1988), 61-70.
62  Alfred Pijpers, "European Political Cooperation and the CSCE Process", *Legal Issues of European Integration*, vol.1, 1984, 135-148.
63  *Cf. infra*, 85-86.
64  On the EPC and sanctions, see Martin Holland, "Sanctions as an EPC Instrument", in *Id.*, *op.cit.*, 180-198.
65  Initially there was a certain reticence to use a Community instrument (i.e. a Council Regulation) to implement sanctions and the Member States implemented them through national, not Community measures. See Simon Nuttall, *op.cit.*, 260-267.
66  On the negotiations leading to the adoption of the Treaty on European Union and its provisions on CFSP, see chapter 4, 92-105.
67  "Report on European Political Cooperation Issued by the Foreign Ministers of the Ten on 13 October 1981 (London Report)", in *European Political Cooperation* (Bonn: Press and Information Office, 1988), 61-70.
68  "European Union. Report by Mr Leo Tindemans, Prime Minister of Belgium, to the European Council" (Brussels: Ministry of Foreign Affairs, 1976), 20.

69  Gianni Bonvicini, "The Genscher-Colombo Plan and the Solemn Declaration on European Union (1981-83)", in Roy Pryce, *The Dynamics of European Union* (London: Croom Helm, 1987), 174-187; Pauline Neville-Jones, "The Genscher/Colombo Proposals on European Union", *Common Market Law Review*, vol. 20, No. 4, 1983, 657-699.
70  For the text of the Solemn Declaration on European Union, see *European Political Cooperation (EPC)* (Bonn: Press and Information Office, 1988), 70-77.
71  David Freestone and Scott Davidson, "Community Competence and Part III of the Single European Act", *Common Market Law Review*, vol.23, No.4, 1986, 793-801.
72  On the reactivation of the WEU, see, Panos Tsakaloyannis (ed.), *The Reactivation of the Western European Union: The Effects on the EC and Its Institutions* (Maastricht: EIPA, 1985).
73  The Platform referred to criteria such as a strategy of deterrence and defence based on a mix of conventional and nuclear forces, strong links with the US, the need for an increased European contribution to defence as well as efforts in the field of arms control and deterrence. See, "Platform on European Security Interests, The Hague, 27 October 1987", in, Alfred Cahen, *The Western European Union and NATO. Building a European Defence within the Context of Atlantic Solidarity* (London: Brassey's, 1989), 91-96.
74  The original WEU member countries are France, the United Kingdom and the Benelux countries. After the failure to establish the European Defence Community, Germany and Italy joined in 1954. Spain and Portugal joined in 1988. At the 1991 Maastricht Summit, the other EC Member States were invited to join, but only Greece accepted the invitation. Ireland and Denmark became observers.
75  Mathias Jopp and Wolfgang Wessels, "Institutional Frameworks for Security Cooperation in Western Europe: Developments and Options", in Mathias Jopp, Reinhardt Rummel, and Peter Schmidt (eds.), *Integration and Security in Western Europe. Inside the European Pillar* (Boulder, San Francisco, Oxford: Westview Press, 1991), 25-73, 32.
76  The participating countries were France, the UK, Italy, Belgium, and the Netherlands. Germany sent extra ships to the Mediterranean and Luxembourg made a financial contribution. The UK, Belgium and the Netherlands closely coordinated their action, but the French and Italian ships operated under national command. *Ibid.*, 30-31.
77  François Duchêne, "Europe's Role in World Peace", in Richard Mayne (ed.), *Europe Tomorrow* (London: Fontana/Collins, 1972), 32-47, 43. On the civilian power concept, see also: Christopher Hill, "European Foreign Policy: Power Bloc, Civilian Model – or Flop?", in Reinhardt Rummel (ed.), *The Evolution of an International Actor. Western Europe's New Assertiveness* (Boulder, San Francisco, Oxford: Westview Press, 1990), 31-55; Finn Laursen, "The EC in the World Context. Civilian Power or Superpower?", *Futures*, vol. 23, No. 7, September 1991, 747-759. The concept was heavily criticised by Hedley Bull, "Civilian Power Europe: A Contradiction in Terms?", *Journal of Common Market Studies*, vol. 21, No. 4, June 1983, 149-170.
78  William Cromwell, *op.cit.*, 42.
79  See Henry Kissinger, *Years of Upheaval* (Boston-Toronto: Little, Brown and Company, 1982), 131.
80  In September 1973, Kissinger would be nominated Secretary of State.
81  For excerpts of the speech, see Henry Kissinger, *op.cit.*, 152-153.
82  Charles Cogan, *op.cit.*, 156.
83  Michel Jobert, *Mémoires d'avenir* (Paris: Grasset, 1974), 259.
84  *Ibid.* 260 and Henry Kissinger, *op.cit.*, 173.

85 See Henry Kissinger, *op.cit.*, 153: "The United States has global interests and responsibilities. Our European allies have regional interests. These are not necessarily in conflict, but in the new era neither are they automatically identical."
86 See Michel Jobert, *op.cit.*, 259: "On se souvient de ce discours fait à New York, qui était un exposé sans prudence de la géopolitique américaine, l'Europe confinée à sa vocation purement régionale et le monde s'ordonnant autour de la puissance américaine comme autrefois l'empire du Milieu s'entourait de sept lunes gravitant autour de lui."
87 In order to avert a possible conflict, the Declaration proposed consultations between the US and the USSR before resorting to a nuclear war. See, Charles Cogan, *op.cit.*, 161-162.
88 Most Western European countries refused to allow American airplanes which were supplying Israel to fly over them. They also declined to deal with the conflict in the framework of NATO. See William Cromwell, *op.cit.*, 86-87.
89 "Document on the European Identity Published by the Nine Foreign Ministers (Copenhagen, 14 December 1973)", in *European Political Cooperation* (Bonn: Press and Information Office, 1988), 48-54.
90 Charles Cogan, *op.cit.*, 167.
91 See Panayiotis Ifestos, *op.cit.*, 181-183.
92 Elfriede Regelsberger, "EPC in the 1980s: Reaching Another Plateau?", in Alfred E. Pijpers, Elfriede Regelsberger, Wolfgang Wessels (eds.), *op.cit.*, 3-48, 28.
93 Henry Kissinger, *op.cit.*, 192.
94 "Declaration by the 17th European Council on the Euro-Arab Dialogue, Lebanon, Afghanistan and the Situation in the Middle East (Venice, 12/13 June 1980)", in *European Political Cooperation* (Bonn: Press and Information Office, 1988), 127-131.
95 On the EPC and the Middle East, see Panayiotis Ifestos, *op.cit.*, 371-587.
96 Stephen Gill, *Atlantic Relations: Beyond the Reagan Era* (London: Harvester Wheatsheaf, 1989), 179.
97 Simon Nuttall, *op.cit.*, 199-207.
98 *Ibid.*, 193.
99 *Ibid.*, 168-171.
100 Anastasia Pardalis, "European Political Cooperation and the United States", *Journal of Common Market Studies*, vol. 25, No.4, June 1987, 271-294, 282-289.
101 Geir Lundestad, "Empire by Invitation? The United States and Western Europe, 1945-1952", in Charles S. Maier (ed.), *The Cold War in Europe. Era of a Divided Continent* (New York: Markus Wiener Publishing, 1991), 143-165.

# 4 American Reactions to Common Foreign and Security Policy (CFSP)

Throughout the post-war period, transatlantic security relations have been characterised by a high degree of continuity. As a result of the perceived Soviet threat, the United States decided to remain in Europe and, through the establishment of the North Atlantic Treaty Organisation (NATO) in 1949, it became involved in European security on a permanent basis. Moreover, backed by a huge nuclear arsenal and massive conventional forces, it became the most important guarantor of Western European security and the key player in the Alliance.

The Western European countries very much welcomed the permanent US presence on their continent. An attack by the Soviet bloc was seen as one of the most important threats to their security and it was generally agreed that only with the support of America's massive military capacity could they enjoy a credible defence. As long as the superpower rivalry continued, the creation of an independent European security organisation outside the Atlantic framework would remain in the realm of wishful thinking. Although there were disagreements and reoccurring tensions, the dominant American position in European security was never seriously challenged. The Western European Union (WEU), the only purely European security organisation, lived entirely in NATO's shadow.

As argued in the introductory chapter of this study, the end of the cold war had the potential of being a real watershed in transatlantic relations, creating uncertainties for both sides. In Europe, it was feared that Washington would use the collapse of communism as a welcome excuse to gradually withdraw its troops and to again become more inward looking. In the United States, on the other hand, there were concerns that the countries of Western Europe would grasp the chance created by the more relaxed international situation to give a more prominent role to independent European security initiatives to the detriment of the existing and well-functioning Atlantic framework of NATO.

This first case study focuses on how the European Communities tried to move beyond European Political Cooperation to develop a joint foreign and security policy. The first section gives an overview of the debates in the framework of the 1991 Intergovernmental Conference (IGC) on Political Union and looks at the positions of the different EC Member States. Special attention is given to the role played by Germany and France in driving the situation. The second section examines the American response to the Twelve's initiatives on security and defence, putting it in the broader context of the emerging US policy towards Europe. Particular attention is given to the Bush administration's policy with regard to German unification: Germany having been identified by the US as one of the keys to stability in post-1989 Europe.

## The Intergovernmental Conference on Political Union

After a year of difficult negotiations in the framework of the Intergovernmental Conferences on Economic and Monetary Union and Political Union, the Ministers of Foreign Affairs of the Twelve met on 7 February 1992 in Maastricht to sign the Treaty on European Union. A new step on the path towards European integration, the Treaty laid down the provisions for the establishment of an Economic and Monetary Union in three phases; enhanced the role of the European Parliament; foresaw increased EU competences; introduced the concepts of subsidiarity and European citizenship; and provided for the gradual development of a Common Foreign and Security Policy (CFSP) as well as for extended cooperation in the field of justice and home affairs (JHA).

It was Title V of the Treaty on European Union, and its provisions on the gradual development of a CFSP among the EU Member States, which attracted most attention in the United States. Although it had always advocated a more active European role in the security area, Washington felt uneasy about the prospect of a foreign and security policy among the Twelve and was anxious to find out what the implications of such a policy were for its own role and position in Europe.

## The Franco-German Linchpin[1]

As has generally been the case with any major leap forward in the European integration process, the main engine behind the proposal to launch negotiations on Political Union was the Franco-German axis. In their joint letter of 19 April 1990 to the Irish Presidency, the German Chancellor, Helmut Kohl, and the French President, François Mitterrand, pleaded for the acceleration of "the political construction of the Europe of the Twelve" and proposed convening an IGC on Political Union to be held in parallel to the IGC on EMU.[2] They defined the main objectives of the IGC as being "to strengthen the democratic legitimation of the union, render its institutions more efficient, ensure unity and coherence of the Union's economic, monetary and political action", and to "define and implement a common foreign and security policy".

Although close Franco-German cooperation is generally seen as one of the main pillars of European integration, the joint initiative which eventually led to the convening of an IGC on Political Union was only possible after a complete U-turn in the French position *vis-à-vis* German reunification. When the fall of the Berlin Wall opened the possibility of the reunification of the two Germanys, the French government, which had officially always supported this goal, could not hide the fact that it was seriously disturbed by the new situation because it would affect its position in Europe in a fundamental way. The delicate balance by which France assumed the role of political leader in Europe, while Germany was the economically dominant partner would be drastically disturbed. Furthermore, the presence of a fully sovereign Germany at the centre of Europe led to fears within the French government that France would become marginalised.[3] It also raised doubts as to future German commitment to European integration, challenging the premise that the Federal Republic of Germany could best be controlled by being integrated in the larger supranational framework of the European Communities.

The speed with which events in both Germanys were proceeding and the French reluctance to face the new political situation led to serious strains in the Franco-German relationship.[4] The first major shock for Paris was the announcement by Helmut Kohl on 28 November 1989, in a speech before the *Bundestag*, of his ten-point plan outlining the stages of gradual German reunification.[5] To the dismay of Paris, the plan was disclosed without prior notification of, let alone consultation with, the French government. The news came as all the more of a surprise since the German Chancellor had not said a word about his future plans at an extraordinary European Council ten days earlier. The ten-point plan based the process of reunification on a two-fold strategy of close cooperation with the German Democratic Republic (points 1 to 5) and on full integration in the European Community and the Conference on Security and Cooperation in Europe (CSCE) (points 6 to 9).[6]

It was at the Strasbourg European Summit on 8 and 9 December 1989 that the Twelve officially discussed the issue of a reunified Germany for the first time.[7] In her memoirs, the former British Prime Minister, Margaret Thatcher, leaves no doubt that Paris and London felt very uncomfortable with the course of events in Germany, but recognises that none of the Heads of State or Government dared to openly express their concerns.[8] The declaration adopted in Strasbourg recognised Germany's right to self-determination, but at the same time firmly linked reunification with Bonn's commitment to deeper European integration.[9] The Member States also exploited the situation to extract German support for Economic and Monetary Union.

Although Paris was one of the main supporters of the prevailing view in Strasbourg, that German reunification had to be counterbalanced by a further deepening of the European integration process, this did not deter the French government from experimenting with alternative strategies aimed at keeping Germany under control. In his New Year's speech on national television on 31 December 1989, President Mitterrand launched the idea of developing a "confederation" of all European countries.[10] By forging links with the countries of Central and Eastern Europe, Paris wanted to prevent Germany from obtaining a dominant position in this region where historically it had played a central role.[11] Fearing that the initiative might be a manoeuvre to preclude them from EC membership and disagreeing with Mitterrand's view that the United States and Canada should not be part of the confederation, the Central and Eastern European countries' reaction was lukewarm and the initiative never really got off the ground.

A further option being explored by Paris was the idea of trying to neutralise Germany's influence by intensifying the Anglo-French relationship.[12] In relation to this there were two private meetings between the French President François Mitterrand and the British Prime Minister Margaret Thatcher, but they did not lead to any concrete results. Mitterrand's above-mentioned strategy of trying to encapsulate the new Germany by deepening European integration was incompatible with the United Kingdom's minimalist view of Europe. According to the UK, a federal Europe would inevitably lead to a German Europe, rather than a European Germany as maintained by Mitterrand.

With the launching of the joint Kohl-Mitterrand letter of 19 April 1990 proposing the convening of an IGC on Political Union, the strategy of addressing the German question by reinforcing Franco-German cooperation and by deepening European integration ultimately prevailed.

## From EPC to a Common Foreign and Security Policy

When on 14 and 15 December 1990, the Heads of State and Government of the Twelve met in Rome to open the IGCs on EMU and Political Union, the well-defined objectives of the IGC on EMU contrasted sharply with the rather vague aims of the IGC on Political Union.[13] It was not accidental that all the preparatory texts of the IGCs had left the term "Political Union" undefined. Earlier discussions during the extraordinary Dublin Summit of April 1990 had revealed that the concept had different connotations in the various Member States and that it would be impossible to reach agreement on a uniform definition.[14]

The text adopted at the Rome Summit defines the major points concerning Political Union on the IGC agenda as the strengthening of democratic legitimacy, the development of a Common Foreign and Security Policy, the examination of the concept of European citizenship, the extension and the strengthening of Community action, as well as the amelioration of the effectiveness and the efficiency of the Union.[15] By further deepening integration among the EC Member States, the Twelve hoped to cope more effectively with the new challenges resulting from German reunification and the changes in Central and Eastern Europe and they wanted to prepare for a further widening of the EC. The end of the cold war had left the word "neutrality" devoid of its meaning, and had removed the final obstacle to the applications for EC membership of the neutral EFTA countries, such as Austria, Sweden, and Finland.[16]

For the purpose of this research our focus has been limited to the negotiations on the provisions relating to the CFSP which besides being one of the most sensitive issues of the IGC on Political Union, was also of most interest to the US.[17] It was a subject given a particular sense of urgency due to the outbreak of the Gulf crisis in August 1990.

The wide variety of foreign-policy proposals put forward at the opening of the IGC on Political Union in December 1990 were illustrative of the Member States' widely diverging views on the matter. The proposals ranged from suggestions for the introduction of small aesthetic changes into European Political Cooperation, as expressed in the Danish memorandum (4 October 1990)[18] and the memorandum of the Portuguese delegation (30 November 1990),[19] to much more radical proposals, such as the Italian proposal on CFSP

(18 September 1990) and the Franco-German letter to the Italian Presidency (6 December 1990). The most radical was undoubtedly the Italian recommendation that the Western European Union and the European Union be merged.[20] In their joint letter of 6 December 1990, Chancellor Kohl, and President Mitterrand, pleaded for Political Union to include "a true common security policy which would in turn lead to a common defence".[21]

Throughout the year of negotiations, first under the Luxembourg (1 January to 30 June 1991) and later under the Dutch Presidency (1 July to 31 December 1991), France and Germany were the main actors in the debate on the development of a CFSP. On two occasions, in the early phase of the IGC and towards its conclusion, Bonn and Paris put forward proposals which had a decisive impact on the course of the negotiations and their final outcome.[22] While the key role played by both of these countries at the IGC cannot be viewed separately from their earlier efforts to develop closer bilateral cooperation in the security and defence field,[23] the end of the cold war and the changing political situation in Europe provided both partners with additional incentives for a further strengthening of the Franco-German security axis. For Bonn, close cooperation with France and active participation in the European security debate was a way to assuage French fears of the development of an independent German security policy. It also allowed the Germans to express their continued commitment to the goal of "an ever closer union among the peoples of Europe".[24] For France, the development of a CFSP was an additional means by which the new Germany could be anchored firmly in the European Union.[25] Furthermore, by closely cooperating with Bonn, Paris hoped to prevent Germany from taking the lead in political affairs in Europe and thus to safeguard France's own position.

The close cooperation between both countries did not imply that their positions were always identical. In line with the Gaullist approach, Paris placed considerable emphasis on the development of an independent European security policy.[26] In a first transitional period, this policy would be developed in close cooperation with the WEU, which would receive its general guidelines from the European Council. Germany supported the objective of an increased security role for Europe but was anxious to prevent potentially adverse effects on relations with the United States and the Atlantic Alliance. As a frontline state without nuclear weapons and a small army, it had been relying fully on the American security guarantee throughout the post-war period and it realised that for the time being NATO and its fully integrated military command would continue to be indispensable for the defence of Western Europe.[27]

## A Europeanist or Atlanticist Approach?

Although both Franco-German proposals submitted at the IGC on Political Union referred to the Atlantic Alliance as being indispensable for the security and stability of Europe, their strong emphasis on the development of an autonomous European security identity seems to suggest that content-wise they were strongly influenced by France. Not surprisingly, such a point of view received strong opposition from the Atlanticist countries, which believed that any strengthening of European security cooperation should take place within the NATO framework.

For the United Kingdom, supported by the Netherlands, Portugal and Denmark, only the United States could credibly guarantee European security – hence, defence questions had to be the exclusive competence of NATO. During the first months of the negotiations, the UK tried to limit the discussions to introducing a number of minor changes to EPC.[28] Under the pressure of the growing threat of American troop withdrawal and impelled by the Italians seeking British support to counterbalance the weight of the Franco-German position in the negotiations, the UK finally became more actively involved in the CFSP debate during the Dutch Presidency in the second half of 1991. On 4 October 1991, together with Italy, the UK submitted a joint proposal on European security and defence, supporting the view that the development of a stronger European defence identity should primarily reinforce the Atlantic Alliance.[29] It was not until the Bush administration explicitly gave the green light for the development of a CFSP at the NATO Summit in Rome in November 1991 that the United Kingdom conceded that security questions should be included in the scope of the competences of the European Union.[30]

The divergence of views between the two groups was also reflected in the way they defined the future role of the WEU. On the one hand, the Europeanists, which apart from France included countries such as Spain, Belgium and Luxembourg, wanted the WEU to develop into the security pillar of the European Union. The Atlanticists, on the other hand, wanted the WEU to become the European security pillar of the Atlantic Alliance and to serve as the bridge between the European Union and NATO. While the first group pleaded for WEU membership to coincide with EU membership, the Atlanticists wanted to expand it to include all the European members of NATO.

The final provisions on the gradual development of a Common Foreign and Security Policy in the Treaty on European Union are the result of a compromise between the two above-mentioned positions. The extremely tortuous formulation of the Article referring to European defence reveals the extremely difficult and long negotiations preceding its adoption:

> The common foreign and security policy shall include all questions related to the security of the Union, including the *eventual* framing of a common defence policy, which *might in time* lead to a common defence.[31] (Article J.4(1))

The text on the Union's relations with the WEU and NATO refers both to the WEU, as an integral part of the development of the European Union (Article J.4(2)), and to NATO (Article J.4(4)).[32] As regards the latter Article, it stipulates that the CFSP will respect the obligations of certain Member States under the North Atlantic Treaty. In a declaration attached to the Treaty on European Union, the members of the WEU solicited their EC partners Denmark, Greece, and Ireland to accede to the WEU or to become observers, and they invited the European members of NATO who were not part of the EU to become associate members.[33]

Of the three EC Member States, only Greece, which had made its support of the Treaty on European Union conditional upon Greek membership of the WEU, opted for full membership.[34] With the coming into power of New Democracy, the former "footnote country"[35] adopted a much more positive attitude towards the development of a European foreign and security policy, a change which was also related to the unstable situation in the Balkans after the end of the cold war.[36]

As a neutral country, Ireland chose observer status.[37] Ireland, which had greatly benefited from EC membership, adopted a pragmatic position with regard to CFSP during the 1991 IGC. The Union's commitment to take into account the "specific character of the security and defence policy of certain Member States" (Article J.4(4)) was accepted as sufficient guarantee of its special status. Likewise, the imminent prospect of other neutral countries acceding to the EU might have had a positive influence in bringing about Dublin's flexible stance.

Denmark, for reasons quite different from those of Ireland, also opted for observer status. The notion of an independent European security identity was in dramatic contrast to the Danish perception of the European Community as a purely economic entity.[38] The Danish government objected in particular to the discussion of defence questions in the framework of CFSP.[39]

Iceland, Norway, and Turkey, which were all members of NATO, but not of the EC, agreed to become "associate members"[40] of the WEU.[41]

## *Why a Temple Proved Stronger than a Tree*[42]

A final, extremely controversial issue during the CFSP negotiations, which however went beyond the division between Atlanticists and Europeanists, was the question of the place of the provisions on CFSP in the Treaty on European Union. Most Member States, not least France, had always favoured maintaining a strict separation between the European Communities and European Political Cooperation. Although the Twelve relatively easily agreed to abandon the artificial distinction between EC and EPC institutions by introducing the principle of a single institutional framework for the European Union, the question of whether CFSP would become part of the European Community or remain a separate entity continued to be an extremely sensitive issue.[43]

The first draft Treaty on European Union, prepared by the Luxembourg Presidency in mid-April 1991, also known as the "Luxembourg Non-Paper",[44] proposed a strict separation between the European Communities, CFSP and cooperation in the field of justice and home affairs.[45] This arrangement, also referred to as the "temple structure", because it proposed a Treaty based on three separate pillars, was a piece of French ingenuity.[46] The purpose of this approach was to ensure that certain of the supranational characteristics of the EC, such as the European Commission's exclusive right of initiative and decisions taken mainly by qualified majority voting (QMV), would not be extended to CFSP. The fact that the French were the brains behind the three-pillar structure is not surprising: France had always regarded the development of a European foreign policy as a means of upgrading its international status and of asserting its political leadership in Europe. Hence, it favoured a purely intergovernmental European foreign policy in which the Member States, and not the Commission, were the main actors. Whereas the three-pillar structure of the "Luxembourg Non-Paper" was acceptable to most Member States, it was radically criticised by the Netherlands, Belgium and the European Commission.[47] They advocated the so-called tree-approach whereby CFSP would be integrated into the EC trunk, in this way expressing the intention that, at least in the long term, CFSP would receive some supranational characteristics.

The second Luxembourg draft Treaty,[48] which the Heads of State and Government at their Summit meeting in June 1991 accepted as the basis for further negotiations,[49] maintained the pillar approach.[50] In late September, the Dutch Presidency nonetheless came up with a proposal introducing a unitary treaty structure, the text of which was adapted to be more in line with its national preferences. However, it was heavily penalised:[51] as it was only supported by Belgium and the European Commission, the proposal had to be withdrawn.[52]

This unhappy episode in the history of the IGC brings to mind an earlier contest between the proponents of a supranational European foreign policy and the advocates of the intergovernmental approach, taking place during the Fouchet negotiations on Political Union in the early 1960s.[53] At the time, the Netherlands, supported by Belgium, objected very strongly to President de Gaulle's proposal to initiate foreign-policy cooperation outside the EC framework. After two years of negotiations, both countries finally vetoed the project in April 1962. It is an irony – and France played a key role in this[54] – that it was the Dutch draft treaty which was rejected many years later. History had come full circle.

Closely linked to the debate on an intergovernmentalist versus a supranationalist approach is the question of the use of QMV in the area of CFSP. While the Netherlands, supported by Belgium, strongly favoured the introduction of QMV,[55] countries such as France, the UK and Denmark defended the *status quo*. Giving up the possibility to block a decision in the area of foreign policy, one of the few remaining bastions of national sovereignty, was a step too far especially for the larger Member States. The Maastricht Treaty maintained unanimity as the general rule (Article J.8(2)), but foresaw the possibility of using a special QMV procedure for the implementation of joint actions. In addition to the 54 votes out of 76 needed, this special QMV system also required the support of at least eight Member States (Article J.3(2)).[56] This was clearly not intended to become the general rule as the Council was to define in advance and by unanimity "those matters on which decisions are to be taken by a qualified majority" (Article J.3(2)).

*CFSP as Defined in Maastricht: A First Evaluation*

The CFSP provisions in the Treaty on European Union can hardly be characterised as a major leap forward. Although the denomination "Common Foreign and Security Policy" evokes high expectations, it reflects wishful thinking rather than reality. Since the end of the Second World War, the process of political integration in Western Europe has always progressed by small steps, while major jumps, like the EDC initiative, have generally failed. The results reached in Maastricht should also be seen in the light of this step-by-step approach.

Indisputably, the most important breakthrough made by the new Treaty was the agreement to gradually extend the scope of CFSP to defence issues. Other positive developments were the introduction of a single institutional framework, the increasing emphasis on joint actions as well as the introduction of a co-right of initiative for the Commission. The major flaw of the compromise reached in Maastricht was that it did not succeed in overcoming the predominantly intergovernmental character of European foreign-policy cooperation. CFSP was not integrated into the EC but became a separate pillar, consolidating, rather than lifting the artificial separation between external economic and political relations. Since most decisions would continue to be taken by unanimity, there was the serious risk that CFSP would continue to be as dynamic as the slowest cog in its mechanism. For the implementation of decisions in the defence area, the European Union had to rely on the WEU, an institution without its own operational capabilities and entirely dependent on the goodwill of its Member States.[57] The inclusion of a clause foreseeing the revision of the CFSP and more particularly the defence provisions at the 1996 IGC can be seen as a gesture to those countries which had hoped for a more far-reaching reform of EPC.[58] The comfort this prospect gave was minimal since the enlargement and consequent inclusion of some of the neutral EFTA countries made the chances of the 1996 IGC adopting a more audacious approach towards CFSP look very slim.[59]

## The Bush Administration and Its Response to CFSP

### *A New Europe, A New Atlanticism*[60]

When, in the course of 1989, the communist regimes of Eastern Europe collapsed one after the other like dominoes, it became imperative for the United States' foreign-policy establishment to radically revise its policy towards the "old continent", which for more than 40 years had been based on a divided Europe. The time had come for a new transatlantic agenda and for new or at least adjusted structures to cope with the changed environment.

One of the first attempts in this direction was President George Bush's appeal for closer consultative links between the US and the European Community made in a speech at Boston University in May 1989.[61] As a result of the success of the 1992 exercise, the image of the EC as a paralysed actor was replaced by that of a vigorous competitor, whose actions could potentially have major implications for the United States. Initially the new European assertiveness was perceived as a direct threat to US interests and led to a real phobia about a so-called "fortress Europe". By 1989, however, Washington was adopting a much more positive and relaxed approach, appreciating the new opportunities the internal market was creating for American business and trade circles.[62] Rather than rejecting the developments on the European scene, the US now resorted to a strategy of trying to influence events by tightening transatlantic links. It hoped to realise this objective by strengthening ties with the European Community.

As events in Eastern Europe gained momentum and the Berlin Wall collapsed, a more elaborate and complete picture of the institutional spectacles through which the United States was seeing its future relations with the emerging new Europe was given in a speech by Secretary of State James Baker in Berlin in mid-December 1989.[63] In the first place, Baker's address was a strong appeal for a "New Atlanticism", which was to be realised through the adjustment of the existing instruments of Western cooperation. In the US view, the three main institutional pillars for transatlantic integration were NATO, the EC and the Conference on Security and Cooperation in Europe (CSCE).[64] The importance of the Baker speech can hardly be overstated: it was a first attempt to articulate the US view with regard to the respective role of the different multilateral institutions in the post-cold war Europe and throughout the four years of the Bush administration its principles served as a major guide for US policy.

One of the principal messages of the Baker address was the continuing importance of NATO, the organisation which for the last 40 years had been the major bridge between the two sides of the Atlantic and the chief channel for US influence in Europe. Washington strongly disagreed with those who argued that this cold war instrument had lost its *raison d'être*, and defended the view that NATO should adapt itself and take on the mission of building "a new security structure in Europe, one in which the military component is reduced and the political is enhanced".

The paper also came up with concrete proposals as to the tasks a more political North Atlantic Alliance should assume. Suggestions were that these should be the establishment of a NATO arms control verification staff, intensified consultations among the allies on regional conflicts, and the development of closer ties with the East. The paper left no doubt that US and European security continued to be indissolubly linked and that Washington would continue to maintain military troops in Europe. It also strongly supported overcoming the divisions of both Europe and Germany.

The second pillar of Baker's New Atlanticism was the European Community. The text especially emphasises the important vocation of the EC in Eastern Europe. At the same time, however, the US Secretary of State warned the Twelve that the EC could never serve as an alternative to transatlantic cooperation. Closer European integration always had to run parallel with the development of deeper US-EC links. Baker repeated the above-mentioned appeal of President Bush to strengthen the institutional and consultative links between the US and the EC "either in treaty or some other form". European integration should be an instrument to bring the US and the Europeans closer together rather than to drive them apart.

As to the future role of the CSCE, the text was rather vague, recommending that new substance be given to its respective security, economic and human rights baskets. In reality the US had rather mixed feelings with regard to the CSCE. The main reason for its inclusion in Baker's speech was its potential function as a link with Russia. Washington hoped to give a clear signal to Moscow that it would not be left out of the emerging transatlantic framework. In addition, the CSCE was seen as an institution that could play an important role in the promotion of democratic values in Eastern Europe, analogous with what it had previously accomplished in the field of human rights.

Baker's Berlin speech is one of the keys to understanding what in the coming years was to become the main course of US policy towards Europe. While fully committing itself to remaining a European power, Washington left no doubt that it was primarily through NATO, the organisation where its position in Europe was the strongest, that it wanted to continue to realise its goals in the old world.[65] Rather than trying to exploit the changed circumstances to withdraw its troops as some Europeans had feared, the US seemed primarily to be looking for new reasons to justify its continued presence on the continent. It wanted NATO to move beyond its traditional military approach and to reinforce its political capacities.

It is striking that the address was silent about the future role of the Western European countries in NATO and did not say a word about an eventual strengthening of their position. The US seemed mainly concerned about safeguarding its own influence. As to the major justification for its continued role in Europe, Washington referred to the need to prevent a return to the unstable Europe of the first half of the century.[66]

Although the Baker address did not explicitly propose a division of tasks between the three institutions that it mentions and only briefly referred to the "increasingly important political roles" of the EC, the function of the political-military arm of European security was primarily attributed to NATO. The EC, which has potentially an important role to play in Central and Eastern Europe, was mainly seen as the economic pillar of the new Europe. Baker recognised the danger of a growing overlap between the EC and NATO, and therefore recommended enhanced communication between the two bodies, without precisely expressing how this could concretely be implemented.

The United States' unequivocal commitment to remain a power in Europe was generally welcomed by the EC Member States and to some extent assuaged increasing fears of a withdrawal of US troops. In Germany, in particular, the appeal for a new Atlantic partnership was received very positively.[67] The German government, anxious to receive US support for reunification, was eager to express its commitment to continued close cooperation with Washington.[68] The enthusiastic reaction of Bonn, which during the first half of 1990 put forward concrete proposals for the conclusion of a US-EC agreement, should also be seen in the light of the German willingness to counterbalance the bilateral "Treaty on good-neighbourness, partnership and friendship" concluded with the Soviet Union.[69]

In France, on the other hand, there was little enthusiasm and even suspicion *vis-à-vis* the American proposals. The French Minister of Foreign Affairs, Roland Dumas, rejected the proposal to transform NATO into a political organisation and suspected that, by tightening the links with the EC, Washington was trying to get a grip on the EC decision-making process.[70]

The United Kingdom was taken by surprise by the Baker speech. During a brief landing in London prior to his visit to Berlin, Secretary of State James Baker had refrained from informing Prime Minister Margaret Thatcher of his design for the new Europe. Although the British Prime Minister did not appreciate the speech's major emphasis on European integration, she fully agreed with the American analysis that the new situation in Europe required the strengthening of the transatlantic links.[71]

## The Transatlantic Declaration

One of the most immediate spin-offs of the Baker speech was the re-examination of the US-EC relationship. Although the United States had been one of the first countries to have an official mission with the European Coal and Steel Community (ECSC), and later with the EC, relations with Brussels had never received high priority. Bilateral relations with the European capitals had always been considered as being more important. With the success of the internal market programme, Washington started to realise the increasing importance of the EC as an international actor and estimated that it would be beneficial for the US to formalise its relationship with Brussels.[72] The potentially very influential role of the EC in Eastern Europe and its function as anchor of a united Germany further reinforced US interest in reinvigorating its ties with the EC.

In the course of 1989, both President Bush and Secretary of State Baker had suggested the institutionalisation of US-EC relations.[73] The decision at the G7 Summit (July 1989) to ask the European Commission to coordinate Western aid to Poland and Hungary and the attribution of full diplomatic status to the Delegation of the European Commission in Washington D.C. were further signs of increased US willingness to recognise the EC as a fully-fledged partner.[74]

A first step towards closer institutional links between both partners was made by the end of February 1990, when President George Bush and the Irish EC Presidency agreed to organise biannual meetings between the Presidents of the European Council and the European Commission on the one side and the US President on the other, and at the same time agreed to hold biannual consultations between the EC Foreign Ministers, accompanied by representatives of the European Commission, and the US Secretary of State.[75] Furthermore, ad hoc consultations were foreseen between the foreign minister of the EC country holding the Presidency or the Troika and the US Secretary of State, plus there would be consultations between the Commission and the US government at cabinet level twice a year. For the first time in the history of US-EC relations, there was a provision for regular consultations between both partners at presidential level.

The Baker speech of December 1989 had advanced the idea of concluding a transatlantic treaty but left it up to the EC to decide what form a tightened US-EC relationship should take. Partly because the EC itself was undergoing important changes and, to some extent, because there continued to be doubts as to the real motives of the US, the Heads of State and Government at the Dublin Summit of June 1990 opted for "a joint transatlantic declaration", rather than for the conclusion of a treaty.[76]

The negotiations between both partners started in the summer of 1990 and led to the adoption of the "Declaration on US-EC Relations" on 20 November 1990.[77] The discussions took place on the basis of a text put forward by the Italian Presidency. On the US side, it was primarily the State Department and the US Mission to the EC in Brussels which were involved.[78]

Among the more sensitive issues of the negotiations was the US proposal to include a reference to the North Atlantic Alliance, an idea which met strong French opposition.[79] In the final text, which was the result of a compromise, the preamble refers to both the CSCE, NATO and to the EC.[80] It was explicitly recognised that the EC was in the process of acquiring its own identity "in foreign policy matters and in the domain of security" and the declaration also included an evolutionary clause stipulating that, as the European Community developed, the transatlantic relationship would be adjusted accordingly.

Content-wise, the declaration is mainly a declaration of intent. It was formulated in very general terms and places major emphasis on supporting common values such as the promotion of democracy, the safeguarding of peace and the advancement of market principles. The declaration refers to the willingness of both partners to inform and consult each other on important economic and political developments, and to cooperate in a number of areas such as education, science, culture, and the environment. As regards the institutional framework for consultation, the text repeats the arrangements adopted during the above-mentioned Bush-Haughey meeting of February 1990.

The Transatlantic Declaration was far from being a watershed in US-EC relations. It was primarily a political gesture, expressing the willingness of the United States and the European Community to strengthen their cooperation and to adjust their relationship to the vastly changed circumstances in Europe. It also reflected the recognition by the US of the increasingly important role of the EC and can be seen as a first step towards a more equal partnership. That the US was the prime instigator of the initiative reflects the fact that it was the partner that had the most to gain from the adoption of the declaration. As the US anticipated a decreased role for NATO, Washington saw that a close relationship with the EC, as one of the key players of the new Europe, was becoming crucial. Washington's eagerness to strengthen its links with Brussels also illustrates its consciousness of the increasing importance of economics in the transatlantic relationship.

The adoption of the Transatlantic Declaration received little attention in the press and went by largely unnoticed by public opinion, which was fully absorbed by the events in the Gulf.[81] If there were any hopes that the declaration signalled the beginning of a revitalised transatlantic relationship they were completely dashed when, barely two weeks after its adoption, the Uruguay Round talks broke down because of the inability of the US and the EC to solve their agricultural disagreements. This incident sharply contrasted with the principles of solidarity and cooperation to which the declaration had subscribed.

*Washington and German Reunification*

If 1989 goes down in the annals of history as the year of the fall of the Berlin Wall, 1990 was undoubtedly dominated by the reunification of the two Germanys and the end of the division of Europe.

As the main guarantor of Western European security and one of the four Second-World-War allies with residual rights over Germany, the United States had a direct interest at stake in the process of German reunification.[82] In contrast to Moscow, London and Paris, which were troubled by fears that reunification might unleash nationalistic forces and that Germany might abuse its economic strength and its newly acquired position in the centre of Europe, Washington soon realised that reunification was becoming an inevitable process and was among the first to express its full support for a single Germany.[83] By adopting a constructive attitude, the United States hoped to influence the course of events in Germany as much as possible.[84]

Although the US had always fully supported the principle of a peaceful and democratic reunification of Germany, there were also a number of other considerations underlying the US stance. The huge stream of refugees daily fleeing to the West clearly demonstrated that the East German population would not be satisfied with idle promises of aid and was calling for a much more substantial solution to its problems.[85] When, by the end of November 1989, Chancellor Kohl produced his ten-point plan suggesting the establishment of confederate structures and ultimately the reunification with Eastern Germany, the US realised that any attempt to obstruct this process would negatively affect Bonn's close links with the West and might be exploited by the Soviet Union.[86] Rather than irritating and exasperating what would become one of the largest countries on the European continent, the US opted for a strategy of support and a tightening of US-German links.

In May 1989, when things had already started to move in several Central and Eastern European countries, President George Bush, during a visit to Mainz, called upon the Federal Republic of Germany (FRG) to strengthen its links with the US and invited Bonn to become "partners in leadership" with Washington.[87] A memorandum of the National Security Council of March 1989 had defined the fate of the Federal Republic of Germany as "the top priority for American foreign policy in Europe".[88] It was not London or Paris, but Bonn that was considered to be the capital that could best defend US interests in Europe.[89] Washington was clearly nourishing high expectations as regards the international role that would be assumed by a fully sovereign Germany.

An ultimate factor which positively influenced the US position towards reunification was the supportive attitude of American public opinion.[90] Polls indicated that 75% of the Americans were in favour of reunification.

While London and Paris were still tinkering with strategies to obstruct the German reunification process, Washington concentrated its energy on designing ways to influence it. At a NATO meeting in December 1989, when briefing the Allies about his first summit with President Gorbachev in Malta, President Bush linked his support for reunification with four main principles.[91] They were that reunification would respect the right to self-determination of the German people; that it included the implication of a continued commitment to NATO and European integration; that it was to be a peaceful and gradual process; and last but not least, that the Helsinki principles concerning the inviolability of borders had to be respected.

Given the pace of events in both Eastern and Western Germany, it became evident that the US did not have the time to take "careful stock of the implications" of unification as the British Prime Minister Margaret Thatcher had suggested earlier.[92] If it wanted to safeguard its interests and influence the course of events, Washington had no choice but to act rapidly.[93]

One of the major challenges was the question of the framework in which the external aspects of German reunification, which also included Germany's future security arrangements, would be negotiated. It was the United States and, more particularly, Secretary of State Baker's principal adviser on Germany, Robert Zoellick, who in January 1990 came up with the proposal to use the "two-plus-four" framework.[94] This formula had the advantage that it brought together the two Germanys as well as the four allied powers of the Second World War that had some residual rights and responsibilities over Germany and Berlin. It also gave a prominent place to the Soviet Union, the country with the most serious reservations about rapid German reunification and German membership of NATO. After having obtained support from Bonn and once it had convinced both France and the United Kingdom[95] of its idea, the US also succeeded in persuading the Soviet Union, which initially pleaded for the use of the forum of the CSCE.[96]

Once there was an agreement on the two-plus-four formula, Washington concentrated all its efforts on the goal of full German membership of NATO and its integrated military structure. The US was wary of Bonn accepting neutral status in exchange for Soviet support for reunification. Such a scenario would not only ruin the work of 40 years of US policy tying Germany to the West; it also contained the seeds of an unpredictable and unstable Europe. Being one of the largest European countries, occupying a central position on the continent, Germany could play an important role in counterbalancing the Soviet Union, and could serve as an important channel for the defense of US interests in Europe. A major argument against a neutral Germany, deprived of being part of a multilateral security framework, was that it might sooner or later be tempted to develop an independent security and defense policy, including its own nuclear force.[97] Furthermore, there were also what Brent Scowcroft has called "practical reasons" for a continued German membership of NATO. Without the American bases in Germany, it would be difficult to maintain a US presence in Europe.[98]

While the principle of the continued German membership of NATO was publicly supported by Chancellor Helmut Kohl at the end of a summit with President Bush in late February 1990,[99] it would take many more efforts, including a whole series of American diplomatic initiatives to overcome the strong Soviet reservations.[100] At a meeting in May 1990, Secretary of State Baker presented President Gorbachev with a list of nine points, aimed at reassuring the Soviet Union with regard to the future intentions of the US, Germany and NATO. The document talked about a continued US commitment to arms reduction talks; a comprehensive review of the NATO strategy; a strengthening of the CSCE; a nuclear-free Germany; a transitional period for the departure of Soviet troops from the GDR as well as a delay in extending NATO forces to its territory; and an explicit recognition by a united Germany of the inviolability of its external borders.[101]

The signing at the Bush-Gorbachev Summit (Washington D.C., Camp David, 30 May to 2 June 1990) of a trade agreement between both countries was primarily aimed at helping Gorbachev overcome domestic opposition with regard to continued German membership of NATO.[102] Although Gorbachev initially tried to convince the US of a double membership, whereby Germany would be anchored to both NATO and the Warsaw Pact, the final declaration of the Summit explicitly recognised that Alliance membership was a matter for the German people to decide themselves.[103]

Also the series of measures adopted at the London NATO Summit (5 and 6 July 1990), giving the Alliance a more friendly face, were primarily aimed at convincing the Soviet Union that NATO was changing.[104] It was *inter alia* proposed that the members of NATO and the Warsaw Pact adopt a joint declaration in which they confirmed that they were no longer adversaries. Furthermore, the Soviet Union and the countries of Central and Eastern Europe were invited to establish "regular diplomatic liaison with NATO" and to intensify their military contacts with the Alliance. The Alliance also announced it would reduce its reliance on nuclear weapons, which would become "truly weapons of last resort".

A further objective of the London Summit was to give a positive signal to the German population. A poll of 22 to 25 June 1990 had revealed that only 51% of the German population favoured a continuing NATO membership for a united Germany. Only 53% approved of the stationing of foreign troops on

German territory, while 54% advocated the removal of nuclear weapons.[105] The agreement in London on the reduced reliance of NATO on nuclear weapons, and the appeal that the CSCE play a more prominent role in European security, were important concessions to the German public and were clearly intended to overcome some of their reservations regarding the continued membership of the Alliance. In addition, the US' agreement not to modernise Lance missiles, the Alliance's short-range nuclear missiles (SRNMs), should be seen in the same light.[106]

However important the US role in securing the continued German membership of NATO may have been, the final Soviet reservations with regard to German reunification were lifted during a bilateral meeting between Chancellor Kohl and President Gorbachev on 16 July.[107] In exchange for the restoration of full German sovereignty, including the freedom of choice concerning Alliance membership, Chancellor Kohl accepted a 370,000 ceiling on German troops, promised to repeat his renouncement of atomic, biological and chemical (ABC) weapons and committed Germany to becoming party of the Nuclear Non-Proliferation Treaty. Finally, he also agreed that NATO structures would not apply to the GDR territory as long as there were Soviet troops present. The financial package consisted of a credit of US$ 3 billion and support for the withdrawal of Soviet troops from East Germany.

On 12 September, the "Treaty on the Final Settlement with Respect to Germany" was signed. It gave the united Germany full sovereignty over both its internal and external affairs and explicitly recognised "the right of the united Germany to belong to alliances".[108] On 3 October, less than one year after the fall of the Berlin Wall, Germany was officially united.[109]

Although the key to successful and rapid reunification lay primarily with the German citizens and their respective governments, the above paragraphs clearly demonstrate that the United States played a decisive role.[110] The fact that the US adopted a very supportive and positive attitude towards reunification from the beginning was of invaluable importance for Germany as it prevented the French, British and Soviet attempts to slow down the reunification process from succeeding.

The major contribution of the US was undoubtedly the achievement that a unified Germany continued to be a full member of the Atlantic Alliance. At the outset of the negotiations it was far from certain that it would be possible to overcome the strong Soviet objections to such an arrangement. At the first ministerial meeting of the two-plus-four group in Bonn (5 May 1990), the Soviet Foreign Minister, Shevardnadze, described continued German membership of NATO as an unacceptable option, both from a military as well as from an internal, political point of view.[111] Other proposals such as the conclusion of bilateral agreements between a united Germany and the Allies, and German membership of NATO based on the French model, were circulating and considered to have a much better chance of being realised.[112]

Washington spared no pains to try to achieve its objective by organising high-level meetings with the major actors involved. Between February and June 1990, President Bush successively received NATO Secretary-General Manfred Wörner, Chancellor Helmut Kohl, Prime Minister Margaret Thatcher and President François Mitterrand. On each of these occasions, German unification was high on the agenda. Once he had made sure that the position of the Western countries was on one line, President Bush concentrated all his efforts on persuading the Soviet Union that it was also in Moscow's security interest that a united Germany be embedded in the NATO structure. Had it not been for the multiple US initiatives aimed at convincing the Soviet Union that East-West relations were being organised on a new basis, Moscow would never have accepted full NATO membership of the single Germany.

An element which certainly contributed to Washington's success was that the process was steered by a very small team of US officials with a strong strategic sense who realised that the future stability of Europe depended to a large extent on the way the German question was addressed.

For President Bush, the question of a continuing German membership of NATO was considered to be crucial as it would "decide future decades of European history". In *A World Transformed*, he warns that "if Germany were permitted to leave the Alliance, the old 'Pandora's box' of competition and rivalry in Europe would be reopened."[113] He defines the fact that the US succeeded in persuading the allies to accept German reunification and managed to convince the Soviets to agree with a continuing membership of the Alliance as "probably the most important moment in the transformation of Europe."[114]

That the United States was willing to invest so much energy in obtaining enduring German membership of NATO clearly reflected the fact that the Alliance would continue to be the major linchpin of US policy towards Europe. Without Germany, the Atlantic Alliance and consequently the US position in Europe would have been considerably weakened. By guaranteeing that Germany would continue to be embedded in Western security structures, the US not only prevented future generations of Germans from feeling singled out and being tempted to pursue the *Sonderweg* again, but it also secured a powerful interlocutor for American interests in Europe, and laid the foundation for a continuing central US role on the European continent.

## NATO and CFSP: Rivals or Partners?

Once the question of German reunification had been settled satisfactorily, both the European Community as well as the Atlantic Alliance focused their attention on adjusting themselves to the changed European security landscape. While the EC, in the framework of the Intergovernmental Conference on Political Union, started negotiations on the development of a European security and defence policy, NATO concentrated on the transformation of the Alliance and the design of a new strategic concept.

Although both the EC and NATO are based in Brussels and the debates they were having were closely interlinked and to some extent overlapped, there was no official framework where representatives of both organisations formally met or exchanged views. Partly because of the lack of official channels, partly because of competition, there was little communication between the European and Atlantic channels and each body looked for its own answers as how to best address the security challenges of the new Europe.

With the intention of making a reformed Atlantic Alliance the crux of its European policy, Washington was anxious to prevent the security initiatives of the EC Member States from jeopardising the primacy of NATO as the central European security organisation and was looking for possible ways to influence the European debate.

The US reactions to the Franco-German proposal on security policy cooperation in the EC (February 1991) are illustrative of Washington's main concerns. The proposal, although referring to a continued commitment to NATO and the need for a permanent US military presence in Europe, called upon the EC Member States to gradually develop a Common Foreign and Security Policy (CFSP) and a common European defence.[115] Shortly after the paper had been made public, the US sent a telegram to the different European capitals in which it urged the EC Member States not to develop the CFSP in a way that would detract them from NATO's position as *primus inter pares*.[116] The text is unequivocal: "the primary yardstick against which proposals and institutional innovations need to be measured is whether they actually enhance Alliance defensive capabilities and make Europe more secure...efforts to construct a European pillar by redefining and limiting NATO's role, by weakening its structure, or by creating a monolithic block of certain members would be misguided." American support for the development of a European security identity is made conditional upon its capacity to strengthen the Alliance.

One of the main concerns expressed in the telegram, also known as the

Bartholomew *"démarche"* after the name of its initiator, the US Under-Secretary of State for International Security Affairs, is the future relationship between the EC and the WEU. The Franco-German proposal that the WEU develops into the security arm of the Union, implementing security decisions by the European Council was regarded with a lot of suspicion. The development of such an independent European security identity, outside the Alliance framework, could lead to the marginalisation of both NATO and the United States.[117] Furthermore, the Americans also voiced the concern that NATO would increasingly be facing a European caucus, which would not be open to further discussion with the other allies and would therefore undermine the transatlantic debate.[118] Washington was wary of being confronted with a situation comparable to that in GATT, where pre-agreed European positions often turned out to be very rigid, leaving little room for further negotiations. The message of Deputy Assistant Secretary of State James Dobbins, who was visiting various European capitals in the same period, was along similar lines.[119]

In April, the Europeans received a further warning from the US Secretary of State, James Baker, in a letter to the Luxembourg EC Presidency outlining the major principles against which the US would judge the proposals for a European security and defence identity. Although it expressed understanding of Europe's ambitions to develop a Common Foreign, Security and Defence Policy, it also insisted that "NATO should remain the principal venue for consultation and the forum for agreement on all policies bearing on the security and defence commitments of its members" and that NATO was to maintain its integrated military structures and command.[120] The letter also cautioned against the exclusion from the security debate of the European NATO members that were not part of the EC. Undoubtedly, the US was mainly alluding to Turkey which, as the Gulf war had illustrated, continued to occupy a major geostrategic position in the European security landscape.[121] Knowing the Twelve's reticence with regard to Turkish membership of the European Community, the US was wary that Ankara would become increasingly marginalised in the debate on the future security arrangements on the European continent.[122]

Not all EC Member States had sympathy for the US' concerns and several of them perceived their above-mentioned interventions as an interference in EC internal affairs. In many European capitals, not least in Paris, the Bartholomew *démarche* provoked angry reactions and transatlantic relations passed through a difficult time. Realising that their approach was counterproductive, the Bush administration decided to change its strategy and tried to indirectly influence the outcome of the 1991 IGC by exerting leverage on some of its traditional allies.

As expected, the US found a willing ear for its concerns in the governments in London, The Hague and Lisbon, which supported the American point of view that increased European security cooperation should take place in the framework of the Atlantic Alliance. They did not hesitate to defend this point of view during the IGC discussions on the development of a CFSP, which not surprisingly caused tensions with countries such as France who favoured the development of an independent European security identity.

Germany was also sensitive to Washington's arguments but, once again, the government in Bonn was squeezed between its two conflicting foreign-policy objectives: on the one hand, full commitment to the deepening of the European integration process and, on the other hand, absolute loyalty to the Atlantic Alliance. Bonn tried to reconcile both objectives by opting for close cooperation with Paris during the 1991 debate on CFSP, while at the same time it tried to make sure that the proposals jointly put forward by the Franco-German axis took due account of the continuing importance of the Atlantic Alliance for Europe's security and defence.

Parallel with its efforts to influence the debate among the EC Member States, Washington fully exploited its influential position in the Alliance to further its own views regarding the future European security architecture. After the transformations adopted at the London Summit (5 and 6 July 1990) – the main purpose of which was to prepare the ground for German reunification and continued German membership of the Alliance – NATO started the process of adjusting its structures to the security challenges of the new Europe. The ministerial meetings of the Defence Planning Committee and the Nuclear Planning Group of late May 1991, were entirely dedicated to revising the NATO strategy and developing a new force structure.[123] Taking into account the new type of security risks, it was decided that NATO should rely on smaller, more flexible and multinational forces. In this light, it was agreed that an Allied Rapid Reaction Corps (ARRC) would be established, composed of forces of most NATO member countries.[124]

The decision on the creation of the ARRC was heavily criticised by France. The French Minister of Foreign Affairs, Roland Dumas, suspected the United States was trying to find new ways to perpetuate its military dominance in Europe.[125] The hasty creation of the ARRC, prior to the completion of the Alliance strategy review,[126] was furthermore seen as a manoeuvre to deepen the divisions among the Europeans and to pre-empt the creation of a separate European multilateral force.[127] By placing the ARRC under British command,

Washington was seen to be trying to motivate London to hinder the gradual development of an independent European security identity.[128] France also rejected proposals for the "double-hatting" of the ARRC, which would allow it in certain cases to be placed under WEU command.[129] The use by the WEU of NATO forces ran directly counter to the idea of an independent European defence.

Taking into consideration that for many years the United States had been advocating a more active European role in the security and defence area, the question arises of why the Bush administration initially objected to these timid European security initiatives. Would the disappearance of the Soviet threat not lead to a reduced American presence in Europe, and consequently require a more significant European contribution? Did the reduced US resources not make the development of a European security identity all the more desirable?

Although these questions receive affirmative answers, it should immediately be added that the US had quite specific views as to the organisation and role of the future European security and defence policy. For Washington, such a policy was only acceptable to the extent that it would be complementary and strengthen the North Atlantic Alliance.

During an address before the International Institute for Strategic Studies in London, William Taft, the US Ambassador to NATO, articulated four main principles that were to govern the relations between the Alliance and a separate European defence and security identity.[130] Any European initiative in the security field was to reinforce the institutional effectiveness of NATO and underscore the allies' common values and interests. None of the Alliance members was to become marginalised in the debate on European security, and the basic principle of collective effort in self-defence was to remain untouched. The text repeated three times that "NATO must remain the principal organisation to provide for European security". It accepted however that, outside the NATO area, the WEU could intervene independently. Trying to convince the Europeans not "to mess" with NATO's role and future, Ambassador Taft invoked the US public who would not accept it "if Europeans stopped using NATO or began replacing it with other structures to perform its historic tasks".

Besides the alleged problems of convincing the American public and Congress of the need for a continued US presence in Europe should NATO's role be reduced, there were of course many other motives underlying the US' reticent position.[131] Twice in the course of the twentieth century American soldiers had given their lives to restore peace on the European continent. By defending the pre-eminence of NATO, the US defended the continued existence of an organisation which had successfully guaranteed stability in

Europe for more than 40 years.

Believing that for the time being only the North Atlantic Alliance was capable of defending Europe in case of an attack, Washington was wary of exchanging a well-functioning NATO for an emerging CFSP which still had to prove itself.[132] If the attempts to establish a European security policy faltered, the nightmare scenario of a return to the unstable Europe of before Yalta and to a renationalisation of Europe's defence policies was no longer impossible. German reunification further strengthened the US' conviction that it should remain a European power.

Although Washington's scepticism of the EC's capacity to develop a viable alternative to NATO might have been well founded, the fact that an independent European security and defence policy would considerably impinge upon the US' influence on the European continent was probably what concerned Washington most. The United States had traditionally occupied a dominant position in NATO and as long as the Alliance was the major framework for European security, American governments had a forum available in which their views could be heard and their interests be defended.[133] It was far less certain whether a separate European security and defence policy would always be willing to take the US' point of view into account.

*France:* l'enfant terrible

American misgivings *vis-à-vis* the development of a CFSP were further reinforced by the fact that the country taking the lead in the debate was France. Although relations between Paris and Washington in the post-war period have always been close, they have at the same time been interwoven with ambiguity and misunderstandings. While the United States found it difficult to understand that French interests did not always coincide with those of Washington, France, for its part, resented its position of dependence on the American superpower and saved no effort in reaffirming its sovereignty and *grandeur*. The relationship between both countries is very well captured in the words of Frank Costigliola who characterises it as the "cold alliance".[134]

Much as it resented US dominance of the Alliance, France realised that only the United States had the capability to provide a credible deterrent to the Soviet military threat. It was the US nuclear umbrella and its continued commitment to Europe's defence that made it possible for the French, who left the integrated military command of NATO in 1966, to develop their own independent security position based on a nuclear deterrent force.[135] The end of the cold war, which carried with it the Europeanisation of the Alliance, raised the expectation that NATO-French cooperation would be given a new impetus and even led to the speculation that France might again become a full member of the Alliance. The issue of bringing France closer to the Alliance was discussed during a series of secret meetings between Washington and Paris, but they did not lead to any concrete results. France made such a development conditional upon the reform of NATO's integrated military command but this was unacceptable to the Pentagon.[136] The Bush-Mitterrand meeting in Martinique, in mid-March 1991, shattered any hopes for a fundamental revision of France's relationship to NATO.[137]

Contrary to Washington, for whom a transformed NATO continued to be the primary instrument for European security, Paris favoured the development of a separate European security identity. France expressed doubts about whether Western Europe could in the long term continue to rely on the United States for its defence. As US vital interests were no longer threatened by the communist challenge, it was increasingly questionable whether the US would continue to be a European power.[138] Reduced financial resources fuelling isolationist tendencies in the US public and in Congress led French politicians and analysts to the conclusion that the time had come for the Europeans to take care of their own security.[139]

During the 1991 IGC, France became the most vocal defender of the development of a distinct European security and defence identity and, together with Germany, it is one of the leading countries in the CFSP debate. There are several underlying factors which help to explain the French viewpoint.

The end of the cold war and the reduced importance of the US military guarantee were seen as providing an exceptional chance for France to boost its own position and to realise its long-awaited dream of becoming the political leader of Europe. German reunification further stimulated France's interest in the development of a European security policy. Wanting to prevent Germany from possibly once again going its *Sonderweg*, France was eager to anchor Germany more tightly in the European Community and hoped to do so by extending the scope of EC activities to security and defence. Conscious of the hesitation of certain Member States with regard to such plans, Paris proposed that the Western European Union become the security arm of the European Union. In the long term, the WEU could become fully merged with the EU.

It was exactly the position of the WEU in the emerging European security architecture which was one of the central points of controversy between Washington and Paris. The response to this question was important because, depending on whether the WEU was part of the EU or served as the European pillar of NATO, an entirely different concept of a European security identity would be realised. In the first option, an independent European security policy would gradually develop, while in the second model the WEU remained subordinate to NATO. At the Rome Summit (7 and 8 November 1991), the NATO allies did not explicitly choose either option. In oracular language they tried to compromise both concepts, welcoming "the perspective of a reinforcement of the role of the WEU, both as the defence component of the process of European unification and as a means of strengthening the European pillar of the Alliance, bearing in mind the different nature of its relations with the Alliance and with the European Political Union".[140]

Throughout the four years of the Bush administration, France's relationship with NATO remained as ambiguous and contradictory as ever. Although it continued to value NATO's stabilising effect on Russia and its anchoring function *vis-à-vis* Germany, and although the French Minister of Foreign Affairs, Roland Dumas, explicitly recognised that NATO remained "*la base de l'organisation de la défense de l'Europe*",[141] the French government did very little to contribute to the organisation's transformation, an operation which had to ensure its continued existence. France, for example, radically opposed the extension of NATO competences to the political and economic areas. It argued that NATO was primarily a military organisation and would continue to be so in the foreseeable future. American efforts to transform NATO into a political body were mainly seen as an attempt to sustain the United States' dominant position in Europe.[142]

A further issue of disagreement between Washington and France in the debate on the adaptation of NATO was the future role of nuclear weapons in Europe's defence. By accepting the principle that nuclear forces were becoming "truly weapons of last resort", the London Summit (5 and 6 July 1990) recognised that NATO's strategy of flexible response had become obsolete.[143] France, whose position of independence and rank in international affairs had been based on the possession of nuclear weapons, fiercely opposed reduced reliance on them.[144] In early 1992, the French President, François Mitterrand, brought up the issue of a European nuclear doctrine for the first time, defining it as one of the major issues in the building of a European defence.[145]

Notwithstanding the diverging perceptions among the NATO member countries and the US reservations with regard to a more assertive European security policy, the NATO Council of Copenhagen (6 and 7 June 1991) succeeded in reaching agreement on a compromise text which endorsed the objective of the development of a European security and defence identity, while simultaneously explicitly recognising the pre-eminence of NATO for European security.[146]

The relationship between the emerging European security policy and the Alliance was further clarified at the NATO Summit of the Heads of State and Government in Rome (7 and 8 November 1991).[147] It defined as the prime objective of the development of a European security identity and defence role the strengthening of the European pillar of the Alliance. An enhanced role for the Europeans was to be paralleled by closer transatlantic links guided by the principles of complementarity and transparency. Although the text recognises that "it is for the European Allies concerned to decide what arrangements are needed for the expression of a common foreign and security policy and defence role", the text leaves no doubt that the Alliance continued to be "the essential forum for consultation among its members and the venue for agreement in policies bearing on the security and defence commitments of Allies under the Washington Treaty".[148]

American support at the Rome Summit for an increased European security role considerably facilitated the reaching of an agreement on the "second pillar" provisions at the EC Maastricht Summit one month later. Having received the go-ahead from Washington, the so-called Atlanticist countries were found more willing to compromise on this very sensitive issue.

*External Events Influencing the European and Transatlantic Security Debate: The Case of the Gulf Conflict*

On two occasions during the Bush administration the euphoria following the end of the cold war was seriously disturbed by conflict, showing that contrary to what some had claimed, the end of history was far from being reached. Firstly, there was the Gulf crisis, which took place in the period August 1990 to February 1991; secondly, there was the conflict leading to the break-up of the Federal Republic of Yugoslavia, starting in June 1991 and going on well into the first Clinton administration.

In both crises, the transatlantic partners became to a larger or lesser extent involved, with their engagement giving an initial indication of their possible roles in the post-cold war world. In this chapter, we limit ourselves to the Gulf conflict and how it has interfered in the transatlantic security debate. The conflict in the former Yugoslavia, which has had a determining impact on the shaping of the new security architecture and the respective roles of the European Community and the United States in it, will be the subject of the next chapter.

In the summer of 1990, while the international community was still digesting the shock of the breathtaking events in Central and Eastern Europe, it was taken by surprise by the Iraqi invasion of Kuwait: a crisis which would very soon assume international dimension. Occurring in the midst of the debate on the development of a European security policy, the crisis had a galvanising effect on the discussions taking place in the framework of the 1991 IGC. At the same time, the many difficulties the Twelve were having to meet in trying to coordinate their positions and to speak with one voice showed that there were still many hurdles to overcome before the goal of a genuine European foreign policy could be approached.

The Gulf crisis was very revealing with respect to the strengths and weaknesses of European Political Cooperation. Initially, the EPC machinery functioned rather well. Within less than one week, the EC Member States issued a statement which condemned the invasion, imposed an embargo against oil imports from Iraq and Kuwait, and suspended military and scientific cooperation with Baghdad.[149] Other measures through which the Twelve tried to assert themselves as a fully-fledged international actor were the decision to expel military personnel in Iraqi embassies in the EC Member States, the supply of emergency aid to refugees, as well as the attribution of a financial aid package to Egypt, Jordan and Turkey, countries whose economies were being seriously affected by the conflict.[150]

Very soon, however, European solidarity also proved to have its limits. An agreement that there would be no unilateral initiatives to liberate the European hostages being held by Iraq did not prevent former Chancellor Willy Brandt and, soon afterwards former Prime Minister Edward Heath, from undertaking so-called "humanitarian missions" to Baghdad.

It was, however, when the crisis threatened to escalate into a military conflict that the Europeans proved to be at their weakest. Since military aspects of security are excluded from the scope of EPC, the contributions of European countries to the military build-up in the Gulf region could only be made on a national basis, with France and the United Kingdom being the main contributors. A joint European military presence in the Gulf crisis was confined to the intervention of the WEU. In total, the WEU member countries deployed more than 30 ships, whose main task was to enforce the UN embargo against Iraq. The role of the WEU was limited to coordinating the naval deployment by the WEU member countries, while the vessels remained under national operational command.[151]

While most European observers agreed that the Twelve's performance in the Gulf had been unsatisfactory, they did not necessarily draw the same lessons. While Atlanticist countries, such as the United Kingdom, interpreted the EC's poor accomplishments as proof that Europe continued to be dependent on the United States for the defence of its security interests, Europeanists, such as the President of the European Commission, Jacques Delors, saw it as "another argument for moving towards a form of political union embracing a common foreign and security policy".[152] The Europeanists, especially France, questioned the Atlanticist assumption that Western Europe could continue to rely on the US for its security, arguing that the Gulf crisis had once again illustrated that European and American interests do not necessarily coincide. While the majority of the EC Member States, in conformity with the EC tradition of being a civilian power, wanted to fully exploit the potential of trade and diplomatic instruments to reach a peaceful solution of the crisis, the US, supported in this by the United Kingdom, was much more inclined to use military instruments to force Iraqi compliance with the UN resolutions.[153]

The Gulf conflict also revived long-standing transatlantic differences over the role of NATO in out of area regions. Looking for a new role for the Atlantic Alliance in the post-cold war era, Washington tried to promote it as the principal forum for Western consultation and cooperation, not only on transatlantic questions but also on a much broader range of issues, including the Gulf. Most EC Member States, with France as its most articulate exponent, had traditionally been very reticent with regard to the proposal to extend NATO's scope, and preferred the United Nations as the main platform for coordination and common action by the Western partners.[154] The American preference for a broader NATO role was seen primarily by the Europeanists as an attempt by the US to keep a grip on European initiatives outside the North Atlantic framework.

The Twelve's performance in the Gulf crisis provided the United States with an interesting case study on European foreign-policy coordination. Whatever the rhetoric on the development of a Common Foreign and Security Policy, it was clear that, at least in the short term, the Europeans still had a long way to go and that, for the time being, they did not have a credible alternative to the North Atlantic Alliance. If as such this might have been a source of relief, Washington's great fear was that the EC Member States would try to bring an end to the American presence on the European continent before they had developed a viable European security and defence policy.

Considering the continuing importance of the national players in the Gulf crisis, it was also very instructive for American political analysts to examine the course of events in the individual European countries. As regards the positions defended by the United Kingdom and France, they were not surprising. London closely aligned its stance with that of Washington,[155] whereas Paris played its traditional role of trying to assert an independent posture while at the same time cooperating with the Western allies. Hopes that the successful Franco-American cooperation, culminating in French troops serving under American command, might have been the start of a return of France to NATO's integrated military structures did not materialise.[156] On the contrary, the smooth interaction between both allies was seen as reinforcing the argument that an integration of the commands of both countries was superfluous.

The most intriguing question for the US, as well as for most European observers, was the role which Germany, who was supposed to become Washington's "partner in leadership" in the post-cold war era, would assume in the crisis. The Bush administration's high expectations were clearly not met. It was primarily domestic, rather than leadership considerations which would determine Germany's position.[157] Occurring in the immediate aftermath of the end of the cold war, the Gulf crisis coincided with a period during which reunification was still the top priority of the Bonn government. Wary about not irritating the Soviet Union, whose support was indispensable in realising this objective and taking into account national public disapproval of any German military involvement in the crisis, the German government adopted a very low-key position and decided against the deployment of German troops in the Gulf.[158] It justified its absence by referring to a debatable interpretation of the constitution according to which the stationing of German soldiers outside the NATO territory was prohibited.[159] Washington's disillusion with Bonn reached its climax when Germany questioned whether Ankara should automatically be helped in case of an Iraqi attack against Turkey.[160]

The strong German reluctance to become involved raised serious questions about the willingness of Europe's largest economy to assume international responsibilities. Especially the Bush administration, which had given high priority to the cultivation of a special relationship with Bonn, was very disenchanted. Financial compensations and the deployment of German troops in Iraq in April 1991 to assist in the construction of Kurdish refugee camps could only partly repair the damage the Gulf crisis had inflicted on the German-American relationship.[161] As Margaret Thatcher was quick to point out, the real European "partner in leadership" for the US during the Gulf crisis still proved to be the United Kingdom – and to be complete we should also add France – rather than the united Germany.[162]

## Implementing Rome and Maastricht

The last year of the Bush administration was characterised by both the European Community as well as the North Atlantic Alliance starting to gradually implement the principles of transformation and the new orientations upon which they had agreed in the two previous years.[163]

Adjusting itself to the security risks of the post-cold war Europe, the Alliance created the Coordination Centre for Humanitarian Assistance (January 1992). Its main purpose was to serve as a clearing-house for Alliance members and international organisations that needed help with transport and coordination of medical or food aid.[164] An important step in adapting NATO to the new European security environment was made at the North Atlantic Council meeting in Oslo (4 June 1992), when it was agreed that, depending on case-by-case decisions, NATO could support peace-keeping activities of the CSCE.[165] The Brussels NATO Council of 17 December 1992 further extended the possibility for such interventions to missions under the mandate of the United Nations.[166] The question of NATO out-of-area actions, which during the Gulf crisis had still succeeded in making feelings run high, no longer seemed to be an issue.

At European level, the most substantial developments took place within the framework of the WEU, which the Maastricht Treaty had defined as "an integral part of the development of the Union" and which it had charged with the elaboration and implementation of the decisions and actions of the Union with defence implications.[167] In the Petersberg Declaration, adopted on 19 June 1992, the Ministers of Foreign Affairs and Defence of the nine WEU member countries started to implement the Maastricht mandate.[168] Like the North Atlantic Council two weeks before, they expressed their willingness to participate in the implementation of conflict prevention and crisis management operations, undertaken not only under the aegis of the CSCE but also by the United Nations. As in NATO, the Member States would decide on a case-by-case basis whether to make troops available. The scope of action for the forces answerable to the WEU (the so-called FAWEU) included humanitarian and rescue tasks, peace-keeping operations as well as peace-making missions.[169] Conscious that for the time being the WEU was no more than a paper tiger, the Ministers discussed how the WEU's operational capabilities could be developed.[170] It was decided to organise twice-yearly meetings of the WEU chiefs of defence staff,[171] and to set up a WEU planning cell.[172] One year earlier, the WEU Council of Vianden (27 June 1991) had already decided on the creation of a WEU satellite data interpretation centre in charge of collecting and interpreting satellite-derived data and with the task of training European experts to interpret these data.[173]

The WEU Council in Petersberg also addressed the question of the status of the associate members and observers of the WEU[174] and gave its fiat to the removal of the WEU Permanent Council and General Secretariat to Brussels, closer to the headquarters of NATO and the European Communities.[175]

In the EC itself, efforts primarily concentrated on the ratification of the Treaty on European Union, an exercise which proved more difficult than at first assumed when the Treaty was signed in Maastricht in February 1992.[176] The European Council of Lisbon (26 and 27 June 1992), which was dominated by the negative outcome of the Danish referendum, adopted a report defining the geographical areas of Central and Eastern Europe, the CIS, the Balkans, the Mediterranean (especially the Maghreb countries) and the Middle East, as priority areas for CFSP.[177] It also included a list of preferred priority areas for joint actions in the field of security, which was a repetition of the list adopted by the European Council in Maastricht (December 1991).[178] It encompassed cooperation in the area of the CSCE, arms control and disarmament in Europe, nuclear non-proliferation, as well as cooperation in the field of the economic aspects of security. Even though the above-mentioned changes and innovations are to be seen as confirmation of the course set in Maastricht, they were not sufficient to reverse the highly negative perception of European public opinion with regard to CFSP since the Yugoslav débâcle, nor did they materialise the *"saut qualitatif"* to which the CFSP report adopted in Lisbon so proudly referred.

The parallel adjustment of both NATO and the EC-WEU to the new European security landscape raises the question as to the interaction between both processes and as to the cooperation and coordination among the different actors. The translation into concrete terms of the concept of "interlocking institutions" put forward by the NATO Rome Summit, and according to which NATO, the CSCE, the European Community, the WEU and the Council of Europe were to work together and complement each other when shaping the new European security architecture, gave rise to the expected problems.[179] The relationship between NATO and the WEU, especially, proved to be initially quite strained. Rather than openness and complementarity, as the first joint meeting between the NATO Council and the WEU Council in May 1992 had proclaimed, it was initially competitiveness which seemed to be the guiding principle of the relations between both organisations.[180] In July 1992, both NATO and the WEU sent naval forces to the Adriatic to monitor observance of the UN embargo against Serbia and Montenegro.[181] The fact that there was coordination between the two Western naval forces was more related to the fortunate coincidence that the WEU as well as the NATO commanders were of Italian nationality rather than the result of deliberate agreement.[182] It was not until June 1993 that a joint session of the Councils of NATO and the WEU finally decided on a combined operation including a single command.[183]

In an attempt to clarify relations between the two organisations, a directive outlining the rules for mutual information and representation at ministerial and other levels, and dealing with the issue of cooperation in planning and coordination of ministerial meetings was adopted in November 1992.[184] In the same month, NATO's Secretary-General, Manfred Wörner, participated for the first time in the WEU Council, and in December, Willem van Eekelen, his counterpart in the WEU, was invited to take part in the Atlantic Council.

Despite the renewed declarations of support for a European security and defence identity,[185] NATO and more particularly the United States continued to exhibit some apprehension about the security developments in the EC and the WEU. A draft version of the Pentagon Defence Planning Guide for the fiscal years 1994 to 99, advancing the view that the US should take into sufficient account the interests of other industrialised nations in order to dissuade them from challenging the American leadership role, was illustrative of the continuing uneasiness of certain US circles with regard to the developments in Europe.[186]

The most important source of friction between both sides of the Atlantic in the last year of the Bush administration was the Franco-German proposal to establish a Eurocorps. First launched during the IGC negotiations in October 1991,[187] the initiative was further elaborated at the Franco-German Summit of La Rochelle (21 and 22 May 1992).[188] It was agreed that the corps, which was to be based on the Franco-German brigade, as well as on a French and a German division, was open to any WEU member country willing to join. The corps was to serve three major functions: the defence of the European territory in conformity with the NATO and WEU Treaties; peace-keeping missions; peace-enforcement and humanitarian action. Proposed as it was in the midst of the Yugoslav crisis, the initiative was in the first place symbolic, expressing the continued commitment of both Bonn and Paris to go ahead with the development of a European security and defence capacity.[189] It also provided a pretence for the continued presence of French troops in Germany and a limited number of German troops on French soil.[190]

The reactions of the other WEU member countries to what might one day become the nucleus of a European army were predictable. While Belgium,

Spain and Luxembourg welcomed the idea and soon expressed their willingness to join the corps, the United Kingdom, the Netherlands, and Denmark opposed it as another French attempt to challenge the continuing existence of NATO.

The most vociferous opposition to the Eurocorps however came from Washington. The idea that the Eurocorps would also be used for the defence of the European territory, one of the core functions of NATO, appalled the United States and was interpreted as a direct assault on the principle of NATO's integrated military command.[191] It was furthermore feared that the Eurocorps would reduce the number of German units available to NATO. For the US government, the Franco-German initiative remained unacceptable as long as it was not clearly stated that the Eurocorps would be placed under NATO command.

Knowing the French reluctance to accept this idea, the Bush administration put enormous pressure on the German government. Once again Bonn was squeezed between its dedication to both a strong Alliance and a strengthened European Community. The German argument that the Eurocorps could be seen as a long-term strategy to bring France back into NATO and the German insistence that the corps could never serve as an alternative to the US presence in Europe, were unconvincing to the US.[192] Finally, France ceded to the American demand and, in January 1993, the SACEUR and the French and German Chiefs of Defence Staff signed an agreement that gave the SACEUR "operational command of the Eurocorps as either main defence or rapid reaction forces of the Alliance".

Retrospectively, the United States seems to have somewhat overreacted to the Eurocorps proposal. Did not the Gulf War experience, which clearly demonstrated Germany's extreme reluctance to commit troops outside the NATO area, and the Twelve's performance in the Yugoslav crisis, provide sufficient grounds to seriously question the feasibility of the Eurocorps? The ultimate acceptance by France to place the Eurocorps under NATO command in case of a crisis is the best indication that Europe continues to rely primarily on NATO for its defence.

## Conclusion

The period preceding the Twelve's decision in Maastricht (December 1991) to embark upon the gradual development of a Common Foreign and Security Policy was a fascinating time for transatlantic relations. Although, strictly speaking, the United States was not a direct participant in the CFSP debate, it is clear that, as the main guarantor of European security since the end of the Second World War, Washington was one of the prime parties concerned when it came to discussing future European security arrangements. As a matter of fact, one of the crucial questions for European security was the extent to which the United States would still be interested in playing a major role on the European continent after the disappearance of the communist threat. Fears that the United States would consider reducing its troops in Europe as an easy way to decrease its budgetary deficit served as an important catalyst in the CFSP negotiations.

The results of the above case study reveal that fears of a return of US isolationist forces have been unfounded. In a keynote speech delivered in Berlin on 12 December, barely one month after the fall of the Wall, US Secretary of State James Baker reassured the allies that the US would remain a European power but, at the same time, acknowledged the need to adjust to the changed European security landscape. Even though Baker's address also referred to the European Community and the CSCE, it left no doubt that NATO was to remain the linchpin of transatlantic security cooperation. Throughout its four years in government, the Bush administration stuck to this policy line and the preservation of the primacy of NATO was the chief guiding principle of American policy towards Western Europe. Taking into account the past 40 years of US investment in this organisation and considering Washington's central role in the Alliance, this position can hardly be seen as surprising.

One of the first prerequisites for the enduring pre-eminence of the Alliance was a continued NATO membership of a reunified Germany. Without the German contribution, the Alliance could hardly survive. Furthermore, a neutral Germany would jeopardise European stability and deprive NATO of one of its principal functions, that of embedding a united Germany in a Western security structure. Between December 1989 and July 1990, Washington spared no effort, including lobbying at the highest levels, to realise this objective. Reassurances about the changing nature of NATO and a package of financial and economic incentives finally convinced the Soviet Union to relinquish its reservations.

A second imperative for safeguarding NATO's position was the adaptation of the Alliance itself and its transformation from a predominantly military organisation to a more political body. Taking into account the disappearance of the Soviet threat and the emergence of a new series of security risks, the US played a leading role in adjusting NATO's strategy and capabilities to the new security environment. This process culminated in the adoption of a "New Strategic Concept" at the Rome NATO Summit in November 1991. While recognising the emerging role of the EC, the WEU and the CSCE in the area of security, the Rome Declaration clearly states that NATO is and remains "the essential forum for consultation among the Allies and the forum for agreement on policies bearing on the security and defence commitments of its members under the Washington Treaty".

Washington's preoccupation with preserving the primacy of NATO explains its distrust with regard to the emerging debate on the development of a Common Foreign and Security Policy. The French blueprint, according to which Europe would develop in the long term an independent European security and defence identity, was a direct threat to the continuing American ambitions on the continent. Although the US administration did not deny that the new circumstances required an increased European role, it primarily wanted to realise this objective through strengthening the European pillar of the Alliance. Concern that Europe would try to go its own way and ultimately send the American troops home, initially provoked rather negative, even hostile, reactions. Through direct interventions, such as the Bartholomew *démarche*, the US government did not hesitate to express its discontent with developments in Europe nor to exert pressure on the EC Member States. Ambassador's Taft's words during an address to the International Institute for Strategic Studies in London are very revealing. While admitting that "it is not for an American to prescribe the means by which Europeans should exercise their collective authority or assume greater responsibility", he immediately adds that "if you do not assume this [defence] role in association with the United States, we will be disappointed".[193] To be sure, the antagonising behaviour of the French, prophesying the departure of American troops and talking about NATO in the past tense as if it had already ceased to exist, was not very helpful in trying to calm American concerns.

Gradually, however, the United States became more relaxed towards Europe's security aspirations and shifted towards a more discreet approach. The realisation that not all EC Member States shared French enthusiasm for developing an autonomous European security policy and the poor performance of the EC, first in the Gulf and later on in the Yugoslav crisis may have reassured the US that, at least in the short term, the EC could not be a credible alternative to the Alliance. Even France, by agreeing to the Eurocorps being placed under NATO command, seemed to recognise implicitly the continuing importance of the Alliance in the case of a major conflict on the European continent.

Undeniably, the message of the Bush administration with regard to Western Europe was clear: the United States remained committed to European security and expressed this continuing engagement through the presence of American troops. Through an active role in guaranteeing a continuing German membership of NATO and the adoption of a new strategic concept, Washington very actively contributed to its goal of preserving the Alliance as Europe's prime security organisation. Its policy however overlooked one factor of crucial importance for its ultimate success, namely the question of how the Alliance could be developed into a real partnership, with the Europeans not only assuming a larger part of the burden, but also playing a more important role in the decision-making process. If the US had advocated that European security initiatives should have been launched within the framework of the Alliance, it could have been expected that Washington would have taken certain initiatives to make it more attractive for the Europeans to do so. The Bush administration was however so obsessed with safeguarding its own predominant role on the European security scene that this issue was entirely neglected.

## Notes

1   Taken from Julius W. Friend, *The Linchpin. French-German Relations, 1950-1990* (Washington D.C: Center for Strategic and International Studies, 1991).
2   "Kohl-Mitterrand letter to the Irish Presidency, 19 April 1990", *Agence Europe*, 20 April 1990.
3   France's difficulty in facing the rapid changes in both Germanys is well illustrated in the following statement by President Mitterrand, accompanied by Chancellor Kohl, at a press conference on 3 November 1989 in Bonn: "A l'allure où vont les choses, je serais étonné que les dix années qui viennent se passent sans que nous ayons à affronter une nouvelle structure de l'Europe". Quoted by Claire Tréan in, "La France et le nouvel ordre européen", *Politique Etrangère,* vol. 56, No. 1, spring 1991, 81-90, 82.
4   Visiting East Berlin and Leipzig at the end of December 1989, President Mitterrand warned against rapid German unification. See Ingo Kolboom, "A la chasse aux vieux démons: la France et l'Allemagne unie", *Politique Etrangère*, vol. 56, No. 3, autumn 1991, 715-721; David Yost, "France in the New Europe", *Foreign Affairs*, vol. 69, No. 5, winter 1990, 107-128.
5   Peter R. Weilemann, "The German Contribution Toward Overcoming the Division of Europe – Chancellor Helmut Kohl's 10 Points", *Aussenpolitik*, vol. 41, No. 1, 1990, 15-23.
6   Horst Teltschik, *329 Tage. Innenansichten der Einigung* (Berlin: Siedler Verlag 1991), 54-58.
7   "Conclusions of the Presidency", *Bulletin of the European Communities*, vol. 22, No. 12, December 1989, 8-18.
8   Margaret Thatcher, *The Downing Street Years* (London: Harper Collins, 1993), 796-797.
9   *Ibid.*, 14.
10  Ernst Weidenfeld, "Mitterrands Europäische Konföderation. Eine Idee im Spannungsfeld der Realitäten", *Europa-Archiv*, vol. 17, No. 1, 1991, 513-518. The first international meeting discussing the French proposal took place from 12 to 14 June 1991 in Prague.

11  During a bilateral meeting with Margaret Thatcher, François Mitterrand said that he "shared my (i.e. Thatcher's) worries about the Germans' so-called 'mission' in Central Europe. The Czechs, Poles, Hungarians would not want to be under Germany's exclusive influence, but they would need German aid and investment." Taken from Margaret Thatcher, *op.cit.*, 798.

12  François Mitterrand and Margaret Thatcher discussed German unification at the Strasbourg European Council and at a private meeting on 20 January 1990. At their first meeting, Mitterrand appears to have said that "at moments of great danger in the past France had always established special relations with Britain and he felt that such a time had come again", in Margaret Thatcher, *op.cit.*, 796-799.

13  On the course of the IGCs, see, Richard Corbett, *The Treaty of Maastricht: From Conception to Ratification: A Comprehensive Reference Guide* (Harlow: Longman, 1993); Andrew Duff, John Pinder, Roy Pryce, *Maastricht and Beyond. Building the Union* (London-New York: Routledge, 1994); Finn Laursen and Sophie Vanhoonacker (eds.), *The Intergovernmental Conference on Political Union. Institutional Reforms, New Policies and International Identity of the European Community* (Maastricht, Dordrecht: EIPA and Martinus Nijhoff Publishers, 1992); Jörg Monar, Werner Ungerer, Wolfgang Wessels, *The Maastricht Treaty on European Union: Legal Complexity and Political Dynamic* (Brussels: European Interuniversity Press, 1993).

14  Margaret Thatcher, *op.cit.*, 759-763. At the Dublin meeting in April 1990, the Italian Prime Minister, Giulio Andreotti, appears to have said: "although we must set up an IGC on political union, it would be dangerous to reach a clear-cut definition of what political union was".

15  "Conclusions of the Presidency", *Bulletin of the European Communities*, vol. 23, No. 12, December 1990, 7-18.

16  Austria was the first country to apply for EC membership in July 1989. The Swedish application came in July 1991, and Finland and Switzerland followed at the beginning of 1992. Norway applied in the second half of 1992. The Swiss application was not followed up due to the European Economic Area Agreement (EEA) being rejected by its population in the referendum of December 1992. The Norwegians rejected accession to the EU in a referendum in November 1994. See Finn Laursen, "The Maastricht Treaty: Implications for the Nordic Countries", *Cooperation and Conflict*, vol. 28, No. 2, 1993, 115-141.

17  For an overview of the debate on CFSP during the IGC on Political Union, see, Mathias Jopp, "The Strategic Implications of European Integration", *Adelphi Paper*, No. 290, 1994; Anand Menon, Anthony Forster, William Wallace, "A Common Defence?", *Survival*, vol. 34, No. 3, autumn 1992, 98-118; Nikolaj Petersen, "The European Union and Foreign and Security Policy", in, Ole Norgaard, Thomas Pedersen and Nikolaj Petersen, *The European Community in World Politics* (London, New York: Pinter Publishers, 1993), 9-30. For a theoretical explanation of the expansion of European integration into the field of military security and defence, see, Alfred van Staden, "After Maastricht: Explaining the Movement Towards a Common European Defence Policy", in Walter Carlsnaes and Steve Smith (eds.), *European Foreign Policy. The EC and Changing Perspectives in Europe* (London: Sage, 1994), 138-155.

18  "Memorandum from the Danish Government, 4 October 1990", in, Finn Laursen and Sophie Vanhoonacker (1992), *op.cit.*, 293-303.

19  "Memorandum from the Portuguese Delegation, 30 November 1990", in Finn Laursen and Sophie Vanhoonacker (1992), *op.cit.*, 304-312.

20 "Italian Proposal on Common Foreign and Security Policy, 18 September 1990", in Finn Laursen and Sophie Vanhoonacker (1992), *op.cit.*, 292.
21 "Text of the Letter Addressed to Andreotti by Kohl and Mitterrand", *Agence Europe*, 10-11 December 1990.
22 "Franco-German Proposals on Political Union: Security Policy Cooperation in the Framework of the Common Foreign and Security Policy of Political Union", *Europe Documents*, No. 1690, 21 February 1991; and "Franco-German Initiative on Foreign Security and Defence Policy, Bonn, Paris, 11 October 1991", *Europe Documents*, No. 1738, 18 October 1991.
23 See David G. Haglund, *Alliance Within the Alliance? Franco-German Military Cooperation and the European Pillar of Defense* (Boulder, San Francisco, Oxford: Westview Press, 1991).
24 Josef Joffe, "After Bipolarity: Germany and European Security", *Adelphi Paper*, No. 285, February 1994, 34-46.
25 Steven Philip Kramer, "La question française", *Politique Etrangère*, vol. 56, No. 4, 1991, 959-974.
26 Philip H. Gordon, *A Certain Idea of France. French Security Policy and the Gaullist Legacy* (Princeton: Princeton University Press, 1993),172-177; Enrico Martial, "France and European Political Union", in Finn Laursen and Sophie Vanhoonacker (1992), *op.cit.*, 115-126.
27 David S. Germroth and Rebecca J. Hudson, "German-American Relations and the Post Cold war World", *Aussenpolitik*, vol. 43, No. 1, 1992, 33-41; Paul Stares (ed.), *The New Germany and the New Europe* (Washington D.C.: The Brookings Institution, 1992); Christa van Wijnbergen, "Germany and European Political Union", in Finn Laursen and Sophie Vanhoonacker (1992), *op.cit.*, 49-61.
28 On the contribution of the UK to the 1991 IGC, see Robert Wester, "The United Kingdom and Political Union", in Finn Laursen and Sophie Vanhoonacker (1992), *op.cit.*, 189-214.
29 "An Anglo-Italian Declaration on European Security and Defence, 5 October 1991", *Europe Documents*, No. 1735, 5 October 1991.
30 *Cf. infra*, 128.
31 Italics added.
32 The texts of Article J.4(2) and J.4(4) reads as follows:
  "2. The Union requests the Western European Union (WEU), which is an integral part of the development of the Union, to elaborate and implement decisions and actions of the Union which have defence implications..."
  "4. The policy of the Union in accordance with this Article shall not prejudice the specific character of the security and defence policy of certain Member States and shall respect the obligations of certain Member States under the North Atlantic Treaty and be compatible with the common security and defence policy established within that framework."
33 "Declaration by Belgium, Germany, Spain, France, Italy, Luxembourg, the Netherlands, Portugal and the United Kingdom of Great Britain and Northern Ireland which are members of the Western European Union", in *Treaty on European Union* (Luxembourg: Office for Official Communications of the European Communities, 1992), 245-246.
34 "Protocol of Accession of the Hellenic Republic to Western European Union", *Europe Documents*, No. 1810, 25 November 1992. It was the WEU Council meeting in Rome on 20 November 1992 which agreed to the Protocol of Accession. On the position of Greece

with regard to the development of a European security and defence policy during the 1991 IGC, see, Yannis Valinakis, *Greece's Security in the Post-Cold War Era* (Ebenhausen: Stiftung Wissenschaft und Politik, 1994), 55-84.
35  This refers to the reservations of Greece about some of the statements in the report of the Dooge Committee and which appeared as footnotes in the final text (1984).
36  Arthur den Hartog, "Greece and European Political Union", in, Finn Laursen and Sophie Vanhoonacker (1992), *op.cit.*, 79-97.
37  See Patrick Keatinge (ed.), *Maastricht and Ireland: What the Treaty Means* (Dublin: Institute of European Affairs, 1992); Paul Gillespie and Rodney Price, *Political Union – Implications for Ireland* (Dublin: Institute for European Affairs, 1991); Christa van Wijnbergen, "Ireland and European Political Union", in, Finn Laursen and Sophie Vanhoonacker (1992), *op.cit.*, 127-138.
38  On Denmark and the development of a European security identity, see, Finn Laursen, "Denmark and Political Union", in Finn Laursen and Sophie Vanhoonacker (1992), *op.cit.*, 63-78; Christian Thune, "Denmark and the Western European Union", in Panos Tsakaloyannis (ed.), *The Reactivation of the Western European Union: The Effects on the EC and Its Institutions* (Maastricht: EIPA, 1985), 87-95.
39  See "Memorandum from the Danish Government", 4 October 1990: "The Government rejects the idea that European Political Co-operation should come to include co-operation in defence policies, *inter alia* the setting-up of common military forces".
40  The rights and obligations of observers and associate members were laid down in the Petersberg Declaration adopted at a WEU Ministerial Council on 19 June 1992. Observers may attend the meetings of the WEU Council, may be invited to meetings of working groups, may be invited on request to speak, and will have the same rights and responsibilities as the full members for functions transferred to WEU from other fora and institutions to which they already belong. Associate members may participate fully in the meetings of the WEU Council; have the right to speak but not to block decisions; can be associated with the Planning Cell and with decisions taken by the member countries; can take part in WEU military operations; will be connected to the member countries' telecommunications systems; and will be asked to make financial contributions to the WEU's budget. For the text of the Petersberg Declaration, see, "WEU Ministerial Council, 19 June, in Petersberg (Bonn)", *Europe Documents*, No. 1787, 23 June 1992.
41  "Document on Associate Membership of WEU of the Republic of Iceland, the Kingdom of Norway and the Republic of Turkey", *Europe Documents*, No. 1810, 25 November 1992.
42  Taken from David Buchan, "Why a Temple Proved Stronger than a Tree", *Financial Times*, 7 and 8 December 1991.
43  See *Treaty on European Union*, Title I, Article C: "The Union shall be served by a single institutional framework which shall ensure the consistency and the continuity of the activities carried out in order to attain its objectives while respecting and building upon the *acquis communautaire*."
Before the adoption of the Treaty on European Union, a strict distinction was made between the Council, which is an EC institution and "the meeting of ministers for foreign affairs in the framework of EPC. The EPC Secretariat was separate from the General Secretariat of the Council, although both were located in the same building. Since the entering into force of the Treaty on European Union, there is only one Council and a single Secretariat, dealing with both EC as well as CFSP matters.

44 "Non-Paper. Draft Treaty Articles with a View to Achieving Political Union", Brussels, 17 April 1991, *Europe Documents*, No. 1709/1710, 3 May 1991.
45 Prior to the negotiations on the Treaty on European Union, cooperation in the field of justice and home affairs had no Treaty basis and was organised in a purely intergovernmental way. The provisions on JHA that were introduced in the Treaty on European Union deal with asylum policy, immigration policy, the fight against drug addiction and fraud on an international scale as well as with judicial cooperation in civil and criminal matters, customs cooperation and police cooperation. On JHA, see Klaus-Peter Nanz, "Der 3. Pfeiler der Europäischen Union": Zusammenarbeit in der Innen- und Justizpolitik", *Integration*, vol. 15, No. 3, 1992, 126-140.
46 The proposal for a temple structure came from Pierre de Boissieu, the grandson of Charles de Gaulle. See Charles Grant, *Inside the House that Jacques Built* (London: Nicholas Brealey Publishing, 1994), 188.
47 For the Commission's point of view with regard to the development of a European foreign and security policy, see "Contribution by the Commission on the Development of a Common External Policy", *Bulletin of the European Communities*, supplement 2, 1991, 89-96.
48 "Draft Treaty on the Union", *Europe Documents*, No. 1722/1723, 5 July 1991.
49 According to Dutch foreign ministry officials, it was only accepted as a possible base for further negotiations.
50 "Conclusions of the Presidency", *Bulletin of the European Communities*, vol. 24, No. 6, June 1991, 8-19.
51 "The Dutch Draft Treaty Towards European Union", *Europe Documents*, No. 1734, 3 October 1991. Further differences with the Luxembourg Draft Treaty concerned increased powers for the European Parliament, and more emphasis on the role of NATO.
52 See Michiel van Hulten, *The Short Life and Sudden Death of the Dutch Draft Treaty Towards the European Union* (Bruges: College of Europe, 1993)(thesis); S. Rozemond, *De gang naar Maastricht* (Den Haag: Nederlands Instituut voor Internationale Betrekkingen, 1991); Robert Wester, "The Netherlands and European Political Union", in Finn Laursen and Sophie Vanhoonacker (1992), *op.cit.*, 172-175.
53 On the Fouchet negotiations, see chapter 3.
54 David Buchan, *Financial Times*, 7 and 8 December 1991. According to Buchan, it was France that convinced Germany, which initially considered supporting the Dutch proposal.
55 See "Text of the Letter Addressed to Mr Giulio Andreotti by R.F.M. Lubbers and H. van den Broek, The Hague, 12 December 1990", in Finn Laursen and Sophie Vanhoonacker (1992), *op.cit.*, 315-317 and *De Europese Politieke Unie*. Document on the Dutch Position towards EPU, 26 October 1990.
56 The Member States have rarely made use of this special QMV option.
57 For a critical evaluation of CFSP, see, Reinhardt Rummel, "Beyond Maastricht: Alternative Futures for a Political Union, in *Id.* (ed.), *Toward Political Union: Planning A Common Foreign and Security Policy in the European Community* (Baden-Baden: Nomos Verlag, 1992), 297-320.
58 See Article J.4(6) and Article J.10 of the Treaty on European Union.
59 The amendments with regard to CFSP agreed by the European Council of Amsterdam (June 1997) were indeed far from revolutionary. See Sophie Vanhoonacker, "From Maastricht to Amsterdam: Was it Worth the Journey for CFSP?", *Eipascope*, No.2, 1997, 6-8.
60 This was the title of a speech by James Baker in Berlin in December 1989. See footnote 63.

61 "Remarks at the Boston University Commencement Ceremony in Massachusetts", 21 May 1989, in *Public Papers of the Presidents of the United States. George Bush. 1989* (Washington D.C.: US Government Printing Office, 1990), vol. 1, 582-585, 583. The speech in Boston was the third of five major foreign-policy speeches given early on in the Bush administration and was aimed at outlining what would become the American grand strategy beyond containment. The first one was delivered on 17 April 1989 in Hamtramck, Michigan, and focused on Eastern Europe; the second one, delivered at Texas A&M University on 12 May dealt with relations with the Soviet Union; the speech in Boston focused on Europe; the fourth speech given on 24 May dealt with the question of arms control; and the final speech was given in Mainz, Germany and was primarily a summing up of the different aspects of the strategy for ending the cold war. For an overview of the different speeches, see, Robert L. Hutchings, *American Diplomacy and the End of the Cold War. An Insider's Account of US Policy in Europe, 1989-1992* (Washington D.C.-London: The Woodrow Wilson Center Press and the John Hopkins University Press, 1997), 38-45.
62 See chapter one.
63 "A New Europe, A New Atlanticism, Architecture for a New Era", *US Policy Information and Texts*, No. 175, 12 December 1989.
64 Some of the basic ideas of the Baker speech had already been mentioned by President Bush at an informal summit meeting of the NATO Heads of State and Government in Brussels on 4 December 1989. The text of Bush's statement was reproduced in *Atlantic News*, No. 2175, 6 December 1989.
65 If the language of the Baker address is very balanced and diplomatic, the US Representative to NATO, William H. Taft, during a speech in Lisbon in November 1989, is much more straightforward: "Let us recognise NATO as a unique institution for the development and coordination of transatlantic policy... In my view, there is only one forum capable of melding the efforts of all these institutions: it is the Atlantic Alliance... Only here can the diverse strengths and resources of North America and Western Europe be coordinated to end the division of Europe." Quoted in *Atlantic News*, No. 2167, 15 November 1989.
66 "But a new era brings different concerns for all of us. Some are as old as Europe itself. Others are themselves the new products of change. Were the West to abandon the patterns of cooperation that we have built up over four decades, these concerns could grow into problems."
67 See, for instance, Minister of Foreign Affairs Hans-Dietrich Genscher: "Wir wollen, dass sich die nordatlantischen Demokratien mit der Politischen Union noch enger verbinden, und dass sie teilnehmen am Bau des einen Europa,... Deshalb mein Vorstoss für eine gemeinsame, feierliche Deklaration zur Besiegelung einer neuen atlantischen Partnerschaft...", in, "Vortrag des Bundesministers des Auswärtigen, Hans-Dietrich Genscher", *Europa-Archiv*, vol.45, No.15, 1990, 473-478.
68 Reinhardt Rummel, "German-American Relations in the Setting of a New Atlanticism", *Irish Studies in International Affairs*, vol. 4, 1993, 17-31.
69 Timothy Garton Ash, *In Europe's Name: Germany and the Divided Continent* (London: Cape, 1993), 355.
70 Philip H. Gordon (1993), *op.cit.*, 169.
71 John Dak, *No More "Special" Anglo-American Relations: Rhetoric and Reality* (London: Weidenfeld and Nicolson, 1994), 215-216.
72 See Youri Devuyst, "European Community Integration and the United States: Toward a New Transatlantic Relationship?", *Journal of European Integration*, vol. 14, No. 1, 1990,

5-29; Martin Lees, "The Impact of Europe 1992 on the Atlantic Partnership", *The Washington Quarterly*, autumn 1989, vol. 12, No. 4, 171-182.
73   See the above-mentioned Boston speech of President Bush (21 May 1989) and the Berlin speech of Secretary of State Baker (12 December 1989).
74   Axel Krause, "What Ever Happened to Bush's Europhoria?", *European Affairs*, June-July 1991, vol. 5, No. 3, 44-47, 45. According to Peter Tarnoff, President George Bush met five times with the Commission President Jacques Delors in 1989, while he met only once with the Japanese Prime Minister. See Peter Tarnoff, "America's New Special Relationships", *Foreign Affairs*, vol. 69, No. 3, 1990, 67-75, 76.
75   For the joint statement issued on that occasion, see *Agence Europe*, 1 March 1990.
76   "Conclusions of the Presidency", *Bulletin of the European Communities*, vol. 23, No. 6, 1990, 14.
77   The declaration was adopted on 20 November and made public on 23 November. For the text, see "Declaration on US-EC Relations", *Europe Documents*, 23 November 1990. One day before, on 22 November 1990, a "Declaration on EC-Canada Relations" had been signed. See *Europe Documents*, No. 1663, 24 November 1990.
78   On the Transatlantic Declaration, see, Desmond Dinan, *US-EC Relations: From the Transatlantic Declaration to Maastricht and Beyond* (Washington D.C.: Unpublished Paper, 1992); Alan K. Henrikson, "The New Atlanticism: Western Partnership for Global Leadership", *Journal of European Integration*, vol. 16, Nos. 2-3, winter-spring 1993, 165-191; Horst G. Krenzler and Wolfram Kaiser, "The Transatlantic Declaration: A New Basis for Relations Between the EC and the USA", *Aussenpolitik*, vol. 42, No. 4, 1991, 363-372.
79   *Financial Times*, 9 November 1990; *Agence Europe*, 12-13 November 1990; *De Standaard*, 24-25 November 1990.
80   The text is formulated as follows: "resolved to strengthen security, economic cooperation and human rights in Europe in the framework of the CSCE, and in other fora, noting the firm commitment of the United States and the EC Member States concerned to the North Atlantic Alliance and to its principles and purposes, ... bearing in mind the accelerating process by which the European Community is acquiring its own identity in economic and monetary matters, in foreign policy and the domain of security...".
81   The White House did not even issue a press release when the declaration was adopted. The Bush administration was wary of attracting attention to the contradiction between the declaration's lofty principles and the impasse in the Uruguay Round of negotiations over the reduction of agricultural subsidies. See Robert L. Hutchings, *op. cit.*, 160-161.
82   For an overview of the events leading to German reunification, see the account by Chancellor Kohl himself as well as that by one of his closest advisers: Helmut Kohl, *Ich Wollte Deutschlands Einheit*. Dargestellt von Kai Diekmann und Ralf Georg Reuth (Berlin: Olsten Buchverlage, 1996); Horst Teltschik, *329 Tage. Innenansichten der Einigung* (Berlin: Siedler Verlag, 1991). See also, Timothy Garton Ash, *In Europe's Name: Germany and the Divided Continent* (London: Cape, 1993); Elizabeth Pond, *Beyond the Wall. Germany's Road to Unification* (Washington D.C.: The Brookings Institution, 1993); Phil Zelikow and Condoleeza Rice, *Germany Unified and Europe Transformed: A Study in Statecraft* (Cambridge, Mass.: Harvard University Press, 1992).
83   See George Bush in the account of his foreign policy: "While Thatcher, Mitterrand, and others feared that Germany might cause more trouble and tragedy, I did not. I did not belittle those fears but, as reunification moved on, I tried to help other leaders to understand my view that this new Germany would be different. I also felt strongly that the United States

ought to follow through on our past pledges of support for German unity when the time came. However complicated or risky the process might be, the pursuit of reunification was something for the Germans themselves to decide." See George Bush and Brent Scowcroft, *A World Transformed* (New York: Alfred A. Knopf, 1998), 187.
Bush's early support for German reunification is also confirmed by National Security Adviser Brent Scowcroft: "In fact, President Bush was the first in the Administration to back reunification unequivocally, as well as the first Western leader – a point Kohl never forgot." *Ibid.*, 188.

84 For a general overview on the role of the United States in the German reunification process, see, Heinrich Bortfeldt, *Washington, Bonn-Berlin. Die USA und die deutsche Einheit* (Bonn: Bouvier Verlag, 1993).
85 In 1989, about 325,000 East Germans or 2% of the population fled the country. See Hanns W. Maull, "German Unity in a European Context", in Otto Pick (ed.), *The Cold War Legacy in Europe* (London and New York: Pinter Publishers and St. Martin's Press, 1992), 96-104, 99.
86 See for example Henry Kissinger quoted in Michael R. Beschloss and Strobe Talbott, *At the Highest Levels. The Inside Story of the End of the Cold War* (Boston-Toronto-London: Little, Brown and Company, 1993), 138: "...a two-Germanys policy would be "disastrous". This would give Gorbachev a golden opportunity to side with Helmut Kohl against the United States in the pursuit of quick unification."
87 "Remarks to the Citizens of Mainz, Federal Republic of Germany, May 31, 1989", in *Public Papers of the Presidents of the United States. George Bush. 1989* (Washington D.C: US Government Printing Office, 1989), vol. 1, 650-654.
88 Robert L. Hutchings, *op.cit.*, 31.
89 Robert L. Hutchings, director for European affairs at the National Security Council describes the US-German dialogue at the beginning of the Bush administration as "surprisingly thin and formalistic, vastly different from the frank, highly substantive discussions we always had with the British." See Robert L. Hutchings, *op.cit.*, 31.
90 Peter Tarnoff, *op.cit.*, 76.
91 *Atlantic News*, 6 December 1989. These four principles were also repeated in Baker's address on a New Atlanticism.
92 Margaret Thatcher, *op.cit.*, 792-796.
93 Michael R. Beschloss and Strobe Talbott, *op.cit.*, 137.
94 Robert D. Blackwill, "German Unification and American Diplomacy", *Aussenpolitik*, vol. 45, No. 3, 1994, 211-225, 214. Ambassador Robert D. Blackwill was Special Assistant to the President for European and Soviet Affairs and the White House's chief action officer on German unification in 1989-90. Other major State Department actors in the process of German unification were the Assistant-Secretary for European Affairs, Raymond Seitz, and Planning Director, Dennis Ross.
95 The British Foreign Minister, Douglas Hurd, expressed his preference for the "four-plus-zero" approach, leaving the Germans out. See Michael R. Beschloss and Strobe Talbott, *op.cit.*, 185. This approach was also favoured by France; see, Robert D. Blackwill, *op.cit.*, 215.
96 Robert D. Blackwill, *op.cit.*, 214. Also the United Kingdom was sympathetic to the idea of making use of the CSCE.
97 Ronald D. Asmus, "A United Germany", *Foreign Affairs*, spring 1990, vol. 69, No. 2, 63-76, 68.
98 See Brent Scowcroft in, George Bush and Brent Scowcroft, *op.cit.*, 196-197.

99  Two weeks before, at a meeting between President George Bush and NATO Secretary-General Manfred Wörner, the exact meaning of the concept of full membership of a unified Germany had been specified. It meant that Germany would participate in the Alliance's integrated military structure, that US troops and nuclear weapons would remain in Germany after reunification; and that the East German territory would be covered by the protection of the NATO treaty. Robert D. Blackwill, *op.cit.*, 216.
100 On the Soviet Union and German membership of NATO, see, Gerhard Wettig, "Moscow's Acceptance of NATO: The Catalytic Role of German Unification", *Europe-Asia Studies*, vol. 45, No. 6, 1993, 953-972.
101 Robert D. Blackwill, *op.cit.*, 219.
102 Michael R. Beschloss and Strobe Talbott, *op.cit.*, 222-224. The conclusion of the trade agreement was strongly opposed by the US Congress, which strongly opposed Soviet policy towards Lithuania.
103 *Ibid.*, 127.
104 "Atlantic Summit, 5-6 July 1990", *Europe Documents*, No. 1635, 10 July 1990. The text adopted at the London Summit had been drafted by the White House and was adopted in almost identical form. According to Robert Blackwill, Gorbachev would later have confirmed that "his eventual decision to accept full German membership in NATO had been largely based on the substance of the London Summit document, which demonstrated decisively to him that NATO was indeed changing." See Robert D. Blackwill, *op.cit.*, 221. On the London Summit, see also Peter Corterier, "Transforming the Atlantic Alliance", *The Washington Quarterly*, vol. 14, No. 1, winter 1991, 27-37.
105 Peter Corterier, *op.cit.*, 32.
106 It was also agreed that negotiations with the Soviet Union on reducing SRNMs could begin once the CFE agreement on cuts in conventional forces had been reached, yet before its implementation had begun. See William C. Cromwell, *The United States and the European Pillar. The Strained Alliance* (London: Macmillan, 1992), 224.
107 Michael R. Beschloss and Strobe Talbott, *op.cit.*, 238-239, and Gerhard Wettig, *op.cit.*, 966-67.
108 Hilmar Linnenkamp, "The Security Policy of the New Germany", in Paul B. Stares (ed.), *op.cit.*, 93-125, 97.
109 For the main documents with regard to the external aspects of German unification, see, Karl Kaiser, *Deutschlands Vereinigung: Die internationalen Aspekte. Mit den wichtigen Dokumenten* (Bergisch-Gladbach: G. Lübbe Verlag, 1991).
110 In the spring and early summer of 1990, President Bush and Chancellor Kohl met four times; and Secretary of State Baker and Minister of Foreign Affairs Genscher met eleven times. See Robert L. Hutchings, *op.cit.*, 92.
111 Quoted by Robert D. Blackwill, *op.cit.*, 218.
112 *Ibid.*, 216.
113 George Bush in George Bush and Brent Scowcroft, *op.cit.*, 242.
114 *Ibid.*, 565.
115 "Franco-German Proposals on Political Union: Security Policy Cooperation in the Framework of the Common Foreign and Security Policy of Political Union", *Europe Documents*, No. 1690, 21 February 1991. *Cf. supra*, 97.
116 For the text of the telegram, see Willem Frederik van Eekelen, *Debating European Security, 1948-1998* (The Hague-Brussels: Sdu Publishers and Centre for European Policy Studies, 1998), 340-344.

117 According to van Eekelen, the telegram had a delaying effect on the European attempts to reach an agreement on the role of the WEU in the emerging CFSP. *Ibid.*, 78.
118 Catherine Guicherd, *A European Defence Identity: Challenge and Opportunity for NATO* (Washington D.C.: Congressional Research Service, 1991), 58; Harry J. Dolton, *The Future Role of the United States in European Security: Determining Factors* (Rome: NATO Defence College, 1991), 92.
119 Catherine Guicherd, *op.cit.*, 58.
120 Willem Frederik van Eekelen, *op.cit.*, 82-83.
121 On the impact of the Gulf war on the European security debate, *cf. infra*, 129-133.
122 Catherine Guicherd, *op.cit.*, 39.
123 "Final Communiqué", *Atlantic News*, No. 2326, May 1991.
124 The ARRC consists of two elements: the smallest component of the size of a brigade (approximately 5,000 troops) should be able to react within 72 hours; the core of the ARRC is a multinational corps of four divisions (50,000 to 70,000 troops), deployable in five to seven days. See Catherine Guicherd, *op.cit.*, 52. The idea of multinational units had been supported earlier by the London Summit of July 1990.
125 David S. Yost, "France in the New Europe", *Foreign Affairs*, vol. 69, No. 5, winter 1990, 107-128, 119.
126 France participated in the Legge Group, established to discuss the reform of the NATO strategy.
127 See speech by Minister for Foreign Affairs, Roland Dumas, and the Minister of Defence, Pierre Joxe, before the WEU assembly, 4-5 June 1991. See also Philip H. Gordon, *French Security Policy After the Cold War. Continuity, Change, and Implications for the United States* (Santa Monica: Rand, 1992), 18-20.
128 François Gere, "L'Europe et l'OTAN dans la stratégie américaine", *Défense nationale*, vol. 47, No. 8-9, August-September 1991, 49-65, 57.
129 Anand Menon, "From Independence to Cooperation: France, NATO and European Security", *International Affairs*, vol.71, No.1, 19-34, 24.
130 William Taft, *The US Role in the New Europe*. Address to the International Institute for Strategic Studies. London, 9 February 1991.
131 Gale A. Meadows, "United States Perspectives on the Growth of a European Pillar", in Michael Clarke and Rod Hague, *European Defence Cooperation. America, Britain and NATO* (Manchester: Manchester University Press, 1990), 127-128.
132 See, for example, Bruce W. Weinrod, Deputy-Assistant Secretary of Defence for European and NATO Policy: "...in the new environment, NATO remains the only credible military force that the democracies of Europe and North America have. We think it would be clearly a mistake to discard that force or do things that would undermine its basic, essential military effectiveness in this time of great uncertainty and unpredictability". Quoted in Stanley R. Sloan, Catherine Guicherd, Rosita Maria Thomas, *NATO's Future: A Congressional-Executive Dialogue* (Washington D.C.: Congressional Research Service, 1992), 19.
133 See, for instance, General John Galvin, the Supreme Allied Commander, Europe: "The US is committed to NATO with a fully deployed force. For that commitment, we get a seat at the table. We get an influence in the shaping of the security situation in Europe, and that's what we want." Quoted in, Robert S. Jordan, "Atlantic Relations and the New Europe. A Conference Report and Analysis of the Committee on Atlantic Studies" (New Orleans: The Eisenhower Center for Leadership Studies, March 1992), 22.
134 Frank Costigliola, *France and the United States. The Cold Alliance Since World War II*

(New York: Twayne Publishers, 1992).
135 Diego A. Ruiz Palmer, "French Strategic Options in the 1990s", *Adelphi Paper*, No. 260, 1991.
136 The idea of appointing a French general as Supreme Allied Commander Europe (SACEUR) was discussed but ultimately rejected by the US in April 1990. See President Bush responding to the question of whether he could envisage the French being Supreme Commander of NATO: "We're very happy with the present arrangements..... People view the US presence as stabilising, as having played a significant role in preserving a peace that, in terms of European history, is a long one.... And part of the command structure, I think, contributes to the view that we have an important role to play and the Europeans want us to have an important role to play." See "Interview with foreign journalists, April 16, 1990", in *Public Papers of the Presidents of the United States. George Bush. 1990* (Washington D.C: US Government Printing Office, 1990), vol. 1, 507.
The idea of a European SACEUR is also rebuffed by some Europeans. See, for example, François Heisbourg: "However flattering to some European egos, or tempting for some neo-isolationists in the United States, there is little to commend such an idea. A SACEUR of US origin is one of the clearest, most effective ways of signalling the indivisibility of the US-European security contract, particularly at a time when there are doubts as to the future of the US commitment, and directly contributes to strategic coupling.", in, François Heisbourg, "The Future of the Atlantic Alliance: Whither NATO, Whether NATO", *The Washington Quarterly*, vol. 15, No. 2, spring 1992, 127-139, 136.
137 Robert L. Hutchings, *op.cit.*, 274-275.
138 François Heisbourg, *op.cit.*, 128.
139 See Edith Cresson as quoted by Philip Gordon (1992), *op.cit.*, 29: "It is evident that the United States is disengaging from Europe... it can't leave and ask us Europeans not to have a defence of our own". In, *Wall Street Journal*, 15 July 1991.
140 "Rome Declaration on Peace and Cooperation", *Europe Documents*, No. 1744, 13 November 1991.
141 "Europe. Débat sur une déclaration du gouvernement", Senat. Séance du 27 juin 1990, 2162-2178, 2164. Even though he expresses the hope that the Europeans will one day be in charge of their own security, he recognises that: "nous en sommes loin et c'est pourquoi l'OTAN demeurera, pour le futur prévisible, la base de l'organisation de la défense de l'Europe".
142 Philip H. Gordon (1992), *op.cit.*, 14-16.
143 "Atlantic Summit, 5-6 July 1990", *Europe Documents*, No. 1635, 10 July 1990.
144 See President François Mitterrand at a press conference at the end of the London NATO summit: "la France ne partageait pas les conceptions stratégiques de l'Alliance, pas plus celles de hier que celles d'aujourd'hui: celles d'hier autour de la défense flexible, la bataille de l'avant, celles d'aujourd'hui sur l'arme de dernier recours..." Quoted in Fréderic Bozo, "La France, l'OTAN et l'avenir de la dissuasion en Europe", *Politique Etrangère*, vol. 56, No. 2, summer 1991, 513-527, 517.
145 *Atlantic News*, 14 January 1992.
146 See especially paragraph 1: "A transformed Atlantic Alliance constitutes an essential element in the new architecture of an undivided Europe; we are agreed that the Alliance must have the flexibility to continue to develop and evolve as the security situation dictates. An important basis for this transformation is the agreement of all Allies to enhance the role and responsibility of the European members. We welcome efforts further to strengthen the

security dimension in the process of European integration and recognise the significance of the progress made by the countries of the European Community towards the goal of political union, including the development of a common foreign and security policy. These two positive processes are mutually reinforcing. The development of a European security identity and defence role, reflected in the strengthening of the European pillar within the Alliance, will reinforce the integrity and effectiveness of the Atlantic Alliance." In "Ministerial Meeting of the North Atlantic Council in Copenhagen, Denmark, 6-7 June 1991, final communiqué", *Atlantic News*, No. 2329, 8 June 1991.

147 "The development of a European security identity and defence role, reflected in the further strengthening of the European pillar within the Alliance, will reinforce the integrity and effectiveness of the Atlantic Alliance". Taken from: "Rome Declaration on Peace and Cooperation", *Europe Documents*, No. 1744, 13 November 1991.

148 See paragraph 6 of the Rome Declaration.

149 On the Twelve and the Gulf Crisis, see, Carlos Closa, "The Gulf Crisis: A Case Study of National Constraints on Community Action", *Journal of European Integration*, vol. 15, No. 1, 1991, 47-67; Geoffrey Edwards, "European Responses to the Yugoslav Crisis: An Interim Assessment", in Reinhardt Rummel (ed.), *Toward Political Union. Planning a Common Foreign and Security Policy in the European Community* (Boulder, San Francisco, Oxford: Westview Press, 1992), 161-186; John Roper and Nicole Gnesotto (eds.), *Western Europe and the Gulf. A Study of West European Reactions to the Gulf War* (Paris: Western European Union, Institute for Strategic Studies, 1992); Trevor C. Salmon, "Testing Times for European Political Cooperation: The Gulf and Yugoslavia", *International Affairs*, vol. 68, No. 2, 1992, 233-253.

150 The money would not arrive till February 1991. See Charles Grant, *op.cit.*, 185.

151 See Willem Van Eekelen, "WEU and the Gulf Crisis", *Survival*, 1990, vol. 32, No. 6, November-December 1990, 519-532; Arnaud Jacomet, "The Role of WEU in the Gulf Crisis", in Nicole Gnesotto and John Roper (eds.), *op.cit.*, 159-169.

152 Jacques Delors, "European Integration and Security", Alastair Buchan Memorial Lecture, London, The International Institute for Strategic Studies, 7 March 1991.

153 Laura Guazzone, "Italy and the Gulf Crisis: European and Domestic Dimensions", *The International Spectator*, vol. 26, No. 4, October-December 1991, 57-74, 63.

154 William C. Cromwell, "Europe, the United States and the Pre-War Gulf Crisis", *International Journal*, vol. 48, No. 1, winter 1992-93, 124-150, 128-130.

155 See Margaret Thatcher, *op.cit.*, 822-828.

156 Philip H. Gordon (1992), *op.cit.*, 33-34.

157 David S. Germroth and Rebecca J. Hudson, "Germany's Response to the Gulf Crisis: The New German Question", *Aussenpolitik*, vol. 43, No. 1, 1992, 33-42; Karl Kaiser and Klaus Becher, "Germany and the Iraq Conflict", in Nicole Gnesotto and John Roper (eds.), *op.cit.*, 39-69; Alan Sked, "Cheap Excuses. Germany and the Gulf Crisis", *The National Interest*, vol.24, summer 1991, 51-60.

158 According to a poll conducted by the Wickert organisation in January 1991, 75% of the German population believed that Germany should not be militarily involved in the Gulf crisis. Taken from David S. Germroth and Rebecca J. Hudson, *op.cit.*, 89.

159 The only restriction in the German constitution is that German armed forces can only be used for "defence purposes" (Article 87a(1)). The Federal Constitutional Court of Germany, in its judgment of 12 July 1994, finally clarified the constitutional basis for the deployment of German forces abroad with the result that the *Bundeswehr* from then

onwards could fully participate in UN, NATO and WEU missions.
160 Some members of the German *Bundestag* argued that Turkey would not qualify for NATO protection because Ankara was fully responsible for its decision allowing American planes to use Turkish airbases for attacking. See Alan Sked, *op.cit.*, 56-57.
161 See Thomas Kielinger and Max Otte, "Germany: The Pressured Power", *Foreign Policy*, vol. 91, summer 1993, 44-62, 53.
162 Margaret Thatcher, *op.cit.*, 769.
163 See Trevor Taylor, "West European Security and Defence Cooperation: Maastricht and Beyond", *International Affairs*, vol. 70, No. 1, January 1994, 1-16.
164 *Atlantic News*, January 1992.
165 "Ministerial Meeting of the North Atlantic Council in Oslo, Norway, 4 June 1992. Final Communiqué", *Atlantic News*, No. 2430, 6 June 1992.
166 "Ministerial Meeting of the North Atlantic Council. NATO Headquarters, Brussels, 17 December 1992", *Atlantic News*, No. 2484, 19 December 1992.
167 See *Treaty on European Union*, Title V, Article J.4.
168 "Petersberg Declaration", *Europe Documents*, No. 1787, 23 June 1992.
169 The third category was not mentioned any more by the communiqué adopted by the WEU Council of Ministers meeting in Rome on 19 May 1993 ("WEU Council of Ministers. Rome, 19 May 1993. Communiqué", *Atlantic News*, No. 2527, 22 May 1993); it took into account the definition of the United Nations Agenda for Peace which delineates peace-making as a political and diplomatic process which does not include the projection of military force. See, *The WEU Planning Cell. Report Submitted on Behalf of the Defence Committee by Mrs Baarveld-Schlamann, Rapporteur* (Paris: Assembly of the WEU, 19 May 1994).
170 All operational capabilities of the WEU had been transferred to NATO with the signature of the modified Brussels Treaty in 1954. The issue of the operational role of the WEU had also been raised by the WEU Declaration adopted in Maastricht.
171 If necessary they could also meet on an *ad hoc* basis.
172 The planning cell was established in Brussels in October 1992. The Petersberg Declaration defines the tasks of the Planning Cell as follows: preparing contingency plans for the employment of forces under WEU auspices; preparing recommendations for the necessary command, control and communication arrangements, including standing operating procedures for headquarters which might be selected; and keeping an updated list of units and combinations of units which might be allocated to the WEU for specific operations.
173 "Council of Ministers – Vianden (Luxembourg), 27 June 1991: Communiqué", *Europe Documents*, No. 5523, 29 June 1991. The satellite centre was ultimately set up in Torrejon (Spain) and officially inaugurated on 28 April 1993.
174 *Cf. supra*, 100-101.
175 The removal took place in early January 1993.
176 The Danish population initially rejected the Treaty as agreed in Maastricht and in France there was only a small "oui". On the ratification process in the different Member States, see Finn Laursen and Sophie Vanhoonacker (eds.), *The Ratification of the Maastricht Treaty: Issues, Debates and Future Implications* (Maastricht and Dordrecht: EIPA and Martinus Nijhoff Publishers, 1994).
177 "Report to the European Council in Lisbon on the Likely Development of the Common Foreign and Security Policy (CFSP) with a View to Identifying Areas Open to Joint Actions vis-à-vis Particular Countries or Groups of Countries", *Europe Documents*, No. 5761, 29-

30 June 1992.
178 "Declaration by the European Council on Areas Which Could Be the Subject of Joint Action", in Finn Laursen and Sophie Vanhoonacker (1992), *op.cit.*, 493-494.
179 "Rome Declaration on Peace and Cooperation", *Europe Documents*, No. 1744, 13 November 1991.
180 *Atlantic News*, 23 May 1992.
181 Both the WEU and NATO Councils took the decision within the sidelines of a CSCE meeting taking place in Helsinki (9-11 July 1992).
182 Fréderic Bozo, "Organisations de sécurité et insécurité en Europe", *Politique Etrangère*, vol. 58, No. 2, 1993, 447-458, 449-450.
183 "An Operational Organisation for WEU: Naval Cooperation – Part One: Adriatic Operations". Report submitted on Behalf of the Defence Committee by Mr Marten and Sir Keith Speed, Joint Rapporteurs (Paris: Assembly of the Western European Union, November 1993), 5.
184 *Atlantic News*, 11 November 1992.
185 See the communiqués adopted at the North Atlantic Council of Oslo (4 June 1992) and Brussels (17 December 1992).
186 See "Excerpts from Pentagon's Plan: Prevent the Re-emergence of a New Rival", *New York Times*, 8 March 1992, A14. James Baker dismissed the document as a low-level internal document, not representative of the administration's view. The final document adopted a more relaxed tone.
187 "Franco-German Initiative on Foreign Security and Defence Policy (Bonn, Paris, 11 October 1991), *Europe Documents*, No. 1738, 18 October 1991. The idea was briefly referred to at the end of the paper: "Franco-German military cooperation will be strengthened beyond the present Brigade. Thus, the reinforced Franco-German units could serve as the core of a European corps, including the forces of other WEU member states. This new structure could also become the model for closer military cooperation between the WEU and the member states."
188 *Atlantic News*, 23 May 1992.
189 On the Eurocorps, see, George Stein, "The Euro-corps and Future European Security Architecture", *European Security*, vol. 2, summer 1993, 200-226, 208-210.
190 Anne-Marie Le Gloannec, "The Implications of German Unification for Western Europe", in Paul B. Stares (ed.), *op.cit.*, 251-278, 269.
191 See, for example, Ambassador William H. Taft, *The NATO Role in Europe and the US Role in NATO*. Speech presented to the Centre for European Policy Studies, 21 May 1992: "...undermining the alliance's integrated military structure in the uncertain process of developing a European security identity would be the height of folly. Like Othello, who "threw a pearl away / Richer than all his tribe", Europe would regret its carelessness too late."
192 At a meeting of the NATO Defence Ministers, the German Minister of Defence, Volker Rühe, tried to convince the US that the Eurocorps would be complementary to NATO, that it would strengthen the Alliance and that it would not endanger the assignment of German troops to NATO. See *Atlantic News*, 27 May 1992.
193 William Taft, "The US Role in the New Europe". Address to the International Institute for Strategic Studies, London, 9 February 1991.

# 5 Transatlantic Relations and the Yugoslav Crisis

## Introduction

When in June 1991 Secretary of State James Baker paid his second state visit to Berlin,[1] the central focus of his speech in the capital of a reunited Germany was on the extension of the transatlantic community and its values to Central and Eastern Europe and the Soviet Union.[2] Baker pleaded for a "Europe whole and free" from Vancouver to Vladivostok, where "old nineteenth century nationalisms" would be transcended by universal values of democracy and economic liberty. As in his 1989 speech on the development of a new Atlanticism, the three main institutions to promote such an enlarged Euro-Atlantic community were NATO, the European Community and the Conference on Security and Cooperation in Europe (CSCE).

That the extension of Western values to the whole of the European continent was not going to be an automatic nor an easy process was soon illustrated by events in Yugoslavia. Posing a serious challenge to the stability in the Balkans, the crisis in Yugoslavia became the first major test for the willingness and capability of the United States and Western Europe to defend their values in the other half of Europe.

As the first major post-cold war European crisis, the break-up of Yugoslavia presents an extremely interesting case for the study of the transatlantic security relationship in the new Europe. Although one has to be prudent in drawing general conclusions and it has to be taken into account that the crisis occurred at a moment when both the European and the transatlantic institutions were still in the midst of their adjustment process to the new European security environment, the way in which the United States and the European Community have responded to the Yugoslav imbroglio have undoubtedly provided important indications as to the readiness as well as to the capability of both partners to address the security challenges in a Europe that is no longer threatened by the risk of a communist attack. Furthermore, as the war in Yugoslavia erupted in the immediate aftermath of the end of the cold war, it had an important impact on the shaping of the new European security architecture and the transatlantic relationship.

The break-up of Yugoslavia clearly raised issues going far beyond the crisis in question. It confronted both sides of the Atlantic with the inability of the cold war structures to address the new type of challenges facing the post-1989 Europe and forced them to urgently confront the security vacuum resulting from the collapse of the communist bloc. The conflict brought up the much broader question of the emerging security order in Europe and the respective role of the Europeans and the Americans in guaranteeing the stability of such order.

The importance of the question of a new division of tasks and more particularly of the need for an increased assumption of responsibilities on the European side was well illustrated by the exclamation of the Luxembourg Foreign Minister, Jacques Poos, at the outbreak of the crisis when he stated that "this is the hour of Europe, not the hour of the Americans".[3] The subsequent failure of the European Community to prevent the escalation of the conflict into a bloody war and the ultimate need for UN, and later US, intervention to rescue the situation illustrated that it was naive and certainly pretentious to believe that after 40 years of US command with respect to European security, the torch of leadership could simply be handed over to the European Community, especially if one takes into consideration that the Twelve had almost no experience in dealing with security matters.

By the end of the Bush administration's term, the war in what had become "former Yugoslavia" was still lingering on and had spilled over from Croatia to Bosnia and Herzegovina. Although it would take the Dayton Agreement of 21 November 1995 before there would be any real hopes for peace, the period starting in June 1991, when both Slovenia and Croatia unilaterally declared their independence until January 1993, when President Bush passed the helm to William J. Clinton, provides ample material, and a sufficiently interesting evolution of the position of the different actors, to constitute an extremely interesting case for this study on transatlantic relations.

This research is primarily interested in how the Bush administration reacted to this first security crisis of the post-cold war Europe and seeks to examine how it responded to the EC's ambitions to play a leading role in addressing the conflict. We start by giving a short introduction to the crisis itself. Subsequently, the respective roles of the European Community and the United States in the crisis are explored and the question of how "Yugoslavia" affected the transatlantic relationship is examined.

## Yugoslavia: An Accident of History?

When future students of history look back at the records of the twentieth century, they will undoubtedly be puzzled by the fact that a small Balkan country, not even 75 years old, was so often at the centre of European events. Even if today Yugoslavia has been reduced to the republics of Serbia and Montenegro, one can argue that there are at least three major events which guarantee that the memory of that country will certainly be kept alive.

In the first place there is Sarajevo, 1914. It was on the territory of what four years later was to become Yugoslavia that following the murder of the Habsburg Crown Prince, Ferdinand, the First World War broke out. As a matter of fact, the creation of Yugoslavia resulted from the territorial reshuffling at the end of this war, with the constitutional monarchy of Yugoslavia being a reward to the Serbs who had been fighting on the side of the victorious *Entente* powers.

During the cold war period, the communist Federal Republic of Yugoslavia, taking an "independent stance" between East and West, was extremely successful exploiting its middle position between the superpowers. As one of the leading countries of the non-aligned movement, Belgrade succeeded in playing a disproportionately important role in international relations.

The third major event which ensures Yugoslavia's place in the annals of twentieth century history is the war of 1991 to 1995, leading to the country's break-up into five independent states. Sadly enough, for Sarajevo 1995, history seemed to have come full circle. The great powers which had been instrumental in the creation of Yugoslavia in 1918 had to intervene once again, this time to mediate in the process of the country's dissolution. And even then peace did not return. In 1999, the ethnic cleansing of the Albanian population of Kosovo instigated by President Milosevic has provoked armed intervention by NATO. However, it remains to be seen whether the massive presence of NATO-led forces will ultimately be able to contribute to stability in the region.

Although history does not provide a full explanation, let alone a justification for the disintegration of Yugoslavia, it certainly provides a basis for a better understanding of some of the underlying factors of the conflict.[4]

### The Two Yugoslavias

The "Kingdom of the Serbs, Croats and Slovenes", better known under the name Yugoslavia, as the country was called from 1929 onwards, was established in 1918 on the ashes of parts of both the Austrian-Hungarian and the Ottoman

Empire. The idea of uniting all "Yugo" or "South" Slavs in one state had gradually taken shape in the nineteenth century as a result of the movements of national awakening sweeping all Europe.[5]

Despite their common southern Slav origin, the inhabitants of the newly established country carried with them considerably different historical experiences.[6] While after the division of the Roman Empire (395), the western part of the later Yugoslavia fell under the sphere of influence of Rome and Roman Christianity, the eastern part came under the control of Byzantium and the patriarch of Constantinople. In the middle ages, the regions that later would make up Yugoslavia were scattered over different kingdoms.[7] From the fourteenth century onwards, Serbia, Montenegro, Bosnia and Herzegovina and Macedonia were gradually incorporated in the Ottoman Empire[8] while both Slovenia and, from the sixteenth century, also Croatia were integrated into the Habsburg Empire.[9]

The fact that the Kingdom of Yugoslavia, also referred to as the "first Yugoslavia" (1918 to 1941), brought together so many different cultures which, because of their different historical courses did not necessarily know each other very well, constituted a significant challenge for the young monarchy. By opting for a very centralised state organisation and by attributing most of the key political functions to Serbs, the Yugoslav government ignored the multinational character of the young state and soon caused strong resentment among the non-Serb population, especially the Croats.[10]

The Second World War, leading to the occupation of Yugoslavia by the Axis powers (1941), brought the underlying tensions between the different nationalities to eruption.[11] A brutal conflict broke out whereby Croat Ustashi, taking the side of Germany, Serb Chetniks and Tito's multi-national communist partisans, both siding with the Allied powers,[12] all fiercely fought each other.[13] The outcome of this black page of Yugoslav history was a victory for the partisans, who after having played an important role in the liberation of their country, took their chance to impose one-party communist rule under the leadership of Josip Broz (1892 to 1980), better known under his code name Tito.[14]

The strong personality of Tito determined the course of communist Yugoslavia or the "second Yugoslavia" (1945 to 1991) for most of the cold war period. While it initially seemed to be the country's fate to become one of Moscow's numerous European satellites, the break between Stalin and Tito in June 1948 totally reversed the situation. Tito did not join the Western camp, but capitalised on the new situation to develop an independent course, expertly exploiting the superpower rivalry into his own advantage.

In the economic field, Tito and his entourage came up with their own interpretation of Marxist-Leninism and developed the so-called system of self-management according to which certain managerial powers were delegated to the workers' councils. Although the system seemed to lead to better results than in the neighbouring communist states, the economic crisis of the 1980s, bringing high levels of inflation and unemployment, demonstrated its deficiencies. Notwithstanding this, the Yugoslav model attracted attention from scholars from all over the world, and was for a long time seen as an interesting alternative to the Soviet one.[15]

In the foreign-policy field, Tito became one of the main promoters of the non-alignment movement. Its programme strongly condemned the division of the world into two opposing military blocs and took a strong anti-colonialist stance, which made it particularly popular with third world countries. The non-aligned movement gave Tito the chance to meet with political leaders from all over the world and allowed Yugoslavia to exert an influence going far beyond its size and its resources.[16]

Of direct interest to this study is the question how communist Yugoslavia dealt with the nationality question. Tito, who himself was half Croat, was very conscious of the flaws of the centralised system of the Yugoslav monarchy and opted from the beginning for the federal model. Under the slogan "brotherhood and unity", which promised equal rights to all nationalities, Yugoslavia became a federation consisting of six republics and two autonomous provinces.[17]

In a first stage, however, the Socialist Federal Republic of Yugoslavia, being based on the Soviet model, was a federation in name only and power continued to be concentrated in Belgrade. The principal asset for the country's different nationalities was the right to use their own language for education and in public affairs. By the late 1960s, the regional entities, taking advantage of the increasing economic decentralisation and the federal structure of the League of Yugoslav Communists (LCY), gradually succeeded in becoming more influential, and in the 1974 constitution they obtained a *de facto* right of veto in the federal decision-making process.[18]

As we know today, Tito's authoritarian regime did not devise any long-lasting solutions for the nationalist problems in Yugoslavia. Growing economic disparities resulted in a situation whereby the more prosperous republics, such as Croatia and Slovenia, increasingly resented the transfer of resources to the economically less advantaged regions, while Serbia and large parts of the Serb population scattered over the different republics regarded the increasing devolution of powers from the centre to the periphery as a threat to the Serb position in Yugoslavia.

The political instability following Tito's death (1980), and the severe economic crisis of the 1980s only exacerbated nationalist tensions. While the collective federal presidency failed to introduce the necessary economic and political reforms to transform Yugoslavia into a democratic state with a market economy, the political elites at the regional level capitalised on the political vacuum to further their own position.

By the late 1980s, two opposing trends had clearly emerged: while both Slovenia and Croatia advocated a transformation of Yugoslavia into a confederation,[19] Serbia wanted to maintain the federation. Bosnia and Herzegovina, with a mixed population of Muslims, Serbs and Croats, as well as Macedonia defended intermediate positions.

In 1990, the different republics[20] organised their first multiparty elections.[21] Bringing to power parties with nationalistic agendas, the chances of a peaceful solution to the escalating crisis further diminished. When on 25 June 1991, both Slovenia[22] and Croatia unilaterally declared their independence, the tense situation escalated into armed conflict and fighting broke out between Slovene militias and the Yugoslav People's Army (JNA).[23]

In Slovenia, where approximately 90% of the population is of Slovene origin and which is the residence of more than 98% of the Slovene population, the warring parties reached an agreement after less than two weeks. In contrast, the conflict in Croatia, a republic with an important Serb minority (12%), continued for more than six months with a durable cease-fire only being reached in early January 1992. It was, however, in Bosnia and Herzegovina, with its mixed population of Muslims, Serbs and Croats, where the conflict was the most brutal and the most difficulty occurred in bringing about a standstill. In the end it was only the Republic of Macedonia which succeeded in breaking away from Yugoslavia without triggering of a major conflict.

Contrary to 1914, the conflict leading to the disintegration of Yugoslavia did not escalate into an all-out Balkan or European war, but remained confined within the country's boundaries. Yet, this does not mean that the conflict can be dismissed as a purely local crisis. Its solution required the intervention of many outside powers, particularly that of the European Community and the US. The following sections will look at their respective roles and examine the implications for their security relationship.

### The EC and the Yugoslav Crisis

When in June 1991, following the unilateral declarations of independence by both Slovenia and Croatia, the long-simmering tensions in Yugoslavia erupted into an open conflict, several in Europe, especially those dreaming of a federal Europe, considered it as presenting the European Community with an "excellent" opportunity to assert itself as a major if not the leading foreign-policy actor on the European scene. After the sobering experience of the Gulf crisis, which had been entirely dominated by the United States and where the EC had merely been a spectator with only individual Member States such as France and the United Kingdom contributing to the US-led alliance, the Twelve were eager to prove that they were capable of handling this first European post-cold war crisis on their own.[24]

The outbreak of the conflict coincided with the 1991 Intergovernmental Conference (IGC) on Political Union and Member States, like France and Germany, which were advocating the development of a fully-fledged European foreign and security policy hoped that the EC's active participation in solving the crisis would strengthen their position and positively influence the IGC's final outcome.[25]

The fervour and the confidence attending the decision of the Luxembourg European Council (28 and 29 June 1991) to tackle the events in Yugoslavia contrasted sharply with the results the Heads of State and Government had so far achieved with regard to the negotiations on the development of a Common Foreign and Security Policy (CFSP). Unable to agree on the ultimate shape of Europe's emerging foreign and security policy, the Member States postponed any decisions on this major and extremely sensitive issue until the final negotiations which were to take place in December 1991 in Maastricht. The Luxembourg European Council mistakenly saw the crisis in Yugoslavia as a welcome distraction, averting attention from the otherwise rather poor results of their meeting and providing a new chance to prove their capacity to act.

Very soon, however, it proved illusory to expect that the Twelve could speak with one voice in a major foreign-policy crisis such as Yugoslavia while having strong disagreements on the further development of a European foreign and security policy. Instead of having the hoped for effect of diverting attention from the Twelve's problems, and rather than being a catalyst for a successful CFSP debate the Yugoslav crisis raised serious questions as to the feasibility of the development of a European security policy and became a real threat to the IGC's success. It brought to the fore the enormity of the difficulties still to be overcome and led to a serious crisis of confidence with European public opinion. The gap between the Member States' rhetoric and their actual capabilities would prove to be huge.

## EC-Yugoslav Relations Prior to the Crisis

The eagerness with which the Twelve in June 1991 decided to address the Yugoslav crisis contrasted strongly with their earlier disregard for the deteriorating situation in that country. Despite early warnings from CIA reports in the autumn of 1990 about Yugoslavia's possible disintegration, and despite US appeals to the European Community in early 1991 to adopt a concerted approach to the mounting political strains among the republics,[26] the Twelve did not undertake any steps to develop a coherent strategy which could help the country in trying to find a political solution to its problems.

In 1990, and the first half of 1991, the EC primarily limited itself to declarations expressing support for the federal government's economic reform programme, appealing for respect for Yugoslavia's territorial integrity and holding out the prospect of the conclusion of an association agreement once the requisite conditions with regard to democratisation and human rights had been met.[27] When, in late May, the President of the European Council Jacques Santer accompanied by Commission President Jacques Delors visited Belgrade, they did not do much more than repeating the same message.[28]

Until the outbreak of the crisis the Twelve stubbornly adhered to this policy of carrot and stick. Up to one day before Slovenia and Croatia declared their independence, European Commissioner Abel Matutes, on behalf of the European Community, signed the third financial protocol, providing federal Yugoslavia with a total of ECU 730 million in European Investment Bank (EIB) loans over five years.[29] Did the Europeans really have the illusion that by throwing large sums of money they could hope to hold Yugoslavia together? Or was it as more cynical observers have suggested that through a lack of agreement on a more comprehensive policy the Twelve resorted to this type of desperate actions? The feeling of helplessness towards the escalating situation in Yugoslavia will certainly have played a role. The light-hearted manner with which the EC Member States by the end of June 1991 decided to become involved in the conflict however also seems to indicate that they seriously underestimated the state of affairs in Yugoslavia and that they certainly had no idea of the huge amount of violence which would attend the break-up of the country.

That the Twelve postponed intervention until the crisis had escalated to a point of no return, was typical for the Member States' reactive approach to foreign-policy problems. In the absence of clear-cut priorities, the agenda of European Political Cooperation was generally determined by the crisis of the moment, rather than by long-term concerns. The case of Yugoslavia has not been different.

A further factor which may have contributed to the Twelve's slow reaction is that Yugoslavia has never been a real priority for the European Community. Since the first contacts in 1965, EC relations with Yugoslavia had always lacked an overall strategy.[30] In the case of both the 1970 and the 1980 EC-Yugoslav agreements,[31] it was external events such as the Soviet invasion in Czechoslovakia (1968) and Afghanistan (1979) which, in the first place, served as the major catalysts for EC action.[32]

With the end of the cold war Yugoslavia's special status of an independent country between East and West had come to an end. As a result there was even less pressure on the EC Member States to come up with a comprehensive approach. It also meant that Yugoslavia now had to compete with the other liberated countries of Central and Eastern Europe for EC aid and attention.

*The Crisis Breaks Out*

After many months of consistently neglecting the multiple signals indicating that the situation in Yugoslavia was going from bad to worse, the outbreak of the war in Slovenia finally seemed to have convinced the Twelve of the need to give the crisis absolute priority. Even more, making a virtue out of necessity, they tried to exploit the crisis for their own purpose of showing the world that Europe had come of age and had political maturity.

The resoluteness with which the Member States launched a series of initiatives contrasted strongly with the traditionally rather slow decision-making process of European Political Cooperation. The Luxembourg European Council (28 and 29 June 1991) immediately dispatched an EC troika of Foreign Ministers which negotiated its first, but unfortunately not its last cease-fire with the Yugoslav parties. On 5 July, the EC was among the first to issue an arms embargo against Yugoslavia and suspended the second and third financial protocol with the country.[33] Two days later, a new troika mission negotiated the so-called Brioni Agreement leading to a definitive cease-fire in Slovenia,[34] the withdrawal of the Yugoslav National Army from that republic and bringing a three-month suspension of the implementation of Slovenia's and Croatia's declarations of independence.[35] The agreement was to be monitored by EC observers, a major novelty for the EPC and its traditional predilection for a declaratory policy.

If these first weeks of EC action were generally considered to be a success for the Twelve and their Dutch Presidency,[36] they also brought to the fore the existence of some underlying tensions. While in the initial phase of the conflict, the EC abided by its earlier position that Yugoslavia's territorial integrity was to be respected, Germany did not hide its sympathy for the cause of Slovenia and Croatia.[37] Especially when in the summer months of 1991, the violence spilled over to Croatia and the Member States' appeal to maintain Yugoslav unity was increasingly overtaken by events, German pressure for recognition became stronger.

For the majority of Member States, however, recognition was at that time still a bridge too far. Although they were willing to drop their earlier position with regard to the preservation of Yugoslavia's territorial integrity, they considered recognition to be too important an instrument for leverage over the warring parties to give up at once. They advocated coming to a negotiated settlement over the new relationship among the different republics, arguing that recognition could only take place if agreed by all republics.

In late August the Twelve decided to contribute to such a negotiated solution of the crisis by convening a peace conference to which representatives of both the federal Presidency, the federal government and the Presidents of the Republics were invited.[38] France, who had been one of the main promoters of the conference hoped that it would calm Germany's propensity to go ahead with unilateral recognition.

Under the chairmanship of the former UK Foreign Secretary Lord Carrington,[39] the opening session of the Conference on Yugoslavia took place on 7 September in The Hague.[40] Two working groups, one in charge of working out constitutional arrangements and one dealing with minority rights were created.[41] An arbitration commission of five experts drawn from the constitutional courts of the Member States and chaired by the French judge Robert Badinter, was in charge of dealing with differences arising among the parties. Among the principles which were to guide the negotiators were the unacceptability of unilateral change of borders by force, the protection of minority rights and the full account of all legitimate concerns and aspirations.[42]

The conditions in which the conference was taking place were far from ideal. The cease-fire which had been concluded prior to the start of the conference was not respected and both Serbs and Croats continued to pursue their objectives through fighting.

Confronted with the inadequacy of traditional diplomatic instruments for coping with the escalating crisis in Croatia, there were increasingly voices pleading for the sending of a peace-keeping force or as the French called it a *"force d'interposition"*.[43] It was argued by the proponents of the development of a European foreign policy that if the EC was to be really serious about becoming a major foreign-policy actor, no option including the military one should be excluded.

## The Military Option

While the idea of sending troops to Croatia had already been floated in late July,[44] it was first seriously discussed in the second half of September 1991 following a Franco-German proposal.[45]

The fact that the Twelve, who had always limited themselves to the use of civilian power instruments such as declarations and trade sanctions, were willing to consider the military option was as such remarkable and has to be seen in the light of the discussions at the time on the development of a European security and defence policy. The initiative was launched by the two countries taking the lead in the European security debate, hoping that their proposal would give an important boast to the IGC negotiations. Both in their letter to the Italian President of the European Council[46] and in their joint proposal on Political Union of February 1991,[47] the French President Mitterrand and the German Chancellor Kohl had pleaded for a common foreign policy encompassing all areas of external relations, including defence and they had advocated making use of a more operational WEU to implement eventual decisions on military action.

The seriousness of the situation in Yugoslavia did, however, not prove to be a sufficient catalyst to realise a decisive breakthrough in the debate on a European security and defence identity and to overcome the traditional opposition of Atlanticist countries such as the United Kingdom and Portugal against independent European military action.[48]

When on 19 September, the Franco-German proposal was discussed at an extraordinary WEU ministerial meeting, the United Kingdom, referring to its experience in Northern Ireland, strongly opposed the idea of a military intervention and also questioned the feasibility of such action.[49] London was also very critical of Germany, who was one of the main advocates of a military intervention but who had argued that it would not be able to participate in the mission because of historical reasons[50] and due to alleged restrictions on out of area operations in its constitution.[51]

The lack of support for an eventual WEU intervention was clearly reflected in the declaration adopted at the subsequent EPC meeting. The Ministers of Foreign Affairs specified that such a mission was to be limited to supporting the activities of the EC monitors, underlining that "it is their understanding that no military intervention is contemplated".[52] The mission was further made conditional on the conclusion of a firm cease-fire and on the approval for the mission by all Yugoslav parties, two requirements which were very unlikely to be fulfilled.[53] The Foreign Ministers also asked for any eventual action on behalf of the WEU to be dependent on their endorsement and that, in case of intervention, the latter would seek the approval of the CSCE and the UN Security Council. This whole range of requirements and conditions indicates that there were still many hurdles on the road, and that it was highly unlikely that military intervention would ever happen.

Taking into account this extremely reticent attitude, it is therefore not surprising that when on 30 September, the ad hoc expert group of the WEU presented four possible military options, going from the mere logistic underpinning of the EC monitors to a peace-keeping force of 20,000 military personnel, not even the most minimal option could get the support of all Member States.[54] The WEU put itself at the disposal of the EC and the EC peace conference but neither would decide to make use of WEU services.

Ultimately, the first WEU contribution to the Yugoslav crisis would only take place after the UN had taken the lead in addressing the conflict. In July 1992, the WEU Member States agreed to participate in the monitoring of the UN embargo against Serbia and Montenegro and sent ships to the Adriatic.[55] The WEU acted on its own initiative, in total independence of the EC.[56]

In October 1991, when the EC was still the leading international actor in the Yugoslav crisis, the sending of troops, even if their mission was to be confined to the protection of the EC monitors, proved a bridge too far. For the Atlanticist countries, the sending of WEU peace-keeping troops implementing an EC decision would have gone radically against their position at the IGC that the WEU was to become the European pillar of NATO.

A further and probably determining factor explaining their reticence was the WEU's total lack of experience with large-scale military operations. So far the WEU had only been involved in small-scale missions like a mine-clearance operation in the Gulf (1987 to 1988) and the naval coordination of the enforcement of the UN embargo against Iraq and Kuwait (1990 to 1991), thus a difficult mission such as the one in Yugoslavia was an extremely risky affair.[57]

The failure of the EC to make the leap forwards to the option of an armed intervention, even if only with a limited mandate, was nevertheless an important, even decisive, moment for the role of the EC in Yugoslavia. It clearly set the limits as to how far the EC was ready and able to go in its efforts to tackle the crisis, and *vis-à-vis* third countries it undoubtedly weakened its position as sole international negotiator.

The decision of the Twelve to restrict themselves to the use of traditional civilian power instruments also had the effect that the two main proponents of the EC handling the crisis started to look for other fora and means to realise their objectives in Yugoslavia. France increasingly turned to the United Nations as the main platform through which it would try to assert its special role in the peace process. As a permanent member of the UN Security Council, Paris occupied a privileged position in the UN forum and did not hesitate to exploit this to find support for its own policy towards Yugoslavia.[58]

Germany, where public opinion was more and more disenchanted with the EC's incapacity to act decisively, would increasingly start to push for what in its eyes was the most effective way to stop the bloodshed in Croatia, namely the recognition of this republic.

*Germany Breaks Ranks*

The episode around the recognition of Slovenia and Croatia is undoubtedly one of the most dark chapters of the EC arbitration in the Yugoslav crisis. More than any other event it illustrated the Member States' divergent interpretations of the conflict and the long way they still had to go before reaching the objective of a Common Foreign and Security Policy.

The recognition question crystallised around two radically opposing opinions with regard to the addressing of the Yugoslav conflict. The first was that the struggle could only be ended following the conclusion of a general agreement among all Yugoslav parties, while the other defended the view that the war could solely be brought to a halt by its internationalisation, i.e. through the recognition of the breakaway republics. The tragedy for the EC was that the two main advocates of these opposing views were France and Germany, precisely the two countries which had been the most ardent supporters of an active EC intervention in the Yugoslav crisis and the development of an independent European foreign policy.

At the outbreak of the crisis in June 1991, most Member States had favoured the option of maintaining Yugoslav unity. Several factors were at the basis of this position. An important consideration was the potential effect of Yugoslavia's disintegration on other Central European countries with different nationalities, not least on the republics of the Soviet Union where especially in the Baltic states, the calls for independence were getting increasingly louder. In addition, there were some EC Member States like France and Spain which were themselves facing serious problems with minorities claiming independence. This made them natural allies of the federal government in Yugoslavia, fighting to preserve its territorial integrity.

Furthermore, it should also be mentioned that both France and the United Kingdom had close historical links with Yugoslavia. During the First World

War, France had fought on the side of the Serbs and had played a major role in the country's creation in 1918.[59] The United Kingdom on the other hand, had been instrumental in bringing Tito to power at the end of the Second World War.[60] Last but not least, the EC's predilection for a united, rather than a disintegrated, Yugoslavia can also be seen as being congruous with its own attempts to form "an ever closer union among the peoples of Europe".

The only EC Member State which from the beginning of the crisis showed sympathy for the decision of Slovenia and Croatia to secede from Yugoslavia was Germany. On 28 June 1991, only a few days after their unilateral declaration of independence, the German Chancellor Helmut Kohl declared that it was "unacceptable that today in Europe people are being shot or that suddenly the rights of self-determination should no longer play a role".[61] At the meeting of Ministers of Foreign Affairs of 5 July in The Hague, the German Minster Hans-Dietrich Genscher for the first time proposed that his colleagues consider the option of recognition as a way of halting the violence[62] but he found himself totally isolated.[63] The divergence of views is clearly reflected in the declaration that was adopted and which refers both to the need to respect the principle of territorial integrity of states as well as to the "right of peoples to self-determination".[64]

When by late July, the further escalation of violence in Croatia made it increasingly clear that the EC's earlier position on a unified Yugoslavia had been overtaken by events, the Twelve recognised that the situation had changed and, pleading for a negotiated settlement of the crisis, they proposed the organisation of a peace conference in which they would mediate between the different parties.[65]

In the meantime, voices in Germany calling for the recognition of Slovenia and Croatia were becoming increasingly loud and had it not been for the pressure of France and President Mitterrand himself,[66] as well as the negative repercussions of unilateral German action on the course of the Intergovernmental Conference and on Germany's highly valued objective of Political Union, Bonn would undoubtedly have proceeded with recognition.

As events unfolded, both partners became more and more vexed and wary about each other's position and Franco-German relations went through a very difficult period. Following the end of the cold war, France had become unduly worried about being marginalised in the new Europe and was extremely vigilant with regard to any foreign-policy actions of the unified Germany. Bonn's pushy attitude to recognition was primarily seen in historic terms and considered as an expression of an old ambition to restore its sphere of influence in "*Mitteleuropa*".[67] The German government on its side, was increasingly upset with Paris's support for the position of the Serbs and its refusal to adopt any measures against this group which it considered to be the main aggressor in the conflict.

More than 40 years of European integration seemed not to have fostered enough confidence to overcome considerations concerning the traditional balance of power. Although the Yugoslav conflict did not ignite an all-European war, the big EC Member States, rather than talking with one voice, did not resist the temptation to take sides with their traditional allies of the First and Second World Wars.

The decision of the Twelve in late September not to intervene militarily in the conflict and the extremely difficult conditions in which the peace conference was taking place further strengthened the German government in its conviction that recognition might be the only way to bring an end to the violence. Because this was still an unacceptable position for the majority of Member States, Germany concentrated its efforts on increasingly isolating the Serbs, which in its eyes was the main group responsible for the continuation of the conflict. At the informal meeting of the Ministers of Foreign Affairs in Haarzuilens, the Twelve at the insistence of Germany, explicitly condemned the aggression by the Yugoslav National Army and criticised the decision of the Presidency of Serbia and Montenegro to seize the Yugoslav federal presidency.[68] Those republics obstructing the peace process (i.e. primarily the Serbs) were furthermore threatened with economic sanctions. For the first time, the text also referred to a possible recognition of the independence of those republics which desired it, although such recognition would be placed in the framework of a negotiated settlement.[69]

By the end of October, the Twelve openly denounced the Serbs' intransigence at the peace conference and threatened to continue negotiations with the cooperative republics, "in the perspective of recognition of the independence of those republics wishing it".[70] A further step towards recognition was made on 2 December when the Member States, after having suspended the Trade and Cooperation Agreement with Yugoslavia, adopted positive measures in favour of Bosnia and Herzegovina, Croatia, Macedonia, and Slovenia. This act implied that the various republics were *de facto* no longer treated as one country.[71]

When, in November 1991, the failure of the EC peace conference had become a reality, it was obvious that it was no longer possible to further withhold Germany from recognition. On 27 November, in a session before the *Bundestag*, Chancellor Kohl announced that any republic expressing the desire, would be recognised before Christmas.[72] Immediately after the European

Council of Maastricht (9 and 10 December 1991)⁷³ when the Yugoslav question could no longer endanger the outcome of the IGC negotiations, the question was placed on the agenda of an extraordinary EPC ministerial meeting, taking place in Brussels on 16 December.

In order to preserve at least some appearance of unity and to disguise the strong contrast with the commitments made a few days earlier in Maastricht to develop a Common Foreign and Security Policy, Paris and Bonn presented their colleagues with a joint initiative for guidelines on the recognition of new states in Eastern Europe and the Soviet Union. At the start of the meeting, only Belgium, Denmark and Italy⁷⁴ were supportive of their proposal.⁷⁵ It was only after long and protracted negotiations that the others followed their lead, not because they were convinced of the positive effects of recognition but to salvage European unity.

The support of Greece, who strongly resisted the recognition of Macedonia, was only obtained after a special paragraph was added to the declaration stating that, prior to recognition, the Yugoslav republics in question had "to adopt constitutional and political guarantees ensuring that it has no territorial claims towards a neighbouring Community State and that it will conduct no hostile propaganda activities versus a neighbouring Community State, including the use of a denomination which implies territorial claims."⁷⁶ It has been suggested that British support for recognition had been assured in exchange for the many concessions John Major had obtained in Maastricht.⁷⁷

In the declaration which was finally adopted, it was agreed that all republics expressing such desire would be recognised by 15 January 1992, on the condition that they fulfilled the necessary conditions of respecting human rights and providing guarantees for minorities.⁷⁸

If the decision by the Twelve allowed the German Minister of Foreign Affairs to exclaim "*einen deutschen Alleingang gab es nicht*",⁷⁹ it did not prohibit the German government from already unilaterally recognising Slovenia and Croatia on 23 December without waiting either for the opinion of the Badinter Commission or for a common decision by the Twelve expected on 15 January. Germany found it apparently more important to keep its promise to the Croatian President, Tudjman, than to adhere to a commitment with its European counterparts. The development of what was to become a European foreign and security policy started under an extremely bad omen and for those who had followed the debate it raised serious questions as to the feasibility of translating the Maastricht Treaty's provisions on CFSP into practice.

Following the unilateral German action, the other Member States had no other choice but to follow suit, even when this implied disregarding the reservations of the Badinter Commission with regard to the recognition of the independence of Croatia.[80] Keeping up the appearance of European unity ultimately proved to be more important than finding the best solution for the former Yugoslav republics. Despite warnings from all sides that the recognition of Slovenia and Croatia would have dramatic consequences for Bosnia and Herzegovina, the Twelve went ahead, entirely neglecting to prepare for the eventual negative repercussions of their action.

## Explaining Germany's Alleingang

Most observers have been appalled and also extremely puzzled by the excessive vigour with which Germany fought for the recognition of Croatia and Slovenia's independence throughout the autumn of 1991. Many interpretations and hypotheses have been advanced trying to clarify this behaviour.

German politicians themselves mostly refer to their determination to defend the principle of self-determination thanks to which they had been able to realise the reunification of their own country. This could, however, not have been the sole explanation for the assertiveness of the Germans and many other factors must also have played a role. The importance of close cultural, historical and religious links with the Catholic republics of Slovenia and Croatia, both of which had been part of the Austro-Hungarian Empire should not be neglected.[81] Certainly for the CSU of Bayern, a fierce supporter of recognition, the religious factor was important. That both young democracies in Slovenia and Croatia were led by Christian Democrats further reinforced the sympathy of the Kohl government for the breakaway republics.

Most observers of the German one-man show also allude to the enormous pressure of public opinion as a determining factor in Bonn's behaviour.[82] Due to the geographical proximity of Slovenia and Croatia, the German population indisputably felt more directly concerned and menaced by the conflict than other EC Member States.[83] Together with Austria, it was directly threatened by the huge streams of refugees the conflict might possibly unleash.[84] The presence of an important Croat population on German soil,[85] and the fact that Yugoslavia and more especially Croatia was a favoured holiday resort for a lot of German citizens, meant that many felt extremely distressed by the violence striking the country. Early in the conflict, influential newspapers such as the *Frankfürter Allgemeine* and *Die Welt* had clearly taken positions regarding the conflict, depicting the Croat population as the poor victims of Serb aggression.[86]

If subsequent research will have to further examine the motives underlying

Germany's pushy conduct it is clear that at the time of the events Bonn's behaviour was not at all appreciated by its European and American partners. The Kohl government had not only exerted extremely strong pressure on the EC Member States to go along with its position, it had totally ignored the pleas of the United States[87] as well as the Secretary-General of the United Nations[88] not to go ahead with recognition.

Being one of the first foreign-policy actions of the recently unified Germany, Bonn's *"Alleingang"* was seen as the expression of a new German assertiveness, and led to serious concerns as to the further willingness of the now fully sovereign country to integrate its foreign-policy activities within multilateral frameworks such as the EC and NATO.[89] Furthermore, the episode raised questions as to the maturity of Germany to take a leading role in the further development of a European foreign and security policy. Although Germany pushed extremely hard for recognition, it did not prepare for the eventual implications of its action. On the contrary, once it had reached its aim, it almost disappeared from the international scene, leaving it to others to take over when the war spilled over to Bosnia and Herzegovina.[90]

A more than 40-year-old policy of "restraint", had clearly had a strong impact on Germany's foreign-policy behaviour and the Yugoslav crisis was the best proof that such legacy could not be overcome overnight.[91] Germany behaved very much as an inexperienced and irresponsible foreign-policy actor without showing much sensitivity for the deep-seated suspicion and the fear its European partners had of the return of a German foreign-policy purely defined by national interests.

*When the UN Comes In*

As in the autumn of 1991, it appeared that the situation in Yugoslavia was getting more and more out of hand and the EC instruments to handle the conflict proved inadequate, the question arose whether the time had not come to invoke the support and the help of the United Nations (UN). In particular, France, who was increasingly exasperated with the incapacity of the EC to act decisively in the crisis, considered the UN forum as an interesting alternative in which to assert a leading role in solving the conflict. In September, Paris took advantage of its position as President of the UN Security Council, and proposed a draft for what would become the UN's first resolution on the Yugoslav crisis.[92]

The UN involvement in the conflict was a step-by-step process. In the early months of the confrontation, the international organisation proved very reluctant to interfere in what it primarily regarded as an internal Yugoslav problem.[93] It is therefore not surprising that although France's above-mentioned proposal included a mandate for the sending of a European force to Yugoslavia,[94] the resolution, while expressing its full support for the EC peace efforts, confined itself to imposing "a general and complete embargo on all deliveries of weapons and military equipment to Yugoslavia".[95]

It was only when the situation further escalated and the calls for the sending of peace-keeping troops became increasingly loud, that on 25 October, the former US Secretary of State Cyrus Vance was nominated as the UN special envoy to Yugoslavia.[96]

While the involvement of the UN had the advantage of bringing the conflict to international attention and of involving other major players such as the United States and Russia, it certainly affected the central role of the EC, which was not directly represented in the UN Security Council. At the same time, it strengthened the position of the two European permanent members of the Security Council, France and the United Kingdom.

Following the poor performance of the EC, the UN provided France not only with an interesting alternative channel in which to realise its ambition to be one of the major international actors in addressing the crisis, it also placed Paris in a more influential position than Bonn.

The UN efforts to bring a halt to the crisis were particularly welcomed by the Serbs, who from the start of the conflict had always expressed doubts about the EC's ability to operate as a neutral broker. When on 5 November, Serbia and Montenegro radically rejected the EC peace plan[97] and the talks within the framework of the EC peace conference stalled, the United Nations became the main mediating force of Yugoslavia's warring parties.[98] By the end of the month,[99] the Croats and the Serbs finally reached an agreement which was implemented from January 1992 onwards.[100] Following the authorisation by UN Security Resolution 743 of 21 February 1992,[101] the first troops of the United Nations Protection Force (UNPROFOR) arrived in Croatia in March.[102] In total, 13,000 UN troops were deployed of which the majority were European.

By 1992, the leadership role in solving the crisis initially assumed by the EC was clearly taken over by the United Nations. The Twelve and their Portuguese Presidency continued their efforts to contribute to the solution of the crisis, by trying to intermediate in the negotiation of a new constitutional arrangement for Bosnia and Herzegovina.[103] However, when in April the war spilled over to that republic, these negotiations also foundered.

At the London Conference of 26 and 27 August, it was decided that the EC peace conference was to become an international and permanent peace conference under the auspices of both the UN and the EC.[104] In particular France, and its Minister of Foreign Affairs, Roland Dumas, who by end of July had publicly declared that he estimated that the EC peace conference had reached its limits, had been pushing hard in that direction.[105]

As the war in Bosnia and Herzegovina further escalated, affecting an ever larger number of victims, the UN becomes increasingly absorbed in the conflict.[106] Under strong US pressure, it adopted a resolution imposing a complete trade embargo on Serbia and Montenegro on 30 May, and condemned them for their involvement in the fighting.[107] In June, the Security Council authorised the deployment of additional UNPROFOR troops to ensure the security and the functioning of Sarajevo airport[108] and in September, it further increased their strength, enlarging their mandate to the protection of humanitarian envoys throughout Bosnia and Herzegovina.[109] One month later a ban was imposed on all military flights in the airspace of Bosnia and Herzegovina.[110]

All above-mentioned resolutions received EC support,[111] but the Twelve were no longer taking the lead. If Europe's voice was heard, it was primarily that of France and the United Kingdom, who as permanent members of the Security Council and major contributors to UNPROFOR actively participated in the debate.[112] When on 28 June, the French President in a heroic gesture flew to Sarajevo, pledging to open the airport for humanitarian flights, he acted on his own initiative, carefully concealing his venture from his European counterparts whom he had met at the European Council in Lisbon the day before (26 and 27 June 1992).[113] What the Twelve had tried so much to prevent – a situation as in the Gulf war whereby the contribution of the EC would be limited to the contributions of individual Member States – was being repeated.

The voice of Germany was muted. Once it had obtained the recognition of Slovenia and Croatia, Bonn's interest in taking an active role in addressing the conflict seemed to have diminished considerably. The fact that Germany did not have a seat in the Security Council and for internal reasons had decided not to contribute to the UN peace-keeping troops, further weakened its position. If at this particular time when Germany was still figuring out the underlying principles of a new foreign policy commensurate with its new and central position in Europe, this might have been convenient, it must nevertheless have given rise to a feeling of isolation among German policy-makers.

It might therefore not be totally accidental that Genscher's successor, Klaus Kinkel raised the question of a permanent seat for his country in the Security Council for the first time at a meeting of the UN General Assembly in September 1992.[114] The UN's earlier assumption that the further development of a European foreign-policy and security identity would make such request superfluous, had been overtaken by events.[115] The developments in Yugoslavia made Germany realise that a unified foreign policy was still far away, and that both France and the United Kingdom might prove extremely reluctant to give up their privileged institutional position in exchange for an EC seat.[116]

*Lessons for the European Community*

The EC mediation efforts in the Yugoslav imbroglio, announced with loud enthusiasm in June 1991, ended less than successfully. By 1992, any illusions that the European Community could manage the conflict on its own had disappeared. Furthermore, most observers were by then fully convinced that the Twelve were unable and badly equipped to address the crisis. Rather than becoming the expected catalyst for the further development of a Common Foreign and Security Policy, the EC's poor performance led to serious questions as to the feasibility of developing such policy and brought to the fore the many challenges still to be overcome.

A first problem facing the Twelve was their great difficulty in speaking with one voice. As a result of their different historical experiences and geographical locations, EC Member States perceived the crisis from totally diverging angles. The fact that the conflict in Yugoslavia presented different risks for the various EC Member States resulted in diverging and often conflicting responses. The strong contrast between the initial indifference and disinterest of the United Kingdom and the eagerness of Germany to get involved can be seen in that light. As has been argued by Nicole Gnesotto, the Yugoslav crisis brought home the point that with the disappearance of the Soviet menace there was no longer a substantial collective threat requiring a collective Western European response.[117]

Most startling, however, is the fact that the two countries who were supposed to become the motor of Europe's emerging foreign policy were entirely at odds as to how to address the crisis. France, haunted by the nightmare of a new *Mitteleuropa*, let itself be seduced by the demons of history and balance of power considerations. Germany on the other hand, was obsessed with the single objective of recognising Slovenia and Croatia and proved unable to withstand strong domestic pressure for the sake of European unity. On the contrary, it did not hesitate to threaten to go its own way, putting at risk the agreement on CFSP reached just before in Maastricht.

The Yugoslav crisis well illustrates that the security interests of the two principal advocates of a European foreign and security policy do not necessarily coincide. While Germany's prime security concern was to guarantee stability along its eastern border, France was particularly preoccupied with developments in the Mediterranean and North Africa. A different historic legacy was a further factor which meant that both countries were looking at the crisis through different lenses. While France had traditionally maintained close links with Serbia, Germany had more affinity with Croatia.

An important weakness in the Twelve's handling of the Yugoslav crisis was their inability to back up their declarations with a credible threat of military intervention. Being confined to the use of "civilian power" instruments such as diplomatic negotiations and trade sanctions, the Member States' leverage over the warring parties was seriously weakened. Although the possibility of sending WEU troops in was discussed, most Member States proved extremely reluctant to make use of military force. It was indeed very much the question of whether the WEU would have had the capacity and the ability to deal with such a challenge. The situation was further complicated by the fact that the German government, although supporting military intervention, refused to participate in such an operation.

A final effect of the Twelve's incapacity to match their rhetoric on Yugoslavia with deeds was that it seriously affected the EC's credibility with the European public. At a time when several countries such as Ireland, Denmark and France were holding referenda on the Maastricht Treaty, citizens were raising serious questions as to the sharp contrast between the prospects held out by the Treaty and the unsettling reality in Bosnia and Herzegovina.[118] In a country like Germany where the citizens were being asked to give up the *Deutschmark* in exchange for an ever closer Political Union, the population felt betrayed and anti-European slogans were increasingly finding very willing ears. Reinforced by the economic crisis, the tragedy in Yugoslavia further strengthened the wave of Europessimism sweeping through Europe in the first half of the 1990s and certainly made European policy-makers more modest and more realistic in their ambitions for the 1996 Intergovernmental Conference.

The question arises as to whether the EC's débâcle in Yugoslavia was entirely unforeseen and whether one could have expected that the handling of such a major foreign-policy crisis would be attended by significant difficulties.

The great confidence with which the Twelve in June 1991 decided to tackle the crisis illustrates very well how seriously they underestimated the gravity of the situation. Although there had been many prior warnings with regard to the potential break-up of Yugoslavia, it was not expected that this would involve so much violence. In hindsight it is therefore almost tragic to see how the European Community practically welcomed the prospect of dealing with the erupting conflict, grasping it as an opportunity to show its citizens and the world that they had grown into a mature foreign-policy actor.

The Twelve started from the wrong assumption that the crisis would serve as an important catalyst for their stalling negotiations on the development of a European foreign and security policy, naively hoping that the Yugoslav conflict would allow them to overcome obstacles which they hitherto had been unable to surmount. They clearly made the mistake of putting the cart before the horse expecting, that as the crisis developed, they would be able to develop the necessary instruments to address it.

Once the Member States had made the link between Yugoslavia and the IGC negotiations on CFSP, they became trapped in their own logic. When they started realising that their intervention was not as successful as they had initially hoped, their principal preoccupation was no longer how they could best contribute to the solution of the crisis, but how they could rescue the IGC negotiations being concluded in Maastricht.

The most tragic example of their obsession with at least keeping an appearance of unity is the saga around the recognition of Slovenia and Croatia. Although there had been ample warning about the disastrous effects of an eventual recognition of Bosnia and Herzegovina and even though several Member States proved extremely reluctant with regard to recognition, they nevertheless ceded to German pressure and went ahead. The aim of maintaining European unity prevailed over the interests of the "Yugoslav" people.

What had to become the show-piece of Europe's emerging foreign and security policy turned out to be a considerable setback for the EC's ambitions to assume increased international responsibilities. After six months, not much of the earlier dream of solving the Yugoslav crisis on "their own" was left and the EC Member States were all too happy to move to the backseat, leaving the place of honour to the United Nations and later to the United States.

## The US and the Yugoslav Crisis

From the outbreak of the Yugoslav conflict in June 1991 until the signature of the Dayton Peace Agreement in December 1995, the American role and involvement in addressing the Yugoslav crisis turned almost 180 degrees. Although the US very closely followed the events in Yugoslavia and was in 1990 among the first to recognise the risk of a violent break-up of the country,

Washington initially adopted a very low-key approach, leaving the initiative almost entirely to the European Community and it was not until late in the first Clinton administration that the US gradually became a central player in the process of bringing peace to Bosnia and Herzegovina.

The Bush administration restricted itself primarily to humanitarian interventions in Yugoslavia and although it gradually became more involved in the crisis, it is obvious that it never reached the level of engagement of the Clinton administration in 1995. The period 1991 to January 1993 was nevertheless an important phase in the process which gradually brought in the United States. Once Bush and his team had evidence that the crisis in the Balkans could not be left to the Europeans alone, it became increasingly difficult and embarrassing to ignore the conflict and to downplay it as a purely local affair. While continuing to refuse to become directly involved into the crisis, the US started to act through the United Nations. Although fears that the crisis might spill over to the wider Balkan region were an important catalyst for increased US interest, military intervention, including the use of airstrikes, was never a serious option for the Bush team.

Before focusing on the policy of the Bush administration towards the Yugoslav crisis, we will first give a brief overview of the relations between both countries prior to the outbreak of the conflict.

*The Cold War Period*

The history of US-Yugoslav relations stands and falls to a large extent with that of the cold war.[119] Prior to the outbreak of the superpower conflict, the United States had shown little interest in Yugoslavia and the Balkans,[120] and during the Second World War, Washington mainly contented itself to following the British policy line with regard to the region.[121]

The beginning of the cold war brought an entirely new situation and the Balkans became a region where the superpowers were fiercely competing to extend their sphere of influence. As a matter of fact, it was the unstable and tense situation in the Balkans, and more particularly fears that the vacuum resulting from the suspension of British aid to Greece and Turkey would be filled by the Soviet Union, which triggered President Truman to announce the famous Truman doctrine, making it "the policy of the United States to support free peoples who are resisting attempted subjugation by armed minorities or by outside pressure".[122]

In the immediate post-war period US-Yugoslav relations were rather tense. Although the Stalin-Churchill agreement on the Balkans (October

1944) was "to go fifty-fifty about Yugoslavia",[123] by the time of the Truman doctrine, the country had clearly opted for the Stalinist model and was part of the Eastern bloc. Other factors overshadowing the relationship between both countries was Tito's claims on Carinthia (Austria) and Trieste (Italy) as well as Yugoslavia's support for the Greek communist rebels in the civil war.[124]

With the Stalin-Tito rupture of June 1948 the parameters of US-Yugoslav relations radically changed.[125] Being the first serious challenge to the strong US conviction that the communist states were a monolithic bloc, the events in Yugoslavia were considered to be a watershed in East-West relations. The US Ambassador in Belgrade talked about the Tito rebellion representing an "outstanding political possibility for the United States' policy inside the Soviet sphere" and he called Yugoslavia the "sole apparent agency for undermining Soviet influence in East Europe".[126] Washington strongly hoped that Tito's defection from the Soviet bloc would set an example for the other communist satellites and mark the beginning of the erosion of Moscow's position in the Balkans and Central Europe.

Yugoslavia's new and independent course was also seen to provide important gains from a strategic point of view. Depriving the Soviet Union of easy access to naval bases on the Adriatic, it was a major asset for the defence of both Italy and Greece.

The developments in Yugoslavia totally reversed US policy towards Belgrade. When the Soviet economic boycott and the stationing of Soviet and Eastern European troops along the Yugoslav border nearly brought the Tito regime to its knees,[127] the US was all too eager to step in with both economic and military assistance.[128] In December 1949, the American government went as far as giving Yugoslavia the guarantee of support in case of an attack by the Cominform countries[129] and in 1951 the possibility of Yugoslavia's membership of NATO was even considered.[130]

The great importance Washington was attaching to the first breach in the communist bloc is also illustrated by the unconditional nature of US support. Although it was hoped that Titoism would ultimately make way for a pluralist democratic regime, this was not made a prerequisite for the receipt of American aid. Despite a normalisation of Soviet-Yugoslav relations in 1954 following Stalin's death,[131] and the unilateral suspension by Tito of military cooperation with the US (1957),[132] the Eisenhower administration decided to continue to provide the country with economic support, an offer which Yugoslavia was all too eager to accept.

Throughout the cold war period, US policy towards Yugoslavia was characterised by a high degree of continuity. Despite the increasing criticism on behalf of Congress,[133] succeeding US administrations, believing that Titoism was far more preferable than a Soviet-dominated Yugoslavia, were ready to close an eye to the faults of Yugoslavia's one party-regime and the strong anti-western tone adopted by the non-alignment movement.

Even when appeals for a redefinition of US policy also started to come from the State Department they were flatly rejected. When Laurence Silberman, US Ambassador to Yugoslavia from May 1975 to January 1977, blamed US policy for having become outmoded and severely criticised the asymmetrical character of the relationship[134] in an article in *Foreign Policy,* the US government was quick to dissociate itself from Silberman's point of view.[135]

It would take the end of the East-West conflict for the US' preferential treatment of Yugoslavia to come to an abrupt end. A pure product of the cold war, US policy was deprived of its foundations and was reformulated on the basis of entirely new criteria. The message of US Ambassador Warren Zimmermann, arriving in Belgrade in March 1989, was totally different from that of his predecessors.[136] Respect for human rights, the application of democratic principles and the development of a market economy were to become the new guiding principles for US-Yugoslav relations.

The US administration, strongly supported by Congress, was especially worried about Serbia's poor record of human rights in Kosovo. In his book on the origins of the Yugoslav crisis, Zimmermann goes as far as calling it "the most serious human rights problem west of the Soviet Union".[137] In Congress, Senators Robert Dole (R., Kansas) and Alfonse D'Amato (R., New York), who during a visit to the region in the summer of 1990 had been prevented from meeting with the Albanian population in Pristina, were particularly active in drawing attention to the problem.[138]

Following the peaceful revolutions in Central Europe, Yugoslavia was very quickly loosing its privileged position in international relations and now faced a situation where it had to compete with its many "liberated" neighbours for US aid and attention. It was no longer the only, nor the best pupil in the class and this had serious implications for its relations with Washington. No longer an important pawn on the international chess-board, Yugoslavia lost its unique place and with it the associated advantages.

When trying to understand the initial US reaction to the Yugoslav crisis, it is very important to keep this changed relationship in mind. By 1991, Yugoslavia was no longer of strategic interest to the US, nor was there an imminent danger that the conflict would spill over into a major East-West conflict. The crisis was dismissed as a local problem, which could best be handled by the Yugoslav peoples themselves.

## Keeping Hands Off

Before elaborating on the role of the Bush administration in the Yugoslav crisis, it is relevant to first rectify the frequent misconception that the outbreak of the conflict took the United States entirely by surprise. Several factors indicate that this was not the case.

Back in the summer of 1990, the US government had received warnings from the CIA that the situation in Yugoslavia was evolving in the wrong direction along with the prediction of a possible breakup of the country, "most probably in the next 18 months".[139]

Also at the highest levels of the Bush administration, there was no lack of knowledge or expertise on Yugoslavia. Both National Security Adviser Brent Scowcroft and Deputy-Secretary of State Lawrence Eagleburger had served in the US embassy in Belgrade in their early careers and spoke Serbo-Croat. They knew the Balkan region and its history very well and were conscious of its explosive character.[140] Warren Zimmermann, the US Ambassador in Yugoslavia, had also previously warned of the possibility of a violent breakup in late 1989.[141]

Despite these warnings and the understanding that the situation was on the verge of escalating into a serious crisis, Yugoslavia continued to be a low priority for the US government. In the late summer of 1990, there was an attempt to bring the possibly dangerous developments in Yugoslavia to the attention of the European allies. A cable was sent out informing them about the grim outlook sketched by the CIA and suggesting discussion of the situation within the NATO framework and at the forthcoming CSCE Summit in November.[142] With the exception of Austria and Hungary, most European governments played down US concerns as being exaggerated, and France fiercely resisted discussing the matter either in NATO or at the next CSCE meeting hosted by Paris.[143] Washington did not insist and was definitely not willing to go it alone.[144] German reunification and events in Central Europe as well as the crisis in Iraq were much more important priorities at the time and were absorbing the full attention of the top-level US policy-makers.

Throughout 1990 and the first half of 1991, the US government restrained itself primarily to a declaratory policy on Yugoslavia, urging respect for human rights, advocating the transition towards a democratic regime and a market economy and expressing support for the continued unity of the country.[145] The main reasoning behind this policy was that the progress towards democracy and economic reform could best be realised by maintaining a unified Yugoslavia. Taking into account the multi-ethnic population of most of the republics, it was expected that the breakup of the country would be accompanied by violence and was therefore rejected. At the same time, however, the US made it clear that it did not intend to intervene in Yugoslavia's internal affairs, nor was it willing to use force to impose continued unity.[146] Coercive unity was associated with Milosevic's design for a centralised, Serb-dominated Yugoslavia and could therefore not be defended by Washington.

The person thought to provide the best guarantee for realising the triple objective of democracy, market reform and unity was Ante Markovic, the reform-oriented Prime Minister of the federal government, who after coming into power in March 1989 launched a major economic reform programme. However, when it came to concrete help for the realisation of his ideas, Markovic had to content himself primarily with verbal support from the Bush administration. When visiting Washington in October 1989, he was brutally confronted with the new reality that Yugoslavia was no longer alone in applying for US funds, but was in fierce competition with other Central European countries which were quickly moving towards a market economy and which seemed to have a higher probability of success than Yugoslavia. Markovic met with several members of the US government, including President Bush, but did not succeed in getting any guarantees for the financial backing of his plans.[147]

That Washington did not intend to develop an activist policy towards the emerging crisis in Yugoslavia is very well illustrated by the message given by Secretary of State James Baker during his one-day visit to Belgrade on 21 June 1991, a few days before Croatia and Slovenia unilaterally declared their independence.[148] Once again expressing support for Yugoslavia's territorial integrity and warning that the United States would not recognise unilateral secession, Baker added that it was "up to the people of Yugoslavia" to overcome their problems.[149] In other words, he did not consider it the task of the United States to intervene or to sort out the country's imminent crisis.[150]

In his memoirs, Secretary of State James Baker refers to his visit as "one of the most frustrating I'd had as Secretary of State". He realised that his appeal for the maintenance of unity was not having the slightest impact on the different leaders. Feeling that he was confronted with a no-win situation, his visit further strengthened his conviction that it was not in the US interest to become too heavily involved in Yugoslavia.

It has also to be taken into account that at the time of the outbreak of the Yugoslav crisis many other important dossiers such as the aftermath of the Gulf war, the resumption of the Middle East peace talks, and the unstable situation in the Soviet Union[151] were fully absorbing US attention.[152] Having just completed a major mission in the Gulf, where it had invested enormous financial and human resources, the US was not eager to embark upon a new rather risky foreign-policy adventure, which, furthermore, could negatively affect the euphoria following the victory in the Gulf.

In addition, the crisis in Yugoslavia was not considered to affect US vital interests. It was seen as a regional conflict which was occurring on Europe's doorstep and therefore could best be handled by the Europeans themselves. In his memoirs, Baker does not deny that US readiness to let the European Community take the lead also had to do with a certain irritation with Europe's political ambitions. Yugoslavia was regarded "as good a test as any" of the Twelve's capacity to "act as a unified power".[153] As a matter of fact, the Bush administration was all too happy that the EC was ready to burn its fingers on Yugoslavia. Many in the US considered the Yugoslav crisis as a real quagmire, feeling that as long as the Yugoslavs themselves were not ready to lay down their arms, little could be done to stop the fighting, taking the attitude of what Susan Woodward described as the typical "new world fatalism about old world nationalism".[154]

A final factor explaining US reticence was the upcoming presidential elections.[155] Taking into consideration that one of the main criticisms of President Bush was that he had concentrated too much on foreign policy and cared too little about domestic problems, one realises that an activist policy towards a conflict in "a faraway country between people of whom the Americans knew nothing" was indeed not a very attractive option for a campaigning President.

*Supporting the European Community*

At the outbreak of the Yugoslav conflict in late June 1991, the United States initially maintained its position of support for Yugoslav unity and issued declarations condemning Slovenia and Croatia's unilateral actions. Although these two breakaway republics were most advanced in their economic reforms and had elected non-communist governments, the United States was in the first place concerned about the negative effects of their acts on the stability of the region, fearing that a dissolution of the country would be attended with a lot of violence. Furthermore, Yugoslavia was considered to set a dangerous precedent for the Soviet Union and other countries of Central Europe with different nationalities.

This cautious US policy can be related to the Bush administration's generally prudent approach *vis-à-vis* revolutionary movements.[156] When for example, President Bush in the beginning of August 1991 visited Kiev and gave what would become known as his "chicken speech", he was very cautious not to support Ukrainian aspirations for independence from the Soviet Union. He warned the Ukrainian parliament that "freedom is not the same as independence" and that "Americans will not support those who seek independence in order to replace a far-off tyranny with a local tyranny".[157] His visit was in the first place meant to express full support for the central government of President Gorbachev, and make it clear that secessionist movements were not to count on the backing of the United States.

When, however, by the end of June the war in Croatia was escalating and the maintenance of Yugoslavia's unity was increasingly associated with the use of violence, the US started to adopt a more flexible approach. On 30 June, Deputy-Secretary of State Lawrence Eagleburger, in an interview on CNN, stated that "We never said never", when asked about the possible recognition of Slovenia.[158] Also President Bush, in an interview with journalists on 8 July, confirmed that if the dissolution of Yugoslavia were peaceful, the United States "would have no difficulties with that".[159]

Throughout the summer and autumn of 1991, the United States limited itself primarily to supporting the European Community's efforts in handling the crisis.[160] It first supported the EC-brokered Brioni Agreement, and then on several occasions endorsed the EC peace conference chaired by Lord Carrington. On 8 November the EC announced the adoption of sanctions against Yugoslavia, and President Bush, visiting The Hague the following day, declared that the US would do the same.[161] In contrast to the EC who afterwards reintroduced positive measures for Bosnia and Herzegovina, Croatia, Macedonia and Slovenia,[162] the US imposed sanctions on the whole of Yugoslavia, arguing that the continuing economic interdependence of the different republics would undermine the efficiency of selective application.[163] This difference in approach reflects the fact that the EC was already increasingly moving in the direction of recognition, while the US was still holding to its preferred option of a loose association among the different republics.

When addressing the question "Can We Do More" before the Senate Foreign Relations Committee, Ralph Johnson, Principal Deputy Assistant-Secretary for European and Canadian Affairs, defended the US low-key role on two grounds.[164] Firstly, he refers to the desperate character of the situation, stating that "the world community cannot stop Yugoslavs from killing one another so long as they are determined to do so". Secondly, he defends the earlier mentioned viewpoint of Secretary of State James Baker that it is appropriate for the EC to take the lead, "because we believe that Europe has the most at stake in this crisis, and because European leverage – economic as well as political – is in general greater than ours".

The statement is not free from contradiction. If the situation in Yugoslavia is so hopeless and can only be reversed by the peoples of Yugoslavia themselves, why does the United States put so much faith in the ability of the Europeans to solve the crisis? Is it not rather cynical to claim that nothing could be done while at the same time urging the EC to take the lead in bringing a negotiated and peaceful solution to the conflict?

The American determination not to become immersed in the crisis against its will is also well illustrated by its initial reluctance with regard to UN involvement. When France, in September 1991, presented the UN Security Council with a draft resolution which also included a mandate for the sending of European peace-keeping troops to Croatia, the US, fearing that sooner or later its own troops might have to intervene, wanted only to go as far as supporting the imposition of an arms embargo.[165] In November the question of the sending of UN peace-keeping forces came up again, but the US only approved the resolution to send the UN special envoy Cyrus Vance to Serbia and Croatia[166] when it was absolutely clear that the eventual sending of troops did not necessarily require a US involvement.[167]

Whether the Bush administration wanted it or not, the increasing involvement of the United Nations indirectly implied enhanced responsibilities for the United States. As a permanent member of the UN Security Council, Washington has a strong influence on the decisions taken within this international framework. Also, the fact that Cyrus Vance, the special UN envoy for Yugoslavia, was a former US Secretary of State, who had close relations with Lawrence Eagleburger, was seen by many as the beginning of an increased US involvement.

*The Recognition Question*

During the first months the United States generally supported the EC's measures in trying to address the crisis and cooperation over Yugoslavia went rather smoothly. It was when it came to the question of recognising Slovenia and Croatia that the first serious tensions started to emerge.

Defending the view that the new framework for relationships between the different Yugoslav republics was to be negotiated peacefully and democratically, the US considered recognition as an important instrument for pressurising the warring parties and therefore deemed that this tool of leverage was to be preserved as long as possible.[168] Washington's position was thus very much in line with that of most EC Member States but opposed to that of Germany, who saw recognition as a way of bringing the conflict to a halt.

By November 1991, the US realised that the EC Member States were increasingly facing difficulties in trying to make Germany keep ranks, therefore the highest levels in the US government, including President Bush himself, tried to convince Bonn not to go ahead with recognition.[169] As was the case for Germany's European partners, their actions were without results. Instead of the majority of EC Member States convincing Germany, it was Bonn, taking advantage of the Europeans' obsession with maintaining unity, who hauled the others into recognition, leaving the US in an isolated position.[170]

That the US was not successful in changing the German position is not surprising. By November 1991, pressure from German public opinion was extremely high and Chancellor Kohl had on several occasions publicly announced that Germany would go ahead with recognition. As with the Yugoslav crisis in general, the US did too little, too late.[171] If it really had wanted to prevent Germany from going its own way, it should have started lobbying at a much earlier stage and the pressure should have been much stronger. In order to be credible, Washington should have developed a strategy and come up with concrete alternatives for dealing with the crisis. However, the Bush administration was not willing to show leadership, nor was it ready to have an argument with a major ally over the recognition question.[172] A good relationship with the newly unified Germany was considered to be more important.

Taking into account the earlier German reticence to support US efforts in the Gulf,[173] the recognition episode was another painful incident in the US' relationship with the reunified Germany, showing that for the time being the dream of "partnership in leadership" was far from being a reality.

The recognition incident confronted the US with the disadvantages of its policy of non-involvement. Having adopted a low profile, it had to face the reality that it would not always be in agreement with the party to whom it had left the handling of the crisis. Less responsibility unmistakenly also implied less influence on the course of events and less leverage over its allies.

The EC's recognition was followed by many other countries and led to increasing pressure on the Bush administration from the well-organised Croatian lobby in the US to do the same. It was, however, clear to Washington that the recognition of Slovenia and Croatia could not be isolated from that of Bosnia and Herzegovina or that of Macedonia. Those republics had not violated international law by seceding unilaterally but had prepared for their independence in a democratic way.[174] It was therefore considered unfair to refuse them recognition. Contrary to the EC, which seemed to have totally lost interest in the recognition question after January 1992, the US wanted to send the message that it was concerned about the fate of the other republics, even when they had populations with a majority of Muslims.[175] The Bush administration argued that recognition would imply the internationalisation of the emerging problems in Bosnia and Herzegovina.[176] This was expected to have an appeasing effect on the Serbs and was seen as a way of preventing the partition of that republic amongst the Serbs and the Croats, a scenario which had been frequently discussed between Tudjman and Milosevic.

The question was further examined with the EC Member States and led to the first joint US-EC declaration in the Yugoslav crisis. The deal agreed between the transatlantic partners was that Washington declared that it would "positively consider" the recognition of Slovenia and Croatia and that the US and the EC would coordinate their policy towards Serbia and Montenegro and examine the requests for recognition of Bosnia and Herzegovina and Macedonia.[177] The ultimate result of these bilateral consultations was that both the EC[178] and the US[179] would recognise Bosnia and Herzegovina in the first week of April. Pressure from the EC and fears for the fall of the pro-American Mitsotakis government in Greece deterred Washington from proceeding with the recognition of Macedonia.[180] Its earlier position against differential treatment of the republics did not seem to count anymore.

The sudden haste with which the US wanted to proceed with the recognition of Bosnia and Herzegovina raises certain questions as to the underlying motives of this act. While a few months before the American government had been criticising Germany for its early recognition of Slovenia and Croatia and had radically refuted the argument that recognition would have an appeasing effect on the warring parties, it was now reasoning along exactly the same lines.

As Germany before, the US government entirely ignored the advise of the UN and Cyrus Vance who were arguing against recognition.[181] Although many, including the CIA,[182] had warned that the recognition of Bosnia and Herzegovina might give the Serbs a pretext to start fighting in this multi-ethnic republic, the US refused to prepare for the eventual negative effects of recognition, rejecting the pleas of the Bosnian President, Izetbegovic, to send peace-keeping troops.[183] The only concession made was that the UN peace-keepers, who were about to arrive in Croatia would set up their headquarters in Sarajevo.[184]

Although the real impulse for the conflict in Bosnia and Herzegovina was given when the EC in January 1992 recognised Slovenia and Croatia, leaving the Bosnian Muslims and Croats in a Serb-dominated rump Yugoslavia, the United States, in the spring of 1992, still refused to defend what it had recognised as a state and was not ready to invest time and effort in the prevention of a conflict many observers had been forewarning. The EC had sent observers and, in the framework of the EC peace conference, had tried to negotiate an agreement on principles for new constitutional arrangements in Bosnia and Herzegovina.[185] An increased US involvement, especially through the sending of UN peace-keeping troops, could have made a difference. However, Washington remained faithful to what was the main guiding principle in its policy towards the former Yugoslavia, namely that no US troops were to be involved. The military option, which was probably the only way through which the outbreak of the conflict in Bosnia and Herzegovina could possibly have been prevented, continued to be closed. As the prime concern when recognising Croatia and Slovenia had been to maintain unity in the European camp, recognition of Bosnia and Herzegovina was much more motivated by the preoccupation with the preservation of transatlantic solidarity than that it was by its effects on the situation on the ground.

*The War Spreads to Bosnia and Herzegovina*

The outbreak of the war in Bosnia and Herzegovina in the spring of 1992 raised fears that the conflict in the former Yugoslavia might spark off a Balkan-wide confrontation and made it increasingly difficult for the US to play down the conflict as a purely local affair where it had no interests at stake.[186]

Rather than increasing its own involvement in the crisis, Washington decided to step up pressure on its European allies to adopt a tougher stance, especially with regard to the Serbs, who were seen more and more as the main aggressors in the conflict.

When meeting with the EC Foreign Ministers in Lisbon on 24 May in the framework of an aid conference for the former Soviet Union, Secretary of State James Baker, talking about "a humanitarian nightmare in the heart of Europe" did not hide his impatience with the Twelve and their impotence to face the Serb aggression. In Baker's words, "anyone who is looking for reasons not to act, or arguing somehow that action in the face of this nightmare is not warranted at this time... is on the wrong wavelength".[187]

While Baker considered that this harsh language was justified because the Europeans needed a "push" and "were to be prodded into action by our private and, more important, public diplomacy", his words provoked the necessary irritation in Europe, especially in France.[188] It was considered all too easy for the US to criticise the EC inaction while Washington itself continued to stay on the sidelines. Paris, which traditionally had defended the position of the Serbs was in addition having difficulties with the US request to isolate Milosevic.

Although it was not welcomed very much, US pressure nevertheless had its effects. A few days after the Lisbon encounter, the EC adopted a sanctions package against Serbia and Montenegro and, on 30 May, France supported the US proposal for UN Resolution 757 imposing a complete trade embargo on Serbia and Montenegro.[189]

The Bush government complemented these acts with a number of unilateral initiatives such as the recalling of Warren Zimmermann, the US Ambassador in Belgrade, the closing of two Yugoslav consulates in the US, and the suspension of the landing rights of the Yugoslav Airlines, JAT.[190]

At no point was there any question of the United States taking the lead in addressing the crisis. Washington adhered to its earlier policy of leaving the initiative to the EC and the UN. It, however, increasingly stepped up pressure on these two actors to take into account its own interpretation of the conflict and did not hesitate to exploit its position as a permanent member of the Security Council to realise a complete trade embargo against Serbia and Montenegro, who in its eyes were the main culprits in the war in Bosnia and Herzegovina.

*Strengthening Humanitarian Relief Efforts*

In the summer months of 1992, public pressure on the US government "to do something" about the deteriorating situation in Bosnia became increasingly strong.

In late July, presidential candidate William J. Clinton made the war in Bosnia and Herzegovina one of the few and most important foreign-policy issues in the election campaign. Exploiting the frustration of the American public with US inaction, Clinton on 26 July issued a statement saying that "the US should take the lead in seeking United Nations Security Council authorisation for airstrikes against those who are attacking relief efforts. The United States should be prepared to lend appropriate military support to that operation."[191]

Although the Bush team tried to capitalise on the proposal to exemplify Clinton's inexperience in the foreign-policy field, it could not prevent the intervention from further intensifying the debate on US policy in Bosnia and Herzegovina, increasing the pressure on the government to abandon its low-key approach to the conflict.

Public indignation with the US' passivity was further raised when, by late

July, the first images of detention camps, evoking memories of the Holocaust, were appearing on television.[192] The caution with which the Bush administration reacted to this information on ongoing cruelties is characteristic of the extreme reluctance to become involved in the crisis displayed by the US. Even though the State Department had been receiving indications of the existence of the camps as early as May 1992,[193] Assistant-Secretary of State for European and Canadian Affairs Thomas Niles, when testifying before the Subcommittee on Europe and the Middle East on 4 August 1992, argued that so far there was not enough information to confirm their existence.[194]

Not wanting to commit troops and become involved in a military conflict in the middle of an election year, the Bush administration tried to appease the increasing criticism by giving its policy towards Bosnia and Herzegovina a humanitarian tinge. In June 1992, following the Serb siege of Sarajevo, the UN Security Council agreed to send 1,000 peace-keepers to protect the city's airport.[195] President Bush agreed that once the airport was reopened American aeroplanes would participate in flying humanitarian aid into Sarajevo. However, no American troops would be committed.[196]

In the meantime, the suffering of the Bosnian people and the question whether or not military intervention could bring an end to the conflict was increasingly being discussed in the press. By late June 1992 some in the State Department, while continuing to exclude unilateral military intervention, were willing to discuss the option of multilateral airstrikes with the purpose of creating the necessary conditions for the delivery of humanitarian relief provided that they took place in the framework of the UN.[197] The question arises how serious this proposal was, as the US continued to refuse to follow the airstrikes with the sending of ground troops necessary to complete the mission.

The Pentagon left no doubt that it adamantly opposed the use of airstrikes, arguing that without a well-defined mission and a clear set of objectives, the use of force was an irresponsible act.[198] The lessons of Vietnam, and even more those of Lebanon 1983, where more than 200 US marines had died in a terrorist attack, were still very much on the military's mind.[199] Another factor reinforcing their reluctance was the realisation that any military intervention would primarily place the burden on the US as it could not possibly be led by Washington's European allies.

Despite the reticence of the military, the US government in early August, nevertheless introduced a draft for a UN Security Resolution demanding permission to use "all necessary means" to protect the delivery of relief supplies in Sarajevo.[200] Besides the pressure of public opinion, a factor playing an important role in the US adopting a firmer position towards the developments in Bosnia and Herzegovina was the increasing concern that the conflict would spill over to the wider Balkan region. If the fighting spread to the largely Albanian-populated region of Kosovo or to the multi-ethnic Republic of Macedonia, it was feared that the war could involve neighbouring countries such as Greece, Bulgaria as well as Turkey. Unlike the conflict in Bosnia and Herzegovina, the prevention of a wider Balkan war was considered to be of "vital interest" to the United States.

The EC Member States, and particularly France, who were willing to provide part of the necessary troops to protect the humanitarian envoys, only supported the US-proposed resolution when it had been clarified that the use of "all necessary means" did not include the use of aerial bombardments against the Serbs, fearing that such action would endanger the lives of its soldiers on the ground.[201]

Following the London Conference (26 to 28 August 1992), the UN Security Council agreed to extend the mandate of UNPROFOR to facilitate the delivery of humanitarian assistance to Bosnia and Herzegovina, but allowed troops to use force only if they were attacked or impeded.[202] As a matter of fact, the United States and more particularly Lawrence Eagleburger, who had succeeded Secretary of State James Baker, played a central role in the meeting, leading to a situation where the EC and UN sponsored conference on the former Yugoslavia would be in permanent session.[203]

A final major UN resolution – in the adoption of which the Bush administration played an important role – was the one imposing a ban on military flights in the airspace of Bosnia and Herzegovina.[204] Again the fact that the European allies were having troops on the ground while the US did not led to a divergence of views among the Atlantic partners.

While Washington advocated the use of force against violators of the ban, both London and Paris vehemently opposed such an option, fearing that it would affect the security of the UN peace-keeping troops. Having no troops on the ground, the US was in a weak negotiating position and it is therefore not surprising that it was the European position which ultimately prevailed.[205]

Towards the end of the Bush administration, the government further tried to increase pressure on the Serb aggressor. It advocated that there should be a start to the identification of those responsible for the massacres and crimes against humanity and a re-examination of the arms embargo against the government of Bosnia and Herzegovina.[206]

The main argument of the US government in favour of the lifting of the arms embargo against the Bosnian Muslims was that the embargo played into the hands of the well-armed Serbs while prejudicing the Muslim population who was being deprived of its sovereign right of self-defence.[207]

The Europeans radically rejected this option as they expected that lifting the embargo would sharply increase the intensity of the fighting, further increasing the number of war victims as well as threatening the security of the UN troops.

As we know today, the question of the lifting of the arms embargo would continue to be the subject of a lively debate in Congress during the first Clinton administration, once again illustrating how the absence of US troops and the involvement of European soldiers led on both sides of the Atlantic to quite different proposals as to how the conflict could best be addressed.

The increasingly tough line adopted during the last two months of the Bush administration had primarily to do with mounting fears that the conflict would spread to cover the entire Balkan region. President Bush was especially concerned that Milosevic might exploit the transitional period between the two administrations to further strengthen the position of the Serbs.[208] Wanting to draw a clear line beyond which the Serb leader was not to move without provoking a harsh American answer, President Bush, on 28 December 1992, issued a clear warning to the Serb leaders in Belgrade not to provoke a conflict in Kosovo.[209]

At least at the time Milosevic seems to have taken the warning seriously. When taking into account the earlier absolute refusal of the US to become involved in the conflict, it is very much the question to what extent the Bush administration would really have been willing to follow up its rhetoric by concrete action.

*Evaluating the Role of the Bush Administration*

In contrast to the first case study where the United States followed a well-defined and engaged policy of trying to maintain NATO as Europe's principal security organisation, the main concern and aim in dealing with the Yugoslav crisis seems to have been not to become involved.[210]

When by the late 1980s increasing tensions among Yugoslavia's different republics made the CIA conclude that a worst-case scenario of a violent break-up of the country was not to be excluded, the United States supported a "unity and democracy" policy, urging the country to move ahead on the road towards democracy and a market economy while at the same time maintaining national unity. In order to realise this double objective Washington primarily counted on the Yugoslav peoples themselves, making it clear that it was not willing to use force to maintain the country's unity. Even though there were attempts to draw the attention of the European allies to the deteriorating situation, no serious mediation efforts to set up a new constitutional framework for Yugoslavia were made. At this moment both the US and the European Community lost an important chance for preventive diplomacy.

When the crisis ultimately erupted in June 1991, Washington adhered to its policy of non-involvement. The eagerness of the European Community to take the lead made it all the more easy to adopt a low-key role and the Bush administration primarily limited itself to supporting the EC position.

The recognition of Slovenia and Croatia did not lead to a change in American strategy, although it was a painful event for the US, who did not agree with the German analysis that independence would bring peace, and also meant Washington had to confront setbacks as a result of its policy of non-involvement. Washington exerted pressure on the European allies and especially on Germany, but did not come up with real alternatives. It continued to follow the conflict from the sidelines.

One of the few moments during which the Bush administration adopted a more active approach was on the question of the recognition of Bosnia and Herzegovina. The major flaw of US policy was that while it argued that recognition would lead to an internationalisation of the conflict and therefore deter Serbian aggression, it refused to provide the necessary troops to guarantee the security of the newly independent state. As most observers had predicted, the war in Bosnia and Herzegovina very soon escalated and the young state was entirely left on its own to defend its borders.

When in May 1992 the US government came under increasing pressure from public opinion to "do something" about the conflict, it opted for a purely humanitarian approach to the crisis. It started to make use of its privileged position in the United Nations to increasingly isolate the Serbs which it considered to be the main culprits of the war and to provide aid to the suffering population of Sarajevo and Bosnia and Herzegovina.

At the same time, however, it made sure that its policy of non-involvement and "prudence and caution" was maintained.[211] If by the end of the Bush administration, the rhetoric had somewhat changed, the essence of US policy had not. At no moment did Washington seriously consider the option of sending troops to Bosnia and Herzegovina and when it supported the sending of humanitarian aid in the framework of the UN, US soldiers were not to be involved. Also when the possibility of airstrikes was discussed, the US was not willing to follow strikes up by a presence on the ground, which seems to indicate that they were never a serious option.

Unlike the EC, which was very keen to take the lead in the crisis but very soon proved not to have the capacities to do so, the policy of the Bush administration was the result of the deliberate choice not to get its fingers burned in what many in this administration considered to be a hopeless conflict. When the fighting spread from Croatia to Bosnia and Herzegovina and risks for an overall Balkan war increased, Washington started to play a more active role in the framework of the United Nations but continued to refuse any leadership position.

The history of US involvement in the Balkans was essentially confined to the cold war period and when the East-West confrontation had been overcome, the United States once again seemed to loose interest in this faraway region. The fact that in the first years of the Yugoslav crisis, Russia was too preoccupied with its own internal problems, made it all the more tempting for the Bush administration to adopt a low-key approach.

It was to take many more unsuccessful attempts to end the fighting before the United States, under the Clinton administration, was finally willing to accept the lessons of the First World War – that what happened in Yugoslavia mattered for European security – and accepted the need to become a central player in the peace process of Bosnia and Herzegovina.

## Yugoslavia and the Transatlantic Relationship

> Nothing is simple in the Balkans. History pervades everything and the complexities confound even the most careful study.[212]

Although Lord Owen, the co-chairman of the Steering Committee of the International Conference on the Former Yugoslavia, is certainly right when he refers to the extreme complexity of the situation in the Balkans as one of the major reasons why the Western powers faced such huge difficulties in addressing the crisis, one should not forget that the situation was further complicated by the fact that the Yugoslav crisis was the first post-cold war conflict in Europe occurring in a period during which the United States and the European Community were still in the middle of the process of adjusting their institutions and instruments to the new world. As a matter of fact, the crisis itself would in the end have an important impact on the shaping of the new European security architecture, providing both allies with a number of interesting lessons about the post-1989 world and having important consequences for the transatlantic relationship.

The first message Yugoslavia undoubtedly brought home was that despite the disappearance of the communist threat and a firm anchoring of the united Germany into NATO, important challenges to European security still continued to exist. Although it was generally agreed that the threats posed by nationalism, terrorism and massive flows of refugees were less serious than those of a nuclear war, they could not simply be ignored but required the European security organisations to develop specific strategies and instruments to deal with them.

The crisis also turned out to be an important test for the capabilities and commitment of the transatlantic partners. The European Community failed to meet the high expectations it had raised. As a civilian power, it was not at all well-equipped to deal with an armed conflict and in addition, the EC Member States were facing tremendous difficulties when trying to speak with one voice. Despite all the rhetoric during the 1991 Intergovernmental Conference, a Common Foreign and Security Policy was still far from being a reality and the many problems the Twelve were having in trying to reach agreement on a common strategy towards Yugoslavia brought the stark reality home to those who hoped that the end of the cold war would serve as a catalyst for the development of an independent European security identity.

However, there was initially not much reason for complacency either for those pleading for the organisation of European security to be continued on an Atlantic basis. The strong reluctance of the United States to deal with the first major post-cold war European crisis contrasted sharply with Baker's pledge in Berlin (December 1989) that the United States would remain committed to playing a central role in European security. If the US and NATO were not ready to deal with Yugoslavia, the question arises as to what were the types of security challenges they were willing to address.

The Bush administration did not make the link between an American involvement in the crisis and the continuing relevance of NATO to European security. The crisis was seen as an isolated event, and its wider implications for the emerging European security architecture were ignored. By identifying the conflict as an out of area question, the US was still thinking in cold-war terms and overlooked the new reality of a unified Europe where there was no longer an iron curtain preventing instability in Central and Eastern Europe from spreading to the West.

With the Europeans disappointed by the lack of US interest in what was happening on their continent and the Americans disillusioned about the poor performance of the EC, one could have expected a major crisis in the transatlantic relationship. Although the conflict caused tensions and the presence of European troops on the ground prompted diverging views as to how the situation could best be addressed, its overall and long-term effect was that it helped to bring about a more realistic view of the respective roles of the Western European countries and the United States in the emerging European security landscape and softened the competition between the Atlantic and European security blueprints, bringing both points of view closer together.

The realisation that for the time being neither the EC nor the WEU had the capacity to embark upon major foreign-policy adventures on their own, not only gave an important boost to those pleading for the continuing organisation of European security on an Atlantic basis, but it also made Europeanists adopt a more supportive attitude towards the transformation of the Alliance. Even a country like France recognised that, rather than isolating itself with its projects for a totally independent European foreign policy, it was better to engage in the debate on the adaptation of NATO to the new European security challenges.

A first major indication that France was increasingly willing to accept the continuing centrality of NATO in the European security architecture was the agreement concluded in January 1993 with the SACEUR that French forces within the Eurocorps were to come under NATO's operational command in case of a crisis.[213] In December 1992, French officers had been given the authorisation to join their NATO colleagues in preparing a potential UN mandate to implement a Bosnian peace agreement or to protect the safe areas.[214] A further expression of France's more cooperative attitude was the combining in June 1993 of the NATO and WEU naval forces enforcing the embargo against Serbia and Montenegro.[215]

The gradual *rapprochement* of France to NATO culminated with the announcement in December 1995 by the French Minister for Foreign Affairs, Hervé de la Charette, that France would fully participate in the Military Committee and that French Defence Ministers would participate in the work of the Alliance.[216] Following the conclusion of the Dayton Peace Agreement, French troops in IFOR (the Bosnian peace implementation force) would be placed under direct NATO command.

The crisis in the former Yugoslavia also strongly influenced and sharpened the US views on the required European security architecture for the post-1989 period. Firstly, the poor performance of the EC made Washington adopt a much more relaxed attitude towards the development of a European foreign and security policy. It was clear that it would still take many years, if not decades, before CFSP could constitute a viable alternative for NATO. Secondly, – and this is the merit of the Clinton administration – the United States realised that if NATO was to remain the linchpin of European security, it had to leave more room for the development of the European pillar of NATO, including the provision of the possibility for the Europeans to intervene without the US. The NATO Summit of January 1994 introduced the concept of Combined Joint Task Forces (CJTF).[217] Such a multinational, multiservice task force was not only meant to increase the mobility and flexibility of NATO's forces, it also explored the possibility of making NATO's assets and capabilities available for purely European military operations in cases where the US did not want to intervene.[218]

As the war in Bosnia and Herzegovina dragged on during the first Clinton administration, the contradiction between the US' alleged continuing commitment to European security and its policy of non-involvement in the Yugoslav crisis became increasingly problematic. If NATO was to survive, it had to be able to address regional European crises like the one in Yugoslavia and it was important to extend stability and security beyond NATO's eastern borders.

When in the summer of 1995 the military balance in Bosnia and Herzegovina shifted in favour of the Muslims and the Croats, the US finally gave up its earlier reluctance to become directly involved and through a successful serious of airstrikes in the first half of September 1995, the Clinton administration decisively contributed to the end of the war and to the conclusion of the Dayton Agreement. As to the implementation of the agreement, Washington, although reluctantly, seemed to be willing to bring into practice what it had learned in the Yugoslav crisis and agreed to participate and contribute a major force to the NATO troops which were to implement the agreement.

The fact that the US initially only committed itself for a period of one year is revealing as regards the prudence of a United States, which was under increasing domestic pressure to give priority to internal challenges first.

## Notes

1   His first state visit to Berlin took place after the fall of the Berlin Wall in December 1989. On that occasion, he pleaded for the development of a new Atlanticism based on an institutional framework consisting of NATO, the EC and the CSCE. See "A New Europe, A New Atlanticism, Architecture for A New Era", *US Policy Information and Texts*, No.175, 12 December 1989. See chapter four, 105-109.
2   James Baker, "The Euro-Atlantic Architecture: From West to East", *US Department of State Dispatch*, vol.2, No.25, 18 June 1991 (reprint).
3   Quoted amongst many others by David Gardner, "EC Dashes into Its Own Backyard", *Financial Times*, 1 July 1991. The same European eagerness was also reflected in the words

of the Italian Foreign Minister, Gianni de Michelis, who, after a troika visit to Yugoslavia, proudly informed the press that Washington and Moscow had been informed rather than consulted about the EC initiatives to address the crisis. Quoted in Ian Traynor and Michael White, "Shuttle Mission Gets Crash Course in Balkan Realities", *The Guardian*, 1 July 1991.

4  For one of the standard works on the history of the Balkans, see Barbara Jelavich, *History of the Balkans*. (Cambridge: Cambridge University Press, 1983)(2 vol.). See also, Georges Castellan, *History of the Balkans. From Mohammed the Conqueror to Stalin* (New York: Columbia University Press, 1992).

5  Barbara Jelavich, *op.cit.*, vol.1, part 2.

6  Georges Castellan, *op.cit.*, 4-9.

7  During the Middle Ages, Bosnia, Croatia, Macedonia, Montenegro and Serbia were at one time or another all independent kingdoms. Mihailo Crnobrnja, *The Yugoslav Drama* (London: I.B. Tauris Publishers, 1994), 22-33.

8  The period of the Ottoman Empire added a third religious group to the population of the future Yugoslavia, that of the muslims. Under the constitution of 1963, the muslim population would be recognised as a separate nationality. See Mihailo Crnobrnja, *op.cit.*, 21.

9  Only Dubrovnik (an independent maritime republic) and North Dalmatia (belonging to Venice), were not part of either of the two empires. By the end of the seventeenth century, Montenegro regained its independence. Following the Congress of Berlin (1878), Bosnia Herzegovina became a protectorate of the Austrian Hungarian Empire and Serbia was recognised as a fully sovereign state. Barbara Jelavich, *op. cit.*, 352-361.

10  *Ibid.*, 134-136 and 143-157.

11  During the Second World War, the territory of Yugoslavia was partitioned among Germany, Hungary, Italy and Bulgaria. Croatia, including part of Bosnia and Herzegovina, became the "Independent State of Croatia", led by the Ustashi or a puppet regime supported by the Nazis. See Mihailo Crnobrnja, *op.cit.*, 65.

12  Although both the Chetniks, under leadership of General Draza Mihailovic and Tito's partisans were opposing German occupation, they strongly disagreed on the required strategy and they had totally different views as to post-war Yugoslavia. *Ibid.*, 66-68.

13  Steven Shelton, "A Tragedy Within A Tragedy: The Yugoslavian Partisan Movement", *Military review*, vol.74, March 1994, 23-31.

14  For Tito's biography, see for example: Stevan K. Pavlowitch, *Tito. Yugoslavia's Great Dictator* (London: C. Hurst & Co., 1992); Jasper Ridley, *Tito* (London: Constable, 1994); Richard West, *Tito and the Rise and Fall of Yugoslavia* (New York: Caroll and Graf, 1995).

15  On the system of self-management, see for example: James H. Gapinski, *The Economic Structure and Failure of Yugoslavia* (Westport: Praeger, 1993).

16  On Tito's foreign policy, see Ranko Petkovic, *Non-Aligned Yugoslavia and the Contemporary World. The Foreign Policy of Yugoslavia, 1945-1985* (Belgrade: Medunarodna Politika, 1986).

17  The six republics were Bosnia and Herzegovina, Croatia, Macedonia, Montenegro, Serbia and Slovenia. The two autonomous provinces Vojvodina (with a large Hungarian minority group) and Kosovo (with a large Albanian minority) were both situated in Serbia. They were created with the objective of preventing the position of Serbia from becoming too predominant in Tito's Yugoslavia. See Mihailo Crnobrnja, *op.cit.*, 70.

18  Lenard J. Cohen, *Broken Bonds. The Disintegration of Yugoslavia* (Westview Press:

Boulder, 1993), 26-38.
19  A concrete proposal for a confederation was submitted in October 1990. See Milan Andrejevich, "Crisis in Croatia and Slovenia: Proposal for a Confederal Yugoslavia", *Report on Eastern Europe*, No.44, 2 November 1990, 28-33.
20  No elections are organised at the national level.
21  The elections resulted in the formation of non-communist governments in Bosnia and Herzegovina, Croatia, and Slovenia. In Macedonia, elections were won by a group of non-communist and communist parties and in Serbia and Montenegro by the communists.
22  Six months before, on 23 December 1990, Slovenia had organised a referendum in which 83% of the electorate had voted in favour of independence.
23  The studies that have been written on the disintegration of Yugoslavia are numerous. See, for example: Mark Almond, *Europe's Backyard War: The War in the Balkans* (London: Heinemann, 1994); Lenard J. Cohen, *Broken Bonds. The Disintegration of Yugoslavia* (Boulder: Westview Press, 1995)(second edition); Mihailo Crnobrnja, *The Yugoslav Drama* (London-New York: I.B. Tauris Publishers, 1994); Paul Garde, *Vie et mort de la Yougoslavie* (Paris: Fayard, 1992); Misha Glenny, *The Fall of Yugoslavia. The Third Balkan War* (London: Penguin Books, 1992); Sabrina P. Ramet, *Balkan Babel: The Disintegration of Yugoslavia from the Death of Tito to Ethnic War* (Boulder: Westview Press, 1995); Laura Silber and Allan Little, *The Death of Yugoslavia* (London: Penguin Books and BBC Books, 1995); Bart Tromp, *Verraad op de Balkan. Een Kroniek.* (Nieuwegein: Uitgeverij Aspekt, 1996); Richard H. Ullman (ed.), *The World and Yugoslavia's Wars* (New York: Council on Foreign Relations, 1996).
24  David Owen, Co-Chairman of the Steering Committee of the International Conference on the Former Yugoslavia speaks about Yugoslavia as "the virility symbol of the Euro-federalists". In David Owen, "The Future of the Balkans. An Interview with David Owen", *Foreign Affairs*, vol.72, No.2, spring 1993, 1-9, 6.
25  For more details on the IGC debate on the development of a European foreign and security policy, see chapter four.
26  Maarten Lak, "The Involvement of the European Community in the Yugoslav Crisis During 1991", in Martin van den Heuvel and Jan G. Siccama (eds.), *Yearbook of European Studies. The Disintegration of Yugoslavia* (Amsterdam: University of Amsterdam, 1992), 175-185, 176 and John Zametica, "The Yugoslav Conflict", *Adelphi Paper*, No.270, summer 1992, 60.
27  See, for example, the joint declaration adopted by the EC-Yugoslavia Cooperation Council on 18 December 1990. In *EC Bulletin*, No.12, December 1990, 118.
28  See Jonathan Eyal, *Europe and Yugoslavia: Lessons from a Failure* (London: Royal United Services Institute for Defence Studies, 1993), 13-14.
29  *Ibid.*, 16.
30  For a historic overview of EC-Yugoslav relations, see Panos Tsakaloyannis, "The Politics and Economics of EEC-Yugoslav Relations", *Journal of European Integration*, vol.5, No.1, 1981, 29-52 and Patrick Artisien and Stephen Holt, "Yugoslavia and the EEC in the 1970s", *Journal of Common Market Studies*, vol.18, No.4, June 1980, 355-369.
31  The first trade agreement, concluded in 1970, covered the period 1970-73. The second trade agreement covered the years 1973-78 and the third trade and cooperation agreement (1980) was concluded for an unspecified period.
32  Panos Tsakaloyannis, *op.cit.*, 36 and 44.
33  "Declaration on the Situation in Yugoslavia. Adopted at the Extraordinary EPC Ministerial

Meeting, The Hague, 5 July 1991", in Snezana Trifunovska, *Yugoslavia Through Documents. From Its Creation To Its Dissolution* (Dordrecht: Martinus Nijhoff Publishers, 1994), 310-311. See also: *EC Bulletin*, July-August 1991, 107-108.

34  Critics observe that Brioni opened the door for the war in Croatia. Having made an end to the conflict in Slovenia, the agreement allowed the Serbs to fully concentrate on Croatia. See Susan Woodward, *Balkan Tragedy. Chaos and Dissolution After the Cold War* (Washington D.C.: The Brookings Institution, 1995), 169.

35  "Joint Declaration of the EC Troika and the Parties Directly Concerned with the Yugoslav Crisis, the so-called 'Brioni Accord', Brioni, 7 July 1991", in Snezana Trifunovska, *op.cit.*, 311-315. Later it would become clear that the Brioni agreement thanked its success primarily to an agreement which the Slovene President Milan Kucan and the Serbian President Slobodan Milosevic had concluded in January 1991. Milosevic accepted Slovenia's right to secede in exchange for Slovene recognition of the right of all Serbs to live in one state. See Laura Silber and Allan Little, *op.cit.*, 122-123; Steven L. Burg, "Negotiating A Settlement: Lessons of the Diplomatic Process", in Stephen J. Blank (ed.), *Yugoslavia's Wars: The Problem From Hell* (Carlisle Barracks: Strategic Studies Institute, 1995), 47-86, 49-50.

36  At that time the EC was still very optimistic about its ability to bring the crisis to a halt. See, for example, the words of the German Foreign Minister, Hans-Dietrich Genscher, who referred to the Brioni Agreement as "the proof of the European Community's ability to act, and its ability to contribute in an operational matter to a solution to the crisis." Quoted in *Atlantic News*, 12 July 1991.

37  The divergence of views among the Member States with regard to the issue of the recognition of the breakaway republics is further elaborated under the paragraph entitled "Germany Breaks Ranks". Cf. *infra*, 159-164.

38  "Declaration on Yugoslavia Adopted at the EPC Extraordinary Ministerial Meeting, Brussels, 27 August 1991", and "Declaration on Yugoslavia Adopted at the EPC Extraordinary Ministerial Meeting, The Hague, 3 September 1991", in Snezana Trifunovska, *op.cit.*, 333-334 and 342-343. See also *EC Bulletin*, July-August 1991, 115-116 and *EC Bulletin*, September 1991, 63.

39  Lord Carrington owed his reputation of being an extremely skilled negotiator to his success in realising a peaceful transfer of power from white to majority rule in Zimbabwe (Rhodesia).

40  Prior to the opening of the peace conference, the Twelve had negotiated a new cease-fire in Croatia, and Belgrade had accepted an extension of the activities of the EC observers to Croatia. As in the past the cease-fire would not hold for long. See "Cease-fire Agreement. Belgrade, 1 September 1991", in Snezana Trifunovska, *op.cit.*, 334-336.

41  Later a third group was created on economic relations between the republics.

42  "Declaration on Yugoslavia Adopted at the EPC Extraordinary Ministerial Meeting, The Hague, 3 September 1991", in Snezana Trifunovska, *op.cit.*, 342-343.

43  The *"force d'interposition"* would be composed of 20,000 soldiers and supported by 10,000 men in charge of logistics. It would be stationed in a *"zone de tampon"* between the warring parties in Croatia. See Hans Stark, "Dissonances franco-allemandes sur fond de guerre serbo-croate", *Politique Etrangère*, vol.57, No.2, 1992, 339-347, 344.

44  At a meeting of the Ministers of Foreign Affairs with representatives of the Yugoslav government and the Yugoslav Presidency on 29 July, France launched the idea of sending a peace-keeping force to Yugoslavia, eventually under WEU auspices. The United

Kingdom and also the Netherlands initially opposed the idea. See James B. Steinberg, "The Response of International Institutions to the Yugoslavia Conflict: Implications and Lessons", in F. Stephen Larrabee, *The Volatile Powder Keg. Balkan Security After the Cold War* (Washington D.C.: The American University Press, 1994), 233-274, 240.

45 At a meeting on 18 September, President Mitterrand and Chancellor Kohl agreed to jointly launch the proposal of a possible military intervention at the EPC and WEU meetings of the following day.

46 "Text of the Letter Addressed to Andreotti by Kohl and Mitterrand, 6 December 1990", *Agence Europe*, 10-11 December 1990.

47 "Franco-German Proposals on Political Union: Security Policy Cooperation in the Framework of the Common Foreign and Security Policy of Political Union", *Europe Documents*, No.1690, 21 February 1991.

48 Although the Netherlands generally sided with the Atlanticists during the 1991 IGC and had opposed the sending of European troops in July, the Dutch Presidency now supported the proposal. They saw it as a way of supporting the peace conference and of preventing unilateral recognition of Slovenia and Croatia by Germany. Italy also strongly favoured sending troops. Geoffrey Edwards, "European Responses to the Yugoslav Crisis: An Interim Assessment", in Reinhardt Rummel (ed.), *Toward Political Union. Planning a Common Foreign and Security Policy in the European Community* (Boulder-San Francisco-Oxford: Westview Press, 1992), 161-186, 172.

49 For a first-hand report on the WEU ministerial meeting of 18 September, see Willem Frederik van Eekelen, *Debating European Security, 1948-1998* (The Hague-Brussels: Sdu Publishers and Centre for European Policy Studies, 1998), 145-147. See also Geoffrey Edwards, *op.cit.*, 170-173 and Trevor C. Salmon, "Testing Times for European Political Cooperation: the Gulf and Yugoslavia, 1990-1992", *International Affairs*, vol. 68, No.2, 1992, 233-253, 250-252.

50 According to the so-called Kohl doctrine, history excluded any participation of German troops in military operations in former Yugoslavia.

51 See the words of a senior British official quoted in the *Financial Times* of 18 September 1991: "If the Germans do not intend to participate, they would do better to shut up." Taken from Geoffrey Edwards, *op.cit.*, 172.

52 "Declaration on Yugoslavia. Adopted at the EPC Extraordinary Ministerial Meeting. The Hague, 19 September 1991", in Snezana Trifunovska, *op.cit.*, 347. See also: *EC Bulletin*, No.9, September 1991, 63.

53 The Serbs had on several occasions expressed their opposition to a foreign military presence in Yugoslavia.

54 The four options for WEU military intervention presented were: (a) logistic underpinning and support of the work of the EC monitors, with 2,000 to 3,000 personnel; (b) escort and protection of EC monitors by armed military forces (3,000 to 5,000 personnel); (c) a peace-keeping force composed of military personnel (10,000 men) in support of monitors; (d) peace-keeping force of 20,000 military personnel. See Willem Frederik van Eekelen, *op.cit.*, 147.

55 "WEU Council of Ministers. Extraordinary Meeting on the Situation in Yugoslavia. Helsinki, 10 July 1992", in Arie Bloed and Ramses A. Wessel (eds.), *The Changing Functions of the Western European Union (WEU). Introduction and Basic Documents*. (Dordrecht-Boston-London: Martinus Nijhoff Publishers, 1994), 155.

56 On the intervention in the Adriatic, *cf. supra*, 135-136.

57  See Luisa Vierucci, "WEU: A Regional Partner of the United Nations?, *Chaillot Papers*, No.12, December 1993, 18-21.
58  *Cf. infra*, 166-167.
59  One of the aims France hoped to realise through the creation of Yugoslavia was to prevent German expansion into south-eastern Europe. See Hans-Dietrich Genscher, *Erinnerungen* (Berlin: Siedler, 1995), 930.
60  On the British relationship with Yugoslavia and more particularly with Tito during the Second World War, see Fitzroy Maclean, *Eastern Approaches* (Harmondsworth: Penguin Books, 1991) (first published in 1949). Maclean became Great Britain's personal representative to Tito in the summer of 1943. See also: Michael Lees, *The Rape of Serbia: The British Role in Tito's Grab for Power, 1943-1944* (New York: Harcourt Brace Jovanovich, 1990).
61  Quoted in John Zametica, *op.cit.*, 64. From then onwards, both Chancellor Kohl as well as Minister of Foreign Affairs Genscher would on several occasions publicly express their support for the recognition of Slovenia and Croatia.
62  For the reasoning behind the German insistence on recognition, see Hans-Dietrich Genscher: "Und was könne den Krieg in Kroatien schliesslich beenden, wenn nicht die Anerkennung und damit die Internationalisierung?, in Hans-Dietrich Genscher, *op.cit.*, 960-961.
63  Heinz-Jürgen Axt, "Hat Genscher Jugoslawien entzweit?", *Europa-Archiv*, vol.48, No.12, 1993, 351-360, 352.
64  "Declaration on the Situation in Yugoslavia. Adopted at the Extraordinary EPC Ministerial Meeting, The Hague, 5 July 1991", in Snezana Trifunovska, *op.cit.*, 310-311. See also *EC Bulletin*, Nos 7-8, July-August 1991, 107-108.
65  *Cf. supra*, 154-155.
66  At bilateral meetings between the German Chancellor and the French President in both late July as well as on 18 September, President Mitterrand exerted very strong pressure on Chancellor Kohl not to act unilaterally, but to respect the EC position with regard to recognition. The compromise declaration reached on 18 September, refers both to the right of peoples to self-determination as well as to the respect of minority rights. Quoted in Hans Stark (1992), *op.cit.*, 343. In August the French Minister of Foreign Affairs Roland Dumas had threatened his German colleague that in case of recognition, "vous renverriez les relations franco-allemandes vingt ans en arrière". *Ibid.*
67  See for example Luc Rosenzweig, "L'Allemagne, puissance protectrice des Slovènes et des Croates", *Le Monde*, 4 July 1991: "Ayant retrouvé son unité et sa souveraineté, l'Allemagne entend aujourd'hui jouer sans complexes un rôle majeur dans une région avec laquelle elle a toujours entretenu d'étroits rapports. On parle toujours, en Allemagne et en Autriche, de Laibach (Ljubljana) et d'Agram (Zagreb), villes liées à la grande époque de la monarchie austro-hongroise."
68  "EC Declaration on the Situation in Yugoslavia. Adopted at the Informal Meeting of Ministers for Foreign Affairs. Haarzuilens, 6 October 1991", in Snezana Trifunovska, *op.cit.*, 351-352. See also *EC Bulletin*, No.10, October 1991, 86-87.
69  On the meeting in Haarzuilens, see also: Hans-Dietrich Genscher, *op.cit.*, 951-954.
70  "Declaration on the Situation in Yugoslavia", in Snezana Trifunovska, *op.cit.*, 368-369. See also *EC Bulletin*, No.10, October 1991, 89-90.
71  "Declaration on Positive Measures", in Snezana Trifunovska, *op.cit.*, 425.
72  Hans-Dietrich Genscher, *op.cit.*, 958.

73  Contrary to the previous summit (Luxembourg, 28-29 June 1991), the Yugoslav question was not placed on the agenda of the Maastricht European Council. Although this decision might have been inspired primarily by the need for the Heads of State and Government to fully concentrate on the final dispositions of the Treaty on European Union, the negative effect of placing such a divisive issue on the agenda has probably also played a role.

74  On the position of Italy vis-à-vis the Yugoslav crisis, see Ettore Greco, "Italy, the Yugoslav Crisis and the Osimo Agreements", *The International Spectator*, vol.29, No.1, January-March 1994, 13-31; Sergio Romano, "L'Italie et l'Europe du Danube et des Balkans", *Politique Etrangère*, vol.57, No.2, 1992, 349-358.

75  John Newhouse, "Bonn, der Westen und die Auflösung Jugoslawiens. Das Versahen der Diplomatie – Chronik eines Skandals", *Blätter für deutsche und internationale Politik*, vol.92, No.10, 1992, 1190-1205, 1197.

76  On Greece and the crisis in Yugoslavia, see Virginia Tsouderos, "Greek Policy and the Yugoslav Turmoil", *Mediterranean Quarterly*, vol.4, No.2, spring 1993, 1-13.

77  See for example Misha Glenny, *op.cit.*, 192. He refers to two opposing positions in the Foreign Office: the British Embassy in Belgrade arguing strongly against recognition, and the Brussels lobby, referring to the many concessions received in the Maastricht negotiations, pleaded for recognition.

78  "Declaration Concerning the Conditions for Recognition of New States. Adopted at the Extraordinary EPC Ministerial Meeting. Brussels, 16 December 1991", in Snezana Trifunovska, *op.cit.*, 431-432.

79  Hans-Dietrich Genscher, *op.cit.*, 966.

80  "Opinion No.5 on the Recognition of the Republic of Croatia by the European Community and its Member States. Paris, 11 January 1992", in Snezana Trifunovska, *op.cit.*, 489-490. The Badinter Commission made a positive decision on Bosnia and Herzegovina dependent on the outcome of a referendum on independence in that republic, to be held under international supervision (*Ibid.*, 486-488). Macedonia was considered to fulfil the criteria but its recognition was opposed by Greece (*Ibid.*, 491-495).

81  Some also relate the pro-Croat attitude of Germany to the German support for the fascist Ustashi-regime in Croatia during the Second World War. Hans Stark however rejects this interpretation, since most Germans ignored the existence of a nazi-oustachi alliance. See Hans Stark (1992), *op.cit.*, 341.

82  Hanns W. Maull, "Germany in the Yugoslav Crisis", *Survival*, vol.37, No.4, winter 1995-1996, 99-130, 102-103 and 111-112; and Heinz-Jürgen Axt, *op.cit.*, 353-354.

83  See also the position of Austria, a direct neighbour of Slovenia and who already prior to the outbreak of the crisis had been pushing for recognition of its independence. In Jonathan Eyal, *op.cit.*, 6.

84  See the words of a German foreign affairs official as quoted in John Newhouse, *op.cit.*, 1195: "Für uns war das ein Problem im eigenen Hinterhof – anders als für Grossbritannien, Frankreich oder Spanien".

85  Of the 700,000 "Yugoslavs" living in Germany, the vast majority was of Croat origin. See Hans Stark (1992), *op.cit.*, 343.

86  It is interesting to note that in France exactly the opposite was taking place: the Serbs were portrayed as being the victims of secessionist Slovenes and Croats. See even President Mitterrand in an interview with the *Frankfurter Allgemeine* on 29 November 1991: "Comme vous le savez, la Croatie faisait partie du bloc nazi, pas la Serbie". Quoted in Alain Finkielkraut, *Comment peut-on être croate?* (Paris: Gallimard, 1992), 110.

87  James A. Baker III (with Thomas A. Defrank), *The Politics of Diplomacy. Revolution, War and Peace 1989-1992* (New York: G.P. Putnam's Sons, 1995), 638. *Cf. infra*, 184-185.
88  In a letter to the Dutch Presidency, the UN Secretary-General warned against the "explosive consequences" of the premature recognition of some of the Yugoslav republics and referred to the potential outbreak of "the most terrible war in Bosnia and Herzegovina". The letter was published in "Letter from the Secretary-General of the United Nations Addressed to the Minister for Foreign Affairs of The Netherlands", 10 December 1991", in Snezana Trifunovska, *op.cit.*, 428-429. Hans-Dietrich Genscher answered the UN Secretary-General that "denying recognition would only encourage the Yugoslav Peoples' Army in its "policy of conquest." Quoted in James E. Goodby, "Peacekeeping in the New Europe", *The Washington Quarterly*, spring 1992, vol.15, No.3, spring 1992, 153-171, 161.
89  The decision in late December 1991 to raise German interest rates without considering the negative effects for other EC Member States further reinforced the impression that Germany was increasingly tempted to go its own way.
90  It is argued that the recognition of Slovenia and Croatia, leaving Bosnia and Herzegovina in a rump Yugoslavia, pushed this multi-ethnic republic to independence, leading to the outbreak of a war between the Serb population of Bosnia which wanted to stay with Serbia and the Muslims and Croats who in a referendum voted for independence.
91  Franz-Josef Meiers, "Germany: The Reluctant Power", *Survival*, vol.37, No.3, autumn 1995, 82-103.
92  Pia Christina Wood, "France and the Post Cold War Order: The Case of Yugoslavia", *European Security*, vol.3, No.1, spring 1994, 129-152, 136.
93  See Article 2.7 of the UN Charter dealing with the non-interference in domestic affairs. See Nicole Gnesotto, "Lessons of Yugoslavia", *Chaillot Papers*, No.14, March 1994, 7.
94  The proposal for the resolution coincided with the discussions in the EC/WEU on the Franco-German proposal to send an "intervention force" to Croatia. See Pia Christina Wood, *op.cit.*, 136.
95  "Resolution 713 (1991) Adopted by the Security Council at its 3009th Meeting, 23 September 1991", in Snezana Trifunovska, *op.cit.*, 349-350.
96  John Zametica, *op.cit.*, 67.
97  The plan proposed a free association among the former republics, based on the European Community model of an internal market, with the free movement of goods and services and possibly also a common currency and with cooperation in the field of foreign affairs and legal matters. The institutional framework consisted of a Council of Ministers, the composition of which varied according to the topic on the agenda, a six-monthly rotating Presidency and a parliamentary assembly. Since the plan recognised the republics' sovereignty and their right to become independent if they so decided, it implicitly recognised the demise of Yugoslavia. This was unacceptable to President Milosevic and the Serbs.
98  On the peace-making efforts of Cyrus Vance in Croatia, see James E. Goodby, *op.cit.*, 159-162.
99  "Geneva Accord", in Snezana Trifunovska, *op.cit.*, 412-413. The accord consists in the Croats agreeing to lift the blockade of all JNA barracks, and in the JNA accepting to withdraw from Croatia. Both parties agree to observe an unconditional cease-fire and to facilitate the delivery of humanitarian assistance.
100 "Accord Implementing the Cease-fire Agreement of 23 November 1991. Sarajevo, 2

January 1992", in Snezana Trifunovska, *op.cit.*, 468-470.
101 "Resolution 743 (1992) Adopted by the Security Council at its 3055th Meeting, 21 February 1992", in Snezana Trifunovska, *op.cit.*, 515-517. The UN peace-keeping force numbered 13 000 military, police and civilian personnel. When later onwards, the UN also deploys troops in Bosnia and Herzegovina, the peace-keeping troops in Croatia are referred to as UNPROFOR I. For a critical evaluation of UNPROFOR I, see Alan James, "The UN in Croatia: An Exercise in Futility", *The World Today*, vol.49, No.5, May 1993, 93-95.
102 The UN troops were concentrated in so-called United Nations Protected Areas (UNPAs): Eastern Slavonia, Western Slavonia, and Krajina. In all three regions, the Serbs were the majority or a substantial minority of the population. UNPROFOR was to protect the inhabitants of the UNPAs and to verify the demilitarisation of the UNPAs. See "Concept for a United Nations Peace-Keeping Operation in Yugoslavia, November/December 1991", in Snezana Trifunovska, *op.cit.*, 418-423.
103 "Statement on Principles for New Constitutional Arrangement for Bosnia and Herzegovina", in Snezana Trifunovska, *op.cit.*, 517-519. On this so-called Cutileiro plan, named after its main EC negotiator, the Portuguese Ambassador José Cutileiro, see Steven L. Burg, *op.cit.*, 56-59. The Vance-Owen plan of January 1993 would to a large extent be inspired by this plan. See Henry Wijnaendts, *Joegoslavische Kroniek. Juli 1991-Augustus 1992* (Amsterdam: Thomas Rap, 1993), 174.
104 From then onwards the conference is jointly chaired by Cyrus Vance (for the UN) and by David Owen (for the EC).
105 Pia Christina Wood, *op.cit.*, 140 and Henry Wijnaendts, *op.cit.*, 191.
106 It is not coincidental that this is the period where the US adopts a more active stance *vis-à-vis* the crisis in the former Yugoslavia. Cf. *infra*, 188-193.
107 "Resolution 757 (1992) Adopted by the Security Council at its 3082nd Meeting, 30 May 1992", in Snezana Trifunovska, *op.cit.*, 593-599.
108 "Resolution 758 (1992) Adopted by the Security Council at its 3083rd meeting, 8 June 1992", in Snezana Trifunovska, *op.cit.*, 601-602.
109 "Resolution 776 (1992) Adopted by the Security Council at its 3114th Meeting, 14 September 1992", in Snezana Trifunovska, *op.cit.*, 720-721.
110 "Resolution 781 (1992) Adopted by the Security Council at its 3122nd Meeting, 9 October 1992", in Snezana Trifunovska, *op.cit.*, 732-733. In mid-October, Hungary and Austria would approve the establishment of an airborne early warning system (AWACS) orbit and allowed overflights so that violations of the airspace could be reported to UNPROFOR by NATO. It is however only from July 1993 onwards that the no-fly zone would also be explored by regular combat patrols. See David Owen, *Balkan Odyssey* (London: Victor Gollancz, 1995), 60.
111 See, for example: "Statement on the UN Security Council Resolution 757 of 30 May 1992. Brussels, 1 June 1992", in Snezana Trifunovska, *op.cit.*, 599. "Declaration on the Situation in Yugoslavia. Brussels, 15 June 1992", *ibid.*, 614. "Declaration on Former Yugoslavia Made by the Foreign Affairs Council of the European Community. Luxembourg, 5 October 1992", *ibid.*, 728.
112 By 1993, there are 22,639 persons serving in UNPROFOR from 32 participating states. The two largest contributors are France with 4,700 troops and the UK with approximately 3,000 troops committed. Other countries contributing are Canada (2,300), Denmark (more than 1,000), Russia (900), the Kingdom of Jordan (900), Spain (800), Nepal (700), Poland (700), Belgium (700), and the Netherlands. See Rosalyn Higgins, "The New United

Nations and the Former Yugoslavia", *International Affairs*, vol.69, No.3, 1993, 465-483, 472.
113 Briefly before Mitterrand's departure, Chancellor Kohl and the Portuguese Presidency had been informed of his move. The fact that Mitterrand did not inform his colleagues is all the more ironic since the issue of the reopening of the Sarajevo airport was discussed at the Lisbon meeting: "The European Council deplores in particular that the reopening of Sarajevo airport for humanitarian purposes, in accordance with UN Security Council resolution 758 (1992), has not been achieved. Further measures are therefore required." In "European Council Declaration on the Former Yugoslavia. Lisbon, 27 June 1992", in Snezana Trifunovska, *op.cit.*, 625-626.
114 On this question, see Wolfgang Wagner, "Le siège permanent au Conseil de Sécurité: Qui a besoin de qui: les Allemands du siège? ou le Conseil de Sécurité des Allemands?", *Politique Etrangère*, vol.58, No.4, winter 1993-1994, 1001-1009; Karl Kaiser, "Devenir membre permanent du Conseil de Sécurité: un but légitime de la nouvelle politique extérieure allemande", *ibid.*, 1011-1022.
115 Peter Schmidt, "A Complex Puzzle – the EU's Security Policy and UN Reform", *The International Spectator*, vol.29, No.3, July-September 1994, 53-66, 54.
116 Karl Kaiser, *op.cit.*, 1017-1018.
117 Nicole Gnesotto, *op.cit.*, 14-15.
118 President Mitterrand's dramatic visit to Sarajevo airport on 28 June 1992 might be seen as an attempt to refute the criticism of the voters in the upcoming referendum that Europe and France were not doing anything to solve the crisis in the former Yugoslavia.
119 For an overview of US-Yugoslav relations in the cold war period, see Nora Beloff, *Tito's Flawed Legacy. Yugoslavia and the West since 1939* (Boulder: Westview Press, 1985); John C. Campbell, *Tito's Separate Road. America and Yugoslavia in World Politics* (New York: Council on Foreign Relations, 1967); Béatrice Heuser, *Western "Containment" Policies in the Cold War. The Yugoslav Case, 1948-53* (London and New York: Routledge, 1989).
120 Barbara Jelavich, *op.cit.*, 284-285. On US-Yugoslav relations in the interwar period, see Linda Killen, *Testing the Peripheries. US-Yugoslav Economic Relations in the Interwar Years* (New York: Columbia University Press, 1994).
121 From 1943 onwards, the British policy line was to give full support to Tito and his partisans rather than to Draza Mihailovic and the Chetniks. See Nora Beloff, *op.cit.*, 87 and 99.
122 Daniel Yergin, *Shattered Peace. The Origins of the Cold War and the National Security State* (Harmondsworth: Penguin Books, 1980), 279-284.
123 Winston S. Churchill, *The Second World War. Triumph and Tragedy* (Boston: Houghton Mifflin Company, 1953), 226-228.
124 Daniel Yergin, *op.cit.*, 288-296. Relations further worsened when, in August 1946, two unarmed American transport planes violating Yugoslavia's national territory were shot down. See Béatrice Heuser, *op.cit.*, 19.
125 On the US and the Stalin-Tito rupture, see Béatrice Heuser, *op.cit.*, 20-35.
126 *Ibid.*, 63. Heuser also quotes a senior official in the State Department saying that the Russian and Cominform experts of the State Department identified the split as "probably the most important single development since the conclusion of hostilities as far as international Soviet and Communist internal affairs are concerned, on a plane with the Trotsky fall from grace." *Ibid.*, 48.
127 According to Nora Beloff, *op.cit.*, 148, it was the firm American reaction to the Korean war

(1950) which led the Soviet Union to abandon its plan to invade Yugoslavia.
128 A first loan, which was to be followed by many others, was provided in September 1949. In 1950, the US Congress adopted the Yugoslav Emergency Relief Act authorising the expenditure of US $50 million. See John C. Campbell, *op.cit.*, 24.
129 Pierre Maurer, "United States-Yugoslav Relations. A Marriage of Convenience", *Studia Diplomatica*, vol.38, No.4, 1985, 429-451, 432.
130 Béatrice Heuser, *op.cit.*, 172-174. In August 1954, Yugoslavia signed a Balkan Pact of Mutual Defence with NATO members Turkey and Greece. The treaty however remained a dead letter.
131 Soviet-Yugoslav relations were normalised in June 1956, following the signature of the Moscow declaration. Pierre Maurer, *op.cit.*, 439.
132 John C. Campbell, *op.cit.*, 39.
133 In 1963, Congress decided to deprive Yugoslavia of its Most Favored Nation (MFN) status. See Nora Beloff, *op.cit.*, 170.
134 "We treat Yugoslavia as a friend, but the Yugoslavs see the United States as the most important impediment to the world changes they seek – and they act accordingly. At the same time, they cleverly encourage our illusions by focusing our attentions on Yugoslav-Soviet relations, with assurance that we will simplistically conclude that if Yugoslavia maintains a measure of independence from Moscow, our interests are fully served." See Laurence Silberman, "Yugoslavia's 'Old' Communism: Europe's Fiddler on the Roof", *Foreign Policy*, vol.26, spring 1977, 3-27, 5.
135 See the words of Patrick Brown, the State Department spokesman in a reaction to Silberman's article: "The US has a fundamental interest in the continued independence, unity and territorial integrity of Yugoslavia". Quoted in Pierre Maurer, *op.cit.*, 449.
136 Warren Zimmermann, "The Last Ambassador. A Memoir of the Collapse of Yugoslavia", *Foreign Affairs*, vol.74, No.2, March-April 1995, 2-20, 2: "...the traditional American approach to Yugoslavia no longer made sense, given the revolutionary changes sweeping Europe... Yugoslavia no longer enjoyed the geopolitical importance that the United States had given it during the Cold War..."
137 Warren Zimmermann, *Origins of a Catastrophe. Yugoslavia and Its Destroyers – America's Last Ambassador Tells What Happened and Why* (New York: Random House, 1996), 14.
138 *Ibid.*, 127-129.
139 Dennison Rusinow, "Yugoslavia: Balkan Breakup", *Foreign Policy*, vol.83, summer 1991, 143-159, 143.
140 Lawrence Eagleburger had been US Ambassador to Yugoslavia (1977-1981) and had served as second secretary in Belgrade in the years 1962-65. Brent Scowcroft had been assistant air attaché at the same embassy in the period 1959-61 and had written his PhD on the theme of congressional attitudes towards foreign aid to Yugoslavia (and Spain). See Susan Woodwards, *op.cit.*, 155.
141 Warren Zimmermann (1996), *op.cit.*, 41.
142 Robert L. Hutchings, *American Diplomacy and the End of the Cold War. An Insider's Account of US Policy in Europe, 1989-1992* (Washington D.C.-London: The Woodrow Wilson Center Press and the John Hopkins University Press, 1997), 306-307.
143 *Ibid.*, 307.
144 Warren Zimmermann (1996), *op.cit.*, 64-65.
145 "US policy toward Yugoslavia is based on support for the interrelated objectives of democracy, dialogue, human rights, market reforms, and unity." See "Statement Released

by Department Spokesman Margaret Tutwiler, May 24, 1991", *US Department of State Dispatch*, vol.2, No.22, 3 June 1991, 395.
146 Warren Zimmermann (1996), *op.cit.*, 62.
147 David Gompert, "How to Defeat Serbia", *Foreign Affairs*, vol.73, No.4, July-August 1994, 30-47, 33.
148 For a personal account of his visit, see Baker's memoirs: James A. Baker, III, (with Thomas A. Defrank), *The Politics of Diplomacy. Revolution, War and Peace 1989-1992* (New York: G.P. Putnam's Sons, 1995), 479-483. During his visit, Baker met with Prime Minister Ante Markovic as well as with the presidents of the different republics.
149 "Excerpts from Remarks at the Federation Palace, Belgrade, Yugoslavia, June 21, 1991", *US Department of State Dispatch*, vol.2, No.26, July 1, 1991, 468.
150 The leader of Montenegro Momir Bulatovic was not impressed by Baker's visit: "When I met Mr Baker I said 'Tell me what you want from me'. He was confused about how to start the conversation with me, until they brought him his briefing book... I peeked into it and there were just two lines:
   – the smallest republic in Yugoslavia.
   – a possible fifth vote for Mesic."
   Quoted in Laura Silber and Allan Little, *op.cit.*, 165.
151 Following the August coup, the Soviet Union would become even more prominent on the US agenda.
152 James A. Baker, *op.cit.*, 636.
153 "There was another reason why we felt comfortable letting the EC handle the conflict. We had been engaged in a political battle in Brussels over the relationship of the Western European Union (WEU) – the EC's defense arm – and NATO. At its heart, this rather theological battle revolved around different conceptions of America's role in Europe. Some Europeans – certain that political and monetary union was coming and would create a European superpower – were headstrong about asserting a European defense identity in which America's role on the Continent was minimised. We had been fighting this for some time, and trying to get them to recognise that, even with a diminished Soviet threat, they still needed an engaged America. But our protestations were overlooked in an emotional rush for a unified Europe. The result was an undercurrent in Washington, often felt but seldom spoken, that it was time to make the Europeans step up the plate and show that they could act as a unified power. Yugoslavia was as good a first test as any." Taken from James A. Baker, *op.cit.*, 636-637.
154 Susan Woodward, *op.cit.*, 155.
155 See Warren Zimmermann on the Yugoslav crisis: "Nobody wanted to touch it. With the American presidential election just a year away, it was seen as a loser". Quote from Warren Zimmermann (1995), *op.cit.*, 15.
156 Michael H. Hunt, *Ideology and US Foreign Policy* (New Haven and London: Yale University Press, 1987), 92-124; Paula Franklin Lytle, "US Policy Toward the Demise of Yugoslavia: The 'Virus of Nationalism'", *East European Politics and Societies*, vol.6, No.3, fall 1992, 303-318, 308.
157 Quoted in Michael R. Beschloss and Strobe Talbott, *At the Highest Levels. The Inside Story of the End of the Cold War* (Boston-Toronto-London: Little, Brown and Company, 1993), 418.
158 Nikolaos A. Stavrou, "The Balkan Quagmire and the West's Response", *Mediterranean Quarterly*, vol.4, No.1, winter 1993, 24-45, 40.

159 "Interview with Foreign Journalists, July 8, 1991", in *Public Papers of the Presidents of the United States. George Bush* (Washington D.C.: United States Government Printing Office, 1992), 833.
160 See for example: "Statement by Press Secretary Fitzwater on Yugoslavia, July 2, 1991", in *Public Papers of the Presidents of the United States. George Bush* (Washington D.C.: United States Government Printing Office, 1992), 814; "The President's News Conference with President Mikhail Gorbachev of the Soviet Union in Moscow, July 31, 1991", *Ibid.*, 995; "Remarks at a Luncheon Hosted by Prime Minister Ruud Lubbers of the Netherlands in The Hague, November 9, 1991", *Ibid.*, 1426; "Remarks Following Discussions With Prime Minister Constantinos Mitsotakis of Greece, December 12, 1991", *Ibid.*, 1594.
161 "The President's News Conference with Prime Minister Ruud Lubbers of the Netherlands and President Jacques Delors of the Commission of the European Community in The Hague, November 9, 1991", in *Public Papers of the Presidents of the United States. George Bush* (Washington D.C.: United States Government Printing Office, 1992), 1429. The US was conscious of the fact that the impact of such sanctions would be limited as US trade with Yugoslavia only represents 5% of total Yugoslav trade.
162 *Cf. supra*, 162.
163 "Announcement of the US State Department Concerning the Trade Embargo on Yugoslavia, 6 December 1991", in Snezana Trifunovska, *op.cit.*, 426-427.
164 "US Efforts to Promote a Peaceful Settlement in Yugoslavia. Ralph Johnson, Principal Deputy Assistant-Secretary for European and Canadian Affairs. Statement before the Senate Foreign Relations Committee, Washington D.C., October 17, 1991", *US Department of State Dispatch*, vol.2, No.42, 21 October 1991, 782-785.
165 Pia Christina Wood, *op.cit.*, 131.
166 "Resolution 721 (1991) Adopted by the Security Council at its 3018th meeting, 27 November 1991", in Snezana Trifunovska, *op.cit.*, 414-415.
167 Thomas Paulsen, *Die Jugoslawienpolitik der USA 1989-1994. Begrenztes Engagement und Konfliktdynamik* (Baden-Baden: Nomos Verlagsgesellschaft, 1995), 54-55.
168 See James A. Baker, *op.cit.*, 639: "...withholding recognition (or conferring it) was the most powerful diplomatic tool available. 'Earned recognition' was one of our key points of leverage over the combatants."
169 James E. Goodby, *op.cit.*, 162.
170 *Cf. supra*, 162-164.
171 Warren Zimmermann (1996), *op.cit.*, 176-177. Zimmermann says that the US did "enough to show that we did something, but not enough to produce results."
172 The presence of an important Croatian community in the US may also have played a role.
173 *Cf. supra*, 129-133.
174 Bosnia and Herzegovina had held a referendum on independence on 29 February and 1 March 1992: 63.4% of the eligible voters participated and 99.7% voted in favour. The referendum was massively boycotted by the Serb population. Macedonia had held a referendum on 9 September 1991: 95% of the population voted in favour of independence.
175 Following the Gulf war where the US had gone to war against a Muslim country, Washington was particularly wary of such criticism. It wanted to send a positive signal to Turkey, who had been very supportive of the US-led alliance in the Gulf.
176 James A. Baker, *op.cit.*, 639-641.
177 "US-EC Declaration on the Recognition of the Yugoslav Republics, Brussels, 10 March 1992", in Snezana Trifunovska, *op.cit.*, 520.

178 "EC Declaration on Recognition of Bosnia and Herzegovina, Luxembourg, 6 April 1992", in Snezana Trifunovska, *op.cit.*, 521. The declaration also includes the adoption of positive measures *vis-à-vis* Serbia. The US however would make the lifting of sanctions against Serbia and Montenegro conditional upon the lifting by Belgrade of the economic blockade against Bosnia and Herzegovina, and Macedonia.
179 "President Bush's Statement on the Recognition of Bosnia and Herzegovina, Croatia and Slovenia, Washington, 7 April 1992", in Snezana Trifunovska, *op.cit.*, 521-522. The US declaration came one day after that of the Europeans, as they had been recommended not to announce recognition on 6 April, the anniversary of the German bombardment of Belgrade which started the outbreak of the Second World War in Yugoslavia. See Susan Woodward, *op.cit.*, 473, footnote 144.
180 Another factor which may have played a role is the presence of the strong Greek lobby in the United States.
181 Thomas Paulsen, *op.cit.*, 62.
182 Patrick Glynn, "See No Evil", in Nader Mousavizadeh, *The Black Book. The Consequences of Appeasement of Bosnia* (New York: Basic Books, 1996), 132-137, 135.
183 David Gompert, *op.cit.*, 37.
184 Warren Zimmermann (1995), *op.cit.*, 16. Zimmermann admits that he should have pushed harder with his government to get peace-keeping troops in Bosnia and Herzegovina.
185 "Statement on Principles for New Constitutional Arrangement for Bosnia and Herzegovina. Lisbon, 23 February 1992", in Snezana Trifunovska, *op.cit.*, 517-519.
186 For a detailed account on the outbreak of the war in Bosnia and Herzegovina, see "The Gates of Hell. The Outbreak of War in Bosnia 1-10 April 1992", in Laura Silber and Allan Little, *op.cit.*, 245-54.
187 James A. Baker, *op.cit.*, 647.
188 Paula Franklin Lytle, *op.cit.*, 314.
189 "Resolution 757 (1992) Adopted by the Security Council at its 3082nd Meeting, 30 May 1992", in Snezana Trifunovska, *op.cit.*, 593-599.
190 Paula Franklin Lytle, *op.cit.*, 314-315.
191 David Owen (1996), *op.cit.*, 13.
192 The first newspaper report had already been published on 19 July 1992 by Roy Gutman of the New York paper *Newsday*. See Laura Silber and Allan Little, *op.cit.*, 274-276.
193 *Ibid.*, 277-278; See also David Owen (1996), *op.cit.*, 20 and Patrick Glynn, *op.cit.*, 134.
194 "Developments in Yugoslavia and Europe – August 1992", *Hearing Before the Subcommittee on Europe and the Middle East of the Committee on Foreign Affairs, House of Representatives. One Hundred Second Congress. Second Session, August 4, 1992* (Washington D.C.: US Government Printing Office, 1993), 5.
195 "Resolution 758 (1992) Adopted by the Security Council at its 3083rd meeting, 8 June 1992", in Snezana Trifunovska, *op.cit.*, 601-602.
196 See, for example, President Bush at a press conference following the G7 meeting in Munich in July 1992: "But in terms of Yugoslavia, our interest is in terms of trying to get humanitarian support in there. I have no plans to inject ourselves into a combat situation in Yugoslavia." Referring to the words of Colin Powell, Bush states that "he expresses administration policy very well on that, the purpose of providing humanitarian aid and not for trying to solve the underlying political issue." Taken from: "The President's News Conference in Munich, Germany, 8 July 1992", in *Public Papers of the Presidents of the United States. George Bush, 1992-1993* (Washington D.C.: United States Government

Printing Office, 1993),1101.
197 James A. Baker, *op.cit.*, 648-651; Thomas Paulsen, *op.cit.*, 75-77.
198 Colin L. Powell, *A Soldier's Way. An Autobiography* (London: Hutchinson, 1995), 558-559.
199 See Colin L. Powell: "When ancient ethnic hatreds reigned in the former Yugoslavia in 1991 and well-meaning Americans thought we should 'do something' in Bosnia, the shattered bodies of Marines at the Beirut airport were never far from my mind in arguing for caution." *Ibid.*, 290-291.
200 Pia Christina Wood, *op.cit.*, 141-142.
201 Thomas Paulsen, *op.cit.*, 88. The resolution was adopted on 13 August 1992. See "Resolution 770 (1992) Adopted by the Security Council at its 3106th Meeting, 13 August 1992", in Snezana Trifunovska, *op.cit.*, 670-672.
202 "Resolution 776 (1992). Adopted by the Security Council at its 3114th Meeting, 14 September 1992", in Snezana Trifunovska, *op.cit.*, 720-721.
203 James Baker had been asked by President Bush to serve as White House Chief of Staff to coordinate the election campaign.
204 "Resolution 781 (1992) Adopted by the Security Council at its 3122nd Meeting, 9 October 1992", in Snezana Trifunovska, *op.cit.*, 732-733.
205 It would take several more months before the Europeans would also agree with the enforcement of the no-fly zone over Bosnia and Herzegovina. See "Resolution 816 (1993) Adopted by the Security Council at its 3191st Meeting, 31 March 1993", in Snezana Trifunovska, *op.cit.*, 874-876.
206 See, for example, "The Need to Respond to War Crimes in the Former Yugoslavia. Secretary Eagleburger. Statement at the International Conference on the Former Yugoslavia, Geneva, Switzerland, December 16, 1992", *US Department of State Dispatch*, vol.3, No.52, 28 December 1992, 923-925. Eagleburger did not hesitate to name prominent war criminals such as Slobodan Milosevic, the President of Serbia, Radovan Karadzic, the self-declared President of the Serbian Bosnian Republic, and General Ratko Mladic, commander of the Bosnian Serb military forces.
207 The support of the Bush administration for the lifting of the arms embargo constituted a change in its earlier policy which rejected the idea that the injection of more arms would bring an end to the conflict. See Thomas Paulsen, *op.cit.*, 81.
208 David Owen (1995), *op.cit.*, 86.
209 Steven J. Woehrel and Julie Kim, "Yugoslavia and US Policy", *CRS Issue Brief*, 1 August 1993, 13.
210 It is interesting to note that George Bush, in "A World Transformed", an account of his foreign policy which he published together with his National Security Adviser Brent Scowcroft, does not deal with the Yugoslav crisis. See George Bush and Brent Scowcroft, *A World Transformed* (New York: Alfred A.Knopf, 1998).
211 See "Statement of Ralph Johnson, Deputy Assistant-Secretary of State for European and Canadian Affairs", in *Hearing Before the Subcommittee on European Affairs of the Committee on Foreign Relations. United States Senate. One Hundred Second Congress, Second Session, 11 June 1992* (Washington D.C.: US Government Printing Office, 1992), 5: "As the President has stated, we will act with prudence and caution when it comes to US involvement in this crisis."
212 David Owen (1995), *op.cit.*, 1.
213 *Cf. supra*, 137-138.

214 Robert P. Grant, "France's New Relationship with NATO", *Survival*, vol.38, No.1, spring 1996, 58-80, 61.
215 *Cf. supra*, 136.
216 *Atlantic News*, 6 December 1995.
217 "Declaration of the Heads of State and Government Participating in the Meeting of the North Atlantic Council Held at NATO Headquarters, Brussels, on 10-11 January 1994", *Atlantic Documents*, No.83, 12 January 1994.
218 Charles Barry, "NATO's Combined Joint Task Forces in Theory and Practice", *Survival*, vol.38, No.1, spring 1996, 81-97.

# 6 Conclusions

The events of 1989 and the end of the cold war have provided enough material and questions to keep several generations of historians and political scientists fully occupied, and it will still take many years before all aspects of their effects and consequences are understood in all their complexity.

This study is a modest contribution to illuminate one of the many consequences of the end of the superpower conflict, namely how it has affected the transatlantic security relationship and more particularly what have been its repercussions on American security policy towards Western Europe. It examines how the Member States of the European Community have taken the chance provided by the ending of the division of their continent to further develop their own security identity and how the United States, as their prime security partner during the cold war, has reacted to these initiatives. Did Washington radically change its security policy towards Western Europe or has there, on the contrary, been a high degree of continuity with the post-1945 period? The time frame of this study is that of the Bush administration, covering the period January 1989 through to January 1993.

In the introductory chapter of this study, it was specified that this research was conducted through the lenses of realism, a theory which is in the first place interested in the impact of systemic forces on US behaviour. The question of the effect of the opportunities and constraints created by the international system is particularly interesting since the period of the Bush administration coincided with one of change in the major players in the international system. The collapse of the Soviet Union ended bipolarity and led to the paradoxical situation whereby the United States was the sole superpower left, while at the same time it faced the increased risk of being challenged by other emerging powers. Realism assumes that unipolarity is no more than an interlude and that sooner or later the unipolar moment will give way to an unstable multipolar world, which will be less conducive to American interests.

The position of the United States in Europe was challenged in two ways. Firstly, the disappearance of the Soviet threat made the NATO allies less dependent on US protection, opening the way for an independent European security policy; secondly, an increasingly economically integrated European Community had become a tough competitor in world markets and a vocal interlocutor in international trade fora, and it was feared that it might develop into a fortress where it would be difficult for American products to have access. This research focuses on how the United States has responded to the first area, and is limited to that of security or high politics.

Realist scholars expect the challenged superpower to defend its position and to strive to maintain the advantages linked to its predominant place in the international system. They do not agree, however, as to how this objective could best be reached. Some anticipate that the US will follow a policy of primacy, which consists of trying to preserve its advantageous position by maintaining the unipolar moment as long as possible. Others defend the view that American interests will best be protected by better balancing commitments and resources, and by reducing Washington's foreign-policy commitments to a number of countries or regions that really matter, and agree that these are primarily the major states of the Eurasian landmass. Both advocates of a primacy policy, as well as those pleading for a policy of selective engagement, share the view that the best way for the US to protect its interests and influence in Europe is by staying engaged, expressing its continuing commitment through the maintenance of NATO, the body in which the US has occupied a central place. In other words, as concerns Western Europe, both groups support a policy that to a large extent continues to be based on US policy as it was developed after the end of the Second World War.

The actual policy of the Bush administration and the relevance of realism in explaining it has been examined through two empirical case studies both of which focus on situations which had the potential of seriously challenging the American position in Europe. Firstly, we have studied the US response to the most important European security initiative following the end of the cold war, namely the decision of the 12 Member States of the European Community, in the framework of the 1991 Intergovernmental Conference (IGC) on Political Union, to move beyond European Political Cooperation and to develop a Common Foreign and Security Policy (CFSP). Secondly, we have focused on the US' reaction to the EC's ambitions to take the lead in addressing the Yugoslav conflict, the first major post-cold war European crisis. Both initiatives, if successful, had the potential of seriously challenging America's central position in Europe and are therefore a good test of US' intentions and policy in the post-1989 Europe. Would Washington try to defend its position and how would it do so? Or would it welcome the European initiatives as an excuse to withdraw from Europe and to radically reverse its post-war policy of engagement?

The four years of the Bush administration were too short to formulate a definitive and complete answer to the momentous changes of 1989 and the process of adaptation to the security challenges of the post-1989 world continued beyond the period examined. Nevertheless, during the years immediately following the collapse of the Berlin Wall, the Bush administration definitely opted for a specific direction, and by doing so had a determining impact on the future course of transatlantic relations and the policy of successive US administrations.

## Maintaining NATO as the Prime European Security Organisation

The end of the division of the European continent sparked off a vivid debate on the future organisation of the European security architecture and led to fierce competition among different international organisations, each claiming that they were best placed to deal with the security challenges of the new Europe.

As the principal European defence organisation during the cold war, NATO was one of the most active participants in the debate. Although it undeniably continued to be the most-developed and best-equipped European security body, NATO was on the defensive, as many were arguing that following the collapse of communism it had become obsolete and would soon cease to exist. Eager to prove the opposite, it invested a lot of effort in defining a new mission and in adjusting its structures to the post-1989 challenges.

A further contender for a place in the new European security landscape was the Conference on Security and Cooperation in Europe (CSCE).[1] The CSCE had the advantage that its membership extended to Russia and the countries of Central and Eastern Europe and as a result it could claim that it was the only available pan-European framework in an undivided Europe. At the same time, however, its large membership and cumbersome structures were a major obstacle for this body to take on major responsibilities in the short term.

The most serious challenge to the central position of NATO was undeniably that posed by the security ambitions of the European Community and the Western European Union (WEU). Several EC Member States hoped to grasp the chances provided by the end of the cold war to develop their own security identity outside the Atlantic framework. The idea was discussed in the framework of the 1991 Intergovernmental Conference (IGC) on Political Union, where the Twelve were debating how to transform European Political Cooperation into a fully-fledged European foreign and security policy. Taking into account the neutral status of Ireland, and the fact that not all Member States shared the same enthusiasm for a European foreign and security policy, it was proposed to develop the WEU, the only purely Western European security organisation, as the EC's security arm.

It is an important initial finding of this research that the Bush administration, despite the general bewilderment surrounding the 1989 events, very soon had a relatively clear picture of how it wanted to address the changing situation in Europe and that it was ready to invest considerable energy and resources in developing a strategy aimed at reaching its favoured design.

In a speech as early as on 12 December 1989 in the symbolic city of Berlin, Secretary of State James Baker clarified the American view on its preferred shape for the new European architecture.[2] He explicitly stated that "America's security – politically, militarily, and economically – remains linked to European security" and that the United States would remain a European power. Referring to the new European security architecture, the US Secretary of State mentioned NATO, the EC and the CSCE, but clearly attributed a pivotal role to the first. Trying to justify a continued US presence in Europe, he proposed a transformed NATO should play a role in the field of arms control, the addressing of regional conflicts, and the building of ties with the East. Although Washington also gave an important place to the European Community, especially when it came to addressing the challenges in Eastern Europe, Baker was quick to add that he wanted "transatlantic cooperation to keep pace with European integration and with institutional reform". Intensified European integration was acceptable and even desirable, but it was not to be developed to the detriment of the US-European relationship.

The American predilection for NATO is not surprising. Unlike the EC and the WEU, the US is a first hand participant in the Atlantic Alliance, allowing it to directly participate in discussions on the future organisation of European security. As its most powerful member and the country providing the members of the Alliance with a nuclear umbrella, Washington's position had always been extremely influential. The fact that the European pillar in NATO was hardly developed and that the European countries regularly defended diverging positions, meant that the United States could in most cases impose its own preferred views. Furthermore, NATO was the only body with a fully operational military command, whereas all other European security organisations were at least for the time being only paper tigers. For more than 40 years the Alliance had successfully ensured peace and stability on the European continent, and the Americans had not forgotten that twice in the course of the twentieth century they had intervened to save Europe from total destruction. It could not to be excluded that now that the communist yoke had disappeared, nationalist forces would once again emerge and the Bush administration therefore considered it to be in the US' interest to remain engaged.

Since the changed international circumstances, the realisation of the Bush administration's central aim of safeguarding NATO as the prime European security organisation required well-directed efforts and active diplomacy. The end of the cold war had led several observers to predict that the Alliance would not survive the defeat of its communist enemy and that sooner or later it would dissolve. Also the prospect that the Europeans themselves would start to play an increased role in the security area possibly constituted a serious challenge to the American objective.

The first and probably the most difficult hurdle to meet in realising the American goal was guaranteeing continued German membership of the Alliance. Being aware of Moscow's strong resistance, Washington feared that Bonn, in exchange for a Russian acquiescence in German reunification, would give in to Soviet pressure and adopt a neutral status and renounce its membership of both NATO and the Warsaw Pact.

For Washington this was considered to be a nightmare scenario as it was hard to conceive how the Alliance, dismembered of one of its principal and most loyal players, could continue to be viable. It was not to be forgotten that NATO had been created to pursue the double purpose of containing both the Soviet Union, as well as Germany.[3] In the longer term, a huge neutral Germany in the centre of Europe was considered to be a recipe for instability, and even war. No longer part of a larger European or Atlantic framework, Germany would soon be overwhelmed by a feeling of insecurity, a situation which once again might provoke a German *Alleingang*.

Conscious that without German membership, the continuing existence of the North Atlantic Treaty Organization was seriously threatened, the Bush administration combined all its forces to prevent such development. After having come up with the proposal to discuss the external aspects of German unification within the framework of the two-plus-four conference of the two Germanys and the four former Second World War allies, US diplomacy concentrated all its efforts on convincing both its Western allies and Moscow to realise German reunification within the Alliance.

To persuade the Soviet Union, where understandably opposition was extremely high, Washington launched a whole series of initiatives, among which were the presentation of a list of nine points aimed at reassuring Moscow about the future intentions of the West (May 1990), as well as a US-Soviet trade agreement (June 1990), directed at domestic opinion in the Soviet Union. The NATO London Summit (5 and 6 July 1990), passed a range of measures trying to demonstrate that the nature of the Alliance was changing and that it was no longer to be feared as an adversary.

The credit for radically changing the Soviet position, leading President Gorbachev to ultimately accept that it was up to the German people themselves to decide whether they would support Germany's continued membership of the Alliance, should to a large extent be given to the active involvement and creativity of US diplomacy. Whether or not the judgement of Robert D. Blackwill, the White House's chief action officer on German unification, that a continued German membership of NATO was "one of this century's pivotal diplomatic accomplishments" is true, it can be considered as one of the Bush administration's principal contributions to the stability of post-1989 Europe.[4]

Once the question of German security had been settled, the United States concentrated its efforts on reforming the Alliance. The waning of the communist threat and the new European security environment required a revision of NATO's strategy and imposed the development of smaller and more flexible structures. A whole range of measures from the creation of an Allied Rapid Reaction Corps (ARRC) to the adoption of a new strategic concept at the Rome Summit (7 and 8 November 1991),[5] and the decision that NATO should have the possibility of supporting peace-keeping activities under the responsibility of the CSCE[6] were all part of the same scheme to prepare NATO for the new type of security challenges it would be facing, cutting short critical voices claiming that in the post-1989 world the organisation had become obsolete.

Another new and major task which NATO appropriated for itself and which further helped justify its continuing existence, was extending the stability of the West to the whole of Europe. One of the instruments contributing to the creation of such "a Europe whole and free" was the establishment in December 1991 of the North Atlantic Cooperation Council (NACC),[7] providing the NATO Member States and the countries of Central and Eastern Europe with an institutional basis for consultation and cooperation on political and security issues.[8]

The above-mentioned initiatives considerably increased the chances of realising the American objective of maintaining NATO as the central European security organisation. Nevertheless, the Alliance was not the only game in town and it was apparent that the success of the US strategy would to a significant extent also be determined by what was happening in other fora.

The traditional reticence and ambiguity with which Washington had generally responded to European ambitions in the security field during the cold war period did not augur well for the US' receptivity towards the undertakings of the European Community in the framework of the 1991 IGC. In the third chapter of this study, it was described how with the exception of the European Defence Community, where the European army was planned to be an integral part of NATO, attempts like those of de Gaulle to establish a Political Union (1960 to 62), or the decision of the Six in 1970 to move beyond economic integration and to start cooperation in the foreign-policy area, were considered as challenges to US leadership and led to American counter-proposals aimed at strengthening the Atlantic community. The question arises as to what extent the United States was willing to adopt a more supportive and relaxed attitude towards European security initiatives following the end of the cold war.

## Washington and CFSP: Mixed Feelings

Very soon after the fall of the Berlin Wall, the Member States of the European Community, primarily under the impetus of France supported by Germany, decided to grasp the chances provided by the new international climate in order to extend the scope of European Political Cooperation (EPC) to the area of security and possibly defence, a field in which the Twelve had hitherto little if no experience. At the Dublin Summit of June 1990, it was agreed to organise, in parallel with the IGC on Economic and Monetary Union, an Intergovernmental Conference on Political Union and the development of a common European foreign and security policy became one of the central themes of the negotiations.[9]

Taking into account Washington's central role in guaranteeing European security, it was natural that it followed the debate with particular attention. Having specific views as to the future European security architecture, the Bush administration was anxious to see to what extent the European plans were compatible with its own blueprint. If successful, the development of a fully-fledged European foreign and security policy could constitute a serious challenge to its plans to maintain NATO as the central European security organisation. Alternatively, if the European attempts failed and NATO had in the meantime disappeared this would lead to a security vacuum and instability would ensue.

A further factor which stimulated the US to closely follow the IGC debate was that the main instigator behind the plans for a European foreign and security policy was France. Paris had never accepted America's dominant position on the European security scene and it was feared that the French government would grasp the opportunity provided by the end of the cold war to boost its own position and to claim the role of being Europe's political leader for itself, marginalising the United States.

Although since 1945 successive US governments had always paid lip-service to the idea of Western Europe taking a larger share in assuming the burden of its security and defence, the Bush administration was quick to make it clear that its support for such an increased role was not unconditional. In the above-mentioned Baker speech on a new Atlanticism, the Secretary of State had explicitly stated that closer European cooperation should not be an alternative to Atlantic cooperation, but on the contrary had to be compensated by enhanced links between the two partners.[10] In that sense the message of the Bush administration seemed to echo that of Presidents Kennedy and Nixon. When the Europeans in the early 1960s and 1970s tried to come up with independent European initiatives for closer foreign-policy cooperation, they had argued that this was only acceptable to the extent that this would strengthen the Atlantic community.

When in the course of the IGC, it realised that the European plans might be more ambitious than was to its liking, Washington did not hesitate to express its apprehensions or to intervene directly in the discussions. Taking into account that for the time-being European defence capacities were almost non-existent and that NATO was the only forum having the capacity to concretely take care of Europe's security and defence, the US government was in a relatively strong position to influence the European debate.

Through such means as the Bartholomew *démarche* of February 1991, the US government opted for a policy of exerting direct pressure on the European capitals, emphasising once again the Baker message that NATO was to remain the central European security organisation. Rather than developing a separate European security identity, the US urged the Western European countries to develop the European pillar of NATO. Besides guaranteeing a more direct US impact, such a policy would also have the advantage that a country such as Turkey, which is not a member of the EC but which during the Gulf war proved to be a key ally, continued to be closely involved in the European security debate.

The misgivings of Washington towards the Franco-German initiative to strengthen European foreign-policy cooperation were further reinforced by the US experience during the Uruguay Round of GATT where the Twelve turned out to be extremely rigid negotiating partners. Once the Europeans, in the framework of the EC, had succeeded in determining a common position, it proved very difficult to make them adopt a different point of view. The Bush administration dreaded a situation whereby the same would happen in the security area and the EC Member States, speaking with one voice in the area of CFSP, would gang up against the United States.

During the early 1990s, two opposing concepts of European security integration – one European, the other Atlantic – were once again competing with each other.[11] The two different wills were impossible to reconcile or merge into one coherent concept. For Europeanists such as France, supported by countries like Germany,[12] Belgium, Luxembourg and Spain, the time had come for the Europeans to finally start taking care of their own security and defence and to considerably reduce their dependence on their American ally. Atlanticists like the United Kingdom, the Netherlands and Portugal thought that Washington should maintain a central role on the European security and defence scene. According to the first blueprint, Europe would gradually have to take its own responsibilities, eventually becoming an independent interlocutor on the international scene, and if necessary would defend a position different from that of the United States. For the Atlanticists in contrast, initiatives for a stronger European identity were to be developed in the NATO framework in close consultation with the United States. Disagreements between the allies were to be smoothed out internally, not on the international scene.

The different philosophy behind the two schools of thought is well illustrated by the debate on the role of the Western European Union. If the Europeanists wanted this organisation to develop into a mature European security and defence institution, which in the long term would be merged with the EU, the Atlanticists wanted it to be the European security arm of the Alliance. In the first case the WEU would gradually become part of the EU, while in the second it would be subordinate to NATO.

Both Europeanists and Atlanticists were making important efforts to enhance the chances of success of their preferred approach. The EC, in the framework of the 1991 IGC, adopted the Treaty on European Union, including a new Title on Common Foreign and Security Policy, which covered "all questions related to the security of the Union, including the eventual framing of a common defence policy, which might in time lead to a common defence".[13] The extension to all aspects of security was certainly an important step forward *vis-à-vis* European Political Cooperation, although the very cautious formulation of the text indicates that an agreement had only been reached after extremely difficult negotiations, and that the implementation of the new provisions would not be an easy task. The European Community had no practice in working in the security field and it is obvious that such expertise cannot be developed from one day to another. Some argued that the high level of integration reached in the economic area would ultimately spill over to the political and security field and that having a tradition as a civilian power, the EC would be very well placed to deal with the non-military challenges of the post-1989 world. The events in Yugoslavia and the problems which the EC faced in addressing the situation seem to challenge this assumption.

The Atlantic Alliance had a comparative advantage over the European Community in that it could look back on a legacy of more than 40 years of security and defence cooperation. But here caution was also required: very much would depend on how NATO would implement the changes it had introduced and how they would pass the test of new security crises in the unified Europe.

The confrontation with the "real world" would be all the more important since the debate on the new European security architecture had not led to an explicit choice of one option to the detriment of the other. Both the Atlantic and the European model would co-exist and depending on their ability to deal with newly arising challenges, they would have to prove their relevance. Whether this might lead to a division of tasks or the ultimate prevalence of one option over the other was not clear, but was left open for the future to decide. It was the conflict in Yugoslavia which, as the first post-cold war crisis in Europe, was to ultimately provide the much-needed test for both the European and Atlantic security model.

## Yugoslavia: The First Test for Europe's Emerging Security Architecture

While the first case study on the development of a European foreign and security policy was primarily situated at the abstract level in the sense that at the time of the Bush administration it consisted mainly of a series of provisions on paper, the second case examined how the European and American allies reacted towards a concrete security challenge, namely the crisis in the Federal Republic of Yugoslavia.

Although both partners were claiming that they wanted to play a central role in the new European security architecture, the EC and the US each responded in an entirely different way to this first major post-cold war crisis in Europe. The EC Member States proved much more eager than Washington to get involved in addressing the escalating situation. Coinciding with the 1991

Intergovernmental Conference and the negotiations on the development of a Common Foreign and Security Policy, the crisis was seen as an opportunity to illustrate the willingness and the capacity of the Twelve to play a reinforced role on the European security scene. The United States on the other hand, decided to stay on the sidelines and adopted a wait-and-see attitude.

When on 25 June 1991, both Slovenia and Croatia unilaterally declared their independence and an armed conflict broke out, the Luxembourg Presidency heralded the EC attempts to address the situation as "the hour of Europe and not the hour of the Americans" and the Troika of Ministers of Foreign Affairs engaged in active shuttle diplomacy. Despite some initial successes such as the Brioni Agreement[14] and the sending of EC monitors, the crisis proved much more difficult to handle than initially expected. When by the autumn of 1991, fighting in Croatia had become increasingly serious and an attempt by the Twelve to agree on WEU military intervention failed, most EC Member States were all too happy to transfer the lead to the United Nations. The EC continued to play a mediating role through a peace conference in The Hague in which all parties in the conflict participated, but it did not have the authority to bring about a negotiated solution. Peace in Croatia would ultimately only come in January 1992 following the mediation of the United Nations.

What the Europeanists had hoped would be an event reinforcing their case for the development of an independent European security identity, turned out to be an illustration of the enormous weaknesses and flaws still inherent in European foreign-policy cooperation. One of the most exasperating aspects of the EC intervention was the enormous difficulty, if not the incapacity, of the Member States to speak with one voice. With their different historic backgrounds and divergent geographic interests, the European countries did not see events through the same spectacles. While France and the United Kingdom for example did not hide their sympathy for the Serbs, Germany was clearly more supportive of the Croatian point of view.

The antagonism reached a climax when it came to the question of the recognition of the breakaway republics of Slovenia and Croatia. While most Member States agreed that recognition constituted an important instrument of leverage over the warring parties and was to be postponed as long as possible, a recently unified Germany argued that these republics could not be denied the right to self-determination. Bonn found itself initially isolated but, by threatening to go it alone, its partners ultimately accepted the German position in order not to damage the recent agreement on the Maastricht Treaty and its provisions on CFSP. On 16 December 1991, the Ministers of Foreign Affairs agreed that all republics which so desired would be recognised by 15 January 1992, on the condition that they fulfilled the necessary conditions of respecting human rights and providing guarantees for minorities.

After the recognition saga, the Twelve continued to be actively involved in trying to bring the crisis to a peaceful end, but also, when in April 1992 the conflict spilled over to Bosnia and Herzegovina, they never really succeeded in recapturing the initiative. Rather than giving it a boost, the Yugoslav adventure had a damaging effect on the credibility of the emerging common foreign-policy, which had consequences far beyond the conflict in question.

The initial reaction of the United States was radically different from that of the Twelve. With experts on Yugoslavia like National Security Adviser Brent Scowcroft and Deputy-Secretary of State Lawrence Eagleburger at the highest levels, the US administration had recognised the seriousness of the situation much earlier than the Europeans and proved to be very reticent about getting trapped in the Yugoslav quagmire. Having just been involved in the Gulf war and with presidential elections around the corner, there was little enthusiasm for involvement in another major and extremely risky foreign-policy, let alone military, operation. Besides, the US attitude cannot be separated from the novel situation created by the end of the cold war. Yugoslavia was no longer a stake in the larger East-West rivalry, and hence the conflict was seen as a regional one, not constituting a threat to American security. It was a European crisis which could therefore best be handled by the Europeans themselves. As a result, the eagerness of the Europeans to become a central player suited the United States very well.

Throughout its years in government, the Bush administration tried as much as possible to stick to this deliberate policy of staying on the sidelines. It could, however, not prevent itself from gradually becoming more and more involved in the Yugoslav imbroglio as a result of the EC's aborted peace attempts.

In particular, the increasingly central role of the United Nations from the autumn of 1991 onwards inevitably also led to enhanced US interference. As a permanent member of the UN Security Council, Washington whether it wished to or not became an important participant in the debate on how the conflict could best be addressed. Increasingly frustrated with the EC's incapacity to act firmly, it played an influential role in the adoption of a series of UN resolutions like the one imposing a complete trade embargo against Serbia and Montenegro,[15] the resolution to protect the delivery of relief support to Sarajevo[16] and the ban on military flights in the airspace of Bosnia and Herzegovina.[17]

Throughout its entire period in office, however, the Bush administration remained adamant when it came to the question of the sending of American troops. Horror scenes in detention camps, pressure from public opinion and heavy criticism on behalf of the presidential candidate William J. Clinton concerning US inertia could not change the position of the US government.

The deliberate decision of the United States not to become involved in the Yugoslav crisis has been heavily criticised both at the national as well as at the international level. Although it has to be admitted in all fairness that the conflict was extremely complex, and one can only speculate as to whether or not earlier US involvement would have made a serious difference, it is clear that a more pronounced American role would have given more weight to the initiatives of the European Community and could perhaps have increased the chances of successful mediation. By some parties such as the Serbs, the United States was seen as a more impartial mediator, a factor which could possibly have facilitated a negotiated settlement at an earlier stage.

On the other hand, certain events such as the US pressure for the recognition of Bosnia and Herzegovina, which ultimately led to the conflict spilling over into that republic, seem to cast doubts over whether Washington would have been more apt at handling the crisis. As Germany in the case of Croatia, the US was not ready to live up to the consequences of its policy and not prepared to defend what it had recognised as a state.

While there seem to have been plenty of good reasons underlying the American choice for a deliberate policy of non-involvement, it raises certain questions. If the US was so anxious to remain present in post-cold war Europe and maintain NATO as the linchpin of European security, could it not have been expected that Washington would grasp the events in Yugoslavia to prove the necessity of its continued presence? Did the United States, by deciding to stay on the sidelines and by not involving NATO, not miss an opportunity to further reaffirm its position on the European security scene?

The Bush administration clearly did not follow this reasoning. Several factors may help to explain this approach. As mentioned before, the US was much more conscious of the extremely risky and complex nature of the conflict than the Europeans. If it were to use the Yugoslav crisis as a way of demonstrating the necessity of a continued US presence in Europe, it was in its absolute interest that its intervention be successful. In light of the nature of Yugoslavia's territory and the conflict's highly complex nature, such success was far from being guaranteed. Furthermore, the crisis occurred at a moment when NATO was still in the middle of the process of adapting its structures and the Alliance was far from being prepared to deal with a security challenge such as the one in Yugoslavia. It could therefore only intervene at the high risk of failure.

Despite its many flaws, the American policy of non-involvement finally worked out to its advantage and contributed to the realisation of its objectives in Europe. It brought home the fact that, at least for the time being, the Europeans were not able to take care of their own security and that active US involvement remained not only desirable but also indispensable. Yugoslavia turned out to be the hour of the Americans, not of the Europeans as the Luxembourg Foreign Minister had claimed.

The decision to intervene in Bosnia and Herzegovina was ultimately taken by the Clinton administration, but only after it had been in office for two and a half years. In late August 1995, Washington supported a series of NATO airstrikes on Serb targets and became the main motor behind the negotiations leading to the conclusion of the Dayton Peace Agreement. To execute the airstrikes and later to implement the peace agreement, the United States to a large extent relied on NATO, implementing its policy of sustaining the Alliance as the central player in European security. Taking into account that by that time the warring parties were reaching a certain degree of war fatigue and seeing the failure of the other players to address the situation, the US came in from a position of strength, giving it higher chances of succeeding where others had failed.

The final denouement of the Yugoslav crisis, and the central role of the United States in addressing it, has had a major impact on the emerging European security architecture and the place of the different players in it. Rather than being a major support for the project of a European security and defence identity, as several European leaders had initially expected, Yugoslavia proved to be a major stepback for CFSP, while at the same time it provided an important boost to the Atlantic blueprint attributing a central role to the United States and NATO in the European security architecture.

However, the balance sheet for the Atlantic model is not entirely positive either. That "Yugoslavia" was ultimately operational in promoting the preferred US scheme for the organisation of European security, was much more the result of the poor performance of the Europeans than of a well-designed policy on behalf of the US and it seems that it was by default rather than by design that the Atlantic blueprint ultimately prevailed. Contrary to events like a continued German membership of NATO, where the United States had an articulate policy and was ready to do the almost impossible to realise its objectives, its ultimate central and successful role in Yugoslavia resulted primarily from the fact that none of the other players had the political weight to bring the conflict to an end. During the Bush administration, the only guiding principle of US policy was to try not to become involved, a rather remarkable policy for a country claiming that it remained fully committed to European security and one pleading for the realisation of "a Europe whole and free".

Secondly, the US' performance in Yugoslavia also very well illustrates the flaws and ambiguities inherent to the Atlantic model as promoted by the Bush administration. Having been originally developed in the immediate postwar period, this model perpetuated an organisation of transatlantic relations based on inequality, whereby the US was the senior and Europe the junior partner. If such an arrangement might perhaps have been attractive from the American point of view, it was questionable whether it was at all viable in the post-1989 period. Having become a major economic power, the Western European countries wanted to translate their economic weight into political influence and were no longer willing to accept an inferior position. Furthermore, the disappearance of the Soviet threat made it more likely that developments in Europe would be perceived differently by the Atlantic partners. A situation like the one in Yugoslavia for example could not possibly be ignored by the Europeans, whereas it could easily be played down by the US as being a regional crisis not requiring any American intervention.

If the Atlantic model was to survive, it was crucial to further develop NATO's European pillar and to provide for the necessary flexibility in cases where only the European members wanted to act. Being obsessed as it was with the survival of the Alliance and the perpetuation of a continuing central role for the US in Europe, the Bush administration paid little attention to this question. It would take until the second Clinton administration before the issue of a more balanced Alliance and the possibility of independent European action in the NATO framework would be explored and elaborated.

## US Policy Towards Western Europe in the Post-Cold War Period

Having described the findings of the two empirical cases, we now return to the question as to what these case studies teach us about the policy of the Bush administration towards Europe. To what extent did the end of the cold war lead to a redefinition of American interests and goals towards the old continent? What were the elements of continuity with the past? What were the new threats and challenges facing the reunified Europe, according to the US, and how could they best be addressed? How did the Bush Presidency react to European initiatives to develop an independent European foreign and security policy, challenging its previously predominant position in Western Europe? Although it once again has to be stressed that the answers given in the period 1989 to January 1993 cannot be considered as final and that they only constituted a first step in adjusting to the changed circumstances, they nevertheless point in a certain direction and already lift part of the veil on America's gradually emerging post-cold war policy towards Europe. If one cannot exclude the possibility that successive governments might decide to radically overturn the track chosen by the Bush administration, it is clear that if they did so, they would have to justify such a policy and have particular reasons for doing so.

One of the conclusions of this research is that the most often heard criticism with regard to the Bush administration, namely that it lacked vision,[18] does not apply to its policy towards Western Europe. On the contrary, very soon after the Wall crumbled, Secretary of State James Baker in his famous Berlin speech (December 1989) presented a first outline of US policy, making it clear that the guarantee of a continued US role in Europe was to be a central foreign-policy objective. Furthermore, the US government promptly engaged in an activist policy to realise this goal. Any speculations and concerns that Washington would become considerably less interested in the developments on the European scene and possibly return to its pre-1945 policy of isolationism proved to be unfounded.

The Bush administration shared the pessimistic views expressed by most realists that the end of the cold war would not necessarily bring peace and stability to Europe. Even if the outbreak of a large-scale conflict was unlikely, new risks such as re-emerging nationalism, nuclear proliferation, a re-nationalisation of defence policies were looming and it was far from certain that the Europeans themselves would be successful in addressing them. The experience of two world wars, in one of which Bush himself had been involved as a soldier, had taught him that sooner or later a major European war would drag the United States in. With significant overseas investments and Europe being one of its main trading partners, the US still believed that it was in its interest to stay engaged. For the Bush administration the best way to do so was through the Atlantic Alliance and a continuing deployment of American troops.

The end of the cold war had, however, raised serious question marks concerning the future position of the US in Europe. Following the disappearance of the communist threat, Europe had become less dependent on the American security guarantee and some European countries, with France taking the lead, argued that as an important player on the international economic scene, the time had come for the European Community to translate its weight into political power and to start taking care of its own security. In such a scenario, there would be little place for a body such as NATO, which was considered to reflect American interests too much.

From this perspective, the plans of the European Community to develop a fully-fledged European foreign and security policy did indeed have the potential of constituting a serious challenge to the position and influence of the United States and it is therefore not surprising that Washington followed the process very closely and did not hesitate to try to influence it.

In his study *"War and Change in World Politics"* (1981),[19] Robert Gilpin identifies two main strategies for a state whose position is being challenged by that of other emerging powers: either it opts for a policy of primacy, trying to sustain its predominant position and refusing to share its influence with others; or alternatively, it reduces its commitments trying to better balance its responsibilities and resources so that further decline can be halted. Both the strategies of primacy as well as that of selective engagement, as they have been labelled in the theoretical chapter, are aimed at defending the position of the challenged state as much as possible.[20] The primacy strategy, however, suggests that by investing the necessary means the country in question can maintain its predominant place. The second strategy, in contrast, accepts that the position of the challenged state has declined and tries to manage the transitional phase as well as possible. For selective engagement, resources are scarce and as a result the available policy options are limited.

In formulating its response towards the EC's initiative to develop a Common Foreign and Security Policy, the Bush administration clearly opted for a strategy of primacy. It wanted to perpetuate the situation of the cold war period where NATO was the central European security organisation and where the United States was the dominant and most influential player on the European security scene.

In order to achieve this objective, Washington simultaneously worked on many different fronts. A first series of initiatives consisted in leading the debate reformulating NATO's objectives and missions, and investing considerably in the adaptation of its structure and its new strategic concept. High priority was given to nurturing the relationship with Germany, who was expected to become one of the main players on the European continent. The Bush administration did its outmost to guarantee the country's continued membership of the Alliance and invited Bonn to become "a partner in leadership", who together with the US would take the lead in addressing the challenges on the European continent. The close links with traditionally Atlanticist oriented countries such as the United Kingdom, the Netherlands and Portugal were an important means in trying to influence the European security debate from within. Efforts were also made to bring France closer to the Alliance but they were not successful.

The main aim of all these endeavours was to try to convince the European allies not to challenge NATO and the American position but to bandwagon with it.[21] The arguments being used by Washington were of a cooperative nature.[22] The US and NATO with its integrated military command were still best placed to provide the Europeans with the collective good of security. NATO had a positive record of more than 40 years, whereas any new European initiatives still had to prove themselves.

Although speaking in more general terms and not specifically about Europe, the rationale for a continuing central US role in Europe is very well expressed at the end of Bush's publication on the major achievements of his foreign-policy. In the concluding pages, he argues:

> As I look to the future, I feel strongly about the role the United States should play in the new world before us. We have the political and economic influence and strength to pursue our own goals, but as the leading democracy and the beacon of liberty, and given our blessings of freedom, of resources, and of geography, we have a disproportionate responsibility to use that power in pursuit of a common good. We also have an obligation to lead. Yet our leadership does not rest solely on the economic strength and military muscle of a superpower: much of the world trusts and asks for our involvement. The United States is mostly perceived as benign, without territorial ambitions, uncomfortable with exercising our considerable power.[23]

The fervour with which the Bush administration tried to defend its position in NATO could not have contrasted more sharply with the reticence it demonstrated with regard to becoming involved in the Yugoslav crisis. Earlier on we referred to the fact that the non-policy towards Yugoslavia was the result of a deliberate choice and we pointed to its inconsistency with the policy of maintaining NATO as the central European security organisation.

The Yugoslav case is important as its contrasting results complete the findings of the first case study and allow us to give a more accurate and nuanced picture of the Bush administration's policy towards Europe. The fact that it invested so much effort in preserving NATO but consistently refused to intervene in Yugoslavia indicates that the policy of the Bush administration towards Europe cannot be described as a crude primacy policy in the strict sense. It is more accurate to refer to it as being a mixture of both elements of primacy and selective engagement. The enormous efforts that have been made to preserve NATO and the repeated refusal to intervene in Yugoslavia shows that certain parts of Europe mattered more than others and that despite its continuing commitment, the US was not ready to become Europe's policeman, and intervene in every single crisis. A clear distinction was made between a key objective such as the safeguarding of NATO and a continuing presence in Western Europe on the one hand and the crisis in Yugoslavia on the other hand. While the former was considered to be the best guarantee for preserving vital US interests, the latter was merely seen as a civil conflict, which could best be addressed by the Europeans themselves. In other words, there were clearly limits as to how much the US wanted to get involved and besides concerns about its future place on the European security scene, other considerations such as availability of resources, chances of success, relevance for US security, domestic politics have also played a role.

Comparing the reaction of the Bush government with that of previous administrations, it is striking how many parallels can be drawn with the past. The main message coming from Washington continued to be that the development of a stronger European security identity should not be to the detriment of the transatlantic relationship and that intensified European cooperation should be counterbalanced by closer links between both sides. The Bush government did not hesitate to try to influence the European debate by lobbying hard for its own preferred design for the new European architecture. As with Kennedy's Grand Design and Kissinger's Atlantic Charter, it is a blueprint for closer European security cooperation within the Atlantic framework rather than within a purely European security organisation. Or to use the words of Dean Acheson 40 years before: the United States supports "a form of European cooperation within and in support of NATO".

The question remained how to recompense Europe for carrying an increased burden by giving the European allies greater weight in NATO and how to develop the Alliance into a more balanced partnership. The Bush government gave surprisingly little thought to this challenge. It was in the first place concerned how to preserve the centrality of NATO and the related predominant role of the United States.[24]

Also on the European side, the fundamentally altered security situation did not lead to an immediate or radical change in the EC Member States' positions. While France once again took the lead in launching the debate on the development of a European security identity, the traditionally Atlanticist countries like the United Kingdom, the Netherlands and Portugal, continued to have more faith in maintaining the centrality of NATO. Also countries with a more sympathetic view towards the French proposals for an independent

European course were at least for the time being not ready to decouple their security from that of the United States and NATO. It soon became clear that they were much more eager to grab the peace dividend than to invest huge amounts in a military apparatus that was already available in NATO. The disadvantages resulting from dependence on an outside power and the realisation during the Yugoslav crisis that American and European interests were not necessarily the same, did not seem to be sufficient to change these positions.

With Paris taking the lead in the European security debate, London defending the view from Washington, and Bonn doing the impossible by trying to reconcile both the Europeanist and Atlanticist view, the policies of the major European countries seem to have been very much guided by the legacy of the past. However, also here one has to be careful in drawing definitive conclusions. The debate in Maastricht on the development of a Common Foreign and Security Policy took place only two years after the fall of the Berlin Wall. Since it was still a period of transition and it was far from clear how the security scene in Europe would further develop, the continuity with the past is perhaps not that surprising. Further research into the developments in the 1990s and beyond should teach us more about the longer-term effects of the end of the cold war on the security policies of European countries and might make it necessary to qualify these first conclusions.

**Evaluating the Results**

Having argued that the Bush administration had specific views with regard to the goals it wanted to reach in Western Europe, the question remains to what extent it was able to attain these objectives. The situation today whereby NATO continues to be the main guarantor of European security and CFSP is merely a slightly upgraded version of the former European Political Cooperation seems to suggest that American policy has been successful. Reality is however more complex and as has been illustrated in the Yugoslav case, has much to do with the failure of the Europeans to come up with a viable alternative.

Although most European governments recognise that at least for the time being, a continuing American presence in Europe is desirable and that NATO is the only body which has the capacity to guarantee European security, the way the Bush administration tried to realise its goals contains certain flaws. The main criticism with regard to the American approach is that it was very much a policy of maintaining the *status quo*. The central concern was how the United States could safeguard its predominant position on the European security scene and its principal premise seems to have been the same as that of the young Sicilian aristocrat in Lampedusa's "*Il Gattopardo*": "*se vogliamo che tutto rimanga como è, bisogna che tutto cambi*", which freely translated means "if we want everything to stay as it is, we will have to change everything", the only aim of the changes being to keep things as they were.[25]

In other words, changes in the organisation of European security aimed in the first place at preserving the existing situation which was characterised by an American predominance of power. The US did not hesitate to take the lead in the discussion of a new strategic concept, the establishment of more rapid and flexible forces, and the definition of a new mission for NATO. All these actions were part of the American strategy aimed at proving that the Alliance and the American presence still continued to be the best possible option. The question of how the Alliance could be adjusted to better reflect the changed power relations in Europe and be transformed into a real partnership did not seem to interest the Bush government.

This is undoubtedly one of the major weaknesses of the Bush administration's policy towards Europe. The adaptation of the Alliance to the changed distribution of power in Europe had been long overdue and, as was discussed in the chapter on the history of the transatlantic security relationship, has been the cause of multiple tensions.[26] After an earlier failed attempt in the 1970s under President Nixon, the end of the cold war provided an excellent opportunity to finally come to grips with this problem, but this chance was missed. The Bush administration was too obsessed with the preservation of its position, and the Europeans were too busy quarrelling amongst themselves.

It is the Yugoslav crisis which ultimately made both Europeans and Americans accept the importance and the urgency of a debate revising their respective roles in the Alliance. The poor performance of the Europeans considerably strengthened the position of the Atlanticists arguing that a stronger European security role could best be realised by further developing the European pillar of NATO. Even France came to the conclusion that the European security debate could not be confined to the EC framework alone and that if Paris did not want to be marginalised, a closer relationship with NATO was inevitable. It is easier to influence a debate from within than from sitting on the sidelines.

To the United States, Yugoslavia has also provided a sobering lesson. While on the one hand it has confirmed the American view that the European Community is not ready to take over the Alliance's tasks, it has also led to a clarification of its own future role on the old continent. It has made Washington realise that in the post-1989 period there may be an increasing number of "small" crises in which the United States does not necessarily want to intervene. If it wants NATO to continue to play a central role, it has to foresee the possibility that in such cases the Europeans can act without American involvement, but with the support of NATO resources.

The debate on how to strengthen the European pillar of NATO finally took off during the Clinton administration. The most categorical expression of the willingness of the new administration to discuss a more important European role within the Alliance framework is the concept of Combined Joint Task Forces (CJTF) according to which the European allies, in addressing a European crisis in which the US does not want to be involved, have the possibility of making use of NATO's assets and capabilities. Although a seemingly simple idea, launched by President Clinton at the NATO Summit of January 1994, its implementation has proved to be complicated as it raised many difficult questions such as to what degree European decision making can really be independent if relying on NATO capabilities.

The difficult negotiations on CJTF illustrate that the further development of NATO's European pillar will not be realised over night. While it remains a real challenge for the Europeans to speak with one voice and to assume larger security responsibilities, it will also demand considerable effort from the United States to adjust to a less dominant role in NATO. Disagreements between both sides of the Atlantic will continue to arise and Washington will have to learn to engage in a real discussion rather than imposing its views. The debate is gradually taking off but undeniably both sides still have a long way to go.

## Is Realism Still Relevant?

The conceptual framework that has been used in this research is that of realism and the final question we would like to address is to what extent its assumptions have been helpful in understanding the policy of the Bush administration. We argue that they have been in several respects.

The realist tenet that a state's foreign-policy is primarily shaped by systemic forces rather than the domestic environment provides compelling explanations of the Bush administration's policy towards Europe and more particularly of its reaction to the development of a European security identity. Unipolarity and the expected transition towards a multipolar system created both opportunities and constraints for US policy and shaped it in an important way. While the end of the cold war placed the sole superpower in a seemingly untouchable position, the projected rise of other states pushed it towards a defensive policy. The United States interpreted the EC's plans to develop an independent foreign and security policy as a direct challenge to its position and its response in the form of a policy of primacy is typically that of a power defending its place and trying to maintain the related advantages. Rather than coming to the conclusion that the disappearance of the Soviet threat no longer required an American presence, Washington's entire policy was based on defending the *status quo* whereby NATO would remain the principal European security organisation and the US would continue to occupy a central place in it.

The end of bipolarity also had a major impact on US policy towards Yugoslavia. The collapse of communism had dramatically reduced the importance of this country in international relations, permitting the US to downplay the crisis as a regional one, not requiring American intervention. In addition, concerns about America's declining position led some to advocate a more cost-conscious foreign-policy, prompting Washington to become more selective with regard to its operations in third countries. While maintaining NATO was defined as a primary US foreign-policy objective, settling the Yugoslav crisis was not.

Considerations of international power, which realism links to the anarchic character of international relations, have played an important, if not a central role in the determination of US policy towards the post-1989 Europe. Fears of a reduced influence on the old continent were one of the principal reasons why the United States proved so reluctant with regard to the development of an independent European security identity and why it was investing so much time and effort in trying to maintain NATO as Europe's prime security organisation. Although America's continuing presence is undoubtedly an important factor in stability, this strong preoccupation with perpetuating an influential US role in Europe seriously limited the available policy options and led to a policy which not only lacked flexibility but which was also out of touch with changed realities. How to take into account the increased European weight on the international scene and to develop a genuine transatlantic partnership was not on the agenda.

Considerations of power do, however, not explain everything. Had this been the case, the American government would probably have intervened at a much earlier stage in the Yugoslav crisis, grasping it as a chance to prove the continuing relevance of NATO. As we have seen, other factors such as the reticence of public opinion to accept possible casualties and Bush's preoccupation with his upcoming election were important in shaping the policy of the US government. So if the international power element proved to be very important in the first case study, it has turned out to be less of a determining element in the second case. Here further research at the domestic level will undeniably add interesting findings to the research results made at the systemic level.

Although institutionalists will be eager to point to the central role of NATO in the European security debate,[27] it can be argued that at least in the area of security, the focus of realism on the state as the central player in international relations continues to be justified. Contrary to the realm of economics where multinational corporations are increasingly powerful players, the provision of security remains one of the core functions of the state. Even though individual states organise themselves in multinational alliances and as a result give up part of their sovereignty, they generally try to limit this "loss" by opting for decision making by unanimity so that no decisions can be imposed against their will. As is illustrated by the example of the European Union, countries remain extremely reluctant to move beyond intergovernmental cooperation and to transfer sovereignty in this sensitive area to supranational bodies.

While it is true that NATO was strongly present in the new European architecture discussions, it has to be recognised that its role has primarily been instrumental. It was used by Washington to guarantee a continued US presence and influence in Europe and it served as an instrument to balance others aspiring to take a role in European security, such as the European Community and the CSCE. Furthermore, the Alliance was the essential forum for discussion through which the Bush administration could signal its future intentions on the continent. The North Atlantic Treaty Organization was however not an autonomous player. Its role was to a large extent confined to the one its member states and more particularly the United States wanted it to fulfil.

We consider that the above findings are sufficiently compelling to allow us to conclude that the realist approach continues to be pertinent when studying international relations, especially when it concerns research which focuses on the security policy of one of the world's most powerful countries. At the same time, however, this study has also unveiled some of the major weaknesses of realism. Having examined the international system during a period of transition, it is striking how little theoretical interest there has so far been with regard to the phenomenon of change in international relations. Realists like Kenneth Waltz, for example, who are fascinated with the durability of the bipolar world, have primarily focused on explaining why the system proved so stable and have not shown any interest in questions related to a period beyond bipolarity.[28]

One of the few exceptions in addressing the question of the conditions under which change occurs and how it affects the behaviour of both the emerging and the challenged states in the international system is Robert Gilpin. Even though *"War and Change"* (1981) represents a huge amount of work and is one of the most systematic attempts to get a better grip on the phenomenon of change, it is clear that one single study, no matter how extensive it may be, can never grasp a phenomenon of such complexity in all its aspects. The end of the cold war has provided a huge amount of new material and should therefore be grasped as an opportunity to further refine our understanding of the causes and consequences of systemic change.

**Beyond the Bush Administration**

Any student interested in the future of Europe and the European Union is inevitably faced with the question of the further evolution of the role of the United States, which since the end of the Second World War has been one of the central players on the old continent.

The results of this study which has examined the transatlantic relationship in the immediate post-1989 period indicate that at least for the short- and medium-term future, US policy will very much be coloured by the legacy of the past. The United States has decided to remain engaged in Europe, and continues to institutionalise this commitment through a permanent alliance. Most European countries, after some initial flirtation with the idea of an independent European security identity, seem to have come to support the American view that at least for the time being the Atlantic model of organising European security continues to be more viable than a purely European one.

Despite the current state of affairs and the relatively smooth transition towards the post-1989 period, there is however little reason for complacency and a number of question marks remain. Firstly, it is debatable whether it is viable to continue to organise transatlantic relations on the same basis as during the cold war. Now that the communist threat has disappeared, the ambiguities underlying both American and European attitudes towards transatlantic cooperation might come to the surface more than before and lead to increased irritation and problems. The United States, which since the Clinton administration seems to have accepted that serious efforts have to be made to attribute greater weight to the Europeans, continues to have difficulties in translating this goal into practice. As we have seen with the debate on NATO's enlargement, Washington does not like to be contradicted and, due to the fact that it still has a powerful position, it succeeds in most cases to get its way. Old habits die hard. The US has been used to the fact that despite regular disagreements, the views of Washington often prevail and it will not be simple for the Americans to engage in a real dialogue with its partners.

Also the attitude of the Europeans continues to be equivocal. Even if the United States were to engage all its efforts in trying to convert the Alliance into a real association of equals, success would be far from being guaranteed. The tortuous negotiations on CFSP during the 1991 IGC and the difficulties the Member States of the European Union have displayed in trying to speak with one voice on foreign affairs illustrate that Europe still has a long way to go before being a unified actor on the international scene. Whether it will be able to become so in the framework of the Alliance under the impulse of the United States remains questionable. A real transatlantic partnership in the security area presupposes a solid European pillar. Currently such a pillar does not exist. Having different geographical situations, with different historical experiences, and differences in size, the hurdles which the European countries have to overcome continue to be enormous.

Secondly, the question of America's long-term strategy remains. Realism warns against over optimism with regard to the endurance of alliances once their common enemy has waned. Will coming generations of Americans with an increasingly important Hispanic component in the population continue to be willing to provide the hegemonic leadership to maintain NATO?[29] Will they be willing to invest in the security of a prosperous Europe if the latter continues to be so reluctant to provide the necessary resources?

Furthermore, we should not underestimate the effect of the rise of China as one of the principal players on the world scene in the next century. This may lead to the reorientation of American priorities towards Asia, a trend which has already started under the Clinton administration.

In the coming years, transatlantic relations will continue to be at a crossroads. Either the United States and Europe carry on the road chosen by the Bush administration, and continue to opt for an American-led Alliance with the risk that in the long term new generations on both sides disengage; or both players concentrate their efforts on developing transatlantic relations into a genuine partnership. The latter option is undoubtedly preferable but also the more challenging one as it requires a considerable change of behaviour on both sides, with the Europeans assuming increased responsibilities and the Americans becoming a real interlocutor. At this moment it is still unclear which direction is being taken. The only certainty we have is that for the Alliance to endure under the new circumstances of the post-1989 period, the necessary adjustments and investments will have to be made.

## Notes

1. In 1994, the name of the Conference on Security and Co-operation in Europe (CSCE) became the Organisation on Security and Co-operation in Europe (OSCE).
2. James Baker, "A New Europe, a New Atlanticism, Architecture for a New Era", *US Policy Information and Texts*, No.175, 12 December 1989.
3. Wolfram F. Hanrieder speaks of "double containment". See Wolfram F. Hanrieder, *Germany, America, Europe. Forty Years of German Foreign-policy* (New Haven: Yale University Press, 1989), 6.
4. Robert D. Blackwill, "German Unification and American Diplomacy", *Aussenpolitik*, vol.45, No.3, 1994, 211-235, 212.
5. "The Alliance's New Strategic Concept", *Atlantic Documents*, No.1742, 9 November 1991.
6. "Communiqué of the Ministerial Meeting of the North Atlantic Council in Oslo, 4 June 1992", *NATO Review*, vol.40, No.3, June 1992, 30-32. At the ministerial meeting of the North Atlantic Council in Brussels of 17 December 1992, it was agreed that the Alliance, on a case-by-case basis, would also support peace-keeping operations under the authority of the UN Security Council. See *Atlantic News*, 19 December 1992, No.2484.
7. "Statement Issued at the Meeting of the North Atlantic Co-operation Council. NATO Headquarters, Brussels, 18 December 1992, *NATO Review*, vol.41, No.1, February 1993, 28-30.
8. Under President Clinton, possibilities for cooperation were further extended through the Partnership for Peace (PfP) initiative and during the second Clinton administration, agreement was reached on the enlargement of the Alliance with Hungary, Poland and the Czech Republic.
9. See Chapter 4.
10. See footnote 2.
11. See chapter 3, especially 73-75; 83-84; 86-88.
12. Germany found itself in a rather difficult situation. Having obtained support for its reunification from both the EC Member States and the United States, Bonn was eager to prove that it continued to be strongly committed to the European integration process, while at the same time it wanted to show that it was a reliable ally in NATO.
13. *Treaty on European Union*, Title V.
14. The Brioni Agreement led to the withdrawal of the Yugoslav National Army from Slovenia, brought a definitive cease-fire in that republic, and brought a three-month suspension of the implementation of the declarations of independence of Slovenia and Croatia.
15. "Resolution 757 (1992) Adopted by the Security Council at Its 3082nd Meeting, 30 May 1992", in Snezana Trifunovska, *Yugoslavia Through Documents. From Its Creation To Its Dissolution* (Dordrecht: Martinus Nijhoff Publishers, 1994), 593-599.
16. "Resolution 758 (1992) Adopted by the Security Council at Its 3083rd Meeting, 8 June 1992", in Snezana Trifunovska, *op.cit.*, 601-602.
17. "Resolution 781 (1992) Adopted by the Security Council at Its 3122nd Meeting, 9 October 1992", in Snezana Trifunovska, *op.cit.*, 732-733.
18. See, for example, Larry Berman and Bruce W. Jentleson, "Bush and the Post-Cold-War Period: New Challenges for American Leadership", in Colin Campbell and Bert A. Rockman (eds.), *The Bush Presidency. First Appraisals* (New Jersey: Chatham Publishers,

1991), 93-128; Michael Duffy and Dan Goodgame, *Marching in Place. The Status Quo Presidency of George Bush* (New York: Simon and Schuster, 1992).
19  Robert Gilpin, *War and Change in World Politics* (Cambridge: Cambridge University Press, 1981).
20  See chapter 2.
21  This aim has been most explicitly stated in the initial draft of the Pentagon's Defense Planning Guidance (DPG) for the fiscal years 1994-99. This document which was leaked to the *New York Times* expressly said, "We must account sufficiently for the interests of the large industrial nations to discourage them from challenging our leadership or seeking to overturn the established political or economic order". "We must maintain the mechanisms for deterring potential competitors from even aspiring to a larger regional or global role." See "Excerpts from Pentagon's Plan: Prevent the Re-emergence of a New Rival", *New York Times*, 8 March 1992, A14. Following critical reactions, the text was watered down and left out the reference to a policy of primacy (see Patrick Tyler, "Pentagon Drops Goal of Dropping New Superpowers", *New York Times*, 24 May 1992) but according to Christopher Layne the draft version was reflective of the thrust of US policy. See Christopher Layne, "The Unipolar Illusion. Why New Great Powers Will Rise", *International Security*, vol.17, No.4, spring 1993, 5-51, 5-6.
22  See the distinction made by Jervis between cooperative and competitive arguments for primacy as explained in chapter 2.
23  In George Bush and Brent Scowcroft, *A World Transformed* (New York: Alfred A. Knopf, 1998), 565-566.
24  *Cf infra*, 231-233.
25  Quoted by Peter Burke, *Venetië en Amsterdam* (Amsterdam: Agon, 1991), 137-138.
26  See chapter 3.
27  See for example: Robert O. Keohane and Stanley Hoffmann, "Conclusion: Structure, Strategy, and Institutional Roles", in Robert O. Keohane, Joseph S. Nye, Stanley Hoffmann (eds.), *After the Cold War. International Institutions and State Strategies in Europe, 1989-1991* (Cambridge, Ma., and London: Harvard University Press, 1993).
28  See Kenneth N. Waltz, *Theory of International Politics* (New York: McGraw-Hill, 1979).
29  According to statistics of the US bureau of census, the proportion of American citizens of European origin will go down from 80% in 1980 to 56% in 2050 and those of Hispanic origin will raise from 6% to 22%. See Philip H. Gordon, "Recasting the Atlantic Alliance", *Survival*, vol.38, No.1, spring 1996, 32-57.

# Bibliography

**Official Documents and Reports**

"Accord Implementing the Cease-fire Agreement of 23 November 1991. Sarajevo, 2 January 1992", in Snezana Trifunovska, *Yugoslavia Through Documents. From Its Creation To Its Dissolution* (Dordrecht: Martinus Nijhoff Publishers, 1994), 468-470.

"An Anglo-Italian Declaration on European Security and Defence, 5 October 1991", *Europe Documents*, No. 1735, 5 October 1991.

"Announcement of the US State Department Concerning the Trade Embargo on Yugoslavia, 6 December 1991", Snezana Trifunovska, *op.cit.*, 426-427.

"An Operational Organisation for WEU: Naval Cooperation – Part One: Adriatic Operations". Report Submitted on Behalf of the Defence Committee by Mr Marten and Sir Keith Speed, Joint Rapporteurs (Paris: Assembly of the Western European Union, November 1993).

"Atlantic Summit, 5-6 July 1990", *Europe Documents*, No. 1635, 10 July 1990.

"Cease-fire Agreement. Belgrade, 1 September 1991", in Snezana Trifunovska, *op.cit.*, 334-336.

"Communiqué of the Ministerial Meeting of the North Atlantic Council in Oslo, 4 June 1992", *NATO Review*, vol. 40, No. 3, June 1992, 30-32.

"Communiqué of the Conference of the Heads of State and Government of the Member States of the European Community (The Hague, 2 December 1969, excerpts)", in *European Political Cooperation* (Bonn: Press and Information Office, 1988), 22-23.

*Completing the Internal Market: White Paper from the Commission to the European Council* (Brussels: Commission of the European Communities, 14 June 1985)(COM (85) 210 final).

"Concept for a United Nations Peace-Keeping Operation in Yugoslavia, November/December 1991", in Snezana Trifunovska, *op.cit.*, 418-423.

"Conclusions of the Presidency", *Bulletin of the European Communities*, vol. 24, No. 6, June 1991, 8-19.

"Conclusions of the Presidency", *Bulletin of the European Communities*, vol. 23, No. 12, December 1990, 7-18.

"Conclusions of the Presidency", *Bulletin of the European Communities*, vol. 23, No.

6, June 1990, 8-24.
"Conclusions of the Presidency", *Bulletin of the European Communities*, vol. 22, No. 12, December 1989, 8-18.
"Contribution by the Commission on the Development of a Common External Policy", *Bulletin of the European Communities*, supplement 2, 1991, 89-96.
"Council of Ministers – Vianden (Luxembourg), 27 June 1991: Communiqué", *Europe Documents*, No. 5523, 29 June 1991.
"Declaration by Belgium, Germany, Spain, France, Italy, Luxembourg, the Netherlands, Portugal and the United Kingdom of Great Britain and Northern Ireland which are members of the Western European Union", in *Treaty on European Union* (Luxembourg: Office for Official Communications of the European Communities, 1992), 245-246.
"Declaration by the European Council on Areas Which Could Be the Subject of Joint Action", in Finn Laursen and Sophie Vanhoonacker (eds.), *The Intergovernmental Conference on Political Union. Institutional Reforms, New Policies and International Identity of the European Community* (Maastricht, Dordrecht: EIPA and Martinus Nijhoff Publishers, 1992), 493-494.
"Declaration by the 17th European Council on the Euro-Arab Dialogue, Lebanon, Afghanistan and the Situation in the Middle East (Venice, 12/13 June 1980)", in *European Political Cooperation* (Bonn: Press and Information Office, 1988), 127-131.
"Declaration Concerning the Conditions for Recognition of New States. Adopted at the Extraordinary EPC Ministerial Meeting. Brussels, 16 December 1991", in Snezana Trifunovska, *op.cit.*, 431-432.
"Declaration of the Heads of State and Government Participating in the Meeting of the North Atlantic Council Held at NATO Headquarters, Brussels, on 10-11 January 1994", *Atlantic Documents*, No. 83, 12 January 1994.
"Declaration on EC-Canada Relations", *Europe Documents*, No. 1663, 24 November 1990.
"Declaration on Former Yugoslavia Made by the Foreign Affairs Council of the European Community. Luxembourg, 5 October 1992", in Snezana Trifunovska, *op.cit.*, 728.
"Declaration on Positive Measures", in Snezana Trifunovska, *op.cit.*, 425.
"Declaration on the Situation in Yugoslavia. Brussels, 15 June 1992", in Snezana Trifunovska, *op.cit.*, 614.
"Declaration on the Situation in Yugoslavia. Adopted at the Extraordinary EPC Ministerial Meeting, The Hague, 5 July 1991", in Snezana Trifunovska, *op.cit.*, 310-311.
"Declaration on the Situation in Yugoslavia", in Snezana Trifunovska, *op.cit.*, 368-369.
"Declaration on US-EC Relations", *Europe Documents*, 23 November 1990.
"Declaration on Yugoslavia. Adopted at the EPC Extraordinary Ministerial Meeting. The Hague, 19 September 1991", in Snezana Trifunovska, *op.cit.*, 347.

"Declaration on Yugoslavia Adopted at the EPC Extraordinary Ministerial Meeting, The Hague, 3 September 1991", in Snezana Trifunovska, *op.cit.*, 342-343.

"Declaration on Yugoslavia Adopted at EPC Extraordinary Ministerial Meeting, Brussels, 27 August 1991", in Snezana Trifunovska, *op.cit.*, 333-334.

"Declaration on EC-US Relations", *Europe Documents*, No. 1662, 23 November 1990.

"Developments in Yugoslavia and Europe – August 1992", *Hearing Before the Subcommittee on Europe and the Middle East of the Committee on Foreign Affairs, House of Representatives. One Hundred Second Congress. Second Session, August 4, 1992* (Washington D.C.: US Government Printing Office, 1993).

"Document on Associate Membership of WEU of the Republic of Iceland, the Kingdom of Norway and the Republic of Turkey", *Europe Documents*, No. 1810, 25 November 1992.

"EC Declaration on Recognition of Bosnia and Herzegovina, Luxembourg, 6 April 1992", in Snezana Trifunovska, *op.cit.*, 521.

"EC Declaration on the Situation in Yugoslavia. Adopted at the Informal Meeting of Ministers for Foreign Affairs. Haarzuilens, 6 October 1991", in Snezana Trifunovska, *op.cit.*, 351-352.

"Europe. Débat sur une déclaration du gouvernement", *Senat. Séance du 27 juin 1990*, 2162-2178.

"European Council in Edinburgh, 11-12 December 1992. Conclusions of the Presidency. Decision of the Heads of State or Government, Meeting Within the European Council, Concerning Certain Problems Raised by Denmark on the Treaty on European Union", *EC Bulletin*, vol. 25, No. 12, December 1992, 25-26.

"European Union. Report by Mr Leo Tindemans, Prime Minister of Belgium, to the European Council" (Brussels: Ministry of Foreign Affairs, 1976).

"Excerpts from Remarks at the Federation Palace, Belgrade, Yugoslavia, June 21, 1991", *US Department of State Dispatch*, vol. 2, No. 26, July 1, 1991, 468.

"External Trade and Balance of Payments. Monthly Statistics", *Eurostat* (Luxembourg: Statitistical Office of the European Communities, 1992-1993).

*External Trade. Statistical Yearbook. Recapitulation 1958-1993* (Luxembourg: Statistical Office of the EC, 1994).

"First Report of the Foreign Ministers to the Heads of State and Government of the Member States of the European Community of 27 October 1970 (Luxembourg Report)", in *European Political Cooperation* (Bonn: Press and Information Office, 1988), 24-31.

"Franco-German Initiative on Foreign Security and Defence Policy, Bonn, Paris, 11 October 1991", *Europe Documents*, No. 1738, 18 October 1991.

"Franco-German Proposals on Political Union: Security Policy Cooperation in the Framework of the Common Foreign and Security Policy of Political Union", *Europe Documents*, No. 1690bis, 21 February 1991.

*Foreign Relations of the United States (FRUS)*, vol. 3, Part I, 1951.

"Geneva Accord", in Snezana Trifunovska, *op.cit.*, 412-413.

"Italian Proposal on Common Foreign and Security Policy, 18 September 1990", in Finn Laursen and Sophie Vanhoonacker (1992), *op cit.*, 292.

"Joint Declaration of the EC Troika and the Parties Directly Concerned with the Yugoslav Crisis, the so-called "Brioni Accord", Brioni, 7 July 1991", in Snezana Trifunovska, *op.cit.*, 311-315.

"Kohl-Mitterrand Letter to the Irish Presidency, 19 April 1990", *Agence Europe*, 20 April 1990.

"Le dossier de l'Union politique. Recueil de documents avec préface de M. Emilio Battista" (Luxembourg: Direction générale de la documentation parlementaire et de l'information, January 1964).

"Memorandum from the Danish Government, 4 October 1990", in Finn Laursen and Sophie Vanhoonacker (1992), *op. cit.*, 293-303.

"Memorandum from the Portuguese Delegation, 30 November 1990", in Finn Laursen and Sophie Vanhoonacker (1992), *op. cit.*, 304-312.

"Ministerial Meeting of the North Atlantic Council in Copenhagen, Denmark, 6-7 June 1991, final communiqué", *Atlantic News*, No. 2329, 8 June 1991.

"Ministerial Meeting of the North Atlantic Council in Oslo, Norway, 4 June 1992. Final Communiqué", *Atlantic News*, No. 2430, 6 June 1992.

"Ministerial Meeting of the North Atlantic Council. NATO Headquarters, Brussels, 17 December 1992", *Atlantic News*, No. 2484, 19 December 1992.

"Non-Paper. Draft Treaty Articles With a View to Achieving Political Union", Brussels, 17 April 1991, *Europe Documents*, No. 1709/1710, 3 May 1991.

"One Market, One Money: An Evaluation of the Potential Benefits and Costs of Forming an Economic and Monetary Union", *European Economy*, No. 44, October 1990.

"Opinion No.5 on the Recognition of the Republic of Croatia by the European Community and its Member States. Paris, 11 January 1992", in Snezana Trifunovska, *op.cit.*, 489-490.

"Petersberg Declaration", *Europe Documents*, No. 1787, 23 June 1992.

"Platform on European Security Interests, The Hague, 27 October 1987", in Alfred Cahen, *The Western European Union and NATO. Building a European Defence within the Context of Atlantic Solidarity* (London: Brassey's, 1989), 91-96.

"President Bush's Statement on the Recognition of Bosnia and Herzegovina, Croatia and Slovenia, Washington, 7 April 1992", in Snezana Trifunovska, *op.cit.*, 521-522.

"Protocol of Accession of the Hellenic Republic to Western European Union", *Europe Documents*, No. 1810, 25 November 1992.

*Report of the Committee for the Study of Economic and Monetary Union* (Luxembourg: European Community, April 1989).

"Report on European Political Cooperation Issued by the Foreign Ministers of the Ten on 13 October 1981 (London Report)", in *European Political Cooperation* (Bonn: Press and Information Office, 1988), 61-70.

"Report to the European Council in Lisbon on the Likely Development of the Common

Foreign and Security Policy (CFSP) with a View to Identifying Areas Open to Joint Actions vis-à-vis Particular Countries or Groups of Countries", *Europe Documents*, No. 5761, 29-30 June 1992.

"Resolution 713 (1991) Adopted by the Security Council at its 3009th Meeting, 23 September 1991", in Snezana Trifunovska, *op.cit.*, 349-350.

"Resolution 721 (1991) Adopted by the Security Council at its 3018th meeting, 27 November 1991", in Snezana Trifunovska, *op.cit.*, 414-415.

"Resolution 743 (1992) Adopted by the Security Council at its 3055th Meeting, 21 February 1992", in Snezana Trifunovska, *op.cit.*, 515-517.

"Resolution 757 (1992) Adopted by the Security Council at its 3082nd Meeting, 30 May 1992", in Snezana Trifunovska, *op.cit.*, 593-599.

"Resolution 758 (1992) Adopted by the Security Council at its 3083rd meeting, 8 June 1992", in Snezana Trifunovska, *op.cit.*, 601-602.

"Resolution 770 (1992) Adopted by the Security Council at its 3106th Meeting, 13 August 1992", in Snezana Trifunovska, *op.cit.*, 670-672.

"Resolution 776 (1992) Adopted by the Security Council at its 3114th Meeting, 14 September 1992", in Snezana Trifunovska, *op.cit.*, 720-721.

"Resolution 781 (1992) Adopted by the Security Council at its 3122nd Meeting, 9 October 1992", in Snezana Trifunovska, *op.cit.*, 732-733.

"Resolution 816 (1993) Adopted by the Security Council at its 3191st Meeting, 31 March 1993", in Snezana Trifunovska, *op.cit.*, 874-876.

"Rome Declaration on Peace and Cooperation", *Europe Documents*, No. 1744, 13 November 1991.

"Statement by Press Secretary Fitzwater on Yugoslavia, July 2, 1991", in *Public Papers of the Presidents of the United States. George Bush* (Washington D.C.: United States Government Printing Office, 1992).

"Statement Issued at the Meeting of the North Atlantic Cooperation Council. NATO Headquarters, Brussels, 18 December 1992, *NATO Review*, vol.. 41, No. 1, February 1993, 28-30.

"Statement of Ralph Johnson, Deputy Assistant Secretary of State for European and Canadian Affairs", in *Hearing Before the Subcommittee on European Affairs of the Committee on Foreign Relations. United States Senate. One Hundred Second Congress, Second Session, 11 June 1992* (Washington D.C.: US Government Printing Office, 1992).

"Statement on Principles for New Constitutional Arrangement for Bosnia and Hercegovina",in Snezana Trifunovska, *op.cit.*, 517-519.

"Statement on the UN Security Council Resolution 757 of 30 May 1992. Brussels, 1 June 1992", in Snezana Trifunovska, *op.cit.*, 599.

"Statement Released by Department Spokesman Margaret Tutwiler, May 24, 1991", *US Department of State Dispatch*, vol.. 2, No. 22, 3 June 1991, 395.

"Text of the Letter Addressed to Andreotti by Kohl and Mitterrand, 6 December 1990", *Agence Europe*, 10-11 December 1990.

"Text of the Letter Addressed to Mr Giulio Andreotti by R.F.M. Lubbers and H. van den Broek, The Hague, 12 December 1990", in Finn Laursen and Sophie Vanhoonacker (1992), *op.cit.*, 315-317.

"The Alliance's New Strategic Concept", *Atlantic Documents*, No. 1742, 9 November 1991.

"The Dutch Draft Treaty Towards European Union", *Europe Documents*, No. 1734, 3 October 1991.

"The Need to Respond to War Crimes in the Former Yugoslavia. Secretary Eagleburger. Statement at the International Conference on the Former Yugoslavia, Geneva, Switzerland, December 16, 1992", *US Department of State Dispatch*, vol. 3, No. 52, 28 December 1992, 923-925.

"The President's News Conference in Munich, Germany, 8 July 1992", in *Public Papers of the Presidents of the United States. George Bush, 1992-1993* (Washington D.C.: United States Government Printing Office, 1993), 1101.

"The President's News Conference with President Mikhail Gorbachev of the Soviet Union in Moscow, July 31, 1991", in *Public Papers of the Presidents of the United States. George Bush* (Washington D.C.: United States Government Printing Office, 1992), 995.

"The President's News Conference with Prime Minister Ruud Lubbers of The Netherlands and President Jacques Delors of the Commission of the European Community in The Hague, November 9, 1991", in *Public Papers of the Presidents of the United States. George Bush* (Washington D.C.: United States Government Printing Office, 1992).

"The WEU Planning Cell". Report Submitted on Behalf of the Defence Committee by Mrs Baarveld-Schlamann, Rapporteur (Paris: Assembly of the WEU, 19 May 1994).

"US-EC Declaration on the Recognition of the Yugoslav Republics, Brussels, 10 March 1992", in Snezana Trifunovska, *op.cit.*, 520.

"US Efforts to Promote A Peaceful Settlement in Yugoslavia. Ralph Johnson, Principal Deputy Assistant Secretary for European and Canadian Affairs. Statement before the Senate Foreign Relations Committee, Washington D.C., October 17, 1991", *US Department of State Dispatch*, vol. 2, No. 42, 21 October 1991, 782-785.

"Vortrag des Bundesministers des Auswärtigen, Hans-Dietrich Genscher", *Europa-Archiv*, vol. 45, No. 15, 1990, 473-478.

"WEU Council of Ministers. Extraordinary Meeting on the Situation in Yugoslavia. Helsinki, 10 July 1992", in Arie Bloed and Ramses A. Wessel (eds.), *The Changing Functions of the Western European Union (WEU). Introduction and Basic Documents* (Dordrecht-Boston-London: Martinus Nijhoff Publishers, 1994), 155.

"WEU Council of Ministers. Rome, 19 May 1993. Communiqué", *Atlantic News*, No. 2527, 22 May 1993.

"WEU Ministerial Council, 19 June 1992, in Petersberg (Bonn)", *Europe Documents*, No. 1787, 23 June 1992.

## Speeches

Baker, James, "The Euro-Atlantic Architecture: From West to East", *US Department of State Dispatch*, vol. 2, No. 25, 18 June 1991 (reprint).
Id., "A New Europe, A New Atlanticism, Architecture for A New Era", *US Policy Information and Texts*, No. 175, 12 December 1989.
Bush, George, "Inaugural Address", January, 20, 1989, in *Public Papers of the Presidents of the United States. George Bush. 1989* (Washington D.C.: US Government Printing Office, 1990), vol. 1, 1-4.
Id., "Interview with Foreign Journalists, July 8, 1991", in *Public Papers of the Presidents of the United States. George Bush* (Washington D.C.: United States Government Printing Office, 1992), 833.
Id., "Interview with Foreign Journalists, April 16, 1990", in *Public Papers of the Presidents of the United States. George Bush. 1990* (Washington D.C: US Government Printing Office, 1990), vol. 1, 507.
Id., "Remarks at a Luncheon Hosted by Prime Minister Ruud Lubbers of The Netherlands in The Hague, November 9, 1991", in *Public Papers of the Presidents of the United States. George Bush* (Washington D.C.: United States Government Printing Office, 1992), 1426.
Id., "Remarks at Dedication Ceremony of the Social Sciences Complex at Princeton University in Princeton, New Jersey, May 10, 1991", in *Public Papers of the Presidents of the United States. George Bush. 1991* (Washington D.C.: US Government Printing Office, 1992), vol. 1, 496-499.
Id., "Remarks at the Boston University Commencement Ceremony in Massachusetts, 21 May 1989", in *Public Papers of the Presidents of the United States. George Bush. 1989* (Washington D.C.: US Government Printing Office, 1990), vol. 1, 582-585.
Id., "Remarks Following Discussions With Prime Minister Constantinos Mitsotakis of Greece, December 12, 1991", in *Public Papers of the Presidents of the United States. George Bush* (Washington D.C.: United States Government Printing Office, 1992), 1594.
Id., "Remarks to the Citizens of Mainz, Federal Republic of Germany, May 31, 1989", in *Public Papers of the Presidents of the United States. George Bush. 1989* (Washington D.C: US Government Printing Office, 1989), vol. 1, 640-654.
Delors, Jacques, "Europe and America in the New Security Environment". Summary Proceedings of a Conference in Washington D.C., 30 September-1 October 1993. Sponsored by the Jean Monnet Council with the Assistance of the Brookings Institution.
Id., "European Integration and Security", Alastair Buchan Memorial Lecture, London, The International Institute for Strategic Studies, 7 March 1991.
Taft, William H., "The NATO Role in Europe and the US Role in NATO". Speech presented to the Centre for European Policy Studies, 21 May 1992.
Id., "The US Role in the New Europe". Address to the International Institute for Strategic Studies. London, 9 February 1991.

## Interviews[1]

*Case One – American Reactions to CFSP*

Cornelis Willem Andreae, Embassy of The Netherlands to the US, Washington D.C., 22 September 1993.
R. Ian Butterfield, Legislative Assistant, Defence, Foreign Policy, Intelligence, Senate Committee on Government Affairs, member of the staff of US Senator Roth (Republican), Washington D.C, 27 September 1994.
Jonathan Raphael Cohen, Executive Secretariat, Office of the Secretary of State, US Department of State, Washington D.C., 26 September 1994.
James Dobbins, Ambassador, US Mission to the European Communities, Washington D.C., 27 September 1994.
Harry J. Dolton, Colonel US Army, Washington D.C., 28 September 1994.
Stephen Engelken, Desk Officer for France, State Department, Paris, 5 April 1995.
Jan Grauls, Minister-Counsellor, Embassy of Belgium to the US, Washington D.C., 23 September 1993.
Pedro Marin, Second Secretary, Deputy Director, Press and Public Affairs, Delegation of the European Commission to Washington D.C., Washington D.C., 21 September 1993.
Robert Pearson, Deputy Chief of Mission, US Mission to NATO, Brussels, 19 April 1995.
John Richardson, Head of Unit, Directorate General I (External Relations), European Commission, Brussels, 14 February 1995.
Stanley R. Sloan, Senior Specialist International Security Policy, Congressional Research Service, Washington D.C., 21 September 1994.
Bob Whiteman, Political Affairs, Delegation of the European Commission to the US, Washington D.C., 23 September 1994.
Yvette M. Wong, Political Officer, US Mission to NATO, Washington D.C., 26 September 1994.
Robert B. Zoellick, Undersecretary of State and White House Deputy Chief of Staff, Washington D.C., 22 September 1994.

*Case Two – The Bush Administration and Yugoslavia*

Christian Braun, Counsellor, Permanent Representation of Luxembourg to the EC, Brussels, 1 April 1996.
Roland Bombardella, Deputy Military Delegate, Permanent Representation of Luxembourg to the WEU, Brussels, 24 January 1996.
Robert De Vriese, Minister Plenipotentiary, Belgian Ministry of Foreign Affairs, Brussels, 10 January 1996.
Lawrence Eagleburger, Deputy Secretary of State, Washington D.C., 27 September

1996.

Hendrik Jan Hazewinkel, Deputy Head Directorate Europe, Dutch Ministry of Foreign Affairs, The Hague, 22 February 1996.

Horst Holthoff, Deputy Secretary General, WEU, Brussels, 13 May 1996.

Jane Holl, Director of European and Security Affairs, National Security Council, Washington D.C., 25 September 1996.

Robert L. Hutchings, Director for European Affairs, National Security Council, Washington D.C., 1 October 1996.

George Kenney, Yugoslav Desk Officer, US Department of State, Washington D.C., 24 September 1996.

William Taft, Ambassador, US Mission to NATO, Washington D.C., 4 October 1996.

Alexander Vershbow, Deputy Chief of Mission, US Mission to NATO, Washington D.C., 26 September 1996.

Steve Woehrl, Congressional Research Service, Washington D.C., 25 September 1996.

## Articles and Books

Acheson, Dean, *Present at the Creation. My Years at the State Department* (London: Hamish Hamilton, 1969).

Allen, David, and Smith, Michael, "West Europe in Reagan's World", in Reinhardt Rummel (ed.), *The Evolution of An International Actor. Western Europe's New Assertiveness* (Boulder, San Francisco, Oxford: Westview Press, 1990), 201-240.

Allison, Graham, *Essence and Decision. Explaining the Cuban Missile Crisis* (Boston: Little Brown, 1971).

Almond, Mark, *Europe's Backyard War: The War in the Balkans* (London: Heinemann, 1994).

Andrejevich, Milan, "Crisis in Croatia and Slovenia: Proposal for a Confederal Yugoslavia", *Report on Eastern Europe*, No. 44, 2 November 1990, 28-33.

Aron, Raymond, *Paix et guerre entre les nations* (Paris: Calmann-Levy, 1984).

Id. and Lerner, Daniel, (eds.), *La querelle de la CED* (Paris: Armand Colin, 1956).

Art, Robert J., "A Defensible Defense. America's Grand Strategy After the Cold War", *International Security*, vol. 15, No. 4, spring 1991, 5-53.

Artisien, Patrick, and Holt, Stephen, "Yugoslavia and the EEC in the 1970s", *Journal of Common Market Studies*, vol. 18, No. 4, June 1980, 355-369.

Asmus, Ronald D., "A United Germany", *Foreign Affairs*, vol. 69, No. 2, spring 1990, 63-76.

Axt, Heinz-Jürgen, "Hat Genscher Jugoslawien entzweit?", *Europa-Archiv*, vol. 48, No. 12, 1993, 351-360.

Baer, M. Delal, "North American Free Trade", *Foreign Policy*, vol. 70, 1991, 132-149.

Baker, James A., III, with Thomas A. Defrank, *The Politics of Diplomacy. Revolution, War and Peace 1989-1992* (New York: G.P. Putnam's Sons, 1995).

Baldwin, David A., (ed.), *Neorealism and Neoliberalism. The Contemporary Debate* (New York: Columbia University Press, 1993).
Barry, Charles, "NATO's Combined Joint Task Forces in Theory and Practice", *Survival*, vol. 38, No. 1, spring 1996, 81-97.
Beloff, Nora, *Tito's Flawed Legacy. Yugoslavia and the West Since 1939* (Boulder: Westview Press, 1985).
Bergsten, C. Fred, "The Primacy of Economics", *Foreign Policy*, vol. 87, summer 1992, 3-24.
Berlin, Isaiah, "The Hedgehog and the Fox. An Essay on Tolstoy's View of History", in Henry Hardy and Roger Hauscher (eds.), *The Proper Study of Mankind. An Anthology of Essays* (New York: Farrar, Straus and Giroux, 1998), 436-498.
Berman, Larry, and Jentleson, Bruce W., "Bush and the Post-Cold War World: New Challenges for American Leadership", in Colin Campbell and Bert A. Rockman (eds.), *The Bush Presidency. First Appraisals* (Chatham, New Jersey: Chatham Publishers, 1991), 93-128.
Beschloss, Michael R., and Talbott, Strobe, *At the Highest Levels. The Inside Story of the End of the Cold War* (Boston: Little, Brown and Company, 1993).
Beugel, Ernst H., van der, *From Marshall Aid to Atlantic Partnership. European Integration as a Concern of American Foreign Policy* (Amsterdam-London-New York: Elsevier, 1966).
Bhagwati, Jagdish, "Jumpstarting GATT", *Foreign Policy*, vol.83, 1991, 105-118.
Blackwill, Robert D., "German Unification and American Diplomacy", *Aussenpolitik*, vol. 45, No. 3, 1994, 211-225.
Bloed, Arie, and Wessel, Ramses A., *The Changing Functions of the Western European Union (WEU). Introduction and Basic Documents* (Dordrecht-Boston-London: Martinus Nijhoff Publishers, 1994).
Bloes, Robert, *Le "plan Fouchet" et le problème de l'Europe politique* (Bruges: College of Europe, 1970).
Bodenheimer, Susanne J., *Political Union: A Microcosm of European Politics, 1960-1966* (Leiden: A.W. Sijthoff, 1967).
Bonvicini, Gianni, "The Genscher-Colombo Plan and the Solemn Declaration on European Union (1981-83)", in Roy Pryce (ed.), *The Dynamics of European Union* (London: Croom Helm, 1987), 174-187.
Bortfeldt, Heinrich, *Washington, Bonn-Berlin. Die USA und die deutsche Einheit* (Bonn: Bouvier Verlag, 1993).
Bosworth, Stephen W., "The United States and Asia", *Foreign Affairs*, vol. 71, No. 1, 1992, 113-129.
Bozo, Fréderic, "Organisations de sécurité et insécurité en Europe", *Politique Etrangère*, vol. 58, No. 2, 1993, 447-458.
Id., "La France, l'OTAN et l'avenir de la dissuasion en Europe", *Politique Etrangère*, vol. 56, No. 2, summer 1991, 513-527.
Buchan, David, "Why a Temple Proved Stronger than a Tree", *Financial Times*, 7 and 8 December 1991.

Bull, Hedley, "Civilian Power Europe: A Contradiction in Terms?", *Journal of Common Market Studies*, vol. 21, No. 4, June 1983, 149-170.
Burg, Steven L., "Negotiating A Settlement: Lessons of the Diplomatic Process", in Stephen J. Blank (ed.), *Yugoslavia's Wars: The Problem From Hell* (Carlisle Barracks: Strategic Studies Institute, 1995), 47-86.
Burke, Peter, *Venetie en Amsterdam* (Amsterdam: Agon, 1991).
Bush, George, and Scowcroft, Brent, *A World Transformed* (New York: Alfred A. Knopf, 1998).
Bush, George (with Victor Gold), *Looking Forward* (New York: Doubleday, 1987).
Cahen, Alfred, *The Western European Union* (London: Brassey's, 1989).
Calingaert, Michael, *The 1992 Challenge From Europe: Development of the European Community's Internal Market* (Washington D.C.: National Planning Association, 1988).
Calleo, David, *Beyond American Hegemony: The Future of the Western Alliance* (New York: Basic Books, 1987).
Campbell, Colin, "The White House and Presidency Under the "Let's Deal" President", in Colin Campbell and Bert A. Rockman (eds.), *The Bush Presidency. First Appraisals* (Chatham, New Jersey: Chatham Publishers, 1991), 185-222.
Id. and Rockman, Bert A., (eds.), *The Bush Presidency. First Appraisals* (Chatham, New Jersey: Chatham Publishers, 1991).
Campbell, John C., *Tito's Separate Road. America and Yugoslavia in World Politics* (New York: Council on Foreign Relations, 1967).
Carlsnaes, Walter and Smith, Steve (eds.), *European Foreign Policy: The EC and Changing Perspectives in Europe* (London: Sage, 1994).
Carr, Edward Halett, *The Twenty Years' Crisis 1919-1939. An Introduction to the Studies of International Relations* (London: Macmillan, 1940)(second print).
Castellan, Georges, *History of the Balkans. From Mohammed the Conqueror to Stalin* (New York: Columbia University Press, 1992).
Cecchini, Paolo, *The European Challenge 1992: The Benefits of A Single Market* (Aldershot: Gower, 1988).
Chancellor, John, *Peril and Promise. A Commentary on America* (New York: Harper and Row Publishers, 1990).
Churchill, Winston S., *The Second World War. Triumph and Tragedy* (Boston: Houghton Mifflin Company, 1953).
Clesse, Armand, *Le projet de CED du plan Pleven au "crime" du 30 août. Histoire d'un malentendu européen* (Baden-Baden: Nomos Verlag, 1989).
Closa, Carlos, "The Gulf Crisis: A Case Study of National Constraints on Community Action", *Journal of European Integration*, vol. 15, No. 1, 1991, 47-67.
Cogan, Charles G., *Oldest Allies, Guarded Friends. The United States and France Since 1940* (Westport-Connecticut-London: Praeger, 1994).
Cohen, Lenard J., *Broken Bonds. The Disintegration of Yugoslavia* (Boulder: Westview Press, 1993)(second edition).
Cook, Don, *Forging the Alliance. NATO, 1945-1950* (London: Secker and Warburg,

1989).

Corbett, Richard, *The Treaty of Maastricht: From Conception to Ratification: A Comprehensive Reference Guide* (Harlow: Longman, 1993).

Corterier, Peter, "Transforming the Atlantic Alliance", *The Washington Quarterly*, vol. 14, No. 1, winter 1991, 27-37.

Costigliola, Frank, *France and the United States. The Cold Alliance Since World War II* (New York: Twayne Publishers, 1992).

Crabb, Cecil C. and Holt, Pat M., *Invitation to Struggle. Congress, the President, and Foreign Policy* (Washington D.C.: Congressional Quarterly Press, 1992)(fourth edition).

Crnobrnja, Mihailo, *The Yugoslav Drama* (London: I.B. Tauris Publishers, 1994).

Cromwell, William C., "Europe, the United States and the Pre-War Gulf Crisis", *International Journal*, vol. 48, No. 1, winter 1992-1993, 124-150.

Id., *The United States and the European Pillar. The Strained Alliance* (London: Macmillan, 1992).

Dak, John, *No More "Special" Anglo-American Relations: Rhetoric and Reality* (London: Weidenfeld and Nicolson, 1994).

David, Dominique, (ed.), *La Politique de défense de la France. Textes et documents* (Paris: Fondation pour les études de défense nationale, 1989).

Davidson, Roger H., and Oleszek, Walter J., *Congress and Its Members* (Washington D.C.: Congressional Quarterly Press, 1994)(fourth edition).

Devuyst, Youri, "European Community Integration and the United States: Toward A New Transatlantic Relationship?", *Journal of European Integration*, vol. 14, No. 1, 1990, 5-29.

Dinan, Desmond, *US-EC Relations: From the Transatlantic Declaration to Maastricht and Beyond* (Washington D.C.: Unpublished Paper, 1992).

Dolton, Harry J., *The Future Role of the United States in European Security: Determining Factors* (Rome: NATO Defence College, 1991).

Duchêne, François, *Jean Monnet. The First Statesman of Interdependence* (New York-London: W.W. Norton and Company, 1994).

Id., "Europe's Role in World Peace", in Richard Mayne (ed.), *Europe Tomorrow* (London: Fontana/Collins, 1972), 32-47.

Duff, Andrew, Pinder, John, and Pryce, Roy, *Maastricht and Beyond. Building the Union* (London-New York: Routledge, 1994).

Duffy, Michael, and Goodgame, Dan, *Marching in Place. The Status Quo Presidency of George Bush* (New York: Simon and Schuster, 1992).

Duke, Simon, *The Elusive Quest for European Security. From EDC to CFSP* (London: Macmillan, 1999).

Eden, Anthony, *Full Circle* (London: Casell, 1960).

Eden, Lynn, "The End of US Cold War History?", *International Security*, vol. 18, No. 1, summer 1993, 174-207.

Edwards, Geoffrey, "European Responses to the Yugoslav Crisis: An Interim Assessment", in Reinhardt Rummel (ed.), *Toward Political Union. Planning a*

*Common Foreign and Security Policy in the European Community* (Boulder-San Francisco-Oxford: Westview Press, 1992), 161-186.

Edwards, George C., "George Bush and the Public Presidency", in Colin Campbell and Bert A. Rockman (eds.), *The Bush Presidency. First Appraisals* (Chatham, New Jersey: Chatham Publishers, 1991), 129-154.

Eekelen, Willem Frederik van, *Debating European Security, 1948-1998* (The Hague – Brussels: Sdu Publishers and Centre for European Policy Studies, 1998).

Id., "WEU and the Gulf Crisis", *Survival*, vol. 32, No. 6, November- December 1990, 519-532.

Ehlerman, Claus Dieter, "The Institutional Development of the EC under the Single European Act", *Aussenpolitik*, vol. 41, No. 2, 1990, 135-146.

Elman, Colin, "Why Not Neorealist Theories of Foreign Policy?, *Security Studies*, vol. 6, No. 1, autumn 1996, 7-53.

Emerson, Michael, et al., *The Economics of 1992. The EC Commission's Assessment of the Economic Effects of Completing the Internal Market* (Oxford: Oxford University Press, 1988).

Evera, Stephen, Van, "Why Europe Matters, Why the Third World Doesn't: American Grand Strategy After the Cold War", *Journal of Strategic Studies*, vol. 13, No. 2, June 1990, 1-51.

"Excerpts From Pentagon's Plan: Prevent the Re-Emergence of A New Rival", *New York Times*, 8 March 1992, A14.

Eyal, Jonathan, *Europe and Yugoslavia: Lessons from a Failure* (London: Royal United Services Institute for Defence Studies, 1993).

Fauvet, Jacques, "Naissance et mort d'un traité", in Raymond Aron and Daniel Lerner (eds.), *La querelle de la CED* (Paris: Armand Colin, 1956), 23-58.

Featherstone, Kevin, and Ginsberg, Roy H., *The United States and the European Community in the 1990s. Partners in Transition* (London: St. Martin's Press, 1993).

Feld, Werner J., "International Implications of the Joint Franco-German Brigade", *Military Review*, vol. 70, No. 2, 1990, 3-11.

Feldstein, Martin, "Europe's Monetary Union. The Case Against EMU", *The Economist*, 13 June 1992, 19-22.

Finkielkraut, Alain, *Comment peut-on être croate?* (Paris: Gallimard, 1992).

Frankel, Benjamin, (ed.), "Roots of Realism", *Security Studies*, vol. 5, No. 2, winter 1995 (special issue).

Freeland, Richard M., *The Truman Doctrine and the Origins of McCartyism. Foreign Policy, Domestic Politics, and Internal Security 1946-1948* (New York and London: New York University Press, 1985).

Freestone, David, and Davidson, Scott, "Community Competence and Part III of the Single European Act", *Common Market Law Review*, vol. 23, No. 4, 1986, 793-801.

Friend, Julius W., *The Linchpin. French-German Relations, 1950-1990* (Washington D.C: Center for Strategic and International Studies, 1991).

Fukuyama, Francis, "The End of History?", *The National Interest*, vol. 16, summer 1989, 3-18.
Fursdon, Edward, *The European Defence Community: A History* (London: Macmillan, 980).
Gaddis, John Lewis, "International Relations Theory and the End of the Cold War", *International Security*, vol. 17, No. 3, winter 1992-1993, 5-58.
Id., "The Long Peace: Elements of Stability in the Postwar International System", *International Security*, vol. 10, No. 4, spring 1986, 99-142.
Gantz, Nanette, and Roper, John (eds.), *Towards A New Partnership. US-European Relations in the Post-Cold War Era* (Paris: The Institute for Security Studies, WEU, 1993).
Gapinski, James H., *The Economic Structure and Failure of Yugoslavia* (Westport: Praeger, 1993).
Garde, Paul, *Vie et mort de la Yougoslavie* (Paris: Fayard, 1992).
Gardner, David, "EC Dashes Into Its Own Backyard", *Financial Times*, 1 July 1991.
Garton Ash, Timothy, *In Europe's Name: Germany and the Divided Continent* (London: Cape, 1993).
Genscher, Hans-Dietrich, *Erinnerungen* (Berlin: Siedler, 1995).
Gerbet, Pierre, "In Search of Political Union: The Fouchet Plan Negotiations (1960-62)", in Roy Pryce (ed.), *The Dynamics of European Union* (London: Croom Helm, 1987), 105-129.
Gere, François, "L'Europe et l'OTAN dans la stratégie américaine", *Défense nationale*, vol. 47, No. 8-9, August-September 1991, 49-65.
Germroth, David S., and Hudson, Rebecca J., "German-American Relations and the Post Cold War World", *Aussenpolitik*, vol. 43, No. 1, 1992, 33-41.
Id., "Germany's Response to the Gulf Crisis: The New German Question", *Aussenpolitik*, vol. 43, No. 1, 1992, 33-42.
Gill, Stephen, *Atlantic Relations: Beyond the Reagan Era* (London: Harvester Wheatsheaf, 1989).
Gillespie, Paul, and Price, Rodney, *Political Union – Implications for Ireland* (Dublin: Institute for European Affairs, 1991).
Gilpin, Robert, *War and Change in World Politics* (Cambridge: Cambridge University Press, 1981).
Glaesner, H.J., "L'acte unique européen", *Revue du Marché Commun*, No. 298, June 1986, 307-321.
Glaser, Charles L., "Realists as Optimists. Cooperation as Self-Help", *International Security*, vol. 19, No. 3, winter 1994-1995, 50-90.
Glennon, Michael J., "The Gulf War and the Constitution", *Foreign Policy*, vol. 70, 1991, 84-101.
Glenny, Misha, *The Fall of Yugoslavia. The Third Balkan War* (London: Penguin Books, 1992).
Gloannec, Anne-Marie, le, "The Implications of German Unification for Western Europe", in Paul B. Stares (ed.), *The New Germany and the New Europe*

(Washington D.C.: The Brookings Institution, 1992), 251-278.

Glynn, Patrick, "See No Evil", in Nader Mousavizadeh, *The Black Book. The Consequences of Appeasement of Bosnia* (New York: Basic Books, 1996), 132-137.

Gnesotto, Nicole, "Lessons of Yugoslavia", *Chaillot Papers*, No. 14, March 1994.

Goldstein, Joshua S., *Long Cycles. Prosperity and War in the Modern Age* (New Haven and London: Yale University Press, 1988).

Gompert, David, and Larrabee, F. Stephen, *America and Europe: A Partnership for A New Era* (Cambridge and Santa Monica: Cambridge University Press and Rand, 1997).

Gompert, David, "How to Defeat Serbia", *Foreign Affairs*, vol. 73, No. 4, July-August 1994, 30-47.

Goodby, James E., "Peacekeeping in the New Europe", *The Washington Quarterly*, vol. 15, No. 3, spring 1992, 153-171.

Gordon, Philip H., "Recasting the Alliance", *Survival*, vol. 38, No. 1, spring 1996, 32-57.

Id., *A Certain Idea of France. French Security Policy and the Gaullist Legacy* (Princeton: Princeton University Press, 1993).

Id., *French Security Policy After the Cold War. Continuity, Change, and Implications for the United States* (Santa Monica: Rand, 1992).

Grant, Robert P., "France's New Relationship with NATO", *Survival*, vol. 38, No. 1, spring 1996, 58-80.

Grant, Charles, *Delors. Inside the House that Jacques Built* (London: Nicholas Brealey Publishing, 1994).

Greco, Ettore, "Italy, the Yugoslav Crisis and the Osimo Agreements", *The International Spectator*, vol. 29, No. 1, January-March 1994, 13-31.

Green, Fitzhugh, *George Bush. An Intimate Portrait* (New York: Hippocrene Books, 1989).

Gretschmann, Klaus, *European Monetary Union: Stairway to Heaven or Dead End Street of Integration?* Paper delivered at the 1993 annual meeting of the American Political Science Association, Washington D.C., 2-5 September 1993.

Grieco, Joseph M., *Cooperation Among Nations: Europe, America and Non-Tariff Barriers to Trade* (Ithaca: Cornell University Press, 1990).

Id., "Anarchy and the Limits of Cooperation: A Realist Critique of the Newest Liberal Institutionalism", *International Organization*, vol. 42, No. 3, summer 1988, 485-507.

Gros, Daniel, and Thygesen, Niels, *European Monetary Integration: From the European Monetary System to European Monetary Union* (New York: Saint Martin's Press, 1992).

Grosser, Alfred, *The Western Alliance. European-American Relations Since 1945* (London: Macmillan, 1980).

Guazzone, Laura, "Italy and the Gulf Crisis: European and Domestic Dimensions", *The International Spectator*, vol. 26, No. 4, October-December 1991, 57-74.

Guicherd, Catherine, *A European Defense Identity: Challenge and Opportunity for NATO* (Washington D.C.: Congressional Research Service, 1991).

Haglund, David G., *Alliance Within the Alliance? Franco-German Military Cooperation and the European Pillar of Defense* (Boulder, San Francisco, Oxford: Westview Press, 1991).

Hanrieder, Wolfram F., *Germany, America, Europe. Forty Years of German Foreign Policy* (New Haven: Yale University Press, 1989).

Hartog, Arthur, den, "Greece and European Political Union", in Finn Laursen and Sophie Vanhoonacker (eds.), *The Intergovernmental Conference on Political Union. Institutional Reforms, New Policies and International Identity of the European Community* (Maastricht, Dordrecht: EIPA and Martinus Nijhoff Publishers, 1992), 79-97.

Heisbourg, François, "The Future of the Atlantic Alliance: Whither NATO, Whether NATO", *The Washington Quarterly*, vol. 15, No. 2, spring 1992, 127-139.

Henrikson, Alan K., "The New Atlanticism: Western Partnership for Global Leadership", *Journal of European Integration*, vol. 16, Nos. 2-3, winter-spring 1993, 165-191.

Heuser, Béatrice, *Western "Containment" Policies in the Cold War. The Yugoslav Case, 1948-53* (London and New York: Routledge, 1989).

Heuvel, Martin, van den, and Siccama, Jan G., (eds.), *Yearbook of European Integration. The Disintegration of Yugoslavia* (Amsterdam: University of Amsterdam, 1992).

Higgins, Rosalyn, "The New United Nations and the Former Yugoslavia", *International Affairs*, vol. 69, No. 3, 1993, 465-483.

Hill, Christopher, "European Foreign Policy: Power Bloc, Civilian Model – or Flop?", in Reinhardt Rummel (ed.), *The Evolution of An International Actor. Western Europe's New Assertiveness* (Boulder, San Francisco, Oxford: Westview Press, 1990), 31-55.

Hoffmann, Stanley, "de Gaulle, Europe, and the Atlantic Alliance", *International Organization*, vol. 18, No. 1, winter 1964, 1-28.

Hogan, Michael, *The Marshall Plan. America, Britain and the Reconstruction of Western Europe, 1947-1952* (Cambridge: Cambridge University Press, 1987).

Holland, Martin (ed.), *The Future of European Political Cooperation. Essays on Theory and Practice* (London: Macmillan, 1991).

Howarth, D., "The Compromise on Denmark and the Treaty on European Union: A Legal and Political Analysis", *Common Market Law Review*, vol. 31, No. 4, 1994, 765-806.

Hufbauer, Gary Clyde, (ed.), *Europe 1992. An American Perspective* (Washington D.C.: The Brookings Institution, 1990).

Hulten, Michiel van, *The Short Life and Sudden Death of the Dutch Draft Treaty Towards the European Union* (Bruges: College of Europe, 1993).

Hunt, Michael H., *Ideology and US Foreign Policy* (New Haven and London: Yale University Press, 1987).

Huntington, Samuel P., *The Clash of Civilizations and the Remaking of World Order* (New York: Simon and Schuster, 1996).

Id., "Why International Primacy Matters", *International Security*, vol. 17, No. 4, spring 1993, 68-118.

Hutchings, Robert L., *American Diplomacy and the End of the Cold War: An Insider's Account of US Policy in Europe, 1989-1992* (Washington D.C.: The Woodrow Wilson Center Press and John Hopkins University Press, 1997).

Ifestos, Panayiotis, *European Political Cooperation: Towards A Framework of Supranational Diplomacy?* (Aldershot: Avebury, 1987).

Jacomet, Arnaud, "The Role of WEU in the Gulf Crisis", in Nicole Gnesotto and John Roper (eds), *Western Europe and the Gulf. A Study of West European Reactions to the Gulf War* (Paris: Western European Union, Institute for Strategic Studies, 1992), 159-169.

James, Alan, "The UN in Croatia: An Exercise in Futility", *The World Today*, vol. 49, No. 5, May 1993, 93-95.

Jelavich, Barbara, *History of the Balkans.* (Cambridge: Cambridge University Press, 1983)(2 vol.).

Jervis, Robert, "International Primacy. Is the Game Worth the Candle?", *International Security*, vol. 17, No. 4, spring 1993, 52-67.

Id., "Systems Theories and Diplomatic History" in Paul Gordon Lauren (ed.), *Diplomacy: New Approaches in History, Theory, and Policy* (New York: Free Press, 1979).

Jobert, Michel, *Mémoires d'avenir* (Paris: Grasset, 1974).

Joffe, Josef, ""Bismarck" or "Britain". Toward an American Grand Strategy after Bipolarity", *International Security*, vol. 19, No. 4, spring 1995, 94-117.

Id., "After Bipolarity: Germany and European Security", *Adelphi Paper*, No. 285, February 1994.

Jones, Joseph M., *The Fifteen Weeks (February 21-June 5, 1947)* (New York: The Viking Press, 1955).

Jopp, Mathias, "The Strategic Implications of European Integration", *Adelphi Paper*, No. 290, 1994.

Jopp, Mathias, and Wessels, Wolfgang, "Institutional Frameworks for Security Cooperation in Western Europe: Developments and Options", in Mathias Jopp, Reinhardt Rummel, and Peter Schmidt (eds.), *Integration and Security in Western Europe. Inside the European Pillar* (Boulder, San Francisco, Oxford: Westview Press, 1991), 25-73.

Jordan, Robert S., "Atlantic Relations and the New Europe. A Conference Report and Analysis of the Committee on Atlantic Studies" (New Orleans: The Eisenhower Center for Leadership Studies, March 1992).

Jorgensen, Knud Erik, "The Western European Union and the Imbroglio of European Security", *Cooperation and Conflict*, vol. 25, No. 3, 1990, 135-152.

Kaiser, Karl, "Devenir membre permanent du Conseil de Sécurité: un but légitime de la nouvelle politique extérieure allemande", *Politique Etrangère*, vol. 58, No. 4, winter 1993-1994, 1011-1022.

Id., *Deutschlands Vereinigung: Die internationalen Aspekte. Mit den wichtigen Dokumenten* (Bergisch-Gladbach: G. Lübbe Verlag, 1991).

Kaiser, Karl and Becher, Klaus, "Germany and the Iraq Conflict", in Nicole Gnesotto and John Roper (eds.), *Western Europe and the Gulf. A Study of West European Reactions to the Gulf War* (Paris: Western European Union, Institute for Strategic Studies, 1992), 39-69.

Kaiser, Wolfram, "The Bomb and Europe. Britain, France, and the EEC Entry Negotiations 1961-1963", *Journal of European Integration History*, vol. 1, No.1, 1995, 65-85.

Keatinge, Patrick (ed.), *Maastricht and Ireland: What the Treaty Means* (Dublin: Institute of European Affairs, 1992).

Kegley, Charles W., "The Neoidealist Moment in International Studies? Realist Myths and the New International Realities", *International Studies Quarterly*, vol. 37, No. 2, June 1993, 131-146.

Kegley, Charles W., and Wittkopf, Eugene R., *American Foreign Policy. Pattern and Process* (New York: St Martin's Press, 1991).

Kennan, George, *American Diplomacy, 1900-1950* (Chicago: University of Chicago Press, 1951).

Kennedy, Paul, *The Rise and Fall of the Great Powers. Economic Change and Military Conflict from 1500 to 2000* (London: Fontana Press, 1989)(first print in 1988).

Keohane, Robert O., "Institutional Theory and the Realist Challenge After the Cold War", in David A. Baldwin (ed.), *Neorealism and Neoliberalism. The Contemporary Debate* (New York: Columbia University Press, 1993), 269-300.

Id. (ed.), *Neorealism and Its Critics* (New York: Columbia University Press, 1986).

Id., *After Hegemony. Cooperation and Discord in the World Political Economy* (Princeton: Princeton University Press, 1984).

Keohane, Robert O., Nye, Joseph S., and Hoffmann, Stanley, (eds.), *After the Cold War. International Institutions and State Strategies in Europe, 1989-1991* (Cambridge, Massachusetts: Harvard University Press, 1993).

Keraudren, Philippe, and Dubois, Nicolas, "France and the Ratification of the Maastricht Treaty", in Finn Laursen and Sophie Vanhoonacker (eds.), *The Ratification of the Maastricht Treaty: Issues, Debates and Future Implications* (Maastricht and Dordrecht: EIPA and Martinus Nijhoff Publishers, 1994), 147-179.

Keukeleire, Stephan, *Het buitenlands beleid van de Europese Unie* (Deventer: Kluwer, 1998).

Kielinger, Thomas, and Otte, Max, "Germany: The Pressured Power", *Foreign Policy*, vol. 91, summer 1993, 44-62.

Killen, Linda, *Testing the Peripheries. US-Yugoslav Economic Relations in the Interwar Years* (New York: Columbia University Press, 1994).

Kindleberger, Charles, *The World in Depression, 1929-1939* (Berkeley: University of California Press, 1973).

King, Nicholas, *George Bush. A Biography* (New York: Dodd, Mead and Company, 1980).
Kissinger, Henry, *Diplomacy* (New York: Touchstone, 1994).
Id., *Years of Upheaval* (Boston-Toronto: Little, Brown and Company, 1982).
Kohl, Helmut, *Ich Wollte Deutschlands Einheit*. Dargestellt von Kai Diekmann und Ralf Georg Reuth (Berlin: Ullstein Buchverlage, 1996).
Kolboom, Ingo, "A la chasse aux vieux démons: la France et l'Allemagne unie", *Politique Etrangère*, vol. 56, No. 3, autumn 1991, 715-721.
Kramer, Steven Philip, "La question française", *Politique Etrangère*, vol. 56, No. 4, 1991, 959-974.
Krasner, Stephen, "Declining American Leadership in the World Economy", *The International Spectator*, vol. 26, No. 3, July-September 1991, 49-74.
Krause, Axel, "What Ever Happened to Bush's Europhoria?", *European Affairs*, vol. 5, No. 3, June-July 1991, 44-47.
Krauthammer, Charles, "The Unipolar Moment", *Foreign Affairs*, vol. 70, No. 1, 1990-91, 23-33.
Krenzler, Horst G. and Kaiser, Wolfram, "The Transatlantic Declaration: A New Basis for Relations Between the EC and the USA", *Aussenpolitik*, vol. 42, No. 4, 1991, 363-372.
Lak, Maarten, "The Involvement of the European Community in the Yugoslav Crisis During 1991", in Martin van den Heuvel and Jan G. Siccama (eds.), *Yearbook of European Studies. The Disintegration of Yugoslavia* (Amsterdam: University of Amsterdam, 1992), 175-185.
Id., "Interaction between European Political Cooperation and the European Community (External)- Existing Rules and Challenges", *Common Market Law Review*, vol. 26, No. 2, 1989, 281-299.
Larrabee, F. Stephen, "La politique américaine et la crise yougoslave", *Politique Etrangère*, vol. 59, No. 4, winter 1994, 1041-1055.
Laursen, Finn, and Vanhoonacker, Sophie (eds.), *The Ratification of the Maastricht Treaty: Issues, Debates and Future Implications* (Maastricht and Dordrecht: EIPA and Martinus Nijhoff Publishers, 1994).
Laursen, Finn, "Denmark and the Ratification of the Maastricht Treaty", in Finn Laursen and Sophie Vanhoonacker (eds.), *The Ratification of the Maastricht Treaty: Issues, Debates and Future Implications* (Maastricht and Dordrecht: EIPA and Martinus Nijhoff Publishers, 1994), 61-86.
Id., "The Maastricht Treaty: Implications for the Nordic Countries", *Cooperation and Conflict*, vol. 28, No. 2, 1993, 115-141.
Id., "The EC in the World Context. Civilian Power or Superpower?", *Futures*, vol. 23, No. 7, September 1991, 747-759.
Id., "Denmark and Political Union", in Finn Laursen and Sophie Vanhoonacker (eds.), *The Intergovernmental Conference on Political Union. Institutional Reforms, New Policies and International Identity of the European Community* (Maastricht, Dordrecht: EIPA and Martinus Nijhoff Publishers, 1992), 63-78.

Id., and Vanhoonacker, Sophie, (eds.), *The Intergovernmental Conference on Political Union. Institutional Reforms, New Policies and International Identity of the European Community* (Maastricht, Dordrecht: EIPA and Martinus Nijhoff Publishers, 1992).
Layne, Christopher, "The Unipolar Illusion: Why New Great Powers Will Arise", *International Security*, vol. 17, No. 4, spring 1993, 5-51.
Id., "Continental Divide: Time to Disengage in Europe", *The National Interest*, No. 13, fall 1988, 13-27.
Id., "Atlanticism Without NATO", *Foreign Policy*, vol. 67, summer 1987, 22-45.
Lebow, Richard Ned, and Risse-Kappen, Thomas, (eds.), *International Relations Theory and the End of the Cold War* (New York: Columbia University Press, 1995).
Lees, Martin, "The Impact of Europe 1992 on the Atlantic Partnership", *The Washington Quarterly*, vol. 12, No. 4, autumn 1989, 171-182.
Lees, Michael, *The Rape of Serbia: The British Role in Tito's Grab for Power, 1943-1944* (New York: Harcourt Brace Jovanovich, 1990).
Lemaitre, Philippe, "Les Etats-Unis contre les Douze", *Le Monde*, 9 July 1991.
Linnenkamp, Hilmar, "The Security Policy of the New Germany", in Paul B. Stares (ed.), *The New Germany and the New Europe* (Washington D.C.: The Brookings Institution, 1992), 93-125.
Lippmann, Walter, *US Foreign Policy: Shield of the Republic* (Boston: Little, Brown, 1943).
Lodgaard, Sverre, "Competing Schemes for Europe: The CSCE, NATO and the European Union", *Security Dialogue*, vol. 23, No. 3, 1992, 57-68.
Louis, Jean-Victor, "A Monetary Union for Tomorrow?", *Common Market Law Review*, vol. 26, No. 2, 1989, 301-326.
Ludlow, Peter, *Europe and North America in the 1990s* (Brussels: Centre for European Policy Studies, 1992).
Id., *The Making of the European Monetary System: A Case Study of the Politics of the European Community* (London: Butterworth Scientific, 1992).
Lundestad, Geir, "Empire by Invitation? The United States and Western Europe, 1945-1952", in Charles S. Maier (ed.), *The Cold War in Europe. Era of a Divided Continent* (New York: Markus Wiener Publishing, 1991), 143-165.
Luttwak, Edward N., *The Endangered American Dream: How to Stop the United States from Becoming a Third World Country and How to Win the Geo-Economic Struggle for Industrial Supremacy* (New York: Simon and Schuster, 1993).
Id., "From Geopolitics to Geo-Economics", *The National Interest*, vol. 20, summer 1990, 17-23.
Lynn-Jones, Sean M., and Miller, Steven E., *The Cold War and After. Prospects for Peace* (Cambridge, Mass., London: MIT Press, 1997)(fourth edition).
Lytle, Paula Franklin, "US Policy Toward the Demise of Yugoslavia: The "Virus of Nationalism"", *East European Politics and Societies*, vol. 6, No. 3, fall 1992, 303-318.

Maclean, Fitzroy, *Eastern Approaches* (Harmondsworth: Penguin Books, 1991)(first edition in 1949).
Mahaney, Mark S., "The European Community as a Global Power: Implications for the United States", *SAIS Review*, vol. 13, No. 1, winter-spring 1993, 77-88.
Mann, Thomas E., *A Question of Balance. The President, the Congress, and Foreign Policy* (Washington D.C.: The Brookings Institution, 1990).
Martial, Enrico, "France and European Political Union", in Finn Laursen and Sophie Vanhoonacker (eds.), *The Intergovernmental Conference on Political Union. Institutional Reforms, New Policies and International Identity of the European Community* (Maastricht, Dordrecht: EIPA and Martinus Nijhoff Publishers, 1992), 115-126.
Martin, Lawrence W., "The American Decision to Rearm Germany", in Harold Stein, *American Civil-Military Decisions. A Book of Case Studies* (Alabama: University of Alabama Press, 1963), 645-665.
Massigli, René, *Une comédie des erreurs 1943-1956. Souvenirs et réflexions sur une étape de la construction européenne* (Paris: Plon, 1978).
Mastanduno, Michael, "Preserving the Unipolar Moment. Realist Theories and US Grand Strategy After the Cold War", *International Security*, vol. 21, No. 4, 1997, 49-88.
Maull, Hanns W., "Germany in the Yugoslav Crisis", *Survival*, vol. 37, No. 4, winter 1995-1996, 99-130.
Id., "German Unity in A European Context", in Otto Pick (ed.), *The Cold War Legacy in Europe* (London and New York: Pinter Publishers and St. Martin's Press, 1992), 96-104.
Maurer, Pierre, "United States-Yugoslav Relations. A Marriage of Convenience", *Studia Diplomatica*, vol. 38, No. 4, 1985, 429-451.
Meadows, Gale A., "United States Perspectives on the Growth of a European Pillar", in Michael Clarke and Rod Hague, *European Defence Cooperation. America, Britain and NATO* (Manchester: Manchester University Press, 1990).
Mearsheimer, John J., "Back to the Future. Instability in Europe After the Cold War", *International Security*, vol. 15, No. 1, summer 1990, 5-56.
Meiers, Franz-Josef, "Germany: The Reluctant Power", *Survival*, vol. 37, No. 3, autumn 1995, 82-103.
Mélandri, Pierre, "Les Etats-Unis et le plan Pleven", *Relations Internationales*, vol. 11, 1977, 201-229.
Melissen, Jan, "Pre-Summit Diplomacy: Britain, the United States and the Nassau Conference", *Diplomacy and Statecraft*, vol. 7, No. 3, November 1996, 652-687.
Menon, Anand, "From Independence to Cooperation: France, NATO and European Security", *International Affairs*, vol. 71, No. 1, 1995, 19-34.
Id., Forster, Anthony, and Wallace, William, "A Common Defence?", *Survival*, vol. 34, No. 3, autumn 1992, 98-118.
Meriano, Carlo Ernesto, "The Single European Act. Past, Present and Future", *The International Spectator*, vol. 22, No. 2, April-June 1987, 89-99.

Milward, Alan S., *The Reconstruction of Western Europe 1945-51* (London: Methuen & Co., 1984).
Monar, Jörg, Ungerer, Werner, Wessels, Wolfgang, *The Maastricht Treaty on European Union: Legal Complexity and Political Dynamic* (Brussels: European Interuniversity Press, 1993).
Monnet, Jean, *Memoirs* (London: Collins, 1978).
Moravcsick, Andrew, "Negotiating the Single European Act: National Interests and Conventional Statecraft in the European Community", *International Organization*, vol. 45, No. 1, 1991, 651-688.
Morgan, Roger P., *High Politics, Low Politics: Toward a Foreign Policy for Western Europe* (Beverly Hills, California and London: SAGE Publications, 1973).
Morgenthau, Hans J., *Politics Among Nations: The Struggle for Power and Peace* (New York: Knopf, 1978)(fifth edition revised).
Morici, Peter, "Free Trade with Mexico", *Foreign Policy*, vol.87, 1992, 88-104.
Muravcik, Joshua, *The Imperative of American Leadership. A Challenge to Neo-Isolationism* (Washington D.C.: American Enterprise Institute, 1996).
Nanz, Klaus-Peter, "Der 3. Pfeiler der Europäischen Union: Zusammenarbeit in der Innen- und Justizpolitik", *Integration*, vol. 15, No. 3, 1992, 126-140.
Nau, Henry R., *The Myth of America's Decline. Leading the World Economy into the 1990s* (New York-Oxford: Oxford University Press, 1990).
Neville-Jones, Pauline, "The Genscher/Colombo Proposals on European Union", *Common Market Law Review*, vol. 20, No. 4, 1983, 657-699.
Newhouse, John, "Bonn, der Westen und die Auflösung Jugoslawiens. Das Versahen der Diplomatie – Chronik eines Skandals", *Blätter für deutsche und internationale Politik*, vol. 92, No. 10, 1992, 1190-1205.
Nijenhuis, Hans, "De Nederlandse tactiek in de onderhandelingen over een Europese politieke unie (1960-1962): Nee tegen de Gaulle", *Internationale Spectator*, vol. 41, No. 1, January 1987, 41-49.
Noris, Pippa, "The 1992 Presidential Election: Voting Behaviour and Legitimacy", in Gillian Peele, Christopher J.Bailey *et al.* (eds.), *Developments in American Politics* (London: Macmillan, 1994)(second edition), 279-280.
North, Douglas C., and Thomas, Robert Paul, *The Rise of the Western World – A New Economic History* (Cambridge: Cambridge University Press, 1973).
Nuttall, Simon, "The Commission: The Struggle for Legitimacy", in Christopher Hill (ed.), *The Actors in Europe's Foreign Policy* (London: Routledge, 1996), 130-147.
Id., *European Political Cooperation* (London: Clarendon Press, 1992).
Id., "Where the Commission Comes In", in Alfred E. Pijpers, Elfriede Regelsberger, and Wolfgang Wessels (eds.), *European Political Cooperation in the 1980's: A Common Foreign Policy for Western Europe* (Dordrecht: Martinus Nijhoff, 1988), 104-117.
Id., "Interaction Between European Political Cooperation and the European Community", in *Yearbook of European Law* (Oxford: Oxford University Press,

1987), 211-249.
Nye, Joseph S., *Bound to lead. The Changing Nature of American Power* (New York: Basic Books, 1990).
Id., "American Strategy After Bipolarity", *International Affairs*, vol.66, No.3, July 1990, 513-521.
Osgood, Robert Endicott, *NATO, the Entangling Alliance* (Chicago: The University of Chicago Press, 1962).
Owen, David, *Balkan Odyssey* (London: Victor Gollancz, 1995).
Id., "The Future of the Balkans. An Interview with David Owen", *Foreign Affairs*, vol. 72, No. 2, spring 1993, 1-9.
Paemen, Hugo, and Bensch, Alexandra, *Du Gatt à l'OMC: la Communauté européenne dans l'Uruguay Round* (Leuven: Leuven University Press, 1995).
Pardalis, Anastasia, "European Political Cooperation and the United States", *Journal of Common Market Studies*, vol. 25, No. 4, June 1987, 271-294.
Parenti, Michael, *Against Empire* (San Francisco: City Light Books, 1995).
Parmet, Herbert S., *George Bush: The Life of A Lone Star Yankee* (New York: Scribner, 1997).
Pattison de Ménil, Lois, *Who Speaks for Europe? The Vision of Charles de Gaulle* (London: Weidenfeld and Nicholson, 1977).
Paulsen, Thomas, *Die Jugoslawienpolitik der USA 1989-1994. Begrenztes Engagement und Konfliktdynamik* (Baden-Baden: Nomos Verlags- gesellschaft, 1995).
Pavlowitch, Stevan K., *Tito. Yugoslavia's Great Dictator* (London: C. Hurst & Co., 1992).
Pelkmans, Jacques, and Winters, L. Alan, *Europe's Domestic Market* (London: Royal Institute for International Affairs, 1988).
Pescatore, Pierre, "Some Critical Remarks on the Single European Act", *Common Market Law Review*, vol. 24, No. 1, 1987, 9-18.
Petersen, Nikolaj, "The European Union and Foreign and Security Policy", in Ole Norgaard, Thomas Pedersen and Nikolaj Petersen, *The European Community in World Politics* (London, New York: Pinter Publishers, 1993), 9-30.
Peterson, John, *Europe and America. The Prospects for Partnership* (London and New York: Routledge, 1996)(first edition in 1993).
Petkovic, Ranko, *Non Aligned Yugoslavia and the Contemporary World. The Foreign Policy of Yugoslavia, 1945-1985* (Belgrade: Medunarodna Politika, 1986).
Pijpers, Alfred E., *Vicissitudes of European Political Cooperation: Towards A Realist Interpretation of the EC's Collective Diplomacy* (Leiden: Rijksuniversiteit Leiden, 1990).
Id., "European Political Cooperation and the CSCE Process", *Legal Issues of European Integration*, No. 1, 1984, 135-148.
Id., Regelsberger, Elfriede, and Wessels, Wolfgang (eds.), *European Political Cooperation in the 1980's: A Common Foreign Policy for Western Europe* (Dordrecht: Martinus Nijhoff, 1988).
Pond, Elizabeth, *Beyond the Wall. Germany's Road to Unification* (Washington D.C.:

The Brookings Institution, 1993).
Powaski, Ronald E., "The Creation of the North Atlantic Alliance, 1947-1950", in Id., *Toward an Entangling Alliance. American Isolationism, Internationalism, and Europe, 1901-1950* (New York-London: Greenwood Press, 1991),195-222.
Powell, Colin L., *A Soldier's Way. An Autobiography* (London: Hutchinson, 1995).
*President Bush. The Challenge Ahead* (Washington D.C.: Congressional Quarterly, 1989).
*Public Papers of the Presidents of the United States. George Bush. 1989-1992* (Washington D.C.: US Government Printing Office, 1990-1993).
Ramet, Sabrina P., *Balkan Babel: The Disintegration of Yugoslavia from the Death of Tito to Ethnic War* (Boulder: Westview Press, 1995).
Rood, Jan Q.Th., *Hegemonie, Machtsspreiding en Internationaal- Economische Orde Sinds 1945* (Den Haag: Nederlands Instituut voor Internationale Betrekkingen, 1996).
Id., *Verzwakking van de Sterkste: Oorzaken en Gevolgen van Amerikaans Machtsverval* (Den Haag: Nederlands Instituut voor Internationale Betrekkingen "Clingendael", 1989).
Regelsberger, Elfriede, Schoutheete, Philippe, de, and Wessels, Wolfgang, *Foreign Policy of the European Union: From EPC to CFSP and Beyond* (Boulder, CO: Lynne Rienner Publishers, 1997).
Remacle, Eric, *La politique étrangère européenne: de Maastricht à la Yougoslavie* (Brussels: Institut européen de recherche et d'information sur la paix et la sécurité, 1992).
Ridley, Jasper, *Tito* (London: Constable, 1994).
Riste, Olav (ed.), *Western Security: The Formative Years. European and Atlantic Defence 1947-1953* (Oslo: Norwegian University Press, 1985).
Rockman, Bert A., "The Leadership Style of George Bush", in Colin Campbell and Bert A. Rockman (eds.), *The Bush Presidency. First Appraisals* (Chatham, New Jersey: Chatham Publishers, 1991), 1-35.
Romano, Sergio, "L'Italie et l'Europe du Danube et des Balkans", *Politique Etrangère*, vol. 57, No. 2, 1992, 349-358.
Roper, John and Gnesotto, Nicole, (eds.), *Western Europe and the Gulf. A Study of West European Reactions to the Gulf War* (Paris: Western European Union, Institute for Strategic Studies, 1992).
Rosecrance, Richard N., (ed.), *America as an Ordinary Country. US Foreign Policy and the Future* (Ithaca and London: Cornell University Press, 1976).
Id., *Action and Reaction in World Politics. International Systems in Perspective* (Boston-Toronto: Little, Brown and Co., 1963).
Rosskamm Shalom, Stephen, *Imperial Alibis. Rationalizing US Intervention After the Cold War* (Boston: South End Press, 1993).
Rozemond, S., *De gang naar Maastricht* (Den Haag: Nederlands Instituut voor Internationale Betrekkingen, 1991).
Rosenzweig, Luc, "L'Allemagne, puissance protectrice des Slovènes et des Croates",

*Le Monde*, 4 July 1991.
Ruiz Palmer, Diego A., "French Strategic Options in the 1990s", *Adelphi Paper*, No. 260, 1991.
Rummel, Reinhardt, "German-American Relations in the Setting of a New Atlanticism", *Irish Studies in International Affairs*, vol. 4, 1993, 17-31.
Id., "Beyond Maastricht: Alternative Futures for a Political Union, in Id., *Toward Political Union: Planning A Common Foreign and Security Policy in the European Community* (Baden-Baden: Nomos Verlag, 1992), 297-320.
Rusinow, Denisson, "Yugoslavia: Balkan Breakup", *Foreign Policy*, vol. 83, summer 1991, 143-159.
Ruyt, Jean, de, *L'acte unique européen* (Brussels: Editions de l'université de Bruxelles, 1989)(second edition).
Salmon, Trevor C., "Testing Times for European Political Cooperation: the Gulf and Yugoslavia, 1990-1992", *International Affairs*, vol. 68, No. 2, 1992, 233-253.
Santis, Hugh, de, "The Graying of NATO", *Washington Quarterly*, vol. 14, No. 4, autumn 1991, 51-65.
Schmidt, Peter, "A Complex Puzzle – the EU's Security Policy and UN Reform", *The International Spectator*, vol. 29, No. 3, July-September 1994, 53-66.
Schoutheete, Philippe, de, *La Coopération Politique Européenne* (Brussels: Labor, 1986) (second edition).
Schwartz, David N., *NATO's Nuclear Dilemma's* (Washington D.C.: The Brookings Institution, 1983).
Shelton, Steven, "A Tragedy Within A Tragedy: The Yugoslavian Partisan Movement", *Military review*, vol. 74, March 1994, 23-31.
Silber, Laura, and Little, Allan, *The Death of Yugoslavia* (London: Penguin Books and BBC Books, 1995).
Silberman, Laurence, "Yugoslavia's "Old" Communism: Europe's Fiddler on the Roof", *Foreign Policy*, vol.26, spring 1977, 3-27.
Silj, Alessandro, *Europe's Political Puzzle. A Study of the Fouchet Negotiations and the 1963 Veto* (Cambridge, Ma.: Center for International Affairs, Harvard University, 1967).
Sked, Alan, "Cheap Excuses. Germany and the Gulf Crisis", *The National Interest*, vol. 24, summer 1991, 51-60.
Sloan, Stanley R., Guicherd, Catherine, and Thomas, Rosita Maria, *NATO's Future: A Congressional-Executive Dialogue* (Washington D.C.: Congressional Research Service, 1992).
Smith, Michael, and Woolcock, Stephen, *The United States and the European Community in a Transformed World* (London: The Royal Institute of International Affairs, 1993).
Smith, Michael Joseph, *Realist Thought from Weber to Kissinger* (Baton Rouge: Louisiana State University Press, 1986).
Snidal, Duncan, "The Limits of Hegemonic Stability Theory", *International Organization*, vol. 39, No. 4, autumn 1985, 579-614.

Snyder, Glenn, "The Security Dilemma in Alliance Politics", *World Politics*, vol. 36, No. 4, July 1984, 461-495.
Staden, Alfred van, "A Return of the Classical Balance of Power", *Studia Diplomatica*, vol. 49, No. 6, 1996, 77-92.
Id., "After Maastricht: Explaining the Movement Towards A Common European Defence Policy", in Walter Carlsnaes and Steve Smith (eds.), *European Foreign Policy: The EC and Changing Perspectives in Europe* (London: Sage, 1994), 138-155.
Id., "De heerschappij van staten: het perspectief van het realisme", in R.B. Soetendorp, K.Koch, A. van Staden (eds.), *Internationale Betrekkingen: Theorieën en Benaderingen* (Utrecht: Het Spectrum, 1994), 11-39.
Id. (ed.), *Tussen Orde en Chaos: de Organizatie van de Veiligheid in het Nieuwe Europa* (Leiden: DSWO Press, 1994).
Stares, Paul B., (ed.), *The New Germany and the New Europe* (Washington D.C.: The Brookings Institution, 1992).
Stark, Hans, *Les Balkans. Le Retour de la guerre en Europe* (Paris: IFRI, 1993).
Id., "Dissonances franco-allemandes sur fond de guerre serbo-croate", *Politique Etrangère*, vol. 57, No. 2, 1992, 339-347.
*Statistical Abstract of the United States 1991* (Washington D.C.: US Department of Commerce, 1991), No. 1387.
*Statistical Abstract of the United States 1993* (Washington D.C.: US Department of Commerce, 1993), No. 1330.
Stavridis, Stelios, *Looking Back to See Forward: Assessing the CFSP in the Light of EPC* (London: London School of Economics and Political Science, 1994).
Stavrou, Nikolaos A., "The Balkan Quagmire and the West's Response", *Mediterranean Quarterly*, vol. 4, No. 1, winter 1993, 24-45.
Stein, George, "The Euro-corps and Future European Security Architecture", *European Security*, vol. 2, summer 1993, 200-226.
Steinberg, James B., "The Response of International Institutions to the Yugoslavia Conflict: Implications and Lessons", in F. Stephen Larrabee, *The Volatile Powder Keg. Balkan Security After the Cold War* (Washington D.C.: The American University Press, 1994), 233-274.
Stewart, Terence P., *The Gatt Uruguay Round: A Negotiating History (1986-1992)*(Deventer: Kluwer, 1993).
Tarnoff, Peter, "America's New Special Relationships", *Foreign Affairs*, vol. 69, No. 3, 1990, 67-75.
Taylor, Trevor, "West European Security and Defence Cooperation: Maastricht and Beyond", *International Affairs*, vol. 70, No. 1, January 1994, 1-16.
Tellis, Ashley J., "Reconstructing Political Realism. The Long March to Scientific Theory", *Security Studies*, vol. 5, No. 2, winter 1995, 2-94.
Teltschik, Horst, *329 Tage. Innenansichten der Einigung* (Berlin: Siedler Verlag 1991).
Thatcher, Margaret, *The Downing Street Years* (London: Harper Collins, 1993).

Thune, Christian, "Denmark and the Western European Union", in Panos Tsakaloyannis (ed.), *The Reactivation of the Western European Union: The Effects on the EC and Its Institutions* (Maastricht: EIPA, 1985), 87-95.

Thurow, Lester, *Head to Head. The Coming Economic Battle Among Japan, Europe and America* (New York: William Morrow and Company, 1992).

Thygesen, Niels, "The Delors Report and European Economic and Monetary Union, *International Affairs*, vol. 65, No. 4, autumn 1989, 637-652.

Tiefer, Charles, *The Semi-Sovereign Presidency. The Bush Administration's Strategy for Governing Without Congress* (Oxford: Boulder, 1994).

Toschi, Simona, "Washington-London-Paris. An Untenable Triangle", *Journal of European Integration History*, vol. 1, No. 2, 1995, 81-109.

Tower, John G., "Congress Versus the President: The Formulation and Implementation of American Foreign Policy", *Foreign Affairs*, vol. 60, No. 2, 1981-1982, 229-246.

Traynor, Ian, and White, Michael, "Shuttle Mission Gets Crash Course in Balkan Realities", *The Guardian*, 1 July 1991.

Tréan, Claire, "La France et le nouvel ordre européen", *Politique Etrangère*, vol. 56, No. 1, spring 1991, 81-90.

Trifunovska, Snezana, *Yugoslavia Through Documents. From Its Creation To Its Dissolution* (Dordrecht: Martinus Nijhoff Publishers, 1994).

Tromp, Bart, *Verraad op de Balkan. Een Kroniek* (Nieuwegein: Uitgeverij Aspekt, 1996).

Tsakaloyannis, Panos, *Towards a European Security Community* (Baden-Baden: Nomos Verlag, 1996).

Id. (ed.), *Western European Security in A Changing World: From the Reactivation of the WEU to the Single European Act* (Maastricht: EIPA, 1988).

Id. (ed.), *The Reactivation of the Western European Union: The Effects on the EC and Its Institutions* (Maastricht: EIPA, 1985).

Id., "The Politics and Economics of EEC-Yugoslav Relations", *Journal of European Integration*, vol. 5, No. 1, 1981, 29-52

Tsouderos, Virginia, "Greek Policy and the Yugoslav Turmoil", *Mediterranean Quarterly*, vol. 4, No. 2, spring 1993, 1-13.

Tyler, Patrick E., "Pentagon Drops Goal of Blocking New Superpowers", *New York Times*, 24 May 1992.

Ullman, Richard H. (ed.), *The World and Yugoslavia's Wars* (New York: Council on Foreign Relations, 1996).

*US-EC Facts and Figures* (Brussels: US Mission to the EC, March 1993).

Valinakis, Yannis, *Greece's Security in the Post-Cold War Era* (Ebenhausen: Stiftung Wissenschaft und Politik, 1994).

Vanhoonacker, Sophie, "From Maastricht to Amsterdam: Was It Worth the Journey for CFSP", *Eipascope*, No. 2, 1997, 6-8.

Id., "La Belgique: responsable ou bouc émissaire de l'échec des négociations Fouchet?", *Res Publica*, vol. 31, No. 4, 1989, 513-526.

Vierucci, Luisa, "WEU: A Regional Partner of the United Nations?, *Chaillot Papers*,

No. 12, December 1993.
Vukadinovic, Radovan, *The Break-Up of Yugoslavia: Threats and Challenges* (Den Haag: Netherlands Institute of International Relations "Clingendael", 1992).
Wagner, Wolfgang, "Le siège permanent au Conseil de Sécurité: Qui a besoin de qui: les Allemands du siège? ou le Conseil de Sécurité des Allemands?", *Politique Etrangère*, vol. 58, No. 4, winter 1993-1994, 1001-1009.
Walt, Stephen N., "The Case for Finite Containment. Analyzing US Grand Strategy", *International Security*, vol. 14, No. 1, summer 1989, 5-49.
Waltz, Kenneth N., "The Emerging Structure of International Politics", *International Security*, vol. 18, No. 2, fall 1993, 44-79.
Id., "America as a Model for the World? A Foreign Policy Perspective", *Political Science and Politics*, vol. 24, No. 4, 1991, 667-670.
Id., *Theory of International Politics* (Reading, Ma.: Addison-Wesley Publishing Company, 1979).
Id., "The Stability of A Bipolar World", *Daedalus*, vol. 93, No. 3, summer 1964, 881-909.
Wayne, Bert, *The Reluctant Superpower. United States' Policy in Bosnia, 1991-1995* (New York: St Martin's Press, 1997).
Weidenfeld, Ernst, "Mitterrands Europaïsche Konföderation. Eine Idee im Spannungsfeld der Realitäten", *Europa-Archiv*, vol. 17, No. 1, 1991, 513-518.
Weidenfeld, Werner, "25 Years After 22 January 1963: The Franco-German Friendship Treaty", *Aussenpolitik*, vol. 39, No. 1, 1988, 3-12.
Weilemann, Peter R., "The German Contribution Toward Overcoming the Division of Europe – Chancellor Helmut Kohl's 10 Points", *Aussenpolitik*, vol. 41, No. 1, 1990, 15-23.
Werner, Pierre, *Itinéraires européens et luxembourgeois. Evolutions et souvenirs 1945-1985* (Luxembourg: Editions Saint Paul, 1991).
West, Richard, *Tito and the Rise and Fall of Yugoslavia* (New York: Caroll and Graf, 1995).
Wester, Robert, "The United Kingdom and Political Union", in Finn Laursen and Sophie Vanhoonacker (eds.), *The Intergovernmental Conference on Political Union. Institutional Reforms, New Policies and International Identity of the European Community* (Maastricht, Dordrecht: EIPA and Martinus Nijhoff Publishers, 1992), 189-214.
Id., "The Netherlands and European Political Union", in Finn Laursen and Sophie Vanhoonacker (eds.), *The Intergovernmental Conference on Political Union. Institutional Reforms, New Policies and International Identity of the European Community* (Maastricht, Dordrecht: EIPA and Martinus Nijhoff Publishers, 1992), 172-175.
Wettig, Gerhard, "Moscow's Acceptance of NATO: The Catalytic Role of German Unification", *Europe-Asia Studies*, vol. 45, No. 6, 1993, 953-972.
Wijnaendts, Henry, *Joegoslavische Kroniek. Juli 1991-Augustus 1992* (Amsterdam: Thomas Rap, 1993).
Wijnbergen, Christa van, "Germany and European Political Union", in Finn Laursen

and Sophie Vanhoonacker (eds.), *The Intergovernmental Conference on Political Union. Institutional Reforms, New Policies and International Identity of the European Community* (Maastricht, Dordrecht: EIPA and Martinus Nijhoff Publishers, 1992), 49-61.

Id., "Ireland and European Political Union", in Finn Laursen and Sophie Vanhoonacker (eds.), *The Intergovernmental Conference on Political Union. Institutional Reforms, New Policies and International Identity of the European Community* (Maastricht, Dordrecht: EIPA and Martinus Nijhoff Publishers, 1992), 127-138.

Winand, Pascaline, *Eisenhower, Kennedy, and the United States of Europe* (New York: St.Martin's Press, 1993).

Woehrel, Steven J., and Kim, Julie, "Yugoslavia and US Policy", *CRS Issue Brief*, 1 August 1993.

Wood, Pia Christina, "France and the Post Cold War Order: The Case of Yugoslavia", *European Security*, vol. 3, No. 1, spring 1994, 129-152.

Woodward, Bob, *The Commanders* (New York: Simon and Schuster, 1991).

Woodward, Susan, *Balkan Tragedy. Chaos and Dissolution After the Cold War* (Washington D.C.: The Brookings Institution, 1995).

Yergin, Daniel, *Shattered Peace. The Origins of the Cold War and the National Security State* (Harmondsworth: Penguin Books, 1980).

Yin, Robert K., *Case Study Research. Design and Methods* (Newbury Park-London: Sage Publications, 1989).

Yost, David S., "France in the New Europe", *Foreign Affairs*, vol. 69, No. 5, winter 1990, 107-128.

Zametica, John, "The Yugoslav Conflict", *Adelphi Paper*, No. 270, summer 1992.

Zelikow, Philip and Rice, Condoleeza, *Germany Unified and Europe Transformed: A Study in Statecraft* (Cambridge, Mass.: Harvard University Press, 1992).

Zielonka, Jan, "Europe's Security: A Great Confusion", *International Affairs*, vol. 67, No. 1, 1991, 127-137.

Zimmermann, Warren, *Origins of a Catastrophe. Yugoslavia and Its Destroyers – America's Last Ambassador Tells What Happened and Why* (New York: Random House, 1996).

Id., "The Last Ambassador. A Memoir of the Collapse of Yugoslavia", *Foreign Affairs*, vol. 74, No. 2, March-April 1995, 2-20.

**Note**

1   The overview lists the persons with the positions they occupied during the Bush administration and adds the place and date of the interview.

# Index

Acheson, Dean, 60, 62, 223
Adenauer, Konrad, 69, 70, 74
Adriatic, 128, 158, 171
Allied Rapid Reaction Force (ARRC), 118, 119, 210
Amato, Alfonso d', 172
APEC, see Asian Pacific Economic Cooperation
Appeasement, 36
ARRC, see Allied Rapid Reaction Force
Art, Robert J., 42
Asian Pacific Economic Cooperation (APEC), 4
Atlantic Charter, 82-84, 223
Atlantic Community, 84, 88, 211, 212
Austria, 99
    Croatia, recognition of, 163
Badinter, Robert, 156
Badinter Commission, 12, 162
Baker, James A., 9-10, 106-9, 112-3, 117, 131, 147, 187, 208, 212, 220
    Berlin speech (1989), 12, 106-9, 112, 131, 147, 187, 208, 212, 220
    Berlin speech (1991), 147
    and Yugoslav crisis, 174-6, 180
Balance of power, 16, 37, 42-43, 85, 161
Bandwagon(ing), 39, 45-6, 222
Bartholomew démarche, 117, 132, 212
Belgium,
    and Common Foreign and Security Policy, 104, 213
    Croatia, recognition of, 162
    and Eurocorps, 129
    and European Defence Community, 62
    and Luxembourg Non-Paper, 103
    and Political Union (1960-62), 67-70, 104

    and WEU, 101
Benelux, 62
    and European Defence Community, 62
Berlin, Isaiah, 9
Bipolarity, 15, 34, 205, 227, 229
Bipolar system, 27, 31, 34-5, 37
Blackwill, Robert D., 210
Bosnia and Herzegovina, 148, 150, 152, 161, 163-6, 168-70, 176, 180, 216, 218
    recognition of, 178-9, 180-3, 185-6, 189, 217
Brandt, Willy, 76, 83, 124
Brioni agreement, 155, 176, 215
Brussels Treaty Organisation, 63
Burdensharing, 3, 13, 33, 36, 46, 82
Bush administration, 1-4, 13-4, 17-9, 28, 31, 34, 36, 39, 46-8, 96, 101, 117, 122, 126-7, 131-3, 148, 205-9, 224-6, 228-9
    and Common Foreign and Security Policy, 105-33, 211-214, 221-222
    and Croatia, recognition of, 177-180
    and Eurocorps, 129-30
    and Germany, 210-221
    and German unification, 110-5
    principal players, 7-11
    sources on, 17-8
    and Yugoslav crisis, 169-86, 214-9, 222-3
Bush, George, 2, 10, 31,105, 107, 109-10, 112-3, 115, 121, 148, 227
    Boston speech, 105
    chicken speech, 176
    and Common Foreign and Security Policy, 219-20
    and Congress, 11

and EC, 108-110
foreign policy of, 9-10
and France, 120-3
and German reunification, 110-5
inaugural address, 8
Mainz visit, 111
memoirs, 17
and Mitterrand, 121
Princeton address, 11
vision thing, 8
Yugoslav crisis, 169-86

Calleo, David, 33
Carr, Edward Hallett, 29
Carrington, Lord, 156, 176
Carter, Jimmy, 9, 86
CFSP, *see* Common Foreign and Security Policy
Charette, Herve de la, 188
Cheney, Richard, 9-10
China, 8, 11, 38, 230
Churchill, Winston, 170
CIA, 8, 154, 173, 179, 184
Civilian power, 6, 81, 125, 157-8, 168, 187, 214
CJTF, *see* Combined Joint Task Forces
Clinton administration, 5, 170, 184, 186, 189-88, 218, 219, 226, 229, 230
Clinton, William J., 31, 148, 181, 217, 226
Colombo, Emilio, 80
Combined Joint Task Forces (CJTF), 189, 226
Commission, *see* European Commission
Common Foreign and Security Policy (CFSP), 47-8, 77, 79, 96, 99-105, 159, 162, 167, 169, 187-8, 206, 213, 215, 218, 224, 230
  and NATO, 116-20
  and US, 105-33
  and Yugoslav crisis, 153-169
Conference on Security and Cooperation in Europe (CSCE), 78, 106, 109, 112-4, 127-8, 131, 147, 158, 173, 207-8, 228
Conference on Yugoslavia, 156
Congress, 10-1, 71, 119, 121, 171-2, 184
Containment, 1, 32, 42, 58
Copenhagen Report, 77, 80

Costigliola, Frank, 120
Council of Europe, 128
Croatia, 148, 150-2, 155-7, 159-63, 165, 174-7, 185-6, 215, 217
  recognition of, 156, 159-164
Cromwell, William C., 18
CSCE, *see* Conference on Security and Cooperation in Europe

Dayton agreement, 148, 169, 188-9, 218
Declaration on EC-US Relations, 5, 109
Denmark, 80
  and CFSP, 99, 101, 104
  and Croatia, recognition of, 162
  and Eurocorps, 130
  and WEU, 81, 102
Delors, Jacques, 125, 154
Dobbins, James, 116
Dole, Robert, 172
Dublin Summit, 99, 109, 211
Duchêne, François, 81
Dulles, John Foster, 61
Dumas, Roland, 108, 118, 122, 166

Eagleburger, Lawrence, 8, 10, 18, 173, 176-7, 183, 216
Economic and Monetary Union (EMU), 96, 98
ECSC, *see* European Coal and Steel Community
EDC, *see* European Defence Community
Eden, Anthony, 63
Eekelen, Willem van, 129
Eisenhower administration, 62, 71, 171
Eisenhower, Dwight D., 61, 66
Elman, Colin, 31
Entanglement, 39, 43, 58-9
Eurocorps, 129-30, 132, 188
European Coal and Steel Community (ECSC), 61-2, 66, 108
European Commission, 66-7, 78-9, 87, 102, 105, 109, 125, 154-5
  and European Political Cooperation, 7
  and Luxembourg Non-Paper, 103
European Community/ies (EC), 2-7, 11, 14, 19, 31-2, 39, 47-8, 65-6, 74-77, 79-81, 83-4, 96, 98-9, 102-10, 116, 118,

Index   265

120-1, 127-8, 130-2
  and German reunification, 173
  and Gulf crisis, 122-6
  and Yugoslav crisis, 152-164
European Court of Justice, 77
European Council, 97, 100, 109, 117, 157
  Lisbon, 128, 166
  Luxembourg, 153, 155
  Maastricht, 128, 161
European Defence Community (EDC), 59-64, 70, 80, 87, 104, 211
European Free Trade Association (EFTA), 99, 105
European Parliament, 77, 96
European Political Cooperation (EPC), 19, 47, 59, 75-86, 96, 101, 103, 105, 124, 154, 157, 162, 206, 208, 211, 213, 224
  and European security, 80-81
  origins, 75-80
  sanctions, 78-9
European Political Union, *see* Political Union
European Union, 38, 80, 100-1, 105, 121, 228-30,
Evera, Stephen Van, 42

Finland, 99
Forces Answerable to the WEU (FAWEU), 127
Ford administration, 8, 10
Fortress Europe, 105, 206
Fouchet, Christian, 66
Fouchet committee, 67
Fouchet negotiations, 70, 74, 104
Fouchet proposals, 82
Fouchet I, 67, 69
Fouchet II, 67
France, 3, 7, 59-1, 64-66, 73, 75, 87-8, 96, 132
  and Allied Rapid Reaction Force (ARRC), 111
  and Atlantic Charter, 83
  and Berlin speech James Baker (1989), 108
  and Common Foreign and Security Policy, 97-8, 100-1, 103-4, 120-3, 211, 213-4

  and Croatia, recognition of, 159, 162
  and Eurocorps, 129-30, 132
  and European Defence Community, 59-64
  and European Political Cooperation, 75-6
  and German rearmament, 60
  and Multilateral Nuclear Force (MNF), 71-2
  and NATO, 120, 188
  and Political Union (1960-62), 66-70, 73-5
  and Yugoslav crisis, 159, 168
  and WEU, 80-1, 101
Fukuyama, Francis, 33

Gaulle, Charles de, 64-70, 72-5, 87, 104, 211
General Agreement on Tariffs and Trade (GATT), 76, 117
Genscher-Colombo initiative, 80
Genscher, Hans-Dietrich, 80, 160, 166
Geo-economics, 38
German rearmament, 60, 64
German (re)unification, 57, 96-7, 99, 110-6, 120-1, 209-10
Germany, 3, 7, 11, 39, 46-7, 58, 61, 65-6, 74, 83, 96, 100, 106, 122, 131
  and Atlantic Charter, 77
  and Berlin speech James Baker (1989), 108
  and Croatia, recognition of, 156, 159-164, 166-169, 217
  and Common Foreign and Security Policy, 97-8, 211, 213
  Eurocorps, 129-30
  and European Defence Community, 62-4
  and European Political Cooperation, 76
  and Gulf crisis, 126
  and Multilateral Nuclear Force (MNF), 72
  and NATO membership, 112-5, 209-10, 218
  and Political Union (1960-62), 67, 69
  and Yugoslav crisis, 157, 159-164, 167
Gilpin, Robert, 16, 35, 40, 221, 229
Gorbachev, Mikhaïl, 3, 9, 112, 114, 176,

210
Grand Design, 19, 32, 65, 70-3, 75, 87, 223
Grand Strategy, 1
Greece, 58, 80
    and Macedonia, recognition of, 162, 176
    and WEU, 81, 102
Gulf, 7, 9, 43, 48, 81, 99, 110, 117, 122-7, 130, 132, 152, 158, 166, 174-5, 178, 212, 216
Gymnich agreement, 84-5

Haarzuilens, 161
Hague Summit, 75
Haughey, Charles, 110
Heath, Edward, 83, 124
Hegemonic stability theory, 37
Hill, Carla, 4
Hobbes, Thomas, 29
Huntington, Samuel, 37, 43
Hutchings, Robert L., 18

Iceland, 102
IFOR, 188
Intergovernmental Conference (IGC) on Political Union, 2, 7, 14, 19, 47-8, 58, 96-105, 116, 118, 121, 124, 129, 153, 157-8, 160, 162, 168-9, 187, 206, 208, 211, 213, 215, 230
Intergovernmental Conference (IGC) on Economic and Monetary Union (EMU), 47, 96-7, 99, 211
Integrated Military Command, 222
Internal market, 3, 75, 108
Iraq, 9, 11, 124
Ireland, 80
    and WEU, 81, 102
Isolationism, 2, 220
Italy, 63
    and CFSP, 99-101
    and Croatia, recognition of, 162
    and European Defence Community, 62
    and Political Union (1960-62), 67, 69
Izetbegovic, Alija, 173, 179

Japan, 4, 5, 31-2, 38, 83
JNA, see also Yugoslav National Army, 152
Jobert, Michel, 43, 83

Joffe, Josef, 43
Johnson, Ralph, 176

Kennan, George, 42
Kennedy administration, 65, 70-1, 73-4, 84
Kennedy, John, 19, 70-3, 75, 87, 212, 223
Kennedy, Paul, 33
Keohane, Robert, 40
Khrushchev, Nikita, 65
Kinkel, Klaus, 166
Kissinger, Henry, 8, 19, 34, 82-4
Kohl, Helmut, 97-8, 100, 111, 113-5, 157, 178
    and recognition of Croatia, 160-1, 163-4
Korean war, 60
Kosovo, 172, 183-4
Krauthammer, Charles, 16, 38
Kimmitt, Robert, 10

Lampedusa, Giuseppe Tomasi di, 225
Lance missiles, 114
Layne, Christopher, 43
Lebow, Ned, 34
Lippmann gap, 41
Lippmann, Walter, 41, 45
London Conference, 165, 183
London Report, 77-8, 80
London (NATO) Summit, 113, 118, 122, 210
Long peace, 15, 40
Luns, Joseph, 68
Luttwak, Edward N., 38
Luxembourg,
    and Common Foreign and Security Policy, 213
    Eurocorps, 129
    and European Defence Community, 62
    and WEU, 101
Luxembourg Non-Paper, 103
Luxembourg Report, 76, 78, 80, 82

Maastricht, 96, 104, 123, 127-8, 130, 153, 161-2, 167, 169, 224
Maastricht Treaty, 104, 127, 162, 168, 215
Macedonia, 150, 161-2, 176
    recognition of, 162, 178-9, 183
Macmillan, Harold, 66, 72, 75

Machiavelli, Nicolo, 29
Major, John, 162
Mansfield amendment, 82
Markovic, Ante, 174
Marshall Plan, 58, 86-7
Matutes, Abel, 154
Mastanduno, Michael, 31
McNamara, Robert, 65
Mearsheimer, John, 39-40
Milosevic, Slobodan, 174, 179, 181, 184
Middle East, 42-3, 78, 83, 85, 174
Mitsotakis government, 179
Mitteleuropa, 160, 167
Mitterrand, François, 97-8, 100, 115, 120, 122, 157, 160
Monnet, Jean, 59-61, 87
Montenegro, 128, 149-50, 152, 161, 165-66, 179, 181, 188, 216
Morgenthau, Hans, 29
Moschbacher, Robert, 4
Multilateral Nuclear Force (MNF), 71-4
Multipolarity, 16, 41
Multipolar system, 15, 34, 41, 226
Multipolar world, 33-4, 37, 45, 205
Muravcik, Joshua, 38-9

NACC, see North Atlantic Cooperation Council
NAFTA, see North Atlantic Free Trade Agreement
National Security Council, 9, 10, 18, 111
NATO, 2, 6, 12-4, 43, 46-7, 58-60, 62, 64-6, 71, 73-4, 81-4, 87, 95, 100, 102, 106-10, 112, 128, 131-3, 147, 158, 164, 173, 184, 188-9, 206, 208-9, 211-4, 217-9, 221-2, 224, 226-8, 230
  and CFSP, 101-2, 116-20
  and Eurocorps, 130
  and France, 120-1
  and German membership, 112-5
  and Gulf, 125
  New Strategic Concept, 131
  and out-of-area, 187
  and Political Union (1960-62), 68-69
  reform, 127, 131-2, 210
  and Yugoslav crisis, 171, 187
  and WEU, 128-9

Nau, Henry R., 33
Neorealism, 31
Netherlands, The,
  and Common Foreign and Security Policy, 101, 104, 213
  European Political Cooperation, 75
  and Eurocorps, 130
  and European Defence Community, 62
  and Luxembourg Non-Paper, 103
  and Political Union (1960-62), 67-70, 104
Niles, Thomas, 182
Nixon administration, 10, 82, 84
Nixon, Richard, 8, 82-4, 87, 212, 225
North Atlantic Free Trade Agreement, 3, 4
North Atlantic Cooperation Council (NACC), 210
Nye, Joseph, 33

Ottawa Declaration, 79
Owen, Lord, 186

Pax americana, 33, 37, 39
Partners in leadership, 111, 126
Petersberg, 60
Petersberg Declaration, 127
Pentagon, 18, 121, 129
Pleven proposal, 60
Pleven, René, 59-60
Poos, Jacques, 148
Political Union (1960-62), 73-75, 211
  and the European Community, 67
  and NATO, 68-9
Political Union (1990s), 96-105, 157, 160, 168
Portugal,
  and Common Foreign and Security Policy, 99, 101, 213
  and Yugoslav crisis, 157
Presidency, 77
  Dutch, 100-1, 103, 155
  Irish, 109
  Italian, 100, 109
  Luxembourg, 100, 103, 117, 215
  Portuguese, 165
Primacy, 5, 16, 33, 36-7, 39, 40-1, 43, 45-6, 206, 221-3, 227

Reagan, Ronald, 3, 9, 10, 85
Realism, see also structural realism, 17-9, 27-8, 40, 47, 205-6, 226-8, 230
Reykjavik, 3
Risse-Kappen, Thomas, 34
Rolodex diplomacy, 9
Rome Summit,
  EC, 99
  NATO, 101, 123, 128, 131, 210
Ross, Denis, 10
Russia, 46, 107, 122, 165, 186, 207

Santer, Jacques, 154
Sarajevo, 149, 179, 182, 185, 216
Scowcroft, Brent, 8, 10, 17, 113, 173, 216
  memoirs, 17
SDI, see Strategic Defence Initiative,
Selective engagement, 36, 43, 45-6, 206, 221, 223
Serbia, 128, 149-52, 158, 161, 165-6, 168, 172, 177, 179, 181, 188, 216
Security Council, see UN Security Council
Short Range Nuclear Forces (SNF), 3
Short Range Nuclear Missiles (SRNMs), 114
Shevardnadze, Eduard, 114
Single European Act (SEA), 77, 80
Silberman, Lawrence, 172
Slovenia, 148, 150-2, 154-6, 159-62, 174-6, 185, 215
  recognition of, 159-64, 166-7, 169
Snidal, Duncan, 37
Snyder, Glenn, 12
Soft power, 33
Solemn Declaration on European Union (1983), 77, 80
Soviet Union, 11, 13, 15, 31, 58-9, 65, 73, 76, 79-80, 85, 87, 111-3, 115, 126, 131, 147, 159, 162, 170-1, 74-6, 180, 205, 209-10
  and German unification, 111-5
Spaak, Paul-Henri, 68
Spain,
  and Common Foreign and Security Policy, 213
  and Eurocorps, 129
  and WEU, 101

and Yugoslav crisis, 159
Stalin, 61, 150, 170-1
State Department, 10, 18, 84, 171, 182
Status quo, 35-6, 40
Strasbourg European Summit, 98
Strategic Defence Initiative (SDI), 3
Structural Realism, see also realism, 15, 19
Sweden, 99

Taft, William, 119, 132
Thatcher, Margaret, 98, 108, 112, 115, 126
Thucydides, 29
Thurow, Lester, 5
Tindemans Report, 80
Tito, 150-1, 160, 171
Transatlantic Declaration, see also Declaration on US-EC Relations, 110
Treaty on European Union (TEU), see also Maastricht Treaty, 78-9, 96, 101-4, 128
Truman administration, 60, 62
Truman doctrine, 58, 170
Truman, Harry, 60, 61, 170
Tudjman, Franjo, 162, 179
Turkey, 58, 102, 117, 124, 126, 170, 183, 212
Two-plus-Four, 112, 114, 209

Unipolarity, 19, 37, 40, 205, 226
Unipolar moment, 16, 37, 39-41, 45, 205-6
Unipolar system, 31, 37, 40
United Kingdom, 3, 43, 60, 64, 67, 72-4, 83, 98, 104
  and Atlantic Charter, 77
  and Common Foreign and Security Policy, 101, 213
  and Berlin speech James Baker (1989), 108
  and Eurocorps, 130
  and European Defence Community, 62-64
  and Gulf crisis, 124-6
  and Multilateral Nuclear Force (MNF), 72
  and Political Union (1960-62), 67-68
  and Yugoslav crisis, 157, 159, 160, 167
United Nations (UN), 8, 38-9, 124-5, 127-

8, 148, 158, 164, 166, 169-70, 177, 179-83, 185-6, 188, 215
and the Yugoslav crisis, 164-7, 215-6
United States, 60, 66
and CFSP, 105-33,
and European Political Cooperation, 82-86
and European Defence Community, 62-63
and German unification, 98, 110-115
and Slovenia, recognition of, 177-80
and Yugoslav crisis, 216-9, 222-4
and Yugoslavia, 170-2
UNPROFOR, 165, 166, 183
UN Security Council, 11, 158-9, 164-6, 177, 181-3, 216
UN (Security Council) Resolution, 125, 165, 181-3, 216
Uruguay Round, 3, 5, 6, 110, 212
US, *see* United States

Vance, Cyrus, 165, 177, 179

Waltz, Kenneth, 29-30, 34-5, 40, 228
Warsaw Pact, 3, 209
Washington, George, 6

Western European Union (WEU), 6, 7, 80, 95, 100-2, 105, 119, 121-2, 127-9, 131 207-8, 213
associate members, 128
Council of Vianden, 127
and Gulf, 124-6
observers, 128
Petersberg Council, 128
reactivation of, 80-1
and Yugoslav crisis, 157-8, 168, 188, 215
Woodward, Susan, 175
Wörner, Manfred, 129

Year of Europe, 19, 82-84, 87
Yeltsin, Boris, 9
Yugoslav crisis, 14, 39, 47, 129, 130, 132, 152-164, 167-8, 224-5, 227
Yugoslavia, 19, 47, 123, 147-8, 214, 216-9, 222, 225, 227
history and break-up, 149-52
and United States (history), 170-2
Yugoslav People's Army, see also JNA, 152, 155, 161

Zimmermann, Warren, 172-3, 181
Zoellick, Robert, 10, 18, 112